PARALLEL ENCOUNTERS

Cultural Studies Series

Cultural Studies is the multi- and inter-disciplinary study of culture, defined anthropologically as a "way of life," performatively as symbolic practice, and ideologically as the collective product of varied media and cultural industries. Although Cultural Studies is a relative newcomer to the humanities and social sciences, in less than half a century it has taken interdisciplinary scholarship to a new level of sophistication, reinvigorating the liberal arts curriculum with new theories, topics, and forms of intellectual partnership.

Wilfrid Laurier University Press invites submissions of manuscripts concerned with critical discussions on power relations concerning gender, class, sexual preference, ethnicity, and other macro and micro sites of political struggle.

For more information, please contact:

Lisa Quinn
Acquisitions Editor
Wilfrid Laurier University Press
75 University Avenue West
Waterloo, ON N2L 3C5
Canada
Phone: 519-884-0710 ext. 2843
Fax: 519-725-1399
Email: quinn@press.wlu.ca

Gillian Roberts
and David Stirrup, editors

PARALLEL
ENCOUNTERS

Culture at the Canada–US Border

**WILFRID LAURIER
UNIVERSITY PRESS**

This book has been published with the help of a grant from the Canadian Federation for the Humanities and Social Sciences, through the Awards to Scholarly Publications Program, using funds provided by the Social Sciences and Humanities Research Council of Canada. Wilfrid Laurier University Press acknowledges the financial support of the Government of Canada through the Canada Book Fund for its publishing activities.

LAURIER
Inspiring Lives.

Library and Archives Canada Cataloguing in Publication

Parallel encounters : culture at the Canada–US border / Gillian Roberts and David Stirrup, editors.

(Cultural studies series)
Includes bibliographical references and index.
Issued in print and electronic formats.
ISBN 978-1-55458-984-5 (bound).—ISBN 978-1-55458-999-9 (epub).—ISBN 978-1-55458-998-2 (pdf)

1. Canada—Civilization—American influences. 2. Northern boundary of the United States—Civilization. 3. Canada—Relations—United States. 4. United States—Relations—Canada. 5. Canada—Boundaries—United States. 6. United States—Boundaries—Canada. 7. Indians of North America—Travel. 8. Globalization—Social aspects. 9. Transnationalism—Social aspects. I. Roberts, Gillian, 1976–, editor of compilation II. Stirrup, David, editor of compilation III. Series: Cultural studies series (Waterloo, Ont.)

FC95.5.P37 2013   303.48´271073   C2013-903862-0
                                          C2013-903863-9

Cover design by Heng Wee Tan. Front-cover image: *Third Bank of the River*, by Alan Michelson. Text design by Angela Booth Malleau.

This book is printed on FSC recycled paper and is certified Ecologo. It is made from 100% post-consumer fibre, processed chlorine free, and manufactured using biogas energy.

Printed in Canada

RECYCLED
Paper made from
recycled material
FSC   FSC® C103567
www.fsc.org

Contents

relevant
to comics
paper

relevant to
comics/
indigeneity

*relevant
to
Coupland
book*

Theorizing the Border: Literature, Performance, Translation

Acknowledgements

THE CONVERSATIONS ABOUT THE CULTURAL implications of the Canada–US border that inform this book began at the Culture and the Canada–US Border Conference at the University of Kent in June 2009. We wish to express our gratitude to our delegates, many of whom travelled a long way from North America in order to discuss that continent's borders. Your fierce intelligence and commitment have fuelled the production of this volume, as well as the Culture and the Canada–US Border special issue of *American Review of Canadian Studies* (40.2, 2010). We would like to thank the institutions that supported the conference, namely DFAIT (through its sadly now-defunct Canada Conference Grant), the Foundation for Canadian Studies in the UK, the University of Nottingham's School of American and Canadian Studies, and the University of Kent's Faculty of Humanities research development fund, School of English, Centre for American Studies, and Kent Institute for Advanced Studies in the Humanities. For their assistance and support during the planning stages and the conference itself, many thanks to Maureen Kincaid Speller, Gonzalo Ceron García, and Christopher Moore.

We thank our contributors for their enormous amounts of hard work, patience, and perseverance. Thanks too to our editor at Wilfrid Laurier University Press, Lisa Quinn, for her faith in this book. We gratefully acknowledge our anonymous readers for their insightful comments and helpful advice, and the following artists and writers for generous permission to reproduce their work: Rebecca Belmore, Daphne Marlatt, Christian Bök, Alex McKay, and Alan Michelson, and the Anne & Gordon Samstag Museum of Art. For their invaluable support during the production of this volume, we would like to thank Steve Cole, Sheryl Groeneweg, Donna Landry, and John Purdy, in particular, and our colleagues at the Universities of Nottingham and Kent in general. Most especially, we thank our families: Matthew Welton; and Jo, Florence, and Ottilie Stirrup.

one

Introduction

Culture at the 49th Parallel

Nationalism, Indigeneity, and the Hemispheric

Gillian Roberts and David Stirrup

he crossed. the border

line in a northern corner

four

cardinal   points

for

a better over there. created a here.

one foot in A   one foot in a

merica   Canada.

Wayde Compton, "Legba, Landed," *49th Parallel Psalm*

IT IS WIDELY ACKNOWLEDGED that the Canada–US border has long been an important symbol in the Canadian imaginary, considered a site of cultural defence for Canadian identity against US hegemony. Yet it is also plainly the case that the Canada–US border provides a prism through which and at which broader questions of political, economic, and cultural relations within the Americas come into focus. Given the ratification of the Free Trade Agreement in 1989 and of NAFTA in 1994, the events of 11 September 2001 and their fallout for Canada–US relations, the challenges to Canadian nationalism from Indigenous and subnational groups, and recent expansions of how American Studies as a discipline is conceptualized, *Parallel Encounters* argues that it is imperative that we revisit the cultural implications of what has traditionally been celebrated as the longest undefended border in the world. Cultural texts continue to invoke the Canada–US border, identifying it variously as a protective barrier for Canada against the threat of Americanization; a site of policing bodies and identities marked by racialization, gender, and sexuality; a threat

1

to Indigenous sovereignties; a dividing line between a welfare state and the epitome of capitalism; a zone where state-funded culture meant to be "good for us" stands guard against imported popular culture; a contact zone where reading and viewing practices might be inflected with national significance; and what appears to be a sharp contrast to the militarized US–Mexico border, even while trade agreements such as NAFTA locate Canada increasingly in relation to Mexico in particular and the Americas more generally. As a result, we see the need for what Bryce Traister terms a "critical borderlands practice" (34) in order to examine thoroughly the implications of the Canada–US border without romanticizing what the border might represent for what is often misconceived of, particularly in popular border texts, as a homogeneous and unified Canada.

Our focus on the Canada–US border both draws on US–Mexico Border Studies, the "birthplace" of the Border Studies discipline (Michaelsen and Johnson 1), and tests the limits of how far site-specific analysis of the border can travel from its point of origin. If the US–Mexico border is, to quote a seminal text in US–Mexico Border Studies, "*una herida abierta* [an open wound] where the Third World grates against the first and bleeds" (Anzaldúa 25), the Canada–US border presents less of a brutal juxtaposition. Yet the subtle distinctions between Canada and the United States have long exercised Canadian cultural producers and Canadian Studies scholars, and now more than ever we argue the 49th parallel represents "at once a barrier, a conduit and a transition zone" (Konrad and Nicol 22), a boundary paradoxically both circumvented and rendered more visible by the forces of globalization. Examination of the cultural import of the Canada–US border, "that literal demarcation of difference [that] takes on almost allegorical status" (Brown 4) from some Canadian perspectives, might be seen in recent decades to overlap with the aims of a reconfigured American Studies in its "new," "post-national," "transnational," and "hemispheric" paradigms, which have sought to dislodge the primacy of a hegemonic (white, Anglo) Americanness in favour of approaches that address the multiplicities of American identity and that challenge the conflation of "America" with the United States by looking beyond US borders. However, despite John Carlos Rowe's entreaty in *Post-Nationalist American Studies* (2000) to "take into account at the very least the different nationalities, cultures, and languages of the Western hemisphere, including Canada" (25), most of the newly reconfigured American Studies work to date has focused its energies southward to the US–Mexico borderlands and the relationship between the United States and Latin America. In proposing that the "new interest in border studies should include investigations of how the many different Americas and Canada have historically influenced and interpreted each other" (25), Rowe betrays a "conceptual slip" (Traister 47) wherein "Americas" is multiple and "Canada" singular, yet also abstracted, or indeed extracted, from the Americas.

Canada has been marginalized in these newer disciplinary incarnations of American Studies, despite its invocation in the litany of locations that mount challenges to the US-centric model. While Canada has been included in recent texts by US-based scholars working within Hemispheric American Studies, such as Claudia Sadowski-Smith's *Border Fictions* and Rachel Adams's *Continental Divides*, many hemispheric projects have often inserted Canada into a pre-existing American Studies framework that, even as an attempt to redefine disciplinary boundaries, fails to take Canadian Studies into account. Moreover, academic interest in Canada–US relations, particularly in the United States, often emerges from political science and international relations frameworks. Canadian Studies *has* long engaged questions about national borders and cultural comparisons between Canada and the United States, as evidenced by such texts as David Staines's collection *The Canadian Imagination* (1977), Robert Lecker's collection *Borderlands* (1991), Ian Angus's *A Border Within* (1997), W.H. New's *Borderlands: How We Talk about Canada* (1998), Laurie Ricou's *The Arbutus/Madrone Files* (2002), Arnold E. Davidson, Priscilla L. Walton, and Jennifer Andrews's *Border Crossings: Thomas King's Comic Inversions* (2003), Katherine L. Morrison's *Canadians Are Not Americans* (2003), and Winfried Siemerling's *The New North American Studies* (2005); however, the offerings of Canadian Studies as a discipline have been largely neglected as many American Studies scholars seek to expand their object, rather than their method, of study. As Traister argues, "Simply wanting to move the grasp of American Studies scholarship beyond U.S. borders because its currently 'embordered' status represents a form of thinking we distrust fails to account for the persistent realities of meaningful cultural difference that national borders entail" (47). These borders, we emphasize, affect and inflect not only cultural products but also disciplinary perspectives. As such, despite their efforts to the contrary, reconfigured American Studies projects often fail to transcend the status of the "additive move" (Adams, "Northern" 314) where Canada is concerned, and have not genuinely transformed Canada–US Border Studies in ways that are useful for Canadianist scholars. In *Continental Divides*, Adams's own positioning is, perhaps necessarily, exclusive in her discussion of Mohawk artist Shelley Niro's installation *The Border*: "Given its title, we might expect it to take on the better-known controversies associated with the U.S.–Mexico border" (30). Adams's unspecified "we" here will come as a surprise to Canadians and Canadian Studies scholars, given the 49th parallel's long-standing function as a metonym for Canada in Canadian culture, not to mention the prominence of the Mohawks' relationship to the border, particularly since the so-called Oka Crisis in 1990. Opening up the Canada–US border as discursive terrain to examine its function in and in relation to cultural texts is therefore, we assert here, a timely and necessary move.

Lost Canadians and Nationalist Constructions

The January–February 2011 issue of the Canadian magazine *The Walrus* includes an article by Grant Stoddard on the "lost Canadians," residents of the Northwest Angle and Islands in Minnesota, "the only part of the continental US north of the forty-ninth parallel" (26). In the Angle, created by a somewhat haphazard process of border surveying, "anything from visiting a doctor to buying fabric softener involves crossing an international border four times" (27). In 1997, the neighbouring Canadian province of Ontario imposed limits on American fishing in its waters, harming the Angle's economy, which is underpinned by walleye fishing. The community, feeling that its concerns were not being addressed by Congress, announced their desire to secede and join Canada. Their action, which they admitted to Stoddart had been a publicity stunt, was ultimately resolved: the Ontario laws were found to be in violation of NAFTA.

Throughout his article, Stoddard underscores the artificiality of the nation-state border, which, due to "a map-maker's error" (24), has seemingly positioned the residents of the Northwest Angle in the "wrong" country. The "blatantly synthetic" (26) border is "nothing if not completely and utterly arbitrary" (24), Stoddard asserts, and the Northwest Angle's national location is the product of a "comically unwieldy" (24) article in the Anglo-American Convention (1818). Yet Stoddard, probing the implications of the "lost Canadians," consistently infuses this blatantly synthetic border with meaning, confessing his desire to persuade the residents of the Angle that Canada is "the better place" (26): "Wouldn't it benefit the Angle to come over to our side?" (30). Stoddart comes armed with an array of statistics about quality of life and economic prosperity, yet he finds that he cannot convince the Angle's residents of the benefits of "a mere flag swap" (31), even if they already drink Canadian Club and listen to the CBC.

Stoddard asserts at the beginning of his article that "[o]ne of the most striking things separating the United States and Canada is the line that divides the United States from Canada" (24). The border, then, is both one element among many that testify to Canada–US difference and a symbol of all the other differences between the two countries. His presentation of the border—arbitrary, artificial, yet culturally significant—echoes the position of many Canadian border texts in its simultaneous acknowledgement of the absurdities of cartography and its insistence upon the national implications engendered by the imaginary line between Canada and the United States.

The notion that the Canada–US border safeguards Canadian distinctiveness and cultural sovereignty is nothing new. More than three decades ago, Eli Mandel argued that "the border between America and Canada is of enormous importance in the imaginative life of any Canadian" (105). The border features in countless Canadian cultural texts, and Mandel's assignation of its importance exclusively to Canadians is telling here, a tacit acknowledgement that it *border of greater significance to Canadians — English Canadians cp Canadians.*

has less cultural significance to US Americans. Yet it is also telling that he does not qualify *which* Canadians see it as significant. Ian Angus, meanwhile, argues that "[a]ll concern with English Canadian identity, formulated abstractly, is engaged in maintaining a *border* between us and the United States" (47). His point—that Anglo-Canadian identity requires the border to function as a kind of buffer—implicitly acknowledges that French Canadian and Québécois identities have another dominant group against which they are defined. But further qualifications to Mandel's and Angus's assertions introduce additional complications regarding the border's relevance to communities living in the territories claimed by the Canadian and American nation-states.

Stoddard's article gestures briefly toward the colonial legacy that is inherent in the Canada–US border. First, he is introduced to Angle Inlet's one-room school's "international student," a "seven-year-old First Nations child [who] lives on Chippewa land that straddles the United States and Canada" (28). But Stoddard focuses more on the student's need to travel to school by motorboat than on the implications of Indigenous land straddling the nation-state boundary. Second, he similarly invokes the injustice of settler-invader demarcations imposed on Indigenous lands, only to drop the issue when he recounts the Angle's (white) residents' announcement of their desire to secede: "Those left in the dark included members of the Red Lake Indian band, who hold 70 percent of the Northwest Angle's land" (30). Although we hear that Red Lake chief Bobby Whitefeather received a "profus[e]" (30) apology, Stoddard does not speak to members of Red Lake themselves, and he continues to ignore the specifically colonial Euro-North American history that produced the cartographic anomaly of the Northwest Angle. It is of course just that—an anomaly—but it offers momentary insight not only into the arbitrary "angles" of demarcation but also into the ongoing impact of that historic process, while simultaneously conjuring a notion of the borderlands as at once stable and cohesive, and contingent and conditional. In a sense, the Northwest Angle provides a highly visible example of borderlands development, insofar as the borderlands "have emerged and have been transformed from distinct places separated by a boundary to a more common place where people co-exist and cooperate across the border" (Konrad and Nicol 23). Regardless of the socio-cultural constitution of the Angle and its immediate neighbours, it is precisely the fastness of the border, even in this most counterintuitive of locations, that maintains its citizens' identities as legally and politically US American.

Indigeneity and Imposition

The above anecdote presents one scenario in which the border figures as "solidly" for US Americans as it has tended to for Canadians (at least in terms of cultural and national identities). But in that tension between the arbitrariness of the line and the determinacy of what it represents—US citizenship—it also highlights the other pervasive role of the Canada–US border in US cultural narratives: as arbiter, mediator, and moderator of the rights and duties of the citizenry. Two of the most potent instances of the border functioning in this manner for Americans since the mid-twentieth century are the Vietnam War draft resistance and 9/11. While the former carries echoes of nineteenth-century iterations of the Canada–US border as liberating agent—from the Underground Railroad through Sitting Bull's escape to Canada, to (albeit for very different reasons) the Fenian invasions of Canada in 1865 and 1870)—the latter in fact spells the potential triumph of rightist perceptions in the United States that ultimately, Canada poses more of a threat than a promise. Nevertheless, during the turbulent years of the Civil Rights and antiwar era, Canada provided a vision of safety to the conscientious objector and the draft resister and was the locus of "the largest politically motivated outmigration of people in the history of the United States" (Hardwick and Mansfield 384). Threat or promise, the border and its crossings signal Canada's perceived greater liberalism, which is often projected onto real events such as the gathering of the Niagara Movement (later to become the NAACP) at Fort Erie, Ontario, in 1905. Whether W.E.B. Du Bois's desire for privacy and a modicum of secrecy led him to the secluded Erie Beach Hotel, or whether, as the apocryphal version has it, they failed to secure a venue in Buffalo, New York, due to prejudice, such instances feed both off and into perceptions that Canada is more tolerant of racial, ethnic, sexual, and gender difference. Such perceptions continue to fuel *mis*perceptions in certain quarters on the US right that the 9/11 terrorists were "admitted" as a consequence of Canada's lax border controls.

are both of these not misperceptions?

That this greater sense of tolerance can be illusory is arguably nowhere more evident than in the two nation-states' current treatment of Indigenous peoples. Events more recent than the Angle's secession publicity stunt emphasize the extent to which the Canada–US border continues to operate as a colonial imposition and contributes to attempts to impose nation-state citizenship on Indigenous communities. In April 2010 a Mohawk delegation from Kahnawake encountered difficulty travelling home from Bolivia, where they had been participating in the World People's Conference on Climate Change and the Rights of Mother Earth. They experienced a small delay leaving Pearson, with the airline consulting a Canada Customs agent to verify their Haudenosaunee passports: "Oh, they're Indigenous, they can go where they want" (Horn), the Customs agent confirmed. However, on their return trip to Toronto via El Salvador, representatives of the Canadian state did not uphold their right to travel without Canadian documents. The Canadian Embassy refused the Mohawks' request for a letter of explanation to the airline: stating that the Haudenosaunee passports were "unsecure document[s]" (Horn), the embassy insisted that the Mohawk required an emergency travel document tying them to the Canadian state. For the Mohawk delegation, whose ten-day trip was extended to twenty-nine days as a result of the obstructions to their travel home, the nation-state border between Canada and the United States, with its attendant policing of nation-state citizenship, functions to undermine their own nationhood. As one member of the delegation stated regarding the emergency travel document prescribed by the embassy, "We said we can't do that ... We can't compromise who we are because we left on these passports; we're not Canadian; we're not American; our political stance has always been that" (qtd. in Horn). Furthermore, for the delegation, resolution of their immediate travel difficulties was superseded by their responsibilities to their nation: "We were sent there by our people. And so any decisions that we were going to make was [*sic*] going to impact our people[,] ... our people who travel on the Haudenosaunee passport, ... [and] our people who say we are who we say were [*sic*] are and act accordingly to that" (qtd. in Horn).

[handwritten margin note: indigenous straddling + outright rejection of border spaces.]

Readers familiar with Thomas King's work will recognize here echoes of his short story, "Borders," in which a Blackfoot woman refuses to identify herself at the Canada–US border as either Canadian or American. Stuck in a limbo between border crossings for a few days, the woman and her son are finally allowed passage into the United States after a television crew appears and broadcasts their story—embarrassing publicity for the two nation-states. In the case of the Mohawk travelling back from Bolivia, the United States proved more accommodating than Canada, and television played a role in the resolution. A Customs and Immigration agent whose father is Apache said, "[A]s soon as I found out about you boys I could hear my father say you get those boys home right now"; after watching "a documentary ... about the Mohawk Ironworks in New York" on the Discovery Channel, she explained to the US embassy that "Mohawks ... helped build New York" (Horn). Ultimately, the delegation travelled home via the United States, bypassing Canada altogether. Just as the narrator of "Borders" acknowledges his mother's refusal to self-identify as Canadian or American, the delegation recognized that "the easiest thing would have been to sign those documents right at the get-go" (qtd. in Horn). But as explained by a representative of the Haudenosaunee Documentation Committee, "The Haudenosaunee Passport is a non-violent expression of our distinct identity as a sovereign people ... While both Canada and the United States claim us as their citizens, the Haudenosaunee Passport is a constant reminder that our people have never acquiesced our citizenship as Haudenosaunee people" (qtd. in Horn). Crucial to this refusal of nation-state citizenship is the fact that "[w]e were here before you and we're our own Nation ... so you can keep your citizenship, we're not you" (qtd. in Horn).

[handwritten margin mark: ✳]

The case of the Mohawk delegation offers a powerful rejoinder to Stoddard's exploration of the Canada–US border and its significance. Not only does it recall the work of the border-crossing Thomas King in its dislodging of dominant assumptions about the Canada–US border's function to protect cultural identities perceived to be at risk, but it also resonates with the last decade's developments in Canada's relationship to the United States and to the Americas as a whole. First, the concern that the Haudenosaunee passport is an "unsecure document" emphasizes anxieties about security in a post-9/11 climate. This same theme is explored in different terms by Onondaga writer Eric Gansworth, whose short story "Patriot Act" (and more recently a play by the same name) explores the ways in which tribal rights are impinged upon and interfered with through mechanisms of control such as the aptly named USA Patriot Act (2001), which stands for "Uniting and Strengthening America by Providing Appropriate Tools Required to Intercept and Obstruct Terrorism." In "Patriot Act," the Onondaga wife of the narrator is specifically targeted, picked up by Canada–US border security screening for harbouring a radioactive substance (she has recently had an X-ray). With this image of policing the female body specifically, particularly given the health-related circumstances that make her "suspicious," Gansworth neatly draws attention to the ways in which such measures at the border explicitly curtail prior rights and freedoms in ways that potentially affect multiple constituencies. A pressing concern for Indigenous people, of course, this issue nevertheless raises urgent questions about potentially insidious delimitations of mobility as a consequence of the War on Terror.

Second, an entirely different conception of security arises in the Mohawk delegation's participation in the Bolivia conference, which was organized "in response to the Climate Conference in Copenhagen" (Horn) of December 2009 to address concerns of "many governments of developing nations [who] were not pleased with the way the Copenhagen conference turned out," ignoring as it did "these developing countries [that] are among the most affected by climate change" (Horn). In participating at the conference, the Mohawk delegates not only affiliated themselves with developing nations rather than with the Canadian nation-state, but also engaged in a hemispheric conception of the Americas, one that disregarded nation-state boundaries imposed on the continent. Both of the contexts from which this anecdote develops—the historic legacy of the treaty relationships that underpin Indigenous rights in North America, which in turn provides the foundation for the legal aspects of Indigenous custodianship of the land and environment—have achieved even more prominence in Canada since late 2012 with the foundation of the Idle No More Movement. Idle No More was launched in November 2012, when Nina Wilson, Sheelagh McLean, Sylvia McAdam, and Jessica Gordon held a teach-in to protest the Harper government's Bill C-45 (see Meekis and Stuteville). Better known as the second omnibus budget bill, Bill C-45 amends sixty-four previous regulations and acts, several of which have a direct impact on Canada's First Nations. These changes include amendments to the Indian Act, making it easier to open access to treaty lands; to the Navigation Protection Act, removing many of the protections against damage caused by the laying of major pipeline and power projects; and the Environmental Assessment Act, speeding up the approval process for projects that have significant impact on the environment.

On 10 December 2012 the women of Idle No More helped organize a National Day of Solidarity and Resurgence, consisting of protests and rallies across Canada, which were timed to coincide with the hunger strike of Chief Theresa Spence of the beset Attawapiskat First Nation in Northern Ontario. Idle No More has drawn significant public attention to First Nations issues in Canada and beyond; importantly for cross-border analysis, it reminds us once again of the constructed nature of Canada's more liberal reputation in the arena of Indigenous rights, while simultaneously engendering a sense of the *differences* either side of the line that Canadian and US American settler-colonialisms have produced. The imposition of that line has clear and readily definable consequences, no matter how arbitrary its tracing, no matter how accidental—or even incidental—the historic location of Native nations on either side may appear to be. Nevertheless, while Idle No More is emphatic-ally rooted in Canadian legal and political contexts, its rallying cries are more widely heard. Demonstrations have been held on and across the border in the United States, and the movement's spread is not confined to the continent; it has generated support gatherings as far afield as Oxford and London in the UK, from Sweden to South Africa, from France to Greenland. On 4 November 2012, for instance, Jessica Gordon took to Twitter, asking: "@shawnatleo wuts being done w #billc45 evry1 wasting time talking about Gwen stefani wth!? #indianact #wheresthedemocracy #IdleNoMore," rapidly turning the move-ment—and certainly the hashtag—into a global phenomenon. Clearly, while the movement has spread far beyond the border, its local concerns—such as those relating to First Nations–Canadian governance and the legacy of treat-ies—are undeniably hemispheric in import. These concerns have riveted the attention of First Nations and Native American people, Canadians and US Americans, on the relationship between Indigenous rights and environmental custodianship in ways that the 2010 Mohawk delegates to Bolivia were not yet entirely alert to, as they themselves conceded.

Canada in / the Americas / in Canada

The Bolivian controversy, however, points to another consequence of the focus on borders in an American context—that is, the attribution of Border Studies' birth to the US–Mexico border. Ifeoma Nwankwo, a contributor to Caroline F. Levander and Robert S. Levine's special issue of *American Literary History* (2006) titled "Hemispheric American Literary History," notes that in this particular branch of the transnational turn, African American concerns have generally been neglected. As Nwankwo explains, hemispherism has "often focused primarily (and appropriately) on the 'unequal relations' between the

US and the Latin-American nations and states," which has led to a "dearth of scholarship on relations between US African Americans and the rest of the Americas" (580–81). The US's long history and strong legacy of constructing and regulating racialized bodies has arguably maintained this tendency for a north–south axis internal to US borders to supersede a more expansive longitudinal paradigm. Nwankwo's move to highlight the hemispheric (and its current discursive limits) in textual encounters between Latin American and African American concerns in Martin Delany's *Blake* and Gayl Jones's *Mosquito* is urgent, but it presents only "half" the story. The other "half" is categorized by George Elliott Clarke as an "immaculate, politic whiteness"(100). From a Canadian vantage point, that whiteness forms the exclusionary politics of white privilege throughout US history, while reversing the gaze reveals an occlusive apparatus effectively articulated in Canada's "ideal whiteness" (Clarke 100).

Canada's participation in the black diaspora is frequently accounted for as either the historic terminus in the Underground Railroad, or as a transition point in political and economic exile from the Caribbean. But black North American border crossing, as articulated in Wayde Compton's *49th Parallel Psalm* and C.S. Giscombe's *Giscome Road*, among other texts, addresses and assesses Canada's role in the shaping of localized, regional, and transnational black subjectivities. School segregation in Ontario and Nova Scotia, the Ku Klux Klan in the Canadian West (see Clarke), forms of slavery in Canada (see Ferguson in this volume), and the influence of hip hop and other urban forms on urban black cultures in Canada (see Compton, *49th* and *After Canaan*): all of these elements invite not only comparative but also transnational frameworks for considering historic shifts and cross-border developments in black North American cultures and identities in hemispheric terms.

If that quotation from Nwankwo's essay in relation to our earlier consideration of the Mohawk in Bolivia prompts us to deliberate on Canada's exclusion from the African Americas in hemispheric terms, his attentiveness to Latin American contexts also gives us pause to consider another facet of the hemispheric. Or, more particularly, it gives us cause to consider the development from a conceptual contact zone, as articulated for instance in Hinchcliffe and Jewinski's *Magic Realism and Canadian Literature* as early as 1986, to a more literal border presence. In *Fronteras Americanas*, Argentinean Canadian playwright Guillermo Verdecchia has his character "Verdecchia" tell his audience (originally at Toronto's Tarragon Theatre), "Somos todos Americanos" (20). A double irony unfolds from this assertion. First, as Clarke reiterates, "English Canadians—whether black, white, yellow, or brown—only agree that they are *not* Americans" (100, emphasis added); the ambiguity of terms itself enables a collapsing of the border. Second, however, an additional irony is implicit in that ambiguity, for throughout the play those other Americans, US Americans, are absent. Indeed, they are deftly elided as a constituting force, decentred,

[handwritten margin notes: Latin vi. NA as a distinction but unspoken when arowned when Coupland is subsumed]

when "Verdecchia" says, "The border is a tricky place. Take the Latin–North America border" (20–21). Here, the border on which he stands is figured as a frame within a frame: within, the US–Mexico border as precisely that border between Latin and North America; and without, the border that constitutes his negotiated identity, the one between Canada and Argentina, a "division between two countries … between two cultures and two memories" (21). The United States, in this context, merges with Canada to form one giant borderland between the land of his birth and the land of his residence. Following Emmanuel Brunet-Jailly's assertion that "borderland communities also bridge … territories" (638), Verdecchia deftly, wryly, effects one daring hemispheric move. That move draws attention to many of the same contexts and questions invoked in *Parallel Encounters:* to the mobility of cultural forms and cultural stereotypes; to the circulation and relationality of cultural products; to the political and economic influence of transnational relations and international agreements; and to the heavy presence of the border as well as to its collapsing under the ebbs and flows of pre- and post-9/11 globalization.[1]

In-Roads and Interventions

The editors of *Hemispheric American Studies* offer potentially productive possibilities for examining the cultures of the Americas from a hemispheric perspective by calling for the study of "the intricately intertwined geographies, movements, and cross-filiations among peoples, regions, diasporas, and nations of the American hemisphere" (Levander and Levine 3). The goals of such a study include "decentering the U.S. nation" and "contextualiz[ing] what can sometimes appear to be the artificially hardened borders and boundaries of the U.S. nation, or for that matter, any nation of the American hemisphere" (3). Although it opens up the nations of the Americas that might be fruitfully re-examined, much of even hemispheric American Studies seems to depend on a return to the United States, with the implications for other countries and cultures appearing as a kind of afterthought. As Winfried Siemerling and Sarah Phillips Casteel write, "'America' tacitly continues to signify 'United States' in a surprising number of avowedly hemispheric academic treatises" (10), which has contributed to the anxiety about "whether the hemispheric turn is itself an imperializing move" (9). Despite the carefully considered hesitation among many Canadianist scholars regarding the hemispheric paradigm, we agree with Siemerling and Casteel that "it seems all but impossible to situate Canada effectively without taking into consideration both its North American and its hemispheric contexts" (5), particularly in examining the cultural implications of the Canada–US border from a post-FTA, post-NAFTA, and post-9/11 position.

With precisely this difficulty in mind, the chapters in this collection seek to redress the balance of the US-centred narratives that continue to dominate the New American Studies by focusing attention on border-specific and comparative issues through largely Canadian cultural lenses. Taking the wider effects of 9/11 into account, for instance, contributors here reflect not only on the issues of surveillance and security that the post-9/11 terrorist threat has posed to the United States specifically and North America generally, but also on the urgent questions that a hardening border raises for Canadian citizenship, for Indigenous rights in Canada and the United States, for trade from a north–south perspective, and for mobility for communities that traditionally straddle the border. Bringing a wide range of methodological apparatuses to bear on these and similar issues, from health policy to law, from art history to reception theory, from Foucauldian theory to garbology, this volume embodies a broad overview of a nascent branch of the interdisciplinary Border Studies conversation. As such, it brings Canadian Studies to bear in significant ways on the developing contexts of Hemispheric American Studies.

The chapters here focus on a range of regional sites along the border and examine a rich variety of textual forms, including poetry, fiction, drama, visual art, television, and cinema produced on both sides of the 49th parallel. Section 1, Popular Culture and/at the Border, examines how popular cultural products—namely television and film—produced on both sides of the 49th parallel construct the significance of the Canada–US border, how examinations of Canada–US difference circulate via popular media, and how audiences are positioned in relation to their national location. The chapters in this section engage with border crossings both within the texts and of the texts themselves. These texts project, and are read in cross-border viewing practices as shaped by, the values popularly understood to infuse Canadianness with meaning, particularly in distinction to Americanness. Yet, as the chapters in this section demonstrate, popular culture, which includes viewers' encounters with it, does not simply validate binary oppositions across the border; as Jennifer Andrews writes in her chapter, "the 49th parallel [is] a slippery space." These cultural products posit and elicit different modes of citizenship in their concerns with national identity but also in their focus on sexuality, security, race, hemispheric affiliations, and health care provision (and the social contract that underpins it). As the chapters suggest, national viewing is itself tied to the position of the citizen, with differently inflected interpellations of the audience encouraging different visions of what it means to be Canadian, in particular, in the twenty-first century.

Andrews's "Queer(y)ing Fur: Reading *Fashion Television*'s Border Crossings" traces the evolution of particular associations with Canada and Canadian-ness into the twenty-first century by examining City Television's long-running *Fashion Television* program in relation to the nation's settler-invader origins—specifically, to the fur trade. Noting that "[f]ur has had a long and complex relationship with Canada, shaping the country's economic, political, and even sexual identity," Andrews explores how the fur trade's "fundamenta[l] shap[ing of] Canada's interactions with Britain, Europe, and the United States" *make reference to this* is reflected in J.W. Bengough's cartoon "A Pertinent Question" (1869), which stages "the economic, political, and cultural triangulation of Britain, Canada, and the United States." This triangulation has persisted into the present, as attested to by the fashion industry, which was mediated for Canadian viewers until recently by *Fashion Television*, and by host Jeanne Beker's determination to foreground Canadian contributions to fashion design. In championing expatriate Canadian twins Dan and Dean Caton, whose DSquared^2 label both invokes and ironizes stereotypical associations with Canada and the wilderness through its use of fur, *Fashion Television* performed a series of cultural border crossings even while it "appropriated and reconfigured Canada's in-between stance." In its coverage of DSquared^2 and the Catens' queering of fur, *drawn on this in my indigeneity piece* *Fashion Television* ultimately "suggested an alternative concept of (Canadian) sexual citizenship" and "cultivat[ed] new global networks and cross-border linkages that support and indeed celebrate queer identities."

Whereas Andrews's essay discusses one foundational element of popular notions of Canadianness—the relationship with fur and its queering in the present day—Jan Clarke's "Meanings of Health as Cultural Identity and Ideology Across the Canada–US Border" examines a more recently produced yet powerful marker of Canadianness, by juxtaposing Canada's universal health care with the private health care system in the United States, as represented by US filmmaker Michael Moore in his documentary *SiCKO* (2007). As Clarke notes, Moore's film offers "the border crossing as the location where these models can be compared." Moore contrasts US health care with the systems in a number of other countries, including Cuba, Britain, and France as well as Canada, and in this regard, his depiction of the differences in health care across the 49th parallel presents a stark juxtaposition of the assumptions that health is a commodity and that health is a human right, "reflect[ing] a form of ideological enclosure across the border." Moore's film bears out the dominant view in Canada that "citizenship [is] linked to access to good health regardless of means to pay." Not only do the diverging models of health care "lin[k] to cultural identity in terms of what it means to be American or Canadian," but also, fundamentally, they appear to be "based on culturally specific individualism in the United States and collectivism in Canada," suggesting even larger ideological differences across the border.

SiCKO projects a cross-border divide insofar as US citizens are depicted as confronting anxieties about health care costs, whereas Canadian citizens are portrayed as assuming that their health care needs will be met without any cost to them individually. In "Television, Nation, and National Security: The CBC's *The Border*," Sarah A. Matheson turns to a different source of anxiety in the contemporary world, focusing on *The Border*'s negotiation of concerns about border security at the 49th parallel. *The Border*, Matheson argues, "emerg[es] from and is shaped by a borderland society," in both its form and its content, produced as it is in "a cross-border televisual environment." Michael Moore's film, as Clarke's essay observes, confirms meaningful differences between Canada and the United States where collective responsibility and health care are concerned; for her part, Matheson notes that although *The Border* "was premised in part on the perceived notion of a conflict between US and Canadian values and institutions," in "adopt[ing] ... some of the most problematic aspects of action genres," the series "ultimately reproduces a similar kind of politics of paranoia and fear of the sort that pervade so much of post-9/11 television." *The Border* ostensibly assures Canadian viewers that "Canadian approaches to national security" are "more ethical and conciliatory" than those of our cross-border neighbours; however, this "articulat[ion of] a sense of difference and resistance to American influence" is compromised by the program's failure "to rise above the constraints of genre, and trouble both its pleasures and politics."

In "'Normalizing Relations': The Canada/Cuban Imaginary on the Fringe of Border Discourse," Joanne C. Elvy and Luis René Fernández Tabío observe a similar tendency in *The Border*: US political concerns are allowed to eclipse Canada's engagement on its own terms with other parts of the hemisphere. Whereas Moore's *SiCKO* implicitly aligns Canada and Cuba in opposition to the United States with regard to comprehensive state-sponsored health care, Elvy and Fernández Tabío note that *The Border* projects "Cuba as a site of tension" for Canadian viewers. *The Border* is "a cultural product made by Canadians and for Canadians," yet in the episode titled "Normalizing Relations," the program's treatment of Cuba enacts "a gross superimposition of an American lens upon the Canadian psyche" by adopting US concerns about Cuba. In this episode, Cuba is not only "imagined from afar" but also constructed as a "problem" to be "normalized" for Canadian viewers. This representation of Cuba and its replication of a US perspective prompts Elvy and Fernández Tabío to ask whether Canadians are "able to view Cuba in a broader hemispheric context independent of the United States." Given *The Border*'s replication of US concerns, notwithstanding the program's celebration of what it perceives to be Canadian values, it appears that "the omnipresence of America itself" figures as "the looming barrier that impedes Canada/Cuba relations" and that this episode "speaks more of the 'normalization' process between Canada and the United States." In this sense, as both Matheson and Elvy and Fernández Tabío argue, *The Border* undermines its own assertions of cross-border difference, particularly if that difference is understood as resistance to dominant US values and perspectives.

In "How, Exactly, Does the Beaver Bite Back? The Case of Canadian Students Viewing Paul Haggis's *Crash*," Lee Easton and Kelly Hewson question their Canadian students about their responses to representations of race in

Crash (2005), the successful Oscar-winning film produced in the United States but directed by Canadian Paul Haggis. In discussing the representations of race and racism in *Crash*, Easton and Hewson observe that their students, "for all their seeming cosmopolitanism—their transnational potential and ease in globalized space—constructed their viewing selves in relation to the 49th parallel." Deploying Frank Manning's concept of "reversible resistance," Easton and Hewson theorize their students' cross-border responses to the film, noting that the students use the border in their viewing practices "as a way to position themselves and Canada paradoxically as both inferior and superior to America." They ask their students what *Crash* might have looked like had it been made and set in Haggis's own country rather than in the United States; the responses this question elicits configure race relations in Canada in terms of the conflict between Indigenous and settler-invader communities. Indeed, this configuration, Easton and Hewson observe, amounts to cross-border validation of Canadian distinctiveness: "reversible resistance requires an Aboriginal presence in order to shape a Canadian identity that resists American assimilation." Ultimately, Easton and Hewson advocate "an Indigenized Métis/Canadian spectatorship" that will move beyond the "protect[ion of] a notion of white Canadianness," the key function that the Canada–US border might be said to fulfil in the dominant Anglo-Canadian imaginary.

Such a function of the Canada–US border participates in the kind of Canadian nationalism that the popular texts under discussion in the first section of this volume posit and/or affirm, either through the texts themselves or through Canadians' viewing practices. As Easton and Hewson's observations indicate, however, Indigeneity undermines comfortable notions about Canada's status as a settler-invader nation-state attempting to position itself as more just than its neighbour across the border. Crucially, as many chapters in Section 2, Indigenous Cultures and North American Borders, point out, Indigeneity troubles the very existence of the border itself. The 49th parallel, which offers a marker of national difference in and in relation to the popular texts, figures as a colonial imposition on Indigenous peoples' lands. The chapters in this section address the illegitimacy of the Canada–US border through lenses provided by Indigenous texts and the ways in which Indigenous authors and artists represent and negotiate the border and the colonial nation-states it claims to demarcate. As Maggie Ann Bowers argues, "[h]owever arbitrary the border is, it has had consequences in terms of the differing experiences of colonization on either side." The chapters in this section examine Indigenous writers and critics' engagements with postcolonial discourse, as shaped by their position in relation to the border, by Indigenous literature about the border and its relation to questions of citizenship and questions of waste and the environment, by Indigenous border art as contrasted with both non-Indigenous border art and state-sponsored attempts to deploy art to shore up a post-NAFTA version of North American culture, and by *mestiza* and Métis writings that, positioned alongside each other, map Indigenous struggles with colonial nation-states and their borders in continental terms.

Bowers's chapter, "Discursive Positioning: A Comparative Study of Postcolonialism in Native Studies Across the US–Canada Border," examines the ways in which postcolonial theory has been deployed and discussed by Indigenous writers and critics on either side of the 49th parallel, as well as how different discourses have affected examinations of the border. As she notes, "the histories and cultural adaptations of the First Nations and Native American nations divided by the 49th parallel are inevitably different and influenced by the border, whether it is recognized as legitimate or not." Canada's and the United States' "different histories of postcolonialism … have influenced the debates concerning the acceptance or rejection of postcolonial theory in Native North American Studies." Bowers argues that these different histories have led to a greater tendency among Indigenous critics working south of the Canada–US border to engage elements of postcolonial theory, both directly and counter-discursively, particularly in their attempts to establish "a critical framework that includes not only the specifically Native American but also the transnational postcolonial." If the status of the border is inflected by the discourse used to interrogate it, "either as existing in terms of colonialism using a postcolonial theoretical framework, or as an imaginary concept lacking legitimacy in tribal thinking," the adoption and adaptation of some postcolonial theory, such as Bhabha's notion of "the in-between space of the borderlands," provides a means "to examine this duality and … articulate a new discursive position."

As Bowers notes, Cherokee writer Thomas King, long resident in Canada, is prominent among critics who reject the postcolonial framework for readings of Indigenous literature. Gillian Roberts's chapter, "Strategic Parallels: Invoking the Border in Thomas King's *Green Grass, Running Water* and Drew Hayden Taylor's *In a World Created by a Drunken God*," compares King's novel with Taylor's play through their characters' simultaneous assertions of Indigenous and Canadian identities. Such expressions of "multiple and (from some perspectives) incommensurate, assertions of identity" invoke debates about the status of Canadian citizenship for Indigenous people, given the clash between the Canadian sovereignty ostensibly protected by the Canada–US border and Indigenous sovereignties infringed upon by both Canada and the United States. In King's novel and in Taylor's play, the deployment of Canadian identity by Indigenous characters demonstrates the texts' resistance to singular understandings of Indigenous belonging. National identities are deployed in distinction from metaphors of US imperialism, yet neither author resolves the tensions implicit in that resistance. Instead, Roberts argues, each author holds the border "open" as "a site of struggle over citizenship and its implications for Native North American peoples."

In "Waste-full Crossings in Thomas King's *Truth and Bright Water*," Catherine Bates extends the discussion of Thomas King's work by closely examining his representation of the border site that divides a community: both the incomplete, wasting bridge across the border and the river that forms the border—a river that is, itself, full of dumped waste. Bates therefore discusses King's portrayal of the border "as a material place that, when policed, holds the Native peoples who cross it accountable to the nation-state" and that "*makes visible the way lives and bodies are inscribed and constrained by the nation-state.*" In the novel's treatment of the border, identity, and story, waste performs different functions. On the one hand, "[b]y clogging the border, the waste in King's novel remains a permanent reminder of the consequences of systematizing culture and identity restrictively"; on the other, waste is not simply coded negatively, for King also suggests "possible ways that we can read, reconstruct, and re-story the waste productively, by affectively reimagining the border using approaches other than violent and systematizing logic." Ultimately, the border in its materiality represents a site of both containment and inscription and a kind of productive seepage across and beyond the artificial line.

David Stirrup's "Bridging the Third Bank: Indigeneity and Installation Art at the Canada–US Border" analyzes representations of the border site in visual art, exploring questions of emplacement and belonging in installations by Six Nations Mohawk artist Alan Michelson and non-Native Canadian Alex McKay. Michelson's and McKay's works "expressly treat bordered states … and navigate the historical territory of the border as both passage and perimeter." Both artists employ and evoke the motif of the two-row wampum, invoking treaty discourse as alternately recuperative and occlusive in works that "map" the territories and passages of the border zone both literally in terms of contemporary political relationships and figuratively in terms of the historic legacy of colonialism. Stirrup argues that Michelson's *Third Bank of the River* celebrates a living tradition and asserts a continued affirmation of cultural and political sovereignty, whereas McKay's works deliberately invoke a sense of appropriated pastness that raises a tension between an anti-colonial narrative of resistance and a more self-consciously internalized co-option of Indigeneity in the settler-colonial state narrative. Both Michelson and McKay engage with questions of citizenship, with McKay's work "ask[ing] perhaps more generally what it means to be Canadian" while Michelson, figuring the border-straddling and -transcending Mohawk nation "at the centre, rather than on the periphery," ultimately "asserts emplaced citizenship at the border."

Whereas Stirrup focuses on visual art located at the Canada–US border, Sarah E.K. Smith, in "Cross-Border Identifications and Dislocations: Visual Art and the Construction of Identity in North America," examines state-sponsored attempts to recruit Canadian, US, and Mexican visual art in order to redraw North America's cultural borders in a NAFTA context. Analyzing visual art exhibitions mounted with the intention of "promot[ing] continental integration in the post-NAFTA era," Smith discusses such exhibitions as "form[s] of cultural diplomacy." Deploying George Yúdice's notion of "transnational cultural brokering," she demonstrates how NAFTA's signatory governments prompted "a reconceptualized North American landscape." If this new continental landscape emerged out of economic ties, Smith provides a counter-example of visual art in North America that both "foregrounds typical economic transactions on the border" and destabilizes, rather than affirms, state-sponsored attempts to project continental parity. She does so through the work of Anishnabe artist Rebecca Belmore. Belmore's installation *Awasinake: On the Other Side*, mounted in San Diego in 1997, self-consciously positioned the artist herself in dialogue with the US–Mexico border and its narratives of crossing, which are circumscribed by privilege and race. By exploring "Indigenous cross-border identification," *Awasinake* exposes "the tenuous relationship between Indigenous culture and national/ist projects" and "offers a lens through which the Canada–US border can be considered in relation to questions of Indigenous ."

Just as Belmore's installation invites a reconsideration of the Canada–US border through *Awasinake*'s positioning in proximity to the US–Mexico border, so Zalfa Feghali's "Conversations That Never Happened: The Writing and Activism of Gloria Anzaldúa, Maria Campbell, and Howard Adams" produces a comparative border study that privileges the possible Indigenous alliances across the continent over the dominant nationalist fictions of Canada and the United States. Imagining a conversation/collaboration between these three writers—a Chicana activist-writer, a Métis writer, and a Métis scholar—Feghali extends a comparative analysis of border(ed) issues from the southern to the northern boundary of the United States, raising vital questions about racialized and gendered identities. Analyzing each of their personal negotiations with history, their analysis of the internalization of colonization (especially through language), and their understandings of Indigenous, she isolates a number of "essential sites of both convergence and divergence within their thought," ultimately concluding that "each of these writers presents a different version of the same hope for community and coalition building across minority groups." Crucially, Feghali's discussion incorporates Anzaldúa while contesting the perpetual primacy of US–Mexico border-based paradigms, interrogating the extent to which "work done on [a] specific border … [can] be transposed to other borders." As such, this chapter forges necessary dialogue between North America's border sites, actively reworking hemispheric approaches to Border Studies.

Just as the hemispheric paradigm offers the potential to reconceptualize nation-state borders in the Americas, so the chapters in Section 3, Theorizing the Border: Literature, Performance, Translation, present a number of possibilities for rethinking the Canada–US border in literary production, translation, and reading practices. As many of the chapters in this final section demonstrate, conventionally anticipated boundaries between national positions on sexuality, race, language, and cultural production across the 49th parallel begin to blur on closer scrutiny. This section interrogates the site of the border, in its textual and extratextual manifestations, in terms of the role it plays—or, in some cases, fails to play—in demarcating Canadian and US territory and culture. The authors in this section demonstrate that conventional understandings of the 49th parallel are complicated by broader hemispheric contexts, by the ambiguous working and location of the border, and indeed, by the very concept of the border. Engaging with the border in both material and theoretical terms, this final section offers a rich diversity of conceptual routes to and across the 49th parallel. In the authors' theorizing of the border, this volume concludes by offering a set of northern responses to the wealth of conceptualizations of the US–Mexico border site, thereby strengthening the dialogue between border studies in North America.

In "'Some Borders Are More Easily Crossed Than Others': Negotiating Guillermo Verdecchia's *Fronteras Americanas*," Maureen Kincaid Speller brings a hemispheric sense of borders to bear on the 49th parallel. Thinking through how a border site actually functions, she argues that "we may need to find new ways of describing the border." Employing Michel Foucault's notion of heterotopias, Speller analyzes the processes of moderating and modulating the border—as crossed line, zone, passage from one country to another, and even individual interaction with others—that arise in Verdecchia's play. Probing the identity crisis of the play's main character, Speller ponders what an Argentinean Canadian—rather than a Canadian–US American or Mexican–US American—border might look like. Ultimately, such a question can only be answered in relation to a hemispheric framework, as this specific hyphenate experience of identity and borders "moves away from the specifics of geographical location to the border as a state of mind, but a state of mind that also transcends the continent." In this sense, the border opens out to an affiliation with the Americas as a whole while simultaneously operating as a site of self-construction rather than a line of national imposition or exclusion.

If Speller demonstrates the possibilities offered by reconceptualizing the Canada–US border in relation to the hemisphere, Jade Ferguson argues that Hemispheric American Studies has yet to develop a methodology of slavery studies that will account for the history and legacy of slavery in Canada. In "Discounting Slavery: The Currency Wars, Minstrelsy, and 'The White Nigger' in T.C. Haliburton's *The Clockmaker*," Ferguson contends that "[i]n order to contest the pervasive discounting of slavery in Canada," scholars must examine how "Canada's investment in slavery, while it did not manifest itself in the plantation system, shares cultural, literary, and historical commonalities with the rest of the Americas." Ferguson argues that Haliburton's cross-border engagement with "the hotly debated issue of monetary policy in the United States" offered him "an ideology of value" to deploy in order "to mobilize Nova Scotians for economic reform." In projecting an "analogy between money and race, employed in early blackface minstrelsy," in his 1836 sketch "The White Nigger," Haliburton "critique[s] paper money and the dispossessions of white privileges it represents." Racializing the form that money takes, and suggesting that the market negotiates not only "the nature and value of money" but also "the meaning of racial difference" in nineteenth-century Nova Scotia, Haliburton "uses the debates about the form of black–white relations across the border to awaken Nova Scotians to the province's economic instability." As Ferguson demonstrates, Haliburton's sketch demonstrates both "[t]he circulation of the figure of the 'white nigger' across the US-Canada border" and "the necessity of exploring constructions of whiteness and white supremacy in hemispheric contexts."

The dominant Canadian narrative of slavery in North America is, of course, that of the Underground Railroad, a narrative that eclipses Canada's own history of slavery and racism and that figures Canada as a haven across the Canada–US border for enslaved African Americans. In "Detained at Customs: Jane Rule, Censorship, and the Politics of Cross the Canada–US Border," Susan Billingham examines Canada as an ambiguous haven for the US-born lesbian writer Jane Rule, whose political rejection of her country of birth and its "super-patriotism" in favour of Canada and its "more self-reflexive forms of allegiance," particularly in the context of the Cold War, coexists uncomfortably with Canada Customs' detaining of Rule's published work on grounds of obscenity. Whereas Andrews's chapter in Section 1 of this volume offers Canada as a site of alternative sexual citizenship, Billingham demonstrates that Rule provides an example of a citizen whose sexuality made her and her work objects of surveillance. Billingham argues, through an analysis of Rule's work as well as its targeting by Canada Customs, that the Canada–US border functions, in an invocation of Foucault, "as an instrument of 'bio-power' in the regulation of citizens' lives." Rule chose "to make Canada her permanent intellectual home," yet she "remained subject to the institutional biases and cultural mechanisms of the Canadian nation-state that served to reinforce heteronormativity."

As Billingham notes, Rule's crossing of the Canada–US border accorded her an "insider/outsider status with respect to both nations." In "Strangers in Strange Lands: Cultural Translation in Gaétan Soucy's *Vaudeville!*," Jeffrey Orr examines a text that, in its authorship and translation, occupies a similar liminal position. *Vaudeville!* offers an "outsider," defamiliarized portrait of New York produced originally in French by Québécois author Soucy and translated into English by Anglo-Canadian Sheila Fischman. Not only has the text itself been translated, but translation is also integral within the text itself.

By "rendering New York alien and frightening," *Vaudeville!* "questions ... the hegemonic landmarks and landscape of the city and the country of which it is part." Orr discusses the novel's interrogation of US cultural power and the position of the cross-border reader through the lens of translation, which "animates the quotidian and overunderstood elements of American cultural production by reminding the reader of his/her foreignness and oddity." However, as Orr emphasizes, the novel does not "simply oppos[e] USian cultural power"; rather, "it asks us to consider the ways in which the exchange of ideas has both been changed, and been changed by, geographical and cultural translation across the border." Ultimately, the encounter between the original text and its translation "opens new possibilities for self-examination, particularly in a readership from the Americas," as readers are "carried across," or translated at, the border, "immigrating to the new and alien world of the text, and metaphorically seeing New York for the first time."

If readers are carried across the border in their engagement with *Vaudeville!*, Nasser Hussain's "Bodies of Information: Cross-Border Poetics in the Twenty-First Century" examines writers who, both physically and poetically, cross the 49th parallel. Hussain's narrative of the development of contemporary cross-border poetics, which features Canada's "outwithness" with regard to the United States, includes the formation of Tish in Vancouver in 1961 via the language poets' "poetry of boundaries," as well as the work of Darren Wershler-Henry, Christian Bök, and Kenneth Goldsmith, as inheritors, in very different ways, of both the Tish and language poetry lineages. Whereas Billingham's chapter in this section demonstrates how literature as a material object can be obstructed by the 49th parallel, the "cross-border transactions" to which Hussain attends consist of flows of poetics that find the border to be porous. A short cross-border trip took Wershler-Henry and Bök, then based in Toronto, to meet Goldsmith at a reading in Buffalo, New York, where they found unexpected common ground, according to Goldsmith: "They were Canadian pataphysicists who were involved with concrete and sound poetry, while I was coming out of a text art tradition, but we all saw our respective paths as dead ends." As Hussain elaborates, this moment, in this place, gave birth to North American Conceptual poetry, making Buffalo "an exciting forum for new writing in new media and formats where traditional formal, bodily, and political boundaries begin to break down and reform into new practices and identities and a refreshed, global sense of citizenship" that allows us to "begin to conceive of ourselves anew."

The final chapter of this section, and of the volume as a whole, Lynette Hunter's "Bordering on Borders: Dream, Memory, and Allegories of Writing," offers a rich theorization of borders, addressing poetics in relation to borders in a manner that reconceptualizes the self. Inviting us to consider borders in a more intimate sense, in analyzing works by Judy Halebsky and Daphne Marlatt,

Hunter distinguishes between borders as "performance[s] of different kinds of identity and self that realize different kinds of rhetoric" and "bordering," which she describes as an "engaged border," one "where we make difference, create identity through embodiment of our recognition that we are not something other/else." Exploring dream "as a place that embodies difference, memory as a process of situating that embodiment, and allegories of writing as a way of building a situated textuality," Hunter contemplates the "significations of 'border' and 'bordering,' or the performativity of the border ... to think further about the embodied social knowledge wrapped up in the process of bordering, and its articulation in the work of dream, memory, and allegory." As Hunter argues of Halebsky and Marlatt, these poets "enact/perform bordering in their writing" through engagements with translation and memory and forgetting, respectively. Bordering, then, refigures relationships between self and other, reading and writing, and poses a challenge to the rigid identities that the borders designed to "chart territory" are formed to create and reinforce.

To speak of territory is to speak of jurisdictions, of the regulation of bodies and spaces in pursuit of the maintenance of specific cultural, political, and economic models. In speaking of borders, however, we shift from an exclusive discourse of territory to one that encompasses terrain. In other words, we commit to considering the country as that space embordered and the *country* both as the natural topography that transcends it quite literally and as a structural metaphor for cultures and peoples. Implicit in Border Studies, then, is that dual sense of the artificial, state-imposed delimitation of transactions, identities, and relations, and the *natural* forms and means by which those things cross, transgress, mutate at, and transform borders. Examination of the border site reveals these things not as binaries, but as complicated webs of interrelated gestures. If Stoddard's *Walrus* article and the experiences of the Mohawk delegation to the World People's Conference on Climate Change and the Rights of Mother Earth remind us of the political processes engendered by and perpetuated at the Canada–US border, the chapters in this collection articulate a variety of ways in which cultural texts negotiate complex and nuanced understandings of politically charged cross-border comparisons. As *Parallel Encounters* demonstrates, then, cultural products, whether from south of, north of, or at the 49th parallel, grapple with pressing issues concerning national identities, citizenship, continental affiliations, the legacies of colonialism, the spectre of neo-colonialism, the contradictions of settler-invader postcolonial culture, and the question of for whom the border performs legitimately in the first place. Ultimately, approaching the 49th parallel variously as boundary, barrier, bridge, as metaphor, mirror, lens, as a way out of a dead end or a scar across the continent, these chapters offer new pathways into reading the border both as a site of analysis and a crucial location in a broader hemispheric conception of America and Canada's position within it.

Note

1   Clearly Verdecchia's play does not raise post-9/11 concerns, but in preceding 2001's shifts of attitude to the border its very lack of attention to later threats such as terrorism, while still invoking cultural stereotypes of suspicion towards darker-skinned border crossers, is potent in and of itself.

Works Cited

Adams, Rachel. *Continental Divides: Remapping the Cultures of North America.* Chicago: U of Chicago P, 2009.

———. "The Northern Borderlands and Latino Canadian Diaspora." Levander and Levine 313–27.

Angus, Ian. *A Border Within: National Identity, Cultural Plurality, and Wilderness.* Montreal and Kingston: McGill–Queen's UP, 1997.

Anzaldúa, Gloria. *Borderlands/La Frontera.* 2nd ed. San Francisco: Aunt Lute, 1999.

Brown, Russell. "The Written Line." *Borderlands: Essays in Canadian–American Relations.* Ed. Robert Lecker. Toronto: ECW, 1991. 1–27.

Brunet-Jailly, Emmanuel. "Theorizing Borders: An Interdisciplinary Perspective." *Geopolitics* 10.4 (2005): 633–49.

Clarke, George Elliott. "White Like Canada." *Transition* 73 (1997): 98–109.

Compton, Wayde. *49th Parallel Psalm.* Vancouver: Arsenal Pulp Press, 1999.

———. "The Reinventing Wheel: On Blending the Poetry of Cultures Through Hip Hop Turntablism." *Horizon Zero 8* (2003). Web. http://www.horizonzero.ca/textsite/remix.php?is=8&file=7&tlang=0. Accessed 28 March 2013.

———. *After Canaan: Essays on Race, Writing, and Region.* Vancouver: Arsenal Pulp Press, 2010.

Gansworth, Eric. "Patriot Act." *Eric Gansworth: Writer and Visual Artist.* http://www.ericgansworth.com/#!stories-poems-and-essays/patriot-act.pdf. Accessed 12 March 2013.

Giscombe, C.S. *Giscome Road.* Champaign and London: Dalkey Archive Press, 1998.

Hardwick, Susan W., and Ginger Mansfield. "Discourse, Identity, and 'Homeland as Other' at the Borderlands." *Annals of the Association of American Geographers* 1 April 2009: 383–405.

Horn, Greg. "Canada Prevents Mohawks from Returning Home on Haudenosaunee Passports." *Iorì:wase: KahnawakeNews.com* 1 June 2010. http://kahnawakenews.com/canada-prevents-mohawks-from-returning-home-on-haudenosaunee-passports-p798.htm?twindow=Default&smenu=1&mad=No. Accessed 8 April 2011.

Konrad, Victor, and Heather N. Nicol. *Beyond Walls: Re-inventing the Canada–United States Borderlands.* Aldershot and Burlington: Ashgate, 2008.

Levander, Caroline F., and Robert S. Levine, eds. *Hemispheric American Studies.* New Brunswick: Rutgers UP, 2008.

Mandel, Eli. "The Border League: American 'West' and Canadian 'Region.'" *Crossing Frontiers.* Ed. Dick Harrison. Edmonton: U of Alberta P, 1979. 105–21.

Meekis, Devon. "Press Release Idle No More." *Idle No More* 2 January 2013. Web. http://idlenomore.ca/about-us/press-releases/item/58-press-release-idle-no-more. Accessed 12 March 2013.

Michaelsen, Scott, and David E. Johnson, eds. *Border Theory: The Limits of Cultural Politics.* Minneapolis: U of Minnesota P, 1997.

Nwankwo, Ifeoma Kiddoe. "The Promises and Perils of US African-American Hemispherism: Latin America in Martin Delany's *Blake* and Gayl Jones's *Mosquito*." *American Literary History* 18.3 (2006): 570–99.

Rowe, John Carlos. "Post-Nationalism, Globalism, and the New American Studies." *Post-Nationalist American Studies*. Ed. John Carlos Rowe. Berkeley: U of California P, 2000. 23–37.

Sadowski-Smith, Claudia. *Border Fictions: Globalization, Empire, and Writing at the Boundaries of the United States*. Charlottesville: U of Virginia P, 2008.

Siemerling, Winfried, and Sarah Phillips Casteel. "Introduction: Canada and Its Americas." *Canada and Its Americas*. Ed. Winfried Siemerling and Sarah Phillips Casteel. Montreal and Kingston: McGill–Queen's UP, 2010. 3–28.

Stoddard, Grant. "The Lost Canadians." *The Walrus* 81 (2011): 24–31.

Stuteville, Sarah. "Idle No More: Indigenous Rights Go Global." *Seattle Globalist*. 1 February 2013. Web. http://www.seattleglobalist.com/2013/02/01/idle-no-more-indigenous-rights-go-global-and-viral/10073. Accessed 12 March 2013.

Traister, Bryce. "Border Shopping: American Studies and the Anti-Nation." *Globalization on the Line: Culture, Capital, and Citizenship at U.S. Borders*. Ed. Claudia Sadowski-Smith. New York: Palgrave, 2002. 31–52.

Verdecchia, Guillermo. *Fronteras Americanas: American Borders*. 1993. Vancouver: Talonbooks, 1997.

POPULAR CULTURE
AND/AT THE BORDER

two

Queer(y)ing Fur

Reading *Fashion Television*'s Border Crossings

Jennifer Andrews

The beaver (*Castor canadensis* Kuhl) was of dominant importance in the beginning of the Canadian fur trade.

Harold Innis, *The Fur Trade in Canada*, 3

The Beaver renamed ... to end porn mix-up.[1]

Headline, Agence France Presse, 12 January 2010

FUR HAS HAD A LONG AND complex relationship with Canada, shaping the country's economic, political, and even sexual identity. Concurrently, fur remains an important part of the North American and indeed global fashion industry, symbolizing luxury and warmth. Julia Emberley reveals some of the intricacies of fur's cultural significance within the fashion industry, noting that the fur coat in the twentieth century operates primarily as a "feminine fashion commodity worn by women to display the twin signs of wealth and prestige" (16). But as Emberley argues in her persuasive study, *The Cultural Politics of Fur*, the fur coat also operates as a sign of "female sexuality and its libidinal profits of exchange" (16). And while Canada has been a crucial source for fur pelts, it remains a traditionally marginalized (and symbolically feminized) nation with respect to fashion innovation. Yet Canada was the birthplace and home of *Fashion Television*, a half-hour television fashion show hosted by Toronto-based journalist Jeanne Beker that ran for a remarkable twenty-seven years. First broadcast in 1985, *FT* was the longest continually running program of its kind. The show became internationally acclaimed and extremely popular with viewers around the globe; its final episode aired on 22 April 2012. Reruns of the show remain central to the programming schedule of FashionTelevisionChannel, a Canadian-based subscription channel devoted exclusively to fashion, art, and design, which was launched in 2001 and strategically renamed *Fashion Television* in the summer of 2012; this name change attests to the sustained popularity of the original *FT* and its potential to attract new subscribers. When asked in 2010 about what makes *Fashion Television* unique, Beker stated that the show's strength lay in the fact that "Canadians have always made for great observers" and that *FT* "tell[s] [compelling] fashion stories" from a uniquely Canadian perspective (personal interview 3). If, as John Hartley argues in *Television Truths*, "nations themselves are the outcome of 'narrative accrual,' and citizenship is bound up with story" (75), what do explorations of Canada and Canadian identity through fur on a program like *Fashion Television* convey about the nation and its identity, especially in relation to its traditional colonial allies and trading partners—the United States and Britain? How might (re)fashioning or (re)thinking fur's myriad connotations in the context of *FT*—a show that itself crossed multiple borders, literally and figuratively—enable a different understanding of Canada on the world stage, particularly in terms of sexuality?

Fur trading—particularly of the much-coveted beaver pelt—was pivotal to Canada's pre-Confederation development. The fur trade also fundamentally shaped Canada's interactions with Britain, Europe, and the United States and its birth as a postcolonial nation with its own history of internal oppression and exploitation of Native peoples (many of whom were fur trappers).[2] The recent renaming of *The Beaver*—the second-oldest magazine in Canada, "launched in 1920 to celebrate the 250th anniversary of the Hudson's Bay Co. and the fur trade that led to the early exploration of Canada"—serves as a pointed reminder of the sexual connotations of fur in the contemporary world (*"Canada's The Beaver"*). According to publisher Deborah Morrison, "there was only one interpretation for the word [beaver]" when the magazine began. The fact that "in modern times" the term has become "slang for women's genitalia" made it very difficult for *The Beaver* to circulate online without having its readers plagued by spam filters or unable to access the magazine at all. This crudely sexualized rendering of the beaver when paired with Canada's colonial history provides a provocative context for examining fur's border crossings. This chapter couples close readings of Canada's nineteenth-century depictions of itself as a youthful and resolutely feminized source of New World natural resources, especially as represented by fur, with Jeanne Beker's efforts to complicate this clichéd vision of the nation through her work as a fashion journalist and long-standing host of *Fashion Television*. Not only did she reposition Canada (and specifically Toronto) in relation to the world of fashion, but she also used the show to explore and champion alterna(rra)tive sexual identities, particularly through her sustained support of Dean and Dan Caten, gay Canadian-born twin brothers who are the creators of the highly successfully label DSquared[2].

Canada has long been located on the periphery of the global fashion industry; its closest neighbour, the United States, often overshadows it. This perception of Canada as a New World source of natural resources, particularly fur, to be exported to and exploited by other imperializing nations—including America—was pointedly articulated nearly 120 years before the inception

A PERTINENT QUESTION.

MRS. BRITANNIA.—" IS IT POSSIBLE, MY DEAR, THAT YOU HAVE EVER GIVEN YOUR COUSIN JONATHAN ANY ENCOURAGEMENT?"

MISS CANADA.—" ENCOURAGEMENT? CERTAINLY NOT, MAMMA. I HAVE TOLD HIM WE CAN *NEVER* BE UNITED."

Fig. 2.1   J.W. Bengough, "A Pertinent Question," 1869.

of *Fashion Television* in British-born, Toronto-based satirist J.W. Bengough's "A Pertinent Question." Bengough's cartoon first appeared in the *Diogenes*, a popular Canadian humour magazine, on 18 June 1869 [see Figure 1]. Published only two years after Canadian Confederation, the cartoon portrays a young Miss Canada sitting on a bench, turned away from the American dandy, Cousin Jonathan—attired in his sartorial version of the American flag—and leaning into Mrs. Britannia. In the caption that appears below, Mrs. Britannia queries the new nation about her conduct, asking, "Is it possible, my dear, that you have ever given your cousin Jonathan any encouragement?", to which the Miss Canada responds: "Encouragement! Certainly not, Mamma. I have told him we can *never* be united."

[handwritten margin note: idea that Miss Canada is hyper-sexualized and also vulnerable]

While Mrs. Britannia places both hands demurely on her lap, Miss Canada offers only one, propping herself up on Mrs. Britannia's shoulder with the other, and looking away from her mother country's face as she articulates her apparently unwavering commitment to the monarchy, suggesting that the young woman's mind may be elsewhere. The cartoon sets up a resolutely heterosexist paradigm, with Mrs. Britannia attempting to ensure her daughter's loyalty and aversion to her potential male suitor, Cousin Jonathan, whose geographic proximity and economic clout make him a compelling husband and New World protector. In this case, Mrs. Britannia is expressing a genuine fear that her colonial offspring—who is an abundant source of cheap natural resources—may stray. Bengough's choice of image and caption emphasizes the importance of this neighbourly relationship between Canada and the United States, cemented by the shared border, in sexual and financial terms. His cartoon anticipates that Miss Canada will soon be enticed into forging alliances with and even producing children with Jonathan, who, as a symbol of the United States, has already demonstrated his revolutionary and imperialistic tendencies. Bengough's depiction of Canada–US relations also evokes the powerful rhetoric of "Manifest Destiny," a term coined by American journalist John O'Sullivan in 1845 to justify the new nation's efforts to annex the Republic of Texas.[3] Canada soon became another target for the United States, which aimed to spread republican democracy and to liberate colonies all over the world from British and European bondage. Not surprisingly, then, Bengough's cartoon couples the overbearing nature of Mrs. Britannia's rule with the slickly alluring aspects of American exceptionalism, as embodied by Cousin Jonathan. The 49th parallel becomes a slippery space, open to manipulation by Canada's southern neighbour as part of the fulfilment of a broader, American-authored narrative of Manifest Destiny.

In Bengough's cartoon, apparel conveys key assumptions about each nation. Cousin Jonathan wears stovepipe-striped trousers, a dark jacket with tails, a waistcoat patterned with stars, and a top hat, garments that literalize the flag-waving Yankee's loyalty to his New World nation. His dishevelled and lanky hair, his beard, and his hardened facial features are coupled with the phallic cigar he holds in his mouth, offering the promise of unrefined Freudian masculine seduction to the young Miss Canada. Jonathan's body may be physically angled away from Miss Canada, but his right hand, which leans on an adjacent pillar, is in proximity to his female neighbour's shoulder. Such a stance suggests that he could easily reach out and touch her, visually echoing the geographical immediacy of the shared Canada–US border and anticipating the close economic ties between the two nations—ties that continue to this day in the form of agreements such as NAFTA (the North American Free Trade Agreement) and, more recently, the Beyond the Border Declaration and the Regulatory Creation Council, both founded in February 2011. Furthermore,

Cousin Jonathan is the only figure standing in the cartoon; the two female figures sit together on a bench, making Jonathan seem larger than life and positioning him as looming over Miss Canada. Jonathan's stance, as portrayed by Bengough, may be read as implying that Manifest Destiny is the inevitable outcome for Canada as a nation as it matures into womanhood.

Like Cousin Jonathan, Bengough's cartoon women are dressed symbolically to articulate the character of their respective nations. Mrs. Britannia wears a Victorian-style gown, with a high neckline and long hemline that modestly conceals her ankles and feet. She has a headpiece that resembles a gladiator helmet, invoking the ancient Roman roots of Britain, which is in keeping with other traditional depictions of this figure of imperial motherhood.[4] Miss Canada is more youthfully attired in a dress with a visible petticoat. Her ankles are exposed to reveal the short leather boots on her feet. She also wears a tailored long-sleeved fur jacket and small felted hat that combines the North American hunter's fur pelts with the formality of a structured hat.

While Miss Canada is somewhat less modestly dressed than her elder companion, what is notable here in sartorial terms is the presence of fur on the younger woman's garments. Beginning in the sixteenth century, the British North American fur trade was a key supplier of furs and pelts to Britain and Europe, including the much-coveted beaver, which was used to create fur-wool for a wide range of felted products. Emberley describes "the hierarchy of fur's material value" in Britain from the Middle Ages onward, which often involved the legislation of fur-wearing; the most expensive and lightest-coloured furs, including the white back-fur of beaver, fox, marten, and grey squirrel, were reserved for royalty, while the darker pelts of otter, hare, beaver, and fox trimmed the clothing of "lesser nobility and the middle class" (47). Emberley notes that "sumptuary legislation declined" with the decreasing "availability of fur-bearing animals" but that its legacy remained, with fashion being perceived, particularly by church leaders, as a potential mode for subverting established class and race hierarchies (66). Indeed, Miss Canada's coat hints at this transgressive possibility. She wears an abundance of fur: her jacket juxtaposes a middle-class, darker-coloured body with the elegance and refinement of the monarchical white trim that extends beyond the collar and cuffs to the entire edge of the garment. Likewise, the felted hat renders the resources of the youthful nation and her female representative highly visible. As Emberley points out, "More than an object of material culture, a commodity, fashion garment, animal skin, or sexual fetish, fur circulates as a *material signifier* in the transnational discourses of political and libidinal exchange" (4). But Miss Canada remains constrained by the context of Canadian economic and political youth and by her nation's relative dependence on its motherland. Through his cartoon, Bengough conveys the layered significance of the fur that adorns Miss Canada as "an article of trade" and "a luxury good" that circulates in and is valued by a capitalist patriarchal society, but that also makes her—along with the First Nations and French Canadian trappers and hunters and the natural resources of Canada that are exploited in order to access these pelts—into objects of sexual desire and fetish for Europeans and Americans (5).[5] For Miss Britannia to align herself with Cousin Jonathan rather than Mrs. Britannia may appear subversive at first glance, as her youthful rebellion and sexual awakening enable new alliances based on physical proximity and sexual desire rather than on maternal loyalty. But Bengough suggests that this cross-border partnership could be simply another instance of power politics, with Miss Canada as the inevitable object of exploitation. Concomitantly, "A Pertinent Question" portrays a pattern of (inter)national political, economic, and cultural triangulation in which fashion serves as a key reference point, which, more than one hundred years later, *Fashion Television* invokes and subverts for its own (queer) purposes.

Despite the use of differing media, Bengough's cartoon provides a crucial framework for situating Jeanne Beker's show within discussions of cultural, political, and economic border crossings because it conveys the historical limitations imposed on Canada (and Toronto) as a source of raw materials rather than a site of fashion creation and consumption, epitomized by metropolises such as London, Paris, and more recently New York. Like Bengough, Beker has leveraged this perceived marginality to her benefit, by doing what Canadians do best, namely, exporting their natural resources, albeit in a refined format: "[M]any of the great journalists are, you know, from Canada. Again, I think it is because we can see the forest for the trees. We're not that caught up in the hype. And we're great storytellers in this country" (personal interview 3).

Through her strategic presentation of self, Beker reworks a clichéd image of Canada as passively observant to suggest the power of storytelling, especially when done from the so-called sidelines. But Beker is—in contrast to the youthful Miss Canada of Bengough's drawing—a mature woman in her mid-fifties and the mother of two girls. Beker studied theatre in New York and Toronto and mime in Paris before ending up in Newfoundland, where she found work as an arts and entertainment reporter. She eventually moved back to her hometown of Toronto to co-host the pioneering rock 'n' roll show *The New Music* for a decade before becoming the first host of *FT*.

As the daughter of Holocaust survivors who immigrated to Canada in 1948, Beker has been deeply motivated by her parents' legacy and achievements. Notably, in her memoir, fur comes to signify her parents' efforts to attain middle-class prosperity in Toronto. As she recounts in *Jeanne Unbottled*, once settled in Toronto, her father and mother found employment in the garment industry—with her father working with furriers—but after considerable planning, he founded Quality Slippers, a small manufacturing business that soon branched out into the production of "Davy Crockett coonskin hats … [and]

sheepskin vests" (Beker 13). The manufacturing of coonskin hats offers an ironic twist to Beker's father's story of immigrant success, for those hats—made of raccoon pelts—were actually invented by Native Americans, before being adapted by nineteenth-century American frontiersmen as hunting caps, only to be revived in the 1950s by the popularity of a Disney live action series depicting Davy Crockett. Thus, the Beker family's business success came in part from a complex series of cross-border relations that involved the manufacturing in Canada of iconic American fur symbols, which were then sold to children in the United States and Britain, where Disney launched an intense and highly profitable marketing campaign for its Crockett cartoons and related products.

In *Jeanne Unbottled*, Beker reflects on her early understanding of fur as a status symbol within her working-class family by paying homage to her father, who would bring home scraps of fur from the factory floor to adorn her imitation-Barbie doll, Mitzi, turning her from a "cheapo doll" into a "gal pal" with "attitude" (8, 6). Beker's mother was a highly skilled seamstress who made her children's clothing (along with Mitzi's) according to the latest styles. She also supported her daughter's early interest in theatre, which was fuelled by the arrival of the family's first television set—a crucial symbol of prosperity—when Jeanne was five years old. Beker even describes marking her success as a radio personality, and then as a music journalist on *The New Music*, with the acquisition of a "red fox coat" that affirmed her status as "a middle-class, Jewish American princess" (65)—an ironic and indeed border-crossing affiliation that counters her typically resolute self-identification as a Canadian.

Winning the position of *FT* host required unique persistence and drive, for she did not fit the executive producer's original vision for the show. As the station manager of CITY-TV explained to her, "Jay [Levine] was thinking of a model. We really just need someone to introduce fashion videos" (78). But Beker saw the broader potential of the show, insisting that even though she was not a model—and had refused to get plastic surgery on her pronounced (and stereotypically Jewish) nose, which her first television producer had compared to that of Jewish American singer and actress Barbra Streisand—she did have the journalistic experience and vision to make the show into "much more" (78). Her determination to create a show that would probe the industries of fashion, art, and architecture, and her resolute commitment to providing a distinctly Canada- (and Toronto-)centric perspective on camera, ensured its longevity, in contrast to many shorter-lived fashion-focused television programs such as MTV's *House of Style* and the CBC's *Fashion File*.[6]

Over its twenty-seven-year run, *Fashion Television* profited enormously from Beker's journalistic roots and Canadian perspective. Bengough's Miss Canada had been torn between duty to the mother country and Cousin Jonathan's seductive cigar; with *FT*, Beker appropriated and reconfigured Canada's in-between stance, turning it into an asset instead of a liability. As the show's host, Beker deliberately positioned herself as someone "in that world but not of that world" when examining the fashion industry (personal interview 1). Then over time, her initially vaunted outsider status changed, as the face and voice of *FT* became an increasingly important arbiter of what was "fashionable" around the globe. Yet in terms of fur, she remained attuned throughout the show's lifetime to Canada's perceived and actual marginality as a fashion centre. In her memoir, she would recall her ambivalence upon receiving a banana-yellow bunny fur jacket as a gift from "a young American designer in the winter of 2000" (Beker 178). She found herself wrestling with both the ethics of wearing fur—which she had stopped doing in the mid-1980s—and her own position as "a forty-something, hard-working fashion reporter with a sensitive public and a twelve-year-old vegetarian daughter to answer to" (178). By narrating the challenge of enjoying this unexpected gift that made her feel at least momentarily "fabulous and funky"—a gift, moreover, that reflected a time when fashion was focused on "luxury"—Beker highlights her ironic self-positioning as a middle-aged Canadian reporter "in the wilds of New York," covering the fashion shows, abundant with furs of all kinds (including hamster and rat), as well as the ethical reality of wearing such a garment in "Canada," where it may be "darn cold" but such visible excess will likely be scrutinized "by those who feel fur is offensive," including her own children (179, 181). Through this account of her relationship to fur, Beker highlights her insider/outsider status as a Canadian, star-struck both by the glamour of the world she portrayed on *FT* (as epitomized by the excesses of the US-designed fur gifted to her) and by the quotidian life she continues to lead in Toronto—a dynamic that paradoxically recalls the relationship of Miss Canada to the more worldly Cousin Jonathan.

With its focus on fashion, Beker's television show can be read as reconfiguring the triangular relationship of transnational commercial exploitation that is central to Bengough's drawing, with Miss Canada as the colonized supplier of raw materials to industrialized nations. With *FT*, Beker exported herself and her globe-trotting coverage worldwide through the medium of television, thereby creating a lucrative, homegrown product that pointedly altered the traditional trade links suggested by Bengough's cartoon. Neither London nor New York is considered to be the world capital of fashion. Instead, Paris remains the "City of Lights" for the fashion industry, through its formalized couture system, run by the Chambre syndicale de la haute couture, established in 1868. Various controversies have erupted over the past several decades as brash and talented London-based designers (such as John Galliano at Dior and the late Alexander McQueen at Givenchy) have been appointed to head several of the most resolutely French couture labels. As well, some successful New York designers have chosen to show in Paris to develop their businesses (such as Ralph Rucci). Beker pragmatically devoted considerable time each season to covering the Parisian couture runway shows, although she also attended the fashion weeks in New York, London, Milan, and Toronto. To ensure that Toronto's fashion weeks were taken seriously, coverage of them usually comprised the first segment of the show, which kept otherwise indifferent viewers who might be waiting for a later segment tuned in. Likewise, Canadian arts, culture, and design events, and even Canadian-born models, were routinely given prominent billing in all of the show's four segments, although this attention to Canada was carefully balanced with an international focus in keeping with the show's commitment to exploring the fashion industry globally by continuing to cross borders.

In particular, the playful tag line for a television ad for *FT* circa 1988 portrays the show's border-crossing stance from its early years in literal and metaphoric terms. A glamorously apparelled Jeanne Beker is shown exiting a limousine and getting on a private jet, where she encounters Isaac Mizrahi, the New York–based fashion designer. In the ad, Mizrahi looks up, sees Beker, and in *faux* horror, disparagingly comments, "Oh look who's on the plane!" The ad concludes with a single phrase appearing on the screen that celebrates Beker's globe-trotting ways and her willingness to do whatever it takes to speak with designers: "The global search for visual stimulation." While the ad's tag line stresses the international dimensions of *FT*, Mizrahi's snide comment can be read more specifically as playfully parodying American presumptions of superiority over Canada and, for those who recognize both faces, as reiterating the fact that Mizrahi is an established designer and that Beker is merely a reporter. The ad may appear to invoke industry (and neo-colonial) hierarchies, but it also undermines those very structures by virtue of Mizrahi's willingness to be part of the ad campaign. Moreover, the choice of Mizrahi is significant in retrospect partly because he is known for his savvy response to anti-fur activism in the 1990s, as depicted in *Unzipped*, a documentary about his rise and fall in the fashion industry. The documentary, made by his then-partner, Douglas Keeve, describes Mizrahi's decision to produce fake furs that self-consciously play with notions of sexual transgression and performativity (much as Dan and Dean Caten might be said to do, as we will see shortly).[7] Thus, the economic, political, and cultural triangulation of Britain, Canada, and the United States depicted in the Bengough cartoon is revisioned by this ad as well as by *Fashion Television*'s content to create a more intricately woven effect in which Paris, Milan, Toronto, and a host of other cities are regularly profiled along with London and New York.

Fur Trading: Sexuality and Citizenship

If, as Emberley suggests, "the investment of power and authority in the fur-clad woman can be read as a displaced fantasy of the European—white—man's fear of loss of power and authority over himself ... and other men" (79–80), then a reading of Bengough's cartoon, in conjunction with Beker's coverage of Dan and Dean Caten, a pair of gay Canadian-born designers whose Milan-based fashion house and brand are strongly shaped by their use of fur on women, and more importantly, on men, provides a fascinating alterna(rra)tive to that earlier colonial and heterosexual representation of fur's significance. Of the Canadian designers whom Beker has championed on *FT* over the past twenty-seven years, the Catens have been arguably the most prominent—and certainly the most globally successful. Not only do the Catens embrace fur as a fabric central to their collections, but they have also incorporated fur into their playfully parodic exported versions of Canadian identity in provocative and sometimes unexpected ways, using fur's fetishistic qualities to sell a lifestyle vision that both embraces and challenges conventional notions of citizenship, which have traditionally legitimized the power of white, affluent, heterosexual men.

Born and raised in a working-class family of nine in the suburbs of Toronto by an Italian immigrant welder who was a single father, the identical Caten twins were awarded stars on Canada's Walk of Fame in 2009 to honour their international achievements in the world of fashion. Their career breakthrough came in 2001, when they garnered instant fame and serious attention from the fashion industry shortly after creating 150 pieces for pop icon Madonna's video "Don't Tell Me" and the subsequent Drowned World tour. Then in June 2002 Dan and Dean Caten decided to show nine female looks as part of their menswear runway show in Milan, in anticipation of launching their women's line in 2003. Within days, DSquared^2 appeared on the front cover of the New York–based fashion industry trade magazine *Women's Wear Daily*, coupled with an in-depth interview with the designers. Following this initial international commercial and critical success, the duo opened their first free-standing retail space in Milan in 2007. Produced in collaboration with the acclaimed Italian design firm Storage, the store (which has become the blueprint for an array of subsequent DSquared^2 retail ventures) parodically invokes Canada's abundant natural resources, with its walls made from stacked blocks of rough-hewn timber, deer-antler chandeliers to illuminate the space, and tree trunks functioning as display areas for their signature perfumes for men and women, aptly called "He Wood" and "She Wood." The fragrance names combine overtly sexual puns (particularly with the male perfume) with a reference to the predominance of trees in rural Canada—a marketing strategy that pointedly blends with DSquared^2's urban aesthetic and the brothers' tenacity in an industry that usually ignores Canadian talent with a playful mockery of how their homeland is perceived abroad. Like Beker, the Catens would become (albeit briefly) international television celebrities in their own right, as co-hosts of the single-season 2009 New York–based reality show *Launch My Line*, in which contestants competed for the opportunity to create and produce their own fashion line. The Catens travelled around the globe in order to tape the show, leaving their home in London, their factory in Milan, their family in Toronto, and multiple retail outlets (in Capri, Istanbul, Kiev, Singapore, Milan, Cannes, Dubai, and Hong Kong) to be physically present in New York when necessary. More recently, DSquared² was selected to design the costumes for the opening and closing ceremonies of the Vancouver 2010 Winter Olympics, reiterating their significance to Canada.

The Caten twins have continued to build their celebrity music clientele, designing costumes for Christina Aguilera's 2003 "Justified and Stripped" tour and outfits for several Italian pop stars and, more recently, outfitting Britney Spears for her 2009 comeback tour, "The Circus Starring Britney Spears." On occasion their collaborations have gone further. For example, DSquared² made a cameo appearance in a video that was shown at the beginning of each Spears concert and that has since become part of the designers' Facebook page. The two-and-a-half-minute video explores sexual performativity in the context of Spears's return to show business; in it, Dan and Dean Caten are the cross-dressed showgirls, adorned in black tuxedo jackets with tails, white shirts, black bow ties, bare legs, and patent high heels. As (flagless Italian Canadian) showgirls, the Catens introduce the American gay television personality and celebrity blogger Perez Hilton, who is dressed in drag as Queen Elizabeth I—wearing both the US and British flags in his plumed wig—and who admits that his previous online critiques of Spears may have been unfair. Hilton promises an orgiastic experience and is eventually shot in the genitalia by the black-corset-clad Spears with a bow and arrow. This video—in which sexual deviance takes central stage—was not part of Beker's coverage of DSquared². However, it can be read as provocatively echoing and reconfiguring Bengough's cartoon in ways that have impacted on Beker's championing of this Canadian brand, for it blurs the boundary between a "respectable gay citizen and his transgressive queer other" (Arthurs 147). As second-generation immigrants to Canada who now reside in London although they work in Milan and occasionally in New York, the Caten twins can be read as consciously invoking their birth nation in their collections and video performances in ways that refashion liberal (meaning white and heterosexual) conceptions of citizenship by building a brand that celebrates and revels in a multitude of border crossings, challenging traditional conceptions of class, sexuality, and nationality.

Throughout her time as *FT*'s host, Beker, who is overtly heterosexual, demonstrated strong support for and interest in the gay community's contributions to the fashion industry worldwide. Borrowing the words of screenwriter Tom Hedley, Beker not only asserts that "fashion is the ultimate drag" but also sees drag as a crucial tool for negotiating the playfulness of fashion, noting that "[d]rag also works on another level that I ultimately subscribe to: fashion should never be taken too seriously" (*Jeanne* 174). In particular, through her coverage of Toronto's "Fashion Cares," the annual Canadian-born MAC makeup company's "fashion gala benefit" (176), and through her profiles of numerous gay male designers, makeup artists, photographers, and other visual artists, *FT* has suggested an alternative concept of (Canadian) sexual citizenship among viewers—one that makes visible and indeed celebrates the creativity of these men.

In *Television and Sexuality: Regulation and the Politics of Taste*, Jane Arthurs contends that "[t]elevision has a significant role to play in the development of sexual citizenship" because it offers "a forum and stimulus for political debate and education, as well as a source of personal meaning with fragmented audiences pursuing their individual needs" (13). As Arthurs notes, "[c]itizenship includes the right to representation as a form of 'recognition'" (32); and certainly, *FT*'s willingness to experiment with genre formats and to explore the sexual politics of television through a variety of border crossings made it a potent (all puns intended) venue for a more expansive and flexible notion of citizenship. *FT* epitomized what Arthurs describes as "[n]ew, more pluralistic 'ways of telling'" stories that incorporated a "feminized aesthetic of subjective perspectives, [and] emotional empathy," both of which were central to Beker's coverage of DSquared² (146). This is epitomized by a 2003 episode of *FT*, in which Beker offers an ironic twist on this "newly discovered" duo by pointing out that, although the Catens' international success has been relatively recent, *FT* has, in Beker's words, "been following their careers since they started designing some eighteen years ago."[8] The segment that follows, which offers a look at the launch of their women's collection, includes an interview in Toronto with the designers, who are filmed embracing Beker as they enter the studio, setting a tone of familiarity and intimacy that pre-empts those who might claim that the Catens have based their recent popularity on the solidity—and solidarity—of a long-standing, Canada-focused (more accurately, Toronto-focused) connection. Subsequent episodes would affirm these strong links among Beker, DSquared², and Canada. *FT* would cover the Caten twins' seasonal runway shows in Milan, the opening of their new store in Milan in 2007, and the Toronto fashion show they held in conjunction with the Toronto International Film Festival in 2008. The Catens' prominence on *FT* was not surprising, for they did exactly what Beker did on air—"tell [compelling] fashion stories" (Beker, personal interview 2).

While Dan and Dean Caten are unabashedly proud of their Canadian roots, explaining to Beker on *FT* that "we always kind of wave our flags" in their fashion shows, their versions of Canadianness can be read as recalling and pointedly "redoing" the historic relations depicted by Bengough, particularly given that their corporate motto is "Born in Canada, living in London, made in Italy" ("Company Profile"). For instance, DSquared²'s fall/winter 2004 show in Milan—enthusiastically covered by *FT*—began with two men in red RCMP uniforms opening the curtains to the catwalk, which had been staged to replicate a Canadian wilderness landscape with fir trees, snow-capped *faux* mountains (complete with a makeshift ski lift), male and female models wearing fur-trimmed lumberjack hats, and scanty ensembles covered by leather and suede fur vests and luxuriously oversized fur coats. The show concluded with a fake snowfall and the two designers arriving on stage by ski lift surrounded by a bevy of beautiful female models wearing their clothing. For their runway appearance, the twins wore custom-made T-shirts, each printed with half of the now-famous phrase from *Second City Television* (*SCTV*) characters, Bob and Doug McKenzie, the ultimate beer-drinking, toque-wearing, hot dog-eating, campfire-loving, proud white heterosexual redneck Canadians: "Why Don't You Take Off" and "Eh."

As Beker has noted, the fact that the Catens are identical twins "is a great marketing ploy" (personal interview 4), and here their T-shirts have become the ideal canvas for reworking the cliché of the unfashionably attired snowbound white overweight heterosexual beer-drinking Canadian male with a powerful but also playful visual pun that recalls that other set of look-alike brothers. In doing so, the Catens have pointedly inserted themselves in Canadian pop culture mythology, which enables "a broadening of 'legitimate' sexual identities" beyond that of the straight white male (Arthurs 146). In contrast to Bob and Doug McKenzie, the creators of DSquared² are sophisticated, stylish, and perpetually tanned thin gay men, surrounded by a bevy of beautiful male and female models, who spend their time in exotic and glamorous locales rather than being relegated to a backwoods television station set. The Catens' choice of subject matter strategically recalls that the McKenzie Brothers sketches were created when CBC executives demanded that *SCTV* add two minutes of explicitly Canadian content to meet Canadian content regulations. Because *SCTV* was already created, produced, and directed by Canadians and starred Canadian comedians, the two-minute segment became an opportunity to mock this seemingly absurd request; the two actors, Rick Moranis and Dave Thomas, taped the segments at the end of the day and never expected their improvised characters to become stars in both the United States and Canada, where Bob and Doug McKenzie found instant fame, with their own record album, movies, spots in television commercials, and other on-air appearances. In particular, American viewers embraced the duo's clichéd behaviour and jokes, and television executives insisted that the McKenzie Brothers segments be included in regular *SCTV* programming sold to US stations. Likewise, Dan and Dean Caten have strategically employed Canadian icons in innovative ways, showing themselves to be self-reflexive and humorous in the invocation of their roots and willing to complicate their citizenship by foregrounding the sexual diversity and multiple identities evoked by their runway shows, print ads, video work, and retail spaces. The use of Canadian references in their work seems especially apt because of Canada's increasing support of same-sex rights; for instance, same-sex unions were recognized as legitimate nationwide in 2005, in direct contrast to the laws in many US states. The Catens' parodic invocation of Canadian cultural icons earned the label extensive coverage on *FT*, because, as Beker explains, "they've been very savvy in terms of their business and ... brand identity ... [T]he whole thing is really quite magical, what they've done" (personal interview 5).

In recent years, the Catens' label has also reconfigured British–Canadian relations, a shift that Beker covered attentively until *FT* was cancelled. This adds another dimension to re-reading Bengough's triangular representation of Canadian, American, and British relations. Although they produce and show their lines in Milan, the Catens reside in the fashionable London neighbourhood of Notting Hill. Beker taped an exclusive interview and house tour with them in 2008, in which she asked them what characterized their brand. The twins' responses echoed their sustained interest in articulating their Canadian identity: "I think we are definitely representing our country ... There's a touch of Canada in our clothes ... We make real clothes for real people." The cost of DSquared^2 clothing—and their close links to celebrity clients—may belie that claim. Even so, the Catens have put on several shows that bring a decidedly Canadian perspective to iconic British symbols, offering border-crossing alterna(rra)tives to Canada as a colonial entity at the beck and call of Mrs. Britannia or waiting to be preyed upon by Cousin Jonathan.

This reworking of traditional trade routes and revisioning of cultural and sexual citizenship was most pronounced in the 2008 collaboration between *FT* and DSquared^2: a fashion show hosted by Beker and held in the parking lot of the CTVglobemedia building in downtown Toronto, scheduled to coincide with the now world-renowned Toronto International Film Festival in order to draw on the presence of celebrities from around the world to publicize and heighten the event's prestige. The event was extensively covered on *Fashion Television* and on a section of the *FT* website (still live) that is devoted to online exclusive backstage access to the show, from the casting of models, the runway rehearsal, and the makeup and hair preparations to the runway show itself, and that includes substantial galleries of photographs of the designers and their creations. Here, DSquared^2 showed their British-themed fall/winter 2008 collection for both men and women in Canada nearly six months after it was first aired on *FT* from a Milan runway, but without the pub backdrop or *faux* snowfall that had closed the original show in pointed homage to their current residence (London) and birthplace (Toronto) respectively. While such a gesture might be seen as overtly colonial—for it brought what was already fashionable in Europe to the New World half a year later—the framing of the runway show with *FT*'s coverage, the designers' assertion that "it is amazing to be home," and the varied presentation of the fur pieces in a new geographical and cultural location can be read as creating a far more complex narrative. The Caten twins' use of fur for their female fashions in this particular show reiterated the notion of fur as a symbol of femininity, social status, and class privilege, with an abundance of dark fur collars on suits and fur car coats covering lingerie-inspired slip dresses. Of course, as Canadian-born designers bringing their finished garments back to Toronto, the Catens were rerouting the historical exportation of fur pelts as a natural resource by asserting their fashion vision at all stages of production. But the integration of fur into the men's line added a decidedly queer dimension to their return to Canada, one that gestured toward a history of British colonization and US Manifest Destiny but ultimately proposed alternative versions of sexual citizenship—which complicated the heterosexual norm embodied by Mrs. Britannia and her offspring, Miss Canada, and embraced or even complicated the potentially deviant dimensions of Cousin Jonathan's sexuality.

For their fall/winter 2008 men's line and the men's looks presented in their subsequent Toronto show, DSquared^2 took their inspiration from the anti-establishment British skinhead fashions of the 1960s and 1970s, designing a custom DSquared^2 tartan, complete with the "House of DSquared^2" logo, and coupling it with ripped jeans, Dr. Marten boots, shirts with sewed-on suspenders, a dark mink fur vest, and bomber jackets with extravagantly wide light-coloured fur collars. The result, especially when shown in the context of a *Fashion Television*–sponsored Toronto-based event, was pointedly subversive in its invocation and refashioning of anti-establishment colonial traditions, which were already infused with their own complex cultural baggage. In *Subculture: The Meaning of Style*, Dick Hebdige outlines the distinct "visual style" of the male skinhead subculture in Britain, which systematically suppressed "bourgeois influences" with its cropped hair and clothes and boots associated with the white working classes, and which incorporated traditionally aristocratic tartan elements to articulate an anti-establishment sentiment (55). Skinhead culture in Britain was also initially influenced by West Indian immigrant communities, although this precarious affiliation (with its transatlantic roots) would eventually collapse. Skinheads became well known for their scapegoating of "alien groups," including other racial minorities and "'queers'" (58).

In reinterpreting skinhead apparel in a high-fashion context, DSquared^2 ironically reworked the subculture's working-class beginnings and gave it a decidedly queer and resolutely Italian Canadian twist by bringing fur embellishments into the mix. In this case, the fetishistic dimensions of fur, typically displaced onto women's bodies over the past two centuries, were squarely returned (again, all puns intended) to the male torso with a luxurious mink vest. Rather than representing the European, white male fear of a loss of power and authority over himself and other men, the vest may be read as suggesting a New World desire to affirm and indeed embrace the fantasy of male-on-male domination, in contrast with Bengough's heteronormative cartoon. Likewise, the fur-embellished jackets for men can be understood as recalling and subverting, at least for this viewer, British royal sumptuary laws that limited the use of light-coloured furs to court robes and monarchical attire. These fur-trimmed coats, much like the banana-coloured fur gifted to Beker, have ushered in a new kind of border-crossing queer Canadian fashion royalty, epitomized by the Catens themselves, who often wear their own designs. If, as *Fashion Television* suggests, Dan and Dean Caten are fashion's latest and greatest queens—a position facilitated by Beker's storytelling abilities and by her desire to challenge Canada's historical marginality as a fashion centre—viewers of this episode from around the world are invited to revel in their affiliation with Toronto—and Canada—and to embrace the playfully subversive ways in which DSquared^2 presents a new (and New World) interpretation of the British skinhead's visual style that is decidedly Canada-centric, while also reclaiming the anti-gay aspects of skinhead subculture in order to celebrate a multiplicity of sexual orientations and practices.

One of the most poignant and revealing moments of this fashion show collaboration between *FT* and DSquared^2 came when Beker, as host of the party, introduced the musical prelude to the runway show itself, a performance by young Jamaican Canadian pop star Kreesha Turner. As part of its all-access coverage, *FT* recorded the Caten twins backstage, wearing the plaid-collared white shirts, jeans, skinny ties, and boots from their fall/winter 2008 collection, dancing and loudly singing the chorus of Turner's hit single, "Don't Call Me Baby Anymore" in a vocal assertion of their return to Canada as seasoned, globally successful designers and not merely "babes in the woods"—a line that affirms Beker's own efforts through her work on *FT* to put Toronto and Canada on the fashion industry's map. So too does this moment on *FT* remind readers that Canada, and Beker's show, have grown to become entities to be reckoned with rather than simply passive sites of exploitation and commodification.

FT remained on the cutting edge of television up to its last episode in part because it offered a seductively voyeuristic look at postmodern consumer culture that remained cognizant of its visual allure for a wide array of viewers, including straight *and* gay men, who together constituted over half the show's viewers. And Beker rightfully championed Dan and Dean Caten because they ably serviced that broad audience base by providing clothing lines for men and women as well as an array of retail items to replicate their version of Canadiana in a highly sexualized (and enticingly marketable) package. Although the Catens may seem to offer a potentially liberatory version of sexual citizenship for Canadian and international viewers, Arthurs cautions that there is often a gap between "images of the self-fashioning consumer and the reality of most people's lives" (147); in other words, "certain kinds of sexual identity are [often perceived of as] compatible with consumerism," meaning that those who lack money may struggle in their efforts at "recognition" regardless of the potential affiliations offered by television programming (147, 146). Arthurs rightly notes that economics play an important part in constructions of television citizenship and that not all viewers possess the financial means to participate in some of the potential avenues of sexual self-articulation put forth by *FT* or DSquared[2]: they cannot afford the clothes or lifestyle. But just as Beker functioned as host, interviewer, journalist, and writer, as well as a voyeur of sorts, wrestling over her own vexed relationship with the gift of the banana-yellow fur coat, so too did *FT* become a site to explore, at least vicariously, the imaginative possibilities offered by the world of fashion.

The "threat of American [cultural] imperialism" remains in the case of the Canadian television industry because—as Bart Beaty and Rebecca Sullivan point out in *Canadian Television Today*—by allowing "simultaneous substitution," Canadian regulators have facilitated the continued domination of the same US television programming they sought to minimize in Canadian markets (144). Moreover, the fashion capitals of the world remain firmly entrenched. In 2010, Beker explained that "as much as a diehard Canadian fan of Canadian fashion that I am [*sic*] … Toronto is not one of the world's fashion capitals … You've got to go to New York or Paris or Milan or maybe even London" (personal interview 4). And in the New World, New York continues to dominate. But *Fashion Television*, especially through its coverage of DSquared[2], has played an important role in "reconstituting citizenship," particularly sexual citizenship, by cultivating new global networks and cross-border linkages that support and indeed celebrate queer identities (Hartley *Television* 119). *FT* was fundamentally Toronto-centric, a result of both its roots at CITY-TV and economic factors that have centralized fashion shows in major cities, including Toronto and Montreal. Yet across Canada, Toronto continues to evoke resentment from people who see this central Canadian city's assertion of its world-class economic and cultural status as absurd and needlessly exclusionary. Paradoxically, within the film and television industries, Toronto has earned the nickname "Hollywood North" because, as Sarah A. Matheson explains, it can so successfully "masquerade as 'Elsewhere,' functioning as a cost-efficient substitute for virtually any North American urban backdrop" (119), rather than as a distinctive and iconic world city in its own right. Moreover, as a participant in and product of the age of late capitalism, *Fashion Television* has been marked by "the aestheticization of commodities and the commercial exploitation of sexuality," which often perpetuates sexist, racist, and classist stereotypes (Emberley 26). Yet the show and its host did manage, on occasion, to upset these hierarchical constructs, particularly by rethinking what one Canadian perspective might offer television viewers around the globe and presenting this vision to the world.

Beker's championing of the Caten twins, gay men who embrace their Canadian roots, often employing iconic national symbols in a parodic fashion, offers (an)Other model of citizenship that overtly redeploys the concept of globalization or global citizen to its own ends. Likewise, television viewers who have been historically conceived of as passive recipients of content are given a venue in which to embrace similarity and difference through the medium of clothing and to express—as viewers and consumers—their own (sexual) identities in ways that do not always accord with clichéd notions of the nation-state. Imagine if Cousin Jonathan was displaced by the Caten twins, taking on New York on their own terms, and accompanied by their male models, adorned with fur vests and extravagant fur-collared parkas? And what would happen if Jeanne Beker morphed into a mature and sophisticated Canadian-designer-wearing Ms. Canada, pushing Mrs. Britannia off centre stage? Perhaps the fact that to this day, there is no fashion television show in the United States or Britain with the reputation or success of *FT* is telling; when your male [Q]ueen wears a mink vest and fur-collared parka, you see the world differently.

Notes

1 It is worth noting that according to medieval traditions, male beavers were often hunted for their testicles, which were regarded as medicinal; when cornered by a hunter, the male beaver would bite off his testicles in an effort to escape being killed. This narrative of emasculation conforms to more modern slang uses of the term "beaver," situating the animal and its significance in a useful historical context.

2 See Boehmer 30–31, 215–17, 220–21, and 228, for a useful overview of Canada's vexed status as a post/colonial nation.

3 See Hietala 255–72 for a helpful summary of the origin and significance of the term "manifest destiny" in an American context.

4 Many thanks to Neil ten Kortenaar for his thoughtful comments regarding Mrs. Britannia at the 2010 CACLALS meeting in Montreal.

5 See Emberley for a sustained discussion of this subject, especially in Chapters 1, 5, and 6.

6 MTV's *House of Style* was an American-focused exploration of the supermodel phenomenon, hosted by Cindy Crawford from 1989 to 1995. *Fashion File* also first aired in 1989 and soon was internationally syndicated. Produced by the Canadian Broadcast Corporation (CBC) as a public television competitor to *FT*, the show struggled to find its audience with an overly cerebral host, Tim Blanks, who devoted his attention primarily to couture, giving relatively little screen time to Canadian subjects or popular culture issues. Blanks departed in 2007, and the show was cancelled in March 2009.

7 See Emberley's persuasive and entertaining analysis of Mizrahi's "approach to anti-fur activism," which involves recreating "the cultural difference of fur's significance for the Inuit in the cultural and political space of the urban metropolis" (169). This strategy, she argues, is "socially and sexually transgressive, designed to take pleasure in the creative force of disengendering the conventions of sexual difference" (169).

8 I transcribed this quotation from an eight-track recording of the episode that I watched at the *FT* studio in the Bell-Media headquarters, previously the iconic CHUM-City building, located on Queen Street West in downtown Toronto, in January 2010. Many thanks to Matthew Almeida and the student interns at *FT* for getting the tapes from the storage facility and providing me with a place to view them.

Works Cited

Arthurs, Jane. *Television and Sexuality: Regulation and the Politics of Taste.* Maidenhead: Open UP, 2004.

Beaty, Bart, and Rebecca Sullivan. *Canadian Television Today.* Calgary: U of Calgary P, 2006.

Beker, Jeanne. *Jeanne Unbottled: Adventures in High Style.* Toronto: Stoddart, 2000.

———. Personal interview. 19 January 2010.

Boehmer, Elleke. *Colonial and Postcolonial Literature.* Oxford: Oxford UP, 1995.

"Canada's The Beaver Mag Renamed to End Porn Mix-Up." Agence France Presse, 12 January 2010.

"Company Profile." DSquared² official website. 28 July 2010. http://www.dsquared .com/html/corporate/profile.

Emberley, Julia V. *The Cultural Politics of Fur.* Montreal and Kingston: McGill–Queen's UP, 1997.

Hartley, John. *Television Truths.* Oxford: Blackwell, 2008.

Hebdige, Dick. *Subculture: The Meaning of Style.* London: Routledge, 1979.

Hietala, Thomas R. *Manifest Design: American Exceptionalism and Empire.* Ithaca: Cornell UP, 2002.

Innis, Harold A. *The Fur Trade in Canada: An Introduction to Canadian Economic History.* 1930. Toronto: U of Toronto P, 1999.

Matheson, Sarah. "Projecting Placeness: Industrial Television and the 'Authentic' Canadian City." *Contracting Out Hollywood: Runaway Productions and Foreign Location Shooting.* Ed. Greg Elmer and Mike Gasher. Oxford: Rowman and Littlefield, 2005. 117–39.

three

Meanings of Health as Cultural Identity and Ideology Across the Canada–US Border

Jan Clarke

THE CANADA–US INTERNATIONAL BORDER is a social space where a juxtaposition of health care systems exposes ideological tensions. Using Michael Moore's political documentary *SiCKO* (2007) as an entry point, this chapter questions the meaning of health in terms of cultural identity and ideology as well as what can be learned from the stark differences in health care systems from one side of the Canada–US border to the other. To locate this analysis, a brief social history traces federal policies as part of the social shaping of Canada's health care system. The Canada Health Act is then analyzed as a policy that inscribes and embeds national identity and ideology. The meaning of health in the context of border crossings is also linked to Michael Moore's activism and politics; this chapter looks north to Canada in order to apply insights from *SiCKO* to current struggles around public and private health care in the United States. This chapter also draws on the argument that "both enclosure and mobility are defined against the other, hence reflecting our sense of borders as ongoing social processes governed through political, economic, and cultural struggles" (Cunningham and Heyman 293). While border crossings reflect mobility in many economic and ideological ways, the juxtaposition of different health care systems based on health as commodity versus health as human right reflects a form of ideological enclosure across the border.

Michael Moore grew up in the 1950s and 1960s in Flint, Michigan, an auto industry town close enough to the international border for him to be aware of contrasts between the United States and Canada that would later become part of several of his films. The first film in which he looked at the Canada–US border through his American eyes was the comedy *Canadian Bacon* (1995); he then returned to Canada for part of his film *Bowling for Columbine* (2002). His exposure of health care practices in *SiCKO* again compares Canada and the United States, this time with regard to the harsh personal consequences of capitalism. Moore's unique style is evident in his first documentary film, *Roger and Me* (1989), a personal and political documentary that traces the decline of the auto industry in Flint through stories of working-class families in Moore's hometown. Moore's down-to-earth, hard-hitting documentaries expose the greed of capitalism hidden behind the American dream of economic opportunity and social mobility. This unique approach often disarms audiences: "Moore is of the left, but it is also important to him that he is mainstream. He wants to change things, and he knows that to do so he must prove to his followers that they are the majority" (MacFarquhar 133).

Moore's documentary *SiCKO*, "infused with Moore's trademark boundary-pushing and in-your-face irreverence" (Kennedy B8), offers an insightful entry point into the meanings of health across the Canada–US border. *SiCKO* focuses on the consequences of the private health care system in the United States, where poverty and loss of savings as a result of the costs of illness or accident are widely feared, even among those who do have private health insurance. Much of the film's content is drawn from personal stories selected from more than 25,000 respondents to Moore's public email request that they explain why 47 million Americans do not have health insurance and why so many who do are routinely denied treatment options (Smith, "Anniversary"). Kennedy aptly describes *SiCKO* as "filled with stories that break your heart at the same time they enrage you" (B8). Unpredictable health care costs are shown to be an ever-present reality for Americans, regardless of class and privilege. To contrast private health care in the United States with different forms of universal health care elsewhere, Moore compares health care costs in the United States, mostly for emergency and surgical cases, to the costs for similar cases in Canada, England, France, and Cuba. He highlights Cuba to demonstrate the significance of socialized universal health care funded entirely by the state. In Cuba, a communist state, health care is a human right that is to be prioritized even when Cuba is under severe economic constraints. As a social activist and populist, Moore is clearly trying to do more than simply compare radically different health care systems: "Moore is making a film for Americans. And what he is telling his compatriots is very true that America's refusal to embrace some kind of universal health care system makes absolutely no sense" (Walkom). In his discussion of the problem of health care access in the United States, which he refers to as a crisis, David Singer has contended that "the issue is fertile ground for consciousness-raising education, since it affects all of us, and really digging out from under the crisis will reveal how the U.S. class structure promotes profits instead of basic rights such as health care" (18).

Moore effectively and dramatically captures how individuals' lives are socially constructed around the model of health care they depend on. He then links this to cultural identity in terms of what it means to be American or Canadian. By gazing across the border to Canada's universal public health care system, he exposes the inequalities of the US privatized health care system. Singer's economic comparison of these two systems is succinct: "The major difference between there and here is that Canada has a single-payer system. The government pays for almost all medical costs. In the United States there are many competing private insurance companies, some operating for profit and some not for profit. The profits amount to a fortune for the owners of the for-profit companies" (22).

Particularly relevant to the comparison Moore is making is the "Oh Canada!" segment of *SiCKO*, during which the camera pans from urban surroundings to intense close-ups of people telling their health care stories. In this chapter, the Canada–US border is represented both as a means to freedom from economic limits on health care and as a barrier to health care owing to economic constraints. Moore does more than gaze across the border; he crosses into Canada by way of the international bridge between Detroit and Windsor. This allows him to film an American woman, a cancer survivor, who is trying to gain access to "free" Canadian health care by claiming a common-law relationship with a Canadian man. When she fails on this occasion, her friend suggests that they "just get married and it would solve everything" (i.e., it would give her access to the Canadian health care system). In this situation, the border crossing amounts to an opportunity for Americans to access universal health care relatively easily. Moore's next stop in Windsor is to visit his Canadian relatives, Bob and Stella, who never visit the United States without additional health insurance: "We could not afford to be without insurance even for a day." For Bob and Stella, then, the border is an economic *barrier* that restricts their movement. The US health care system is expensive not only for Americans whether they are insured or not, but also for any visitors to the United States who lack additional travel insurance and who must pay up front before receiving any medical treatment. Clearly, Canadians who visit the United States view the health care crisis there as an economic one.

To contrast US privatized health care with Canada's semi-socialized model, Moore interviews Canadians in southern Ontario about the health care to which they are universally entitled. He marvels at their lack of financial concern, at their ease of access to health care, and at the relative efficiency of Canada's public health care system. The Canadians he interviews also make cross-border comparisons: "We know that in America people have to pay for the health care; we don't understand that concept." Moore's film challenges accounts in the US media that stereotype Canada's semi-socialized medicine as inefficient and incompetent. This need to challenge stereotypes is reinforced by Pauline M. Villaincourt Roseneau's content analysis of US newspaper coverage of the Canadian health care system, which highlights how journalists miss both the complexities of Canada's health care system and its differences from the US model: "Too often U.S. journalists appear to interpret what they observe in the Canadian health system based on what they know best and are familiar with—their own U.S. health system. This leads to oversimplification and to misunderstanding" (37). Moore's interviews with Canadians generally capture optimistic views of health, which he underscores with his obvious astonishment at the apparent economic freedom allowed by universal public health care. He shows how patients in a not-for-profit system are not compelled to link illness to the cost of every possible aspect of health care. He interviews new parents in Canada, who are able to marvel at their newborns without connecting their arrival to immediate worries about paying for the delivery. In stark contrast, Moore shows through painful personal stories how every action taken in the for-profit US health care system is linked to awareness of cost, most strikingly to the out-of-pocket expenses before treatment, even for emergencies.

In the "Oh Canada!" segment, people's dramatic experiences contribute to an entertaining documentary, but they also show some of the contrasts between views of health from one side of the border to the other. Moore's style of documentary also serves as a cautionary tale for people with universal health care: "all Canadians should see it, especially those who—recognizing the obvious flaws and deficiencies in our system—look to the profit-making model south of the border as an answer to our prayers" (Kennedy B8). As a cultural product, then, *SiCKO* is meaningful to both Canadians and Americans as they try to make sense of their different health care systems: "On both sides of the US–Canada border, *SiCKO* may do more to galvanize consumers into thinking and caring about what they want in health care delivery ... than any politician's speech or news story could" (Hass 380). Moore's interviews also show how nation-state borders divide groups of citizens from each other and accord different rights to the people living on either side. Moore does more than entertain viewers; he also exposes meanings of health that differ sharply depending on citizenship and on which side of the side of the border one is located: "He's trying to whack his fellow Americans on the head and say to them Hey! Wake up. Why do we run our health care system in such an insane way? No one else does" (Walkom). This documentary compares the economics of public and private health care, and in that sense, it is overly simplistic, for it does not explain how Canada and the United States, whose economies are similar (i.e., capitalist), have developed health care systems that have fostered very different meanings of health. Missing from Moore's analysis are the links between meanings of health, health care systems, and the state evident even in a general comparison of the US and Canadian systems. These meanings of health are framed by a model of health as either commodity or human right, with the border crossing as the location where these models can be compared. These different models of health also lead to different views of one's body in relation to health care systems.

Health care in the United States is a business with a complex, multiple-payer structure, although some US health care programs are state-funded. Access to health care is based on the ability to pay for insurance; as a result, health has come to be viewed as a commodity and is linked directly to dollar value. The direct connection of health to dollar value is repeatedly emphasized in tragic stories recounted in interviews with Americans in *SiCKO*. As a consequence of the system that has developed, the maintenance of health is viewed as an individual responsibility based on ability to pay and on a multitude of self-help measures. This picture of health care is often hidden, although not to US nurses such as Rose Ann DeMoro: "If we are ever going to build a genu-inely humane society, we need to discard the notions of consumerism when it comes to the most basic factor of our humanity—our health … Somehow our health, our life, has become a commodity" (9).

In contrast, while some aspects of health care in Canada are privatized and doctors dominate the state's decisions, health care there is, generally speak-ing, a semi-socialized, single-payer system that provides universal coverage. Most doctors are paid on a fee-for-service basis. This has led to health being seen as a human right and to Canadian citizenship being linked to access to good health regardless of means to pay. Roy Romanow, the former premier of Saskatchewan, who led the Royal Commission on the Future of Health Care, reinforces this view: "In their discussions with me, Canadians have been clear that they still strongly support the core values on which our health care sys-tem is premised—equity, fairness and solidarity. These values are tied to their understanding of citizenship. Canadians consider equal and timely access to medically necessary health care services on the basis of need as a right of cit-izenship, not a privilege of status or wealth" (xvi).

This model of health care establishes a collective responsibility for health, with a number of social programs supporting individuals and communities. This is reinforced by Larry, a Canadian golfer interviewed in *SiCKO*, who says that universal health care allows people collectively to support those less for-tunate. Given that US Republicans vehemently resist state health care, Moore is shocked when Larry reveals that he is a member of the Canadian Conservative Party. "Somebody has to take care of [those less fortunate]," Larry tells him. "Where medical matters are concerned I don't think it would matter what party you're a part of."

The meaning of health in Canadian culture, also apparent in *SiCKO*, is linked to the semi-socialized structure of the health care system. Several Can-adian participants in *SiCKO* quite automatically link Canadian citizenship to a right to health care; for them, access to health care is taken for granted, and they do not question how that access actually happens. This support for uni-versal health care fosters a trust that one's body will be fixed when necessary as well as the attitude that health care is a shared collective responsibility. Canadians as a whole fear the US privatized model of health care, which has commoditized health.

The meaning of health in American culture, also apparent in *SiCKO*, is linked to the fact that access to health care is unreliable and often difficult to achieve, especially for the poor or unemployed. Fears of getting sick, losing one's life savings, and becoming dependent on family or charity often become realities for many. Under a commodity model of health, fragile health can lead to economic ruin. This has fostered a view of health as an individual responsibility—that is, it is up to the individual to stay healthy. As Ross D. Silverman observes: "Underlying the health care debate in the United States is a fundamental question: Is access to care a privilege or a right?" (9). All the while, politicians and the media encourage Americans to fear and misunderstand Canadian-style "socialized" medicine.

The link between social structure and the meaning of health helps clarify how perceptions of health vary with cultural identity and ideology. It also helps explain why American politicians like Bill Clinton in the 1990s and Barack Obama more recently have struggled to introduce a health care system that confronts rather than exacerbates social inequalities. To frame this comparison between the Canadian and US health care systems, I will provide a brief overview of the state's role in the social construction of the meanings of health. This analysis will focus on the Canada Health Act, which is the "founding document" of Canada's health care system (a similar analysis could be applied to other texts that inscribe and embed a nation's identity and ideology).

Before the 1950s, the Canadian and US health care systems were similar—essentially private, which meant that Canadian as well as US families could lose their savings to support ill family members. After the 1950s, Canada began reforming its system, beginning with hospital services—the first aspect of health care to be covered by public funding. This change in model was sparked by Tommy Douglas, a highly respected politician who at various times was premier of Saskatchewan, leader of the Co-operative Commonwealth Federation (CCF), and first leader of the New Democratic Party (NDP). He is remembered fondly even by Larry, the proud Conservative Canadian golfer interviewed in *SiCKO*. Douglas, renowned as "'the father of Medicare' in Canada, always maintained that covering doctors' services and hospital care was only the first step. His vision was ultimately to extend Medicare to cover drugs, dentistry, vision, and most other aspects of health care" (Evans). Douglas is so closely connected to the history of Canadian medicare that in 2004 he was voted to first place in the CBC's The Greatest Canadian Contest (CBC).

The federal Medical Care Act was introduced in Canada in 1966 and was implemented in all provinces by 1970. This led to a public health care system that covered hospital and physician costs through Canadian taxes—a model that made health care feel more or less free. The American response, as expressed by President Richard Nixon in the 1960s, was that this health care model amounted to socialism. Canada's current legislation, the Canada Health

Act, was enacted in 1984 as a federal policy that was to be implemented by the provinces. The Canada Health Act structures the health care system and links meanings of health to social structure. The differently structured health care systems in the United States and Canada became divided by nation-state borders as a consequence of decisions made in the 1960s. These different health care systems in turn constructed different meanings of health based on culturally specific individualism in the United States and collectivism in Canada.

Moore's economic comparison assumes that capitalism structures both the US and Canadian health care systems, yet this only explains the health-as-commodity model, not the health-as-human-right model. Invisible in the economic comparison—at least for Moore's audience—is an acknowledgement and understanding of the place of national social policy in structuring universal health care systems within a capitalist market. To demonstrate this link, we must trace the relevance of the Canada Health Act to the social construction of the Canadian health care system in reference to the meaning of health and links to cultural identity and ideology. The Canada Health Act is a federal policy that structures the universal health care system and that links state to ideology. Pat Armstrong and Hugh Armstrong claim: "As the *Canada Health Act* made clear when it brought together the *Hospital Insurance and Diagnostics Act* and the *Medical Care Act*, Canadians must have reasonable access to health services without facing financial or other barriers" (151).

The Canada Health Act is based on five principles and two annual conditions for all Canadian provinces (Armstrong and Armstrong). Only when these principles have been met are the federal funds that are essential for health care transferred to the provinces. The federal government can and does use its economic power to withhold transfer funds when the principles are not met. State enforcement of these five principles—universality, accessibility, comprehensiveness, portability, and public administration—is key to the social construction of the health care system as well as to Canadians' understanding of the meaning of health in their communities and everyday lives.

The principle of *universality* ensures that everyone is covered under the same terms and conditions; it also defines health care as a human right. This particular principle is politically popular as a focus of Canadian identity and is often quoted during election debates about public and private health care. In the "Oh Canada!" segment of *SiCKO*, Canadian patients in a doctor's waiting room assume they have equal access to care, as do patients interviewed in hospital about access to emergency surgical procedures. The principle of *accessibility* means that services must be similar for everyone and must be offered without financial or social barriers. Accessibility gives Canadians a vested interest in making the health care system work. This principle, which prohibits extra-billing and user fees, is regularly challenged by various provinces as they attempt to move the health care system closer to a health-as-commodity model. It is also the principle that when violated leads to federal threats to deny transfer payments to the provinces. This principle is becoming increasingly difficult to enforce; however, when a province has tried to violate it, provincial politicians have usually reversed their decisions when the federal government has shown itself to be serious about withholding transfer payments. This was an effective strategy in 1986, when Ontario doctors went on strike because their extra-billing rights were denied. However, "the federal government held firm and the popular interpretation of the struggle as one undertaken by greedy doctors helped make it easier for the province to enforce the ban on extra-billing" (Armstrong and Armstrong 58).

Health care in Canada is *comprehensive* with respect to medically necessary services from medical practitioners and dentists in hospitals, but not to all health services. This principle has as its goal that everything medically necessary for care will be provided without charge in hospitals. "Everything" here includes drugs, tests, nursing, accommodation, food, facilities, and supplies. Ideally, there is no obvious billing to patients in hospitals; however, it is doctors who decide what is medically necessary, so there is some leeway for them. In *SiCKO* this principle is illustrated by a patient who had emergency surgery for severed fingers: this was Canada, so all hospital expenses were covered, unlike in a similar US case, where the uninsured patient could only afford to have one of two fingers reattached.

In Canada, *portability* under the Canada Health Act means that while health insurance is a provincial jurisdiction, an individual can "carry" rights to coverage from one province to another. This obviously has an impact on perceptions of illness or injury for travellers, for those who are moving out of province, and for those who wish to access complex procedures in another province. In such cases, billing is automatically directed to the home province so that the cost of health care through taxes is invisible to Canadians. Health care coverage is also portable from job to job, for it is not linked to one's employment. In *SiCKO,* much of the discussion around health care coverage for Americans focuses on the fear of job loss, even beyond retirement age, and loss of health care coverage; similar fears were not expressed by the Canadian interviewees.

The final principle, *public administration,* means that the Canadian health insurance system is administered by a not-for-profit agency, responsible to provincial governments, and subject to audit. This fits with the Canadian ideology of democratic control and public scrutiny of health care as a human right. From the health care industry's perspective, this principle is the sticking point of the Canadian health care system, for it makes privatization and commodification difficult to insert. This principle is often undermined by public–private partnerships for new hospital development and by the growing number of privatized health services that are being charged back to the public system.

With this set of five principles, the Canada Health Act has socially constructed the health care system in Canada, as well as the meaning of health for individuals using this system. Romanow's report on the future of Canadian health care emphasizes the impact of the Canada Health Act for Canadians: "They view it as a hallmark of Canadian society and the five principles closely match their values. All of this has made the *Canada Health Act* virtually immune to change. In fact, most Canadians would not stand idly by and accept changes that would destroy this symbol of Canadian identity" (58). This analysis demonstrates the state's power to structure its health care system and thereby (perhaps unintentionally) frame a meaning of health for a nation; at the same time, though, this structuring process results in a meaning of health that becomes difficult to change. While the Canadian state hangs on to the Canada Health Act, using it largely to contain growing privatization efforts, the United States struggles to find a way to inject some universality into the US system to get beyond the health-as-commodity model—the model that *SiCKO* reveals as having become so problematic. In the United States, a process of change to include different payment systems has involved social activism to demystify universal health care (Goodnough), as well as Barack Obama's policy interventions and persistence over three years to pass the Affordable Care Act in 2012, often referred to as Obamacare ("Health Care Reform"). The entrenchment of individualism and capitalism in the US health care system, which is so evident in the resistance from insurance companies and Republican politicians to Obamacare, has made it extraordinarily difficult for Americans to change the meanings they ascribe to health. This difficulty with making seemingly minor changes to the US health care system points to the close links between individualism, capitalism, and American identity that inform the meaning of health in the US social context. This difficulty has become evident both in activist projects and in politicians' efforts to transform the US health care system from a health-as-commodity model to one of health as a human right.

Michael Moore is known for confronting dilemmas of capitalism head on and with humour in documentaries like *SiCKO*, but as a social activist he also uses these films politically. His films are intended to be both entertaining and explicitly political. Marmor, Okma, and Rojas claim that Moore does this consciously: "Better than anyone in the debate, Moore skillfully manages this interplay between media and politics. He has turned himself into an effective populist politician" (50). While *SiCKO* has been used politically in a variety of ways, it is the way that nurses' organizations in California have appropriated it for debates on public health care reform that reflects the gazing across the northern border that frames Moore's film. In 2007, a nurses' campaign quickly recognized *SiCKO* as an activist tool that could be used to lobby for universal health care for Americans through the US Health Insurance Act, H.R. 676. Connie Curran highlights the emotional impact of *SiCKO:* "As a nurse, a member of our country's largest health profession, I felt ashamed of the American health care industry. I felt nurses should be involved in improving health care, but unclear about what we should or could do" (253). H.R. 676 focuses on full health services coverage for life and health care as a basic right in a democratic society, and its insists that all people are created equal even in terms of access to health. Singer highlights what the consequences for capital of the single-payer universal system would be, as outlined in H.R. 676: "Single-payer would almost eliminate insurance companies, copayments, and premiums. Controlling drug costs would mean that pharmaceutical companies, ballooned by profits from monopolizing patents and exploiting publicly funded research, would have to dream up new con games" (25).

As an advocacy project, the attempt to pass H.R. 676 is the basis of Healthcare-NOW and at the forefront of the US National Nurses Organizing Committee campaign, particularly in California (DeMoro). US nurses have been effective advocates for single-payer health care; they have legitimized *SiCKO*'s message and thereby acquired a profile in the media. A description of a day-long event in California that included a screening of *SiCKO* captures Moore's film's relevance in activist work conducted by the US health care reform movement: "In conjunction with the release of *SiCKO* on hundreds of screens across the nation, CNA/NNOC enlisted thousands of RNs to join a 'Scrubs for *SiCKO*' campaign that brought nurses to nearly 50 theaters to talk to moviegoers and encourage them to get active in lobbying for guaranteed, national healthcare—similar to an improved and expanded Medicare for all" ("Nurses" 4).

The health care reform social movement is promoting single-payer (i.e., Canadian-style) universal health care in an attempt to change cultural ideology and identity in a tangible way and thereby transform the US health care system. Donna Smith describes her experience of this kind of political action, where people meet to fight for a shared cause: "That's the sense I got as I and four other healthcare advocates scrambled onto a hand painted school bus Nov. 12 to embark on a tour of the United States to promote single payer universal healthcare as part of the Healthcare-Now SiCKO Cure National Road Show" ("Taking" 9).

In a more recent context in the United States, lobbying for universal health care and a single-payer system is a long-term project that is now part of Barack Obama's political agenda. Making these changes is far more complicated than at first appears because health care has become part of the United States' capitalist cultural identity and individualistic ideology; thus, H.R. 676 has more far-reaching consequences than simply an individual's health. Singer points out that "the version of single-payer (H.R. 676) proposed by Representative Conyers, is different. It would come close to eliminating the private insurers' roles, insure everyone, contain medical costs (including negotiating lower drug prices), and save both private industry and the public billions in its first year"

(24). In 2009, Obama did try to introduce legislation to move the US health care system toward universality. During election debates he used many of the same arguments evident in *SiCKO*, but his strategies as president have been quite different from Moore's. In an interview, Obama described Canada as a classic example of universal health care: "Basically, everybody pays a lot of taxes into the health-care system, but if you're a Canadian, you're automatically covered … You go in and you just say 'I'm sick' and somebody treats you and that's it" (qtd. in Goodman). Obama acknowledges how difficult implementing universal health care would be for Americans in politics and at work. He has also discovered that health care is such a fundamental ideological issue for Americans that shifting quickly to universal health care would be political suicide. Obama did succeed in passing the Affordable Care Act prior to his re-election in 2012, but it was not ratified at the Supreme Court level until weeks after his re-election, and even then only by a slim margin ("Health Care Reform").

Obama's first step toward universal health care continues to include the insurance companies while also trying to ensure coverage for all Americans. It is a small step toward changing the health care system and the meaning of health—a step that has been informed by looking north to Canada: "'We're not going to get the *Canada Health Act*,' Timothy Jost, a professor of health law at Washington and Lee University in Lexington, Va., quipped. 'But it's very important and historic because we've never gotten this far before'" (Yakabuski). To make these gains Obama made many concessions, including leaving control mostly with health insurance companies, allowing each state to choose control over Medicaid funding rather than be under federal control, and requiring those who can afford health insurance to purchase it themselves. Nonetheless, with the passing of the Affordable Care Act, Obama did succeed in reining in the insurance companies' excessive profit margins, implementing taxes on individuals with unusually generous health insurance policies, and requiring all Americans to have some form of insurance ("Health Care Reform"). This strategy may lead to coverage for most Americans when implemented in 2014, and it appears to embrace ideological mobility by enabling individuals to change their ideology, but it still leaves the US health care system in control of insurance companies, thereby perpetuating the health-as-commodity model.

Canadians' and Americans' experiences with health care—experiences that are evident at the Canada–US border—open up a complex social space for questioning the different meanings of health in similar capitalist economic systems. In *SiCKO*, Moore begins to open up this social space by exposing how the US privatized health care system is framed by a health-as-commodity model. In contrast, Canada's semi-socialized health care system is framed by a health-as-human-right model. Moore's populist documentary films are an effective way to expose controversies within capitalism to a wide audience. This element of his films offers a political tool for activists in the US health care reform social movement to imagine possibilities of a model of health as a human right. To move this debate beyond imagined possibilities, this chapter has highlighted how in a Canadian context the meaning of health is linked to a human right and has become part of the Canadian identity. This social construction of the meaning of health can be unpacked by unravelling the links between meanings of health, health care systems, and the state. The analysis here of the Canada Health Act demonstrates links between the Canadian health care system and an ideology of collectivity. The US health care system, which is a complex multi-payer private system, is more difficult to unravel, though the model of health as commodity is visible. The juxtaposition of two health care systems based on different meanings of health at the Canada–US border provides a social space that exposes the underlying social structures that shape those meanings differently within a similar capitalist social structure. While most Canadians struggle to maintain a universal health care system that ensures health as a human right, some Americans try to imagine how to untangle the multi-payer private system, which reinforces health as a commodity. The Canada–US border is one social place where these different interpretations can continue to be questioned.

Works Cited

Armstrong, Pat, and Hugh Armstrong. *Wasting Away: The Undermining of Canadian Health Care.* 2nd ed. Toronto: Oxford UP, 2003.

Bowling for Columbine. Dir. Michael Moore. Dog Eat Dog, 2002.

Canadian Bacon. Dir. Michael Moore. Polygram, 1995.

CBC. "Tommy Douglas and the NDP." CBC Archives. http://archives.cbc.ca/politics/parties_leaders/topics/851. Accessed 5 April 2011.

Cunningham, Hilary, and Josiah McC. Heyman. "Introduction: Mobilities and Enclosures at Borders." *Identities: Global Studies in Culture and Power* 11.3 (2004): 289–302.

Curran, Connie R. "SiCKO." *Nursing Economics* 25.5 (2007): 253, 292.

DeMoro, Rose Ann. "Sharp Focus." *Registered Nurse* May 2007: 9. http://www.calnurses.org. Accessed 23 July 2010.

Evans, Robert G. "The Unsustainability Myth." *Monitor* 1 July 2010. http://www.policyalternatives.ca/publications/monitor. Accessed 8 August 2010.

Goodnough, Abby. "Next Challenge for the Health Care Law: Getting the Public to Buy In." *New York Times* 19 December 2012. http://www.nytimes.com/2012/12/20/us/officials-confront-skepticism-over-health-law.html?ref=healthcarereform. Accessed 30 December 2012.

Goodman, Lee-Anne. "Obama Health Plan Won't Look Like Canada's." *Canadian Press* 26 March 2009. http://www.medbroadcast.com. Accessed 8 August 2010.

Hass, Janis. "SiCKO Strikes a Chord." *Canadian Medical Association Journal* 177.4 (2007): 380.

"Health Care Reform." *New York Times* 8 November 2012. http://topics.nytimes.com/top/news/health/diseasesconditionsandhealthtopics/health_insurance_and_managed_care/health_care_reform/index.html. Accessed 30 December 2012.

Kennedy, Janice. "'Is This What We'll Become?" *Ottawa Citizen* 8 July 2007: B8.

MacFarquhar, Larissa. "The Populist: Michael Moore Can Make You Cry." *The New Yorker* 80.1 (2004): 133.

Marmor, Theodore R., Kieke G.H. Okma, and Joseph R. Rojas. "What It Is, What It Does and What It Might Do: A Review of Michael Moore's *SiCKO*, 113 Minutes, Dog Eat Dog Films, USA, 2007." *American Journal of Bioethics* 7.10 (2007): 49–51.

"Nurses, Moore Launch Campaign to Expose the Real Sickos." *Registered Nurse* June 2007: 4. http://www.calnurses.org. Accessed 23 July 2010.

Roger and Me. Dir. Michael Moore. Warner Bros., 1989.

Romanow, Roy J. *Building on Values: The Future of Health Care in Canada.* Ottawa: Queen's Printer, 2002.

Roseneau, Pauline M. Villaincourt. "U.S. Newspaper Coverage of the Canadian Health System—A Case of Seriously Mistaken Identity?" *American Review of Canadian Studies* 36.1 (2006): 27–58.

SiCKO. Dir. Michael Moore. Dog Eat Dog Films, 2007.

Silverman, Ross D. "Access To Care: Who Pays for Health Care for the Uninsured and Underinsured? A Symposium Introduction and Overview." *Journal of Legal Medicine* 29 (2008): 1–9.

Singer, David. "The Healthcare Crisis in the US." *Monthly Review* February 2008: 16–29.

Smith, Donna. "Anniversary of an American SICKO." 21 June 2010. http://www.michaelmoore.com/words/mike-friends-blog/anniversary-american-sicko. Accessed 23 July 2010.

———. "Taking the *Sicko* Cure to the People." *Registered Nurse* November 2007: 9. http://www.calnurses.org. Accessed 23 July 2010.

Walkom, Thomas. "Moore Is Right on Medicare: Director's Sicko Shows Folly of U.S. Hostility to Health Care for All." *Toronto Star* 9 June 2007: A19.

Yakabuski, Konrad. "Obama Health Care Victory Takes Major Compromise." *Globe and Mail* 9 November 2009: A12.

four

Television, Nation, and National Security
The CBC's *The Border*

Sarah A. Matheson

IN THE MIDST OF THE INFAMOUS WikiLeaks release of classified documents from the US State Department in November 2010 were reports of confidential cables from the US embassy in Ottawa to officials in Washington that supposedly raised concerns about the portrayal of Americans on Canadian television. In the documents published by *The New York Times*, two CBC series were highlighted in particular: the situation comedy *Little Mosque on the Prairie* and the action-drama *The Border*. They were identified as examples of CBC programs that contained "insidious negative popular stereotyping" of Americans. The public broadcaster, one cable claimed, had "long gone to great pains to highlight the distinction between Americans and Canadians in its programming, generally at our expense" ("A Selection"). The offending material in *Little Mosque* was apparently found in episodes that dealt with Muslim characters encountering problems with border security or finding themselves on US "no-fly" lists. In reference to *The Border*, one cable complained about the representation of "US border agents as insensitive and bullying," apparently in reaction to the series' frequent focus on conflicts between US and Canadian security agencies (Vlessing). An article in *The Hollywood Reporter* quoted the cable: "While the war is supposed to be against criminals and terrorists trying to cross the border, many of the immigration team's battles end up being with the U.S. government officials ... [The] clash between the Americans and Canadians got started early in the season and has continued unabated" (qtd. in Vlessing).

In a sense, what these cables are identifying is a common convention of Canadian TV, which often expresses national differences in terms of broad national stereotypes—a device that would be familiar to most Canadian viewers. For example, Canadian comedy has a history of presenting satirical takes on US politics and popular culture, which often involves poking fun at the differences between Americans and Canadians (usually relying on popular stereotypes of both nations).[1] Series such as *Bordertown* (1989–91) and *Due South* (1994–99), which were premised on US–Canadian partnerships, self-consciously engaged with national stereotypes in storylines that routinely dealt with how national differences frustrated and interfered with cooperation. It may not be an especially surprising revelation, therefore, that national stereotypes can be found on Canadian television. What is more interesting about the cables is their emphasis on the border and national security. The series that appear to raise particular concern are the ones dealing with security initiatives (*Little Mosque*, which addresses racial profiling) and that address US–Canadian conflicts related to border security (*The Border*). In an interesting way, the cables are drawing attention to the fact that these TV series are responding to popular anxieties related to national security, its politics and policies.

This chapter focuses on *The Border* (2008–10), a program that reflected the contemporary heightened awareness of the US–Canada border and the security issues surrounding it. The series follows the activities of Immigration and Customs Security (ICS), an elite—and fictional—squad of agents who fight crime and tackle national security threats in the context of cross-border relations. The program's premise rests on the notion that "in this post-9/11 world, the once 'undefended border' that divides Canada and the US is no longer considered soft. *The Border* lifts stories from the headlines to fuel action-packed episodes about maintaining security in today's world" (CBC Shop). The ICS team is comprised of capable, dedicated, and highly skilled agents. At their helm is Major Mike Kessler, the handsome, principled ex-military man who is guided by a sense of social justice and personal integrity. He finds himself frustrated by the interference of both Homeland Security agent Bianca LaGarda and the shadowy, duplicitous Canadian intelligence agency CSIS (represented by his devious rival Mannering). The ICS team consists of an ensemble of characters, who include ex-customs officer Maggie Norton; former police detective Al "Moose" Lepinsky; brash young ladies' man Gray Jackson; ex-CSIS agent Darnell Williams; beautiful, multilingual, and Muslim agent Layla Hourani; and geeky computer expert Hieronymous Slade. The program relies on the familiar "American–Not American" binary, with Kessler and LaGarda constructed as "national types" who appear to embody very different values and world views.[2] In its first season *The Border* won two Gemini Awards; it has been broadcast in Britain, Italy, Germany, Finland, Norway, Denmark, Netherlands, France, Belgium, Luxembourg, South Korea, Sweden, Estonia, Bulgaria, and South Africa ("CBC's *The Border*").

The Border was also shaped by a cross-border televisual environment, and as such, it reflected the international flow of popular genres and formats. *The Border* is clearly indebted to the American series *24*, yet it is also informed by what can be characterized as a Canadian documentary sensibility. Thus, its depiction of national boundaries is played out through its negotiation of and response to American television and its conventions. In this chapter I consider the following questions: In what ways is this series shaped by the tension between Hollywood conventions and a Canadian "inflection," and what effect does this have on the ways that crime and Canada's participation in the international "War on Terror" are depicted? What does the series suggest about the changing nature of Canada–US relations, and how is this played out in the ways that generic boundaries are traversed? I will argue that despite claims by the series' creator and producer Peter Raymont that *The Border* is "*24* with a conscience" (Dixon R1), the adoption of some of the most problematic aspects of action genres—specifically, so-called "terror television" programs such as *24*—undermine and contradict this objective. Furthermore, while the series is premised in part on the perceived notion of a conflict between US and Canadian values and institutions (which perhaps provided Canadian audiences with a comforting and familiar sense of distance and difference), *The Border* operates within a framework that ultimately reproduces a similar kind of politics of paranoia and fear of the sort that pervade so much of post-9/11 television. I will limit my attention to the program's first season in order to trace how its debut was greeted in the popular press, to examine the critical and promotional discourses surrounding it (which framed its intentions and its relationship to American series in particular ways), and to identify how, as the series established its premise and launched its initial episodes, its significance was discussed and debated.

The Canada–US border has been immensely important to how English Canadian television has been discussed, studied, and theorized. As television from the south floods across the so-called "electronic border," fears about Americanization and the loss of Canadian cultural sovereignty have historically motivated calls for institutions and policies designed to produce forms of national culture that, it is thought, could help protect and maintain national boundaries. Referencing early broadcasting lobbyist Graeme Spry and his famous proclamation, "The State or The United States," Aniko Bodroghkozy points out that public broadcasting in Canada was established on the premise that it could "serve as a weapon to keep seductive American mass culture on the other side of the border" (566). Canadians' preference and enthusiasm for American television has fuelled calls for government support of domestic television production, the view being that Canada needs homegrown series in order to defend what David Taras has described as "the cultural frontier" (174). Yet as Frank E. Manning argues in his discussion of the influence of American popular culture in Canada, "Canadian culture is less the product of its own separate evolution than of its interactive relationship with an American Other. This relationship ... is diffuse, ambiguous, and contradictory. It involves imitation and resistance, infatuation and repugnance, collusion and condemnation, submission and subversion, identification and differentiation, and myriad other forms of acceptance and rejection" (26). Manning here is pointing to the complexity involved in this cultural exchange and the variety of possible responses.

Drama has often been privileged as a form especially crucial to meeting the national imperatives associated with Canadian television. For example, Miller describes TV drama as "one of the few elements in Canadian life that marked our southern border, distinguishing 'here' from 'there'" (*Turn Up* 3). Jen VanderBurgh further notes that "so entrenched is the belief in drama's abilities to consolidate a sense of 'culture' that funding strategies are rhetorically said to be a form of national defence" (269). Yet despite the national stakes frequently associated with it, Canadian dramas are commonly received with indifference, and producers have had a difficult time attracting audiences. In attempts to court a popular audience, one common approach has been to produce programming based on popular genres, formats, and formulas adopted from the United States (and elsewhere) and to conform to American aesthetics and production values. The best of these series, critics contend, are adapted to a Canadian context, and inflected with "distinctive" Canadian elements or sensibilities (Miller, *Turn Up*, "Inflecting"). This suggests that English Canadian television is characterized by an ongoing negotiation with Hollywood genres and forms. Much of it is defined by the tension that results from attempts to appeal to a popular audience whose tastes have been explicitly shaped by the consumption and enjoyment of American television, and by the expectation that series should work to maintain or articulate some kind of difference in terms of national content. This tension is especially pronounced at the CBC, which, as a public broadcaster that also depends on advertising revenue, has to balance commercial pressures with its national mandate, which is to "contribute to shared national consciousness and identity" (1991 Broadcasting Act). Thus, television drama in Canada is arguably a form of culture *defined* by cross-border negotiation, yet it is consistently framed by a discourse that suggests its most important role is to maintain and defend national boundaries and distinctions.

As it grapples with the significance of this negotiation, Canadian television criticism has often turned to the notion of "inflection," which Miller defines as "the grafting of new ideas, dramatic conventions and technical advances on to old conventions" ("Inflecting" 104). Scholars have sought to identify the differences and similarities between particular series (often through comparison with American forms) in order to reveal the ways the border is both crossed and (more importantly) resisted in these programs. Within criticism, emphasis is typically placed on the significance of meaningful differences that point to a distinctive approach (rather than a simple imitation of US formulas).[3] However, as this analysis will demonstrate, it is equally important to consider the parallels, similarities, and correspondences that exist across television cultures that are likewise meaningful.

The Border was part of a broader shift at the CBC under Richard Stursberg, who was appointed in 2004 as the new Executive Vice-President of Television, and then as Executive VP of English Services from 2007 to 2010. Under its new direction, the CBC began to put more emphasis on entertainment genres and on developing popular programming that would compete with American programming. Stursberg used *The Border* as an example of the success of this strategy, describing it as part of the CBC's new "Golden Age," characterized by a prime-time schedule that was attracting larger audiences than ever before (Stursburg A15). In its first season it was scheduled in the same time slot as *24* would have had on Global, a rival Canadian network. *24* was delayed, however, by a writer's strike in the United States. Thus, *The Border* debuted amidst discussions about the opportunities the strike might open up: Canadian drama series might take the place of absent popular American programming, reach audiences that might not normally watch Canadian programs, and perhaps even tap into the lucrative US market. Jason Anderson situates *The Border* and CTV's *Flashpoint* (a similar action drama that also debuted in 2008 and that aired on CBS in the United States) as successful new English Canadian television dramas that replicated the pace, style, and production values of American series: "With their emphasis on heated confrontations and ticking-clock scenarios, *Flashpoint* and *The Border* are imitative of the action-heavy model epitomized by *24* and *NCIS*." At the same time, according to Anderson, the producers of both series defended the Canadian elements and values that—they argued—could be identified in the programs, reflecting the tension between popular appeal and national specificity.

The series' trailer offers a clear summary of the program and how it was marketed to the public. It opens with an aerial image of North America. The camera zooms in, moves through the clouds, and zeroes in on the grid that forms the Canada–US border. A voiceover, deadly serious, explains: "It spans 3,000 miles, separating two massive countries, and its protection is a worldwide concern." The next sequence begins with the image of a massive plane screaming past overhead. The first glimpse of the series features a tense standoff in an airport as a terrorist, wired with explosives, holds an ICS agent at gunpoint. The voiceover continues: "A new dramatic series following the lives of an elite security unit. Their goal: to protect a border from all manner of threat." This is followed by a rapid montage of images from various episodes, designed to excite the audience's interest: explosions, chases, gunfire, references to terrorists, fake passports, and "Taliban-related violence," comprise the sequence. A few images of steamy love scenes and scantily clad women are thrown into the mix. The music pounds and pulsates, driving home the danger, urgency, action, and high-stakes drama the program promises.

The advertisements and promotional discourse surrounding *The Border* situated the series in the context of the post-9/11 climate of fear and paranoia. And as the trailer demonstrates, a key feature of the series was its fast-paced, technology-laden visual style and action-oriented format, both familiar from

American programs. Reviews in the popular press made frequent comparisons between *24* and *The Border*, and the producers, writers, and cast often affirmed this link in interviews. In many ways the series reproduced elements from *24*, and obviously attempted to appeal to audiences by adopting the urgency, stylized spectacle, and thrills associated with action genres. Like *24*, it focused on dangerous threats to national security; also like *24*, it depended on the logic of "exceptional times demand exceptional measures" that accompanied the post-9/11 consensus that "everything has changed." A billboard in downtown Toronto advertising *The Border* emphasized this in its tag line: "This is a new war. These are the few who fight it."

As "Canadian TV's answer to *24*" ("A Run"), *The Border* was also a response to the American myth that Canada's border was permeable and its security lax—a myth that continues to circulate and that is used to justify calls for strengthened border security. *The Border* spoke to popular anxieties about Canadian sovereignty in the context of the War on Terror and the accompanying pressure on Canada to "harmonize" its border security practices with those of the United States (Whitaker 50). It suggested that Canada was prepared to do what it took to ensure national security, while articulating a sense of difference and resistance to American influence.[4]

The Border's difference from its American counterpart was discussed in specific ways in critical and promotional discourse. In particular, the program's connection to documentary was highlighted as part of its distinctive approach.[5] The participation of Peter Raymont and Lindalee Tracey (who co-created the series along with Janet MacLean and Jeremy Hole) was consistently highlighted as central to the program's creation. Raymont and Tracey (now deceased) were both accomplished documentary filmmakers whose work included investigations into immigration and border enforcement issues. According to Raymont, the series was inspired by their investigation of immigration policing in their TV Ontario documentary *The Undefended Border* (Dixon R1). The DVD commentary accompanying the pilot episode of *The Border* consistently reinforces this connection to documentary with regard to pace and visual style, drawing attention to the "hand-held" and "jittery" quality of the camerawork, its use of location shooting, and the sense of immediacy or liveness created through its fast pace. Alluding to the series' connection to *cinéma vérité*, director John Fawcett notes that "one of the keys to *The Border* is that it feels real, it feels like it is really happening" (DVD commentary, "Pockets of Vulnerability"). This sense of documentary realism was further connected to the way its narratives were anchored in references to real events and people outside of its fiction. According to Raymont, the series' storylines were "informed by and drawn from reality ... none of the incidents or situations or actors are really brought out of thin air. They're based on something that might've happened or did happen, so there's a kind of documentary reality to the whole thing" (DVD commentary, "Pockets of Vulnerability"). The "ripped from the headlines" topical approach asserted a claim to authenticity and relevance—that the narratives were anchored in some sense of a Canadian reality.

English Canadian television has a history of inflecting popular genres with elements of documentary realism.[6] This Canadian tradition is "associated with the CBC and National Film Board, a tradition of documentary realism and social responsibility" (Leach, "*E.N.G.*"). Leach identifies a "Canadian mode" in film and television: "its major achievements in television include drama anthologies like the CBC's *For the Record* (1976–85) and series like *Wojeck* (1966–68) that blend documentary and fiction techniques" ("Reading" 114). David Hogarth similarly notes that "documentary programming has shaped Canada's television *aesthetic*" (emphasis in the original). According to Hogarth, "this aesthetic has been organizationally sustained by flexible department structures encouraging public service producers ... to move back and forth from documentary to drama productions, bringing their techniques with them" (5). Documentary ideals, he asserts, have also shaped television criticism, resulting in critics judging even fiction programs for their "documentary as opposed to dramatic value" (6). He writes that "[television documentary] has served to uphold or resolve distinctions made in Canadian cultural discourse between 'quality' and 'commercial' television, between the 'public' and the 'popular,' and between the 'national' and the 'foreign'" (4). In relation to *The Border*, this documentary aspect was often evoked as the site where the series' apparent "conscience" might be located; this, it was implied, set it apart from other series. For example, in framing *The Border* as part of a larger body of work, Raymont suggested that it was informed by the same sense of social justice and human rights advocacy that had informed his (and Tracey's) filmmaking (Dixon R1). In an interview, Raymont further implied a distinction between the series' social value and its entertainment value: "I feel myself as being more of an activist than a filmmaker. I make films to try to make the world a better place. And although *The Border* is very entertaining, fast-paced and should reach a big audience ... at its core, it's about human rights and social justice" (qtd. in Dixon R1).

The Border's storylines do reference a variety of contemporary international human rights issues. For example, the pilot episode addresses racial profiling, with allusions to the Maher Arar case;[7] another episode deals with the trauma experienced by a child soldier from Sudan; yet another focuses on abduction, sexual abuse, and child pornography; and still other episodes deal variously with human trafficking, including organ theft. Within these storylines, the series also frequently alludes to the complicity of the Canadian government and the business community and to the culture of secrecy that enables these crimes and human rights violations to persist. And the central characters themselves wrestle regularly with moral and ethical dilemmas that surface in the course of their work. The character of Hourani is a good example. As a Muslim woman, she is often shown struggling to balance her job with her religious beliefs. In "Enemy Contact" for instance, she is asked to interrogate a Muslim woman; later, she expresses regret that she had to act in ways that she felt violated the woman's rights.

The series' similarities to *24* and its fast pace and action format were used to suggest the program's popular appeal, excitement, and entertainment value. At the same time, documentary ideals and a focus on human rights and social justice themes were used to help differentiate it from the perceived reactionary politics of its US counterpart. The promotional discourse pointed to the series' moral complexity (or so-called "conscience") as a marker of its distinctive approach, which was often framed in national terms. As producer David Barlow noted, *The Border* offered the same energy, action, and "international stakes" as *24*, but with important differences. Among those differences were the program's more collective, ensemble-based mode and its questioning narratives ("A Run"). In interviews, the producers and cast often mentioned the "ethical questions" posed by the various episodes; viewers were being asked to "[track] your own moral and ethical stance on the issues"[8]—the suggestion being that *The Border* offered a more complex and less black-and-white approach to the issues it tackled. As Barlow explained: "We're into the questions a little bit more because, hey we're Canadian" ("A Run"). Within this discourse, therefore, the discussion of the series' inflection followed a traditional tendency to frame differences in broad national terms (which were naturalized and stereotyped). This is paralleled in the storylines, which routinely pit Kessler against LaGarda. Specifically, the "Canadian way" (apparently more level-headed, by the book, and conciliatory) is contrasted with the aggressive, "anything goes" American approach. In her analysis of *The Border*, Yasmin Jiwani draws on the notion of "soft power," arguing that "what is quintessentially Canadian about *The Border* is its softer approach to issues of power and conflict that erupt in the various episodes. Lead actor, James McGowan described the show as 'a clash between classic American and Canadian' approaches to security" (275). She describes this approach as "tending more toward diplomacy, 'smart action,' and collaboration" (275). Jiwani's analysis examines the hegemonic function of soft power in the series, which she argues reinforces hierarchies of race and gender (288).

It is true that, through its storylines, *The Border* articulates a sense of difference between American and Canadian approaches and values, thus appealing to a popular nationalism and reflecting "a Canadian self-image that is tempered with compassion, with humanity" (Jiwani 288). But I would argue that the program's action-oriented framework and emphasis on spectacle also overwhelms and contradicts this theme. *The Border* may be different from *24* in many ways, but it is equally important to understand the similarities between the two—to consider the tropes, conventions, and styles they share. These were often downplayed, or explained by some simply as efforts to appeal to popular tastes, or criticized by others as examples of imitating an American form; even so, they are central and meaningful elements that should be considered. In adopting core aspects of the action and terror television genres, *The Border* depicts the Canada–US border within a framework consistent with rather than disruptive of the politics of paranoia and fear that underpin series such as *24*.

Central to *The Border* was the "action-packed" entertainment it offered viewers, which replicated the thrills and excitement that drew audiences to series like *24*. Many of the reviewers in the popular press commented on its far-fetched narratives and its overblown action scenes. *Globe and Mail* TV critic John Doyle, for example, described *The Border* as "overcooked, noisy and unsubtle" ("Border" R3), "all toxic paranoia and inflated, clench-jawed arguments" and "the usual absurd and raging melodrama" ("Canadian" R3). Reviewer Kate Taylor, even as she acknowledged the ways the show spoke to "Canadian geo-political realities," noted that it was "sometimes burdened by the improbable plots and equally improbable babes that seem to be a staple on most crime shows these days" (R3). Others, like reviewer Maria Kubacki, poked fun at its depiction of immigration and customs officials as action heroes: "And you thought border guards spent all their time slowing down traffic and rooting out contraband Gap hoodies bought on sale at US outlet malls ... But the elite agents on *The Border* ... are all about sleeper cells, corporate spies, international assassins and African drug traffickers. They're also prone to lots of sexy glaring—both at the bad guys and each other—and excitable shouting and flashing of badges" (D10). These comments point to an interesting tension in the series: the claims to realism are countered by recognition of the ways in which the codes and conventions of action genres frame these events and issues.

As Yvonne Tasker points out, action television has been underexamined in television studies. She suggests that recent scholarship on action films may be useful in particular for theorizing the relationship between narrative and spectacle, an issue that has received significant attention in film studies (Tasker, "Action Television").[9] Elsewhere, Tasker takes issue with the tendency in film studies to emphasize the significance of narrative over spectacle. She argues that "[t]he spectacle of action cinema has if not a narrative, then a thematic significance that is too often overlooked" ("Introduction" 3). She adds that "[n]arrative themes and concerns can be developed as much through visual and aural spectacle as through characterization and dialogue" (3). Thus action sequences are not simply empty moments of exaggeration; they are not merely efforts to incorporate more entertaining scenes that can keep audiences on the edge of their seats; rather, they should be examined as significant and expressive elements. Therefore, if, as Jennifer M. Bean argues, "the action film 'speaks' through visual spectacle" (17), what then is *The Border* saying through its mobilization of the aesthetics of the spectacular?

To address this question, it is helpful to consider the importance of genre and form. The term "terror television" was coined by John Kenneth Muir to describe "the entertainment form of horror television programs" (Nakamura 110). It has since been adopted by critics such as Lisa Nakamura to describe popular narrative programs such as Showtime's *Sleeper Cell* and Fox's *24* (111). Terror television, according to Nakamura, "has a paranoid relationship to the real that is fundamentally different from relations seen in ... other genres" (127). Sara Ahmed has demonstrated the ways in which "anxiety and fear create the very effect of borders" (132): "Borders are constructed and indeed policed in the very feeling that they have already been transgressed ... The transgression of the border is required in order for it to be secured as a border in the first place" (132). She writes, "more specifically, it is through announcing a crisis in security that new forms of security, border policing, and surveillance become justified" (132). Terror television provides such "narratives of crisis," provoking fear and anxiety and dramatizing its containment (through its performance of cycles of fear and reassurance). True to the form, *The Border* is steeped in this culture of fear, defining the Canada–US border through what Anna Pratt describes as the "crime-security nexus" in which "the logic of 'security' has been increasingly linked to that of criminality" (220). "In the present day," she writes, "crime-security has become a central occasion for the production, reproduction, and enforcement of borders" (221). Situated firmly in the context of the terror TV genre, *The Border* unquestioningly adopted this logic, using this crime/security nexus as the basic premise animating each episode. This theme is arguably most powerfully expressed through its action sequences.

Like *24*, *The Border* portrays a world constantly on the brink of disaster, a place of crisis and chaos (Monahan 109). Through its storylines, *The Border* repeatedly dramatizes the transgression of the border, often by dangerous outsiders, a violation that threatens to erupt violently into Canadians' everyday spaces. Suicide bombers take hostages in Toronto's Pearson Airport ("Pockets of Vulnerability"); terrorists on the run in rural Quebec prompt a heart-pounding chase through the woods that culminates in dramatic shootouts and a car explosion detonated by a suicide bomber ("Bodies on the Ground"); in a dramatic narrative climax, a former child soldier from Sudan holds his commander at gunpoint in Toronto's Yonge-Dundas Square while frightened pedestrians scream and run ("Family Affair"); "Compromising Positions," about illegal Russian exotic dancers, provides the opportunity for a number of provocative scenes set in a Toronto strip club. In arguably the most over-the-top episode of the season, "Enemy Contact," Kessler orders Gray to take the infant son of the leader of a terrorist sleeper cell into the Toronto subway in order to pressure her to reveal where an imminent anthrax attack is to take place. ICS agents chase terrorists through TTC subway trains and across the platforms of Bloor Station. Surrounded by armed agents, one of the men holds up a jar of homemade anthrax and declares that he is ready to die. Gray arrives with the baby strapped to his chest and attempts to persuade him to give himself up. When that fails, Tasers are used to subdue the man and the attack is thwarted. Gray breathes a heavy sigh of relief as he clutches the baby and leans down to kiss his head.

Episodes of *The Border* are replete with these moments of exaggeration, action, and overblown spectacle. In her analysis of post-9/11 American television, Stacy Takacs notes that *24* varied ideologically from season to season. However, she points to the importance of its structure and to the significance of affect in the series. She likens *24* to an amusement park ride in the way it immerses the viewer in a visceral, physical (rather than mental) experience, noting the way it "appeals to the gut." The affective dimensions of the program, Takacs argues, works to generate a sense of urgency and anxiety that provides justification for the War on Terror; "by mobilizing emotions and sensations, it conscripts viewers into the war effort" (88). She writes: "Spy TV programs construct an expansive regime of fear that seems to necessitate new, more aggressive security measures" (81). In *The Border,* action sequences similarly rely on sensation, shock, and visceral effects over contemplation, and this arguably overwhelms any sense of nuance that may be suggested in the narratives. These sequences exist in an unsettling tension with the narrative elements. The series' storylines raise questions and pose ethical dilemmas, but these are answered by the extreme circumstances and the violent responses they evidently require. And that these scenes are staged in ordinary and recognizable locations suggests that threats are imminent and close to home.

The significance of spectacle also extends to the series' "high-tech style." In reviews, *The Border* was consistently praised for its slick style and high production values, which are showcased predominantly through the visual effects associated with technology. The ICS headquarters, with its chrome-and-glass partitions, serves as a virtual display case for technology; Slade's workstation features multiple computer screens on which he seems effortlessly to employ the latest cutting-edge programs with seemingly instantaneous results. With its foregrounding of technology, *The Border* created an aesthetic similar to what Nakamura describes as *24*'s "terrorist look." This style is produced through the visual spectacle of surveillance and biometric technologies, which are deployed to identify and apprehend terrorist threats that lurk undetected (115). Viewers are dazzled by the display of images and captivated by the ways in which surveillance, data retrieval, and facial recognition systems are used to heighten suspense and complement narrative arcs that typically culminate in dramatic moments when hidden identities are revealed and dangers are unearthed (117). In *The Border,* screens displaying images from surveillance cameras, mobile phones, and databases saturate the visual landscape and underscore the mounting tension surrounding the agents' efforts to identify and apprehend their suspects. Nakamura notes that in the case of *24*, technology is used to create an "aesthetics of astonishment" similar to Tom Gunning's notion of a "cinema of attractions" (114). *The Border* exploits this popular high-tech style for similar ends—that is, for dramatic and sensational effect.

As Nakamura points out, these technologies are not neutral; rather, they are "deeply imbricated with new forms of state power" (113) and are employed in *24*, she argues, "to persuade a paranoid television viewer of the systems' own effectiveness and integrity" (115). In *The Border*, the pervasive use of surveillance and biometric technologies as a response to threats to national security is similarly framed as necessary and reasonable given the urgent circumstances. Very rarely in the series are questions raised about the potential abuses of this technology, the rights issues surrounding it, or the ways it increasingly encroaches on and violates citizens' privacy. Canadian viewers, it seems, can enjoy the spectacle of technology, while being reassured that this power is placed in the hands of people who are working in the best interests of the nation.

Episode 12, "Grave Concern," is an ideal example for analysis, for it contains many of the series' central themes and recurring tropes. The episode begins with the ICS team apprehending a suspect whom they believe is smuggling child pornography across the border. In searching the photos on his computer, the agents discover an image from a surveillance camera that shows a little girl being held captive in a dungeon-like basement. The exact location is at first unknown. They identify the girl as a kidnap victim from Michigan, an eleven-year-old grabbed from her bed eighteen months prior. It is revealed that this had been LaGarda's last case at the FBI and that her inability to solve it has haunted her ever since. She persuades Kessler to let her join the investigation so that she can fulfil the promise she made to the girl's family to bring their daughter home alive.

Technology is central to the narrative arc of this episode. We learn that the kidnapper, Skinner, posed as a teenager online in order to learn where the child lived and then kidnapped her and locked her in the room. His plan is to auction the girl to the highest bidder through a pedophile chat room. Skinner is a skilful computer hacker who is able to hide his tracks and conceal his identity and location; thus, he poses a formidable challenge for Slade, who helps Agent Gray pose as a pedophile in an attempt to infiltrate the group and discover the girl's location. Much of the narrative focuses on things like data retrieval, identity traces, chat room dialogues, attempts to trace computers to their locations, GPS tracking of vehicles, and so on. Slade's inability to identify Skinner and his location is a central tension. At one point LaGarda confronts Slade:

LaGarda: I thought you were the best.
   Slade: I am.

LaGarda: Why don't we know where Skinner Is? You've got his email, voice protocol, why is it so difficult?

Slade: Look, he doesn't want to be found, okay, he's made it virtually impossible.

LaGarda: The FBI's got a guy out of Quantico.

Slade: Crazy Larry Lennox? Please.

LaGarda: Cal Tech?

Slade: Vandals and skateboard punks.

LaGarda: Microsoft?

Slade: Don't even finish that thought! Look, you can turn over every circuit board from Palo Alto to Pakistan and you're not going to find anyone better or faster than me.

LaGarda: I hear you talking and all I hear is a guy making excuses (*she walks away*).

Slade: (*yelling after her*) That was very harsh!

This dialogue represents a significant moment: Slade's abilities are being called into question, and the conflict is framed in national terms. Perhaps, as LaGarda suggests, American experts from these leading institutions are better equipped to do the job. And it is also a moment when the supposedly American way of doing things—aggressive, direct, insensitive—is shown to be unnecessarily tough and out of sync with the usual (Canadian) way of doing things. In the end, during a tense scene as Gray races to rescue the girl, Slade (with the help of his computer wiz ex-girlfriend), works feverishly to discover the girl's location and does so just in the nick of time. The site, in Sault Ste. Marie, Michigan, is shown on a satellite map, which demonstrates its positioning just across the bridge from Sault Ste. Marie, Ontario. Documents from border security reveal that Skinner had a NEXUS pass that enabled him to move freely across the border.

Throughout this episode, data retrieval, biometric, and surveillance technologies are used in ways akin to what Nakamura describes in relation to *24*, as an intricate part of the narrative and as devices for creating suspense and heightening drama. The episode suggests that these technologies are necessary in order to apprehend criminals who themselves are sophisticated computer experts. This episode further suggests the fallibility of current border security programs such as NEXUS, which was introduced as part of the "Smart Border" agreements between the United States and Canada following 9/11.[10] The narrative supports the notion that increased vigilance is necessary while suggesting that Canada is well prepared to face these new threats—perhaps even more prepared than the Americans, who had failed to solve the case. It addresses anxieties about Canadian sovereignty and border security through an appeal to nationalism, yet it also reflects the series' tendency to represent national security through this "crime/security nexus." The series depends on the premise that the border is insecure—a situation that, according to generic conventions, has dire consequences that demand immediate action.

The Border reflected a common strategy in English Canadian television drama—that of inflecting popular Hollywood genres and forms with Canadian elements or sensibilities. It was a good example of a program emerging from and shaped by a borderland society. Furthermore, it continued a Canadian tradition of blending elements of documentary with fiction. In doing so, it satisfied both the commercial objectives associated with TV drama (to attract and entertain a popular audience, and generate advertising revenue), while also articulating a sense of difference and nationhood that fulfilled the CBC's mandate. While the storylines often suggest the more ethical and conciliatory nature of Canadian approaches to national security in contrast to American methods and attitudes, some of the central elements and conventions of action television that are adopted consistently contradict this theme. Moreover, as I've attempted to reveal through this analysis, *The Border* is deeply complicit in the rhetoric of fear and paranoia on which terror TV depends. Perhaps it enacted a meaningful inflection of a popular form, but ultimately, it failed to rise above the constraints of genre, and trouble both its pleasures and politics. *The Border* incorporated not only some of the entertaining techniques and styles of terror TV but also some of its most worrying assumptions.

Notes

1   For example, Rick Mercer's popular "man on the street" sketch "Talking to Americans" (featured first on *This Hour Has 22 Minutes* and later as a CBC special) poked fun at Americans' apparent lack of knowledge about Canada and Canadians. The sitcom *An American in Canada* is another good example of a comedy organized around national stereotypes and based on a "culture clash" premise.

2   Aniko Bodroghkozy identifies this binary as a common way of framing Canada's "national self-in-relation to the American other" (575).

3   See Miller's comparison of *L.A. Law* and *Street Legal* in "Inflecting the Formula." In her discussion of Canadian TV, a central question Bodroghkozy asks is "What happens when Canadian cultural producers mimic the forms and conventions of American popular culture?" (568). She suggests that it may be possible to note a similar postcolonial strategy of "positive unoriginality" described by Meaghan Morris: "borrowing, stealing, plundering, as well as recoding, rewriting and reworking American forms" (Bodroghkozy 568).

4   According to Reg Whitaker, Canada's response to 9/11 had "both to assure an anxious public concerned about threats to their security, and to pre-empt the Americans from taking more drastic measures that would directly threaten Canadian sovereignty" (61).

5   Yasmin Jiwani notes that the referencing of contemporary events "[blurs] the lines between fiction and reality-based programming" (274). Joanne C. Elvy and Luis René Fernández Tabío also note the influence of documentary in *The Border*. See "'Normalizing Relations': The Canada/Cuban Imaginary on the Fringe of Border Discourse" in this volume.

6   Chapters in the recent anthology *Programming Reality: Perspectives on English-Canadian Television* (Wilfrid Laurier University Press, 2008) explore the relationship

between reality and fiction in Canadian television. See also Jim Leach's discussion of the "national-realist tradition" in Canadian cinema in Chapter 1 of *Film in Canada*. Don Mills: Oxford University Press, 2011.

7 Maher Arar is a Syrian-born Canadian citizen who was detained in New York on his way home from a vacation in Tunisia. He was suspected of having ties to al-Qaeda and, even though he had lived in Canada for fifteen years and had a Canadian passport, he was deported to Syria where he was jailed for over a year and tortured. A Canadian judicial inquiry cleared Arar in 2006, finding no evidence of links to terrorist organizations. He received a $10 million settlement and an apology from the Canadian government. However, despite this Arar still remains on the US watch list.

8 DVD special features, interviews.

9 See, for example, King. Like Tasker, King questions the privileging of narrative in film studies and examines the relationship between narrative and spectacle. He points out that there are various ways that they may relate. Spectacle, for example, may reinforce the narrative, interfere with or disrupt it (3, 4).

10 According to Reg Whitaker, the "Smart Border" agreements "involve a series of ongoing negotiations with the United States on such matters as pre-clearance of container traffic at the point of origin; fast-tracking of safe persons and goods; collection and retention of a wide range of data on persons traveling by air across the border; the application of high-tech surveillance equipment along the border; expansion of Integrated Border Enforcement Teams; and, controversially, a 'safe third country' agreement to reduce the flow of refugees across the border" (51).

Works Cited

Ahmed, Sara. "Affective Economies." *Social Text* 22.2 (2004): 117–39.

Anderson, Jason. "Point of No Return: Making Canadian Television Worth Watching Remains a Challenge." *The Walrus* September 2009. http://www.walrusmagazine.com/articles/2009.09-television-point-of-no-return-flashpoint-canadian-television-jason-anderson/1. Accessed 25 April 2011.

Bean, Jennifer M. "'Trauma Thrills': Notes on Early Action Cinema." Tasker, ed. 17–30.

Bodroghkozy, Aniko. "As Canadian as Possible … Anglo-Canadian Popular Culture and the American Other." *Hop on Pop: The Politics and Pleasures of Popular Culture*. Ed. Henry Jenkins, Tara McPherson, and Jane Shattuc. Durham: Duke UP, 2002. 566–88.

The Border. DVD Commentary (Season 1), Episode 1, "Pockets of Vulnerability."

"CBC's The Border Heads for U.S. TV Screens." *CBC News* 24 February 2009. http://www.cbc.ca/arts/tv/story/2009/02/24/border-tvseries.html. Accessed 5 January 2011.

CBC Shop. "The Border Season One DVD." http://www.cbcshop.ca/CBC/shopping/product.aspx?Product_ID=ETART00166&Variant_ID=ETART00166&lang=en-CA. Accessed 20 June 2009.

Dixon, Guy. "24, but with a Conscience." *Globe and Mail* 2 January 2008: R1.

Doyle, John. "The Border Overcooks Its Stew of Paranoia, Bombast and Guns." *Globe and Mail* 29 September 2008: R3.

———. "Canadian Stereotype Not Shared on Our Shows." *Globe and Mail* 6 October 2008: R3.

Hogarth, David. *Documentary Television in Canada: From National Public Service to Global Marketplace*. Montreal and Kingston: McGill–Queen's UP, 2002.

Jiwani, Yasmin. "Soft Power: Policing the Border through Canadian TV Crime Drama." *The Political Economy of Media and Power*. Ed. Jeffery Klaehn. New York: Peter Lang, 2010. 273–92.

King, Geoff. *Spectacular Narratives: Hollywood in the Age of the Blockbuster*. London and New York: I.B. Tauris, 2000.

Kubacki, Maria. "Canadians Like What They See in The Border." *Calgary Herald* 15 December 2008: D10.

Leach, Jim. "*E.N.G.*" *The Museum of Broadcast Communication*. http://www.museum.tv/eotvsection.php?entrycode=eng. Accessed 14 January 2012.

———. "Reading Canadian 'Popular' Television: The Case of *E.N.G.*" *Slippery Pastimes: Reading the Popular in Canadian Culture*. Ed. Joan Nicks and Jeannette Sloniowski. Waterloo: Wilfrid Laurier UP, 2002. 111–26.

Manning, Frank E. "Reversible Resistance: Canadian Popular Culture and the American Other." *The Beaver Bites Back? American Popular Culture in Canada*. Ed. David H. Flaherty and Frank E. Manning. Montreal and Kingston: McGill–Queen's UP, 1993. 3–28.

Miller, Mary Jane. "Inflecting the Formula." *The Beaver Bites Back? American Popular Culture in Canada*. Ed. David H. Flaherty and Frank E. Manning. Montreal and Kingston: McGill–Queen's UP, 1993. 104–22.

———. *Turn Up the Contrast: CBC Drama since 1952*. Vancouver: UBC P, 1987.

Monahan, Torin. "Just-in-Time Security: Permanent Exceptions and Neoliberal Orders." *Reading 24: TV Against the Clock*. Ed. Steven Peacock. London and New York: I.B. Tauris, 2007. 109–18.

Nakamura, Lisa. "Interfaces of Identity: Oriental Traitors and Telematic Profiling in *24*." *Camera Obscura* 24.70 (2009): 108–33.

Pratt, Anna. *Securing Borders: Detention and Deportation in Canada*. Vancouver: UBC Press, 2005.

"A Run for the Border." *Canadian Press* 20 November 2007. TheRecord.com. http://news.therecord.com/arts/article/276287. Accessed 26 September 2010.

"A Selection from the Cache of Diplomatic Dispatches." *New York Times* 3 January 2011. http://www.nytimes.com/interactive/2010/11/28/world/20101128-cables-viewer.html#report/canada-08OTTAWA136. Accessed 5 January 2011.

Stursberg, Richard. "A Memo to Its Detractors: CBC TV's Never Been Better." *Toronto Star* 3 May 2009: A15.

Taras, David. "Defending the Cultural Frontier: Canadian Television and Continental Integration." *Seeing Ourselves: Media Power and Policy in Canada*. Ed. Helen Holmes and David Taras. Toronto: Harcourt, Brace and Jovanovich, 1992. 174–86.

Takacs, Stacy. *Terrorism TV: Popular Entertainment in Post-9/11 America*. Lawrence: UP of Kansas, 2012.

Tasker, Yvonne. "Action Television/Crime Television: Sensation and Attraction." *Flow* 29 October 2010. http://flowtv.org/2010/10/action-television-crime-television. Accessed 25 April 2011.

———. "Introduction." Tasker, ed. 1–13.

———, ed. *Action and Adventure Cinema*. London and New York: Routledge, 2004.

Taylor, Kate. "Gritty Cop Shows Work Better Without the Sultry Babes." *Globe and Mail* 17 March 2008: R3.

VanderBurgh, Jen. "Imagining National Citizens in Televised Toronto." *Programming Reality: Perspectives on English-Canadian Television*. Ed. Zoe Druick and Aspa Kotsopoulos. Waterloo: Wilfrid Laurier UP, 2008. 269–89.

Vlessing, Etan. "WikiLeaks: Canadian TV Shows Mock America." *Hollywood Reporter* 2 December 2010. http://www.hollywoodreporter.com/news/wikileaks-canadian -tv-shows-mock-55668. Accessed 5 January 2011.

Whitaker, Reg. "How Canada Confronts Terrorism: Canadian Responses to 9/11 in Historical and Comparative Context." *Understanding Terror: Perspectives for Canadians.* Ed. Karim-Aly S. Kassam. Calgary: U of Calgary P, 2010. 37–66.

five

"Normalizing Relations"

The Canada/Cuban Imaginary on the Fringe of Border Discourse

Joanne C. Elvy and Luis René Fernández Tabío

THE BORDER BETWEEN CANADA and United States, often referred to as the longest undefended frontier in the world, is a visual reminder of a peculiar tension between the two nations with respect to national identity and historical memory. Within our respective imaginaries, the 49th parallel may be emblematic of our "special" relationship as neighbours, but the events of 9/11 have generated waves of uneasiness with respect to national security. This has influenced how otherness is constructed in visual representations, and that otherness has taken on heightened meaning in the collective unconscious of people on both sides of the border. Depending on the context in which visual information is presented and received, these representations can shift meaning and blur reality and fiction; so can the "enemy" as it is perceived in the context of North/South relations. American foreign policy has attempted to bring about a regime change in Cuba using "soft" and "hard" policy instruments, and this has had an indirect impact on Canadian/Cuban relations over the past fifty years. Our focus in this chapter is on how the issue of Cuba has been constructed for the Canadian public.

This chapter discusses how visual media and communication technologies are able to instill and reinforce particular values in the collective unconscious. Our example of this will be how a television production in Canada constructed and managed a credible voice "of" and "for" Canadian viewers in relation to the United States. This discussion may prove useful when examining the complex relationship between the framing of identity and the construction of otherness, and how these two intersect in the broader sphere of North/South hemispheric relations. The easy exchange of media across the border may leave Canadians unaware of the extent to which they consume American ideology even while they are being "entertained" by popular productions that are celebrated as "Canadian." Even now, many Canadians construe Cuba as an enemy—a mindset left over from the Cold War era, when the containment of "communism" was a priority of US foreign policy.

Canadian television viewers may want to believe that Canada is a sovereign state that holds itself separate from US international policies and interests, but this may not be so. This will be illustrated in our discussion of Episode 10 of *The Border*, a television series funded by the CBC, which presented Cuba as a site of tension. "Terrorism" has long been a hot issue in US–Cuban relations, but not in Canadian–Cuban relations. The US government has listed Cuba a "terrorist" country since 1982, even though the Cuban government has insisted that there is no justification for it, ideological or political. In 1977, the Carter administration declared that the US government would never conduct terrorist activities from its own territory (see "James Carter"), yet for many years, CIA-supported terrorist groups based in Miami have been targeting Cuban citizens for death in orchestrated terrorist attacks.

The plot of Episode 10 of *The Border*, which the CBC ran on 10 March 2008, revolved around a visiting Cuban official "marked for murder" on Canadian territory by a hardline Cuban American from Miami. The episode reflected the extent to which deeply embedded ideologies and power asymmetries can play out in the collective unconscious of a nation. Just the episode's title, "Normalizing Relations," raised questions about how the viewing audience understood Cuba. What was being normalized, for whom, and for what reasons? Most viewers would not have picked up on the significance of this wording unless they had a broad knowledge of US–Cuban relations. The fact that an episode of a CBC action series referred to Cuba in the context of borders and security would have distorted Canadian viewers' perceptions about Cuba and its leaders in a very particular way. Since Fidel Castro had resigned from the presidency a mere three weeks before the episode aired, Cuba's future was already making headlines in the north. The broad assumption was that without Castro, Cuba would quickly embrace a market economy and liberal democracy.

To examine the possible impact of this episode on the Canadian audience, we discuss how domestic cultural production defines and projects Canada's core psyche; we then contrast these domestic productions with those in the United States, where culture is an economic commodity. In this regard, Episode 10 of *The Border* included cultural icons that Canadian viewers would have recognized instantly. For us, the question is whether the average Canadian viewer saw past these overt symbolic gestures to notice the episode's ideological framing—specifically, the way it reflected American perceptions of Cuba. It is worth noting that for Cubans, cultural production and national identity are tightly bound, symbolic of all that it means to be Cuban. That is why Cubans are so concerned that their otherness is so often misunderstood and misrepresented in media productions by their neighbours to the north.

We then discuss how visual information that appeals to and has value for Canadian audiences plays on the collective unconscious and public memory over time. In the case of *The Border*, the series was written sequentially. Prior to the screening of Episode 10, "Normalizing Relations," viewers would have been exposed to specific visual information as signifiers in each of the nine previous episodes, and this would have familiarized them with the characters, the setting, and the overall storyline. Given that each new episode built upon the ones screened earlier, the visual output from the season's premiere onward set the tone and focus for the series as a whole. In this way the audience was guided through a cinematic routine every week so that they learned how and what to take in from each episode. Every week started off with tightly edited flashbacks critical to the upcoming episode to provide a historical prelude to new challenge now facing by the Canadian ICS team.

The Border was loosely structured around headline news in post-9/11 Canada, and viewers would likely have picked up on this referencing. But as they watched for "clues" that would trigger memories of "real" Canadian events, they would have been drawn into visual referencing that was identifiably Canadian. The dramatic premise of "Normalizing Relations" involved Cuban nationals on Canadian territory. Events in Cuba (i.e., the change of government) at the time this fictionalized account was being screened as entertainment in Canada, coupled with the impact of American soft power on the Canadian imaginary over time, would have resulted in a particular framing with regard to how Canadian viewers took in the events of this episode as they unfolded. The issues presented in that episode were framed by long-standing tensions between United States and Cuba outside the bounds of contemporary relations between Canada and Cuba. Canada had maintained diplomatic relations with Cuba post-1959 on its own terms, but would Canadians viewers of the episode be able to view Cuba in a broader hemispheric context independent of the United States? Perhaps the greatest impediment to Canada/Cuba relations has always been the omnipresence of America itself, which functions as the "border" between Canada and Cuba in North/South terms.

Finally, from our respective positions as Canadian and Cuban, we ask how Canadians understand Cuba in collective or historical memory, compared to how *The Border* constructed and popularized Cuba for entertainment purposes. Who was the intended audience for that episode, and what did they learn about Cuba by watching it, as they took in these visual representations as entertainment without reflecting critically? They would have grasped that Cuba posed no security risk to Canada in "border" terms and that Cuba was a popular tourist destination, in part due to its beautiful beaches, but as well because it has been regarded as a safe place for tourists to travel on their own.[1] Yet in the narrative of "Normalizing Relations," not one Cuban national was drawn out as a "real" character, and this left the audience to engage only with those who were part of the Cuban exile community currently living in Toronto.

Similarly, regarding how the story was filmed, the viewing audience was invited into a familiar space to engage with those who had left the island, while those who had chosen to stay in Cuba to support the revolution were kept at a filmic distance, as if they could not be trusted. As edu-tainment, these stereotypes permeated the audience's collective memory, in this way encouraging a particular set of relations as hegemonic referencing. This sort of tactic, over time, will normalize how outsiders to the Cuban Revolution have come to "know" the Cuban people. Such representations—this *coding* of otherness— may serve official American policy and the Cuban exile community, but they will be rather unsettling for Cuban nationals. Although there are several definitions of popular culture—by Raymond Williams, for instance (see below)—if popular culture is intended to reflect the internal dynamics and values of a people, under what conditions could Canada come to accept Cuban sovereignty on its own terms, if the Canadian imaginary with respect to Cuba is blurred with mixed messages?

First, however, since *The Border* was a cultural product intended to show the Canadian perspective on national security, it is important to establish the connection between culture and identity in a Canadian context. In classical terms, Raymond Williams has described culture as consisting of "the works and practices of intellectual and especially artistic activity," which would refer to "high" culture (qtd. in Gagné 161). When he links the production of culture with national identity in Canadian terms, Gagné extends the list to include "books, magazines, newspapers, movies, video and music recordings, radio, and television" as vital components in the realm of mass or popular culture, as means for individuals or groups to "develop a sense of *who they are* in relation to their shared psychological, sociological, and political attachments to each other" (161, emphasis added). Regionalism and ethnic diversity being valued as they are in Canada, and cultural production being viewed as a vital means for expressing and projecting identity, this is in sharp contrast to the American framing of culture as a capitalist commodity that happens to be uniquely "American."

The Canadian national identity, in its evolution from colonial past to contemporary multiculturalism, has generally not been synchronized with broader technological advances in visual media and communications; by contrast, the Hollywood "industry" has been politically and culturally powerful in the United States throughout the past century. This, in tandem with Canada's proximity to the US media industry, has established the context for Canadian cultural production, which finds itself measured nationally and internationally in relation to Hollywood's products, even while being celebrated regionally for its unique qualities. The value of Canadian media productions will always be viewed in relation to the dominant Other, whose style and "look" can hardly be contested in the marketplace. The obstacles for Canadian production are also complicated by the links between the US government and the culture "business," given that Hollywood has played a prominent role in structuring American hegemony throughout the twentieth century.

Cubans' identity has been influenced by the United States since colonial times. Thus, cultural reclamation and preservation has been a priority of the Cuban government since 1959, and has been a tool of self-preservation in the revolutionary battle of ideas. Given Cuba's proximity to the United States—it is only ninety miles from Florida—Cubans throughout the nineteenth century looked north to the United States as a commercial partner, a desirable vacation spot, and a place to educate their children (Pérez). The reasons why the United States became a reference point for Cuba are historically complex, but generally speaking, the American Revolution and the values and aspirations stemming from it were an early inspiration for Cuban independence from Spain. Even then, Cuban merchants were developing economic ties with their northern neighbour. Key figures in the nineteenth-century Cuban independence movement, from Father Felix Varela y Morales (1788–1853) to José Martí (1853–1895) are still revered figures for their efforts to establish a Cuban identity, *cubanidad.* But at the same time, it was recognized even during Cuba's early years of independence that the United States' powerful ideology had the potential to threaten Cuban identity.

Popular culture has become intertwined with capitalist media production to form what Dallas Smythe has referred to as the "consciousness industry," an industry, moreover, with ideological intentions. Fuyuki Kurasawa aptly describes popular cultural production as a powerful instrument "supporting American imperialism and capitalism by manipulating or distracting the 'masses'" (475). To help end colonial domination and to stimulate critical dialogue in post-1959 Cuba, film production was nationalized, and its production standards rewritten, with the goal of extending the revolution to the entire population. Thus was founded the Instituto Cubano de Arte e Industría Cinemátograficos (ICAIC) in March 1959. Culture and national identity in Cuba are now woven tightly together, and cultural production is revered as the sword and the shield of the Cuban nation.

With respect to free trade (the FTA and NAFTA), Canada's cultural policy has long been predicated on the belief that culture is not merchandise and that it should be exempt from free trade agreements. However, in the North American market for high-powered television drama, entertainment trumps culture in terms of popular appeal. Despite the Canadian government's steps to protect and promote its cultural industries, in 1998 alone 95 percent of feature films and 60 percent of television programs shown in Canada were imports, overwhelmingly from the United States. Clearly, the entertainment industry has been a powerful tool for the Americans to project their global hegemony; indeed, that industry is "a central pillar of US foreign policy" (Gagné 161).

By contrast, Canadian cultural production is tied to identity, to processes of self-examination—to "taking stock," as Holman and Thacker put it—and this has left Canadian productions vulnerable to American ones with their superior production and marketing capacity (127). In addition to that, the Internet and satellite television have largely erased communication borders and threaten to do the same to national cultural projects. Social awareness and national identity, as both of these are rooted in culture and language, are coming under stress as Canadian audiences take in the "American" way out of sheer convenience and familiarity.

Most Canadians know little or nothing about the cultural provisions of the FTA and NAFTA, or about their government's measures to protect Canadian broadcasting. At a time when globalization and neoclassical economic approaches are enjoying an ascendance, Canada has taken pains to defend its cultural interests from the free market. It has succeeded in doing so even though the planet's cultural colossus is just across the border. Yet all the while, American productions and their "entertainment" value define the short-term market value of any given Canadian production, overriding any long-term identity-building function it might have in Canada.

The 9/11 terrorist attacks on New York and Washington heightened American anxieties about national security, and as a result, the Canadian border became a significant concern in bilateral relations. Canadian cultural products reinforce how Canadians understand themselves in relation to the United States—and, more broadly, how they see their country as a player on the world stage. These circumstances provided a cultural space for *The Border,* which had a heightened meaning for its viewing audience as emblematic of the Canadian way. Yet in terms of style, critics compared it to American series like *24, CSI,* and *Law & Order.* Its marketers described it as "probably the best Canadian show that has ever been made ... combined into one non-stop, heart pounding thriller that leaves you on the edge of your seat the entire time" (CBC Shop). But as Sarah Matheson details in her chapter in this volume, that *The Border* took on the "look" of American television highlights the fact that it partly embraced American ideology and then left it to Canadian viewers to separate its Canadian from its American content. In terms of national identity, *The Border* showcased the Canadian perspective on security issues affecting the country as well as how Canadians were more open-minded and understanding than Americans typically are in the "War on Terror" (an American term).

The show's executive producers, Peter Raymont and the late Lindalee Tracey—Canadian journalists well versed in immigration and border issues—conceived of *The Border* in 2006, five years after the 9/11 attacks, when they were approached by the CBC to develop a series. Set in Toronto, *The Border* followed a team of agents of the fictitious "Immigration and Customs Security" (ICS). It dealt with transborder security, terrorism, and smuggling. All of the stories it told were all fiction, but they were inspired by actual events that audiences would have remembered, and their Canadian content was buttressed by the use of Canadian television actors and other Canadian visual signifiers. As docudrama, this was television "with a conscience" (Raymont, qtd. in Dixon R1), or perhaps with the pretense of influencing the conscience of the audience, given that the production values would be largely American, including in terms of ideological referencing, deliberate or not.

Documentaries occupy a significant space in the history of Canadian film and broadcasting, and Canadians generally believe that their political and institutional practices are fairly transparent. These two factors suggest why *The Border* had such a strong visual appeal. Canadians were already accustomed to its *cinéma vérité* style, so they instinctively knew how to "read" the series, including its characters, and the more so the longer they watched ("Normalizing Relations" was the 10th episode of the first year's 13). Also, they would have long been attuned to the program's "gritty realism"—its hand-held cameras, tightly angled shots, and kinetic editing. All of this contributed to the program's "believability," in that audiences were accustomed to the style it had adopted.

The series was filmed in Toronto and made strong use of that city's familiar icons: the CN Tower, downtown streets and buildings, the transit system, the waterfront and airport. The scenes in Ottawa resorted to similar icons, such as the Peace Tower on Parliament Hill. The Canadian flag was often visible in the transition shots that were woven into each episode; also visible were a number of Canadian pop cultural references, such as characters drinking Tim Hortons takeout coffee and munching on Timbits while a Toronto streetcar trundled past in the background. All of these visual clues made it clear to the viewer that the program had been made by *and* for Canadians (and that they could, it follows, find comfort in this). The tokens of national memory evident in the series did much to celebrate Canadian identity as expressed through strongly Canadian spaces. In a sense, the series was reclaiming space from American productions that Canadians so often watched on television. The set itself was full of windows and mirrors, suggesting that everyone was being watched all the time, that everyone was under surveillance, but also that everyone could watch what the ICS agents were doing. This amounted to a "democratic" process, one that could be perceived as the "Canadian" way.

The technologies the ICS characters used when accessing and transmitting information as part of the narrative, together with the series' "design"—for example, its use of split-screen techniques and visuals within visuals—heightened the drama but distracted from the underlying message, unless the viewer had the luxury of watching the episode several times. Mary Jane Miller has asked why Canadian television productions would want to do anything that "looks" American (qtd. in Anderson 2), but unless they try, Canadian productions risk appearing lightweight, even when thematically they are not. *The*

Border also acquired "edge" through the use of inserts that strengthened the illusion that real information was being presented to the audience; this heightened the illusion that the viewers were actual participants. Debriefings among ICS agents were shot from a distance, reinforcing the viewer's supposed privileged access to "inside" information as "truth." The viewer was also allowed to eavesdrop on personal conversations and private, intimate moments that humanized the show's characters.

Various backroom scenes in *The Border* revealed the key players weighing moral and ethical choices. Viewers were invited to observe those choices being made, and this added to their sense of participation. All of this encouraged them to believe that these characters actually existed and that they could choose to trust them, or not. In this way, Canadians felt themselves connected not only to the characters but also to world events.

By the time viewers were presented with the episode involving Cuba, they had been actively engaged—visually and experientially—in the lives of the series' characters and had learned to place them in a real-world context. Each case so far in the series had drawn from a multitude of actual historical events: suspected jihadi terrorists in Toronto, Canada's involvement in Afghanistan, drug smuggling through Mohawk territory, human trafficking in Vancouver, international arms dealing ("legal" or not), Russian strippers, child soldiers from Darfur, and so on. Each case unfolded on Monday evening on TV sets across the country to remind Canadians who they were in the world, especially relative to the United States. However indistinct Canadians' position in the world might seem, perhaps their social tolerance and their humility marked them as different from the Americans. The stories *The Border* told were based on headline news stories in Canada, and as such, they stimulated Canadians' collective memory and supported the idea that their approach to securing 49th parallel was inevitably different from the American one. All of this positioned Canadian television viewers to contemplate the "problem" of Cuba in a "normalizing" manner.

That said, what was normal, for Canadians, about Cuba before Episode 10 of *The Borders* was broadcast? In Episode 2, we had been introduced to Special Agent Bianca LaGarda of the US Department of Homeland Security, a stunning woman of Italian/Cuban extraction from Miami, who as a ten-year-old had fled Cuba during the Mariel boat lift of 1980 and who perhaps had been helped at that time by an ex-Marine, who appears to remember her twenty-five years later, in Episode 9 ("Restricted Access"). From a Cuban perspective, it is interesting that someone who fled Cuba in 1980 is now an American official with a great deal of authority to wield against the Canadians. The prologue to Episode 10 consists of tightly edited clips highlighting LaGarda's background; for Canadian viewers, this immediately sets the tone for dark misgivings about "the Castro brothers." Apparently, LaGarda's father had been a high-ranking

Cuban military officer. After being falsely accused of betraying the revolution, he had been executed after a "puppet" trial. The young Bianca and her mother had then fled the island. Cubans may be accustomed to anti-Castro stories like this emanating from Miami's Cuban enclave; Canadians might feel uneasy. In any event, the prologue served as a lens through which all Cubans, wherever they lived, would be viewed throughout the episode.

In Episode 10, an anti-Castro hit man out of Miami slips into Canada illegally with the intention of murdering a visiting Cuban politician, Ulisses Parada, who heads the Cuban Ministry of Economic Modernization. There is no such ministry in Cuba, and that this name is given to a fictitious one in *The Border* implies that Cuba should be progressing toward capitalism. We soon learn that Parada had testified against LaGarda's father during the latter's show trial in Havana. Soon after, the viewing audience and the Canadian ICS team are pointedly excluded from a "need to know" meeting between LaGarda, the visiting Cubans, and US officials. The meeting's purpose is never fully explained to the ICS team, or for that matter to the viewers, except to note that Parada is an economist with strong links to the military who could be in line to lead Cuba after the rule of the Castro brothers has ended. We later learn that the order to eliminate Parada originated in Havana, not in Miami. The implication is that Parada is negotiating a "transition" with US officials behind closed doors, which suggests that the Cuban Revolution is unstable.

But the narrative focuses mainly on Roberto Abrantes, a young boxer of Cuban descent who is currently seeking landed immigrant status so that he can box for Canada in the next Olympics. Abrantes's father, Luis Martinez, a hardliner from Miami, has slipped into Canada for the sole purpose of eliminating Parada. The ICS team believes that Martinez will attempt to make contact with his son, although the two have been estranged for many years. The viewer is introduced to Roberto and his girlfriend Andrea in the opening scene of "Normalizing Relations" as they return unexpectedly to their darkened apartment at the same moment ICS Sergeant Layla Hourani and Detective Sergeant Gray Jackson are installing and testing surveillance equipment as part of a covert mission. Except for a brief shot of an Art Nouveau Cuban poster[2] on the apartment wall and some sultry Latin dance music—these two clues having an appeal to those who have visited the island as tourists—nowhere in the entire episode is any reference made to anything positive or memorable about Cuba. In fact, the harder the ICS team works to track down Martinez, the more negative the accounts become. For example, a female journalist is granted amnesty in Canada after being detained for two years in a Cuban jail; a waiter attempts to present the Cuban perspective but then gives in to the more pressing matter of freedom of expression; and Roberto makes it clear to the viewing audience that he has left Cuba behind. In short, even though Canada and Cuba have a well-established commerical relationship that generates around $1 billion of trade annually, and even though the island is a popular destination for more than a million Canadian "snowbirds" flying south in the winter, the scriptwriters make no attempt to present a more balanced view of the Cuban experience.

Even more significant, however, is the extent to which Cuba is being depicted as the "other" in a Canadian media production. This "otherness" goes by unquestioned and unresolved; indeed, by the end of the episode it has been normalized. Parada, the high-ranking Cuban politician, and his "personal army" come under attack in two significant scenes in this episode—as victims themselves of terrorist activity—yet not once is there any personal or "human" interaction between the Cuban nationals and the Canadian ICS team. Moreover, *The Border* as a whole is built on headline news in Canada, with the focus on security issues, yet this episode stands apart from the previous ones in that it makes no direct reference to the border. Furthermore, it frames the visiting Cuban delegation as inherently suspicious, as non-persons to be scrutinized from afar—a framing that in other shows had been reserved for "terrorists." Given that Canadian viewers are probably unaware that Cuban nationals have been targets of terrorist attacks on Canadian soil—including two bombing incidents at the Cuban Embassy in Ottawa and seven more in Montreal—it would have been better had the writers shifted their the lens sufficiently to mention that, out of respect to Cuban nationals.[3] Admittedly, the *The Border* is fiction, but having said that, what are Canadians meant to take from this episode, especially considering that the Cuban characters in it have not been allowed to speak for themselves? That the ICS agents (and by default the audience as well) have been deliberately excluded from the mysterious meeting between the US State Department and the Cuban officials means that viewers are not privy to any information that might be politically or contextually significant to the story's theme. This contrasts sharply with how *The Border* as a whole has been presented as inclusive.

Instead, the script as a whole is built around how Cuba is imagined from afar, with ICS agents relying on information second-hand from those who have chosen to "flee" the island in recent times as political or economic refugees. This in itself positions the Canadian audience to view Cuba through an American lens—that is, through a Cuban American lens—even though the series has up till then embedded itself in the Canadian historical memory. Over time, even Canadian viewers who have though well of Cuba—as tourists there, perhaps—may find themselves swayed, and their understanding corrupted, by the picture of that island as reflected in Episode 10 of *The Border*. Cuba has always extended respect to other countries, regardless of social, political, and cultural differences, and in return it would like to be treated with the same respect. Anything less would be to present the Cuban as *less*.

Perhaps, as Peter Raymont points out, *The Border* series gets "closer to the truth" than a documentary on border and security issues in a post-9/11 world. And perhaps dramatizations "informed by and drawn from reality" may allow viewers access to pressing issues that they might not otherwise have explored ("Longtime"). But in the case of "Normalizing Relations," the episode has been framed in a way that badly misrepresents hemispheric history. Viewers are being entertained by the episode; in turn, the episode is misrepresenting Cuban history by offering it from the American perspective. So it is ironic that the episode's title, "Normalizing Relations," is a specific term of American policy toward Cuba. This "normalization" in fact entails imposing US policy on Cuba, notwithstanding that it is a sovereign nation. "Entertainments" can have insidious effects on real-world attitudes—in this chapter's example, when it comes to national security and broader hemispheric relations. Perhaps direct personal exchanges with Canadians, through tourism and immigration, will over time improve Canadian and American perceptions of Cuba.

Notes

1 In 2007 Cuba was the fifth preferred tourist destination for Canadians after the United States, Mexico, the UK, and France. With 724,000 Canadian visitors in 2007, this represents about $629 million in spending power in Cuba (see Statistics Canada). Current statistics show that in 2012, 1,071,696 Canadians visited Cuba, representing 39 percent of all foreign visitors as the largest source of incoming tourists to the island (see ONE 6, 5).

2 "Cuba: Holiday Isle of the Tropics," as renascent from Episode One, "Pockets of Vulnerability."

3 At the Cuban consulate, the Cuban trade delegation, and Expo 67, respectively (see Allard).

Works Cited

Allard, Jean-Guy. "The Miami Mafia in Canada: A Drug Trafficking 'Right-hand Man.'" *Digital Granma Internacional* 16 April 2004. http://www.granma.cu/ingles/2004/abril/vier16/16morales-i.html. Accessed 15 August 2009.

Anderson, Jason. "Point of No Return: Making Canadian Television Drama Worth Watching Remains a Challenge." *The Walrus*, September 2009.

CBC Shop. "The Border Season 1 DVD." http://www.cbcshop.ca/CBC/shopping/product.aspx?Product_ID=ETART00166&Variant_ID=ETART00166&lang=en-CA. Accessed 26 February 2011.

Dixon, Guy. "24, but With a Conscience." *Globe and Mail* 2 Jan. 2008: R1.

Gagné, Gilbert. "North American Integration and Canadian Culture." *Capacity for Choice: Canada in a New North America.* Ed. George Hoberg. U of Toronto P, 2002. 159–83.

Holman, Andrew, and Robert Thacker. "Literary and Popular Culture." *Canadian Studies in the New Millennium.* Ed. Patrick James and Mark Kasof. Toronto: U of Toronto P, 2008. 244–76.

"James Carter Presidential Directive NSC 6." White House, Washington, DC 15 March 1977. http://www.gwu.edu/~nsarchiv/news/20020515/cartercuba.pdf. Accessed 1 February 2011.

Kurasawa, Fuyuki. "Finding Godot? Bringing Popular Culture into Canadian Political Economy." *Changing Canada: Political Economy as Transformation*. Ed. W. Clement and L.F. Vosko. Montreal and Kingston: McGill–Queen's UP. 467–74.

"Longtime Documentarian Peter Raymont in Spotlight with New Film, TV Show." *CBC News*. http://www.cbc.ca/theborder/blog/2007/12/longtime_documentarian_peter_r.html. Accessed 21 December 2009.

"Normalizing Relations." *The Border: Season One*. CBC, 2007. DVD.

Oficina Nacional de Estadísticas (ONE). *Turismo Internacional Indicadores Seleccionados enero-diciembre* 2012. Edición Febrero 2011, La Habana. http://www.one.cu/publicaciones/06turismoycomercio/indturismointernac/publicaciondic12.pdf. Accessed 23 June 2013.

Pérez, Louis A., Jr. *On Becoming Cuban: Identity, Nationality, and Culture*. New York: HarperCollins, 1999.

Smythe, Dallas W. *Dependency Road: Communications, Capitalism, Consciousness, and Canada*. Norwood: Ablex, 1981.

Statistics Canada. "Travel and Tourism." http://www41.statcan.ca/2007/4007/ceb4007_000-eng.htm. Accessed 26 February 2011.

six

How, Exactly, Does the Beaver Bite Back?

The Case of Canadian Students Viewing Paul Haggis's *Crash*

Lee Easton and Kelly Hewson

IN HIS ESSAY "CANADA: THE BORDERLINE CASE," Marshall McLuhan famously cast the Canada–US border as an "interval of resonance," porous and charged with historical and emotional intensities (227). Janine Marchessault further refined McLuhan's "interval" as an "interface where two objects meet, often in a kind of mutual irritation, and where identity finds its shape in difference" (100). But the description with perhaps the most powerful purchase, articulating as it does this interface's psychic dimensions, is Roger Gibbins's: the world's longest undefended border "penetrates the Canadian consciousness, identity, economy and polity to a degree unknown and unimaginable in the United States" (317)—until 11 September 2001, that is. In 9/11's aftermath, the northern border's permeability generated considerable concern among our neighbours to its south. The 4,000-mile line, with its relatively relaxed security (points of entry being protected by orange cones), began looking like a portal for terrorists. Subsequently, "smart border" measures were adopted on both sides of the line. Territoriality, that coldly efficient strategy of using borders to delimit area, control movements, and classify peoples, and, whether malignantly or benignly, to express and implement relations of power, is making a comeback. Concretized via easily understood symbolic markers like passports, pumped-up policing, and increased water, air, and land surveillance, the Canada–US border is being seen and felt in new ways.

However, this is not to suggest that some of the "old ways" in which the border gets framed and enacted by Canadians, particularly through attempts to support and protect Canadian popular culture, aren't still operating. Indeed, the view that the Canada–US border is Canadians' defensive line, shielding us from the presumed ill effects of exposure to the cultural products of that behemoth to the south, is a pervasive one, as is the view that the border is always too porous, with Canadians unable to resist the influx of things American. These and other anxieties are evident in scholarship about Canadian popular culture. As Aniko Bodroghkozy indicates, there is a tendency in Canadian media studies to bemoan the tidal wave of American cultural products that overwhelm any Canadian identity (571). This perspective, deeply influenced by Harold Innis, positions the border as too fragile to halt the unfortunate dependence we have developed on American cultural products even though, paradoxically, it remains the only buffer we have. Any number of federal initiatives—from Canadian content regulations to various funding envelopes—can be traced to a sense that a strong "Canadian" identity depends on a fortified border that protects Canadians from American culture. Refreshingly, Bodroghkozy discards this deeply entrenched narrative to posit an alternative that sees Canadians as active participants, engaging with American cultural products and using them to their own ends. "It is important," she writes, "to pay attention to what Canadians 'do' with the products of those [American cultural] industries" (572)—to which we would add, it is important to pay attention to what Canadian students do with these products.

"Reversible Resistance" and the Border: Canadian Students Imagine Race

> How is this movie supposed to help? What does it teach? Everything's on the level of coincidence or accident and the character constructs are deplorable ... simply tools whose specific purposes were designed to be around their intent. Haggis identifies stereotypes, yeah, but the film also perpetuates them.

We begin with this student comment partly because this chapter arose out of an earlier project in which we investigated students' written and verbal responses to the treatment of American race relations in Paul Haggis's 2005 film *Crash* (Easton and Hewson, "Emergent"). At the conclusion of our investigation, we were surprised by, but then skeptical of, our Canadian students' critical assessments of the film's representations. Surprised by their sophistication:

> Racism is so often latent and institutionalized in the real world that a character like Matt Dillon's cop is a red herring—it suggests racism easily spotted and easily addressed.

> No sense of structural racism. He's equalizing or neutralizing or avoiding the fact that racism is systemic. By saying we are all racists he let's [*sic*] everybody off the hook. No need for anyone to do anything to change things.

> I dispute the film's suggestion that there are gradations of racism. Racism is not major or minor. It IS.

but skeptical of the authenticity of their comments. While it was tempting for us to believe that our students' responses were due to our pedagogical prowess, we kept lighting on the thought that perhaps the students were *performing* the kinds of nuanced readings we had trained them to produce and hence weren't experiencing "deep" learning. After further investigation, we arrived at the hopeful hypothesis—which we've since come to question—that their critically informed readings of race might be products of an emergent cosmopolitan mindset of which we, as wary and often cynical educators, are on the periphery.

The question of "borders" seemed a way for us to explore further the extent to which our students, for all their seeming cosmopolitanism—their trans-national potential and ease in globalized space—constructed their viewing selves in relation to the 49th parallel, a line that is increasingly visible, div-isive, and undertheorized. We were interested in better understanding those moments when the student viewers might implicitly and perhaps explicitly invoke the border as a dividing line between practices that identify Canadians *as* Canadians, usually in opposition to an imagined, often American, Other. We decided to continue our investigations with Paul Haggis's Oscar-winning film *Crash*, which, despite our individual conflicts over its achievements, is a particularly rich film text with which to work.

First, Haggis is a Canadian who found success writing and producing American television series; among other accomplishments, he created the police comedy-drama *Due South*. Initially a Canadian/American co-produc-tion, *Due South* was the first Canadian TV series to be shown on an American broadcast network, CBS. Drawing upon Canadian stereotypes embodied by RCMP Constable Benton Fraser, *Due South* self-consciously played with the complexities of the American–Canadian relationship. Haggis followed up his American TV successes by working as a writer/producer of the Oscar-winning *Million Dollar Baby;* he then extended his achievements to include writing and directing *Crash*, a high-profile "serious" film that addressed the complex-ities of American race relations. *Crash* has been criticized for its sentimental and simplistic representations of race, but we were intrigued that a Canadian writer/director had created this film, and at least one of us thought that evi-dent in it were playful markers of Canadiana that had also been part of *Due South*'s appeal. We wondered, then, whether *Crash* might provide Canadian filmgoers with similar viewing positions that Aniko Bodroghkozy posits *Due South* offered its Canadian television audiences. That is, would *Crash* give Can-adian film viewers an "opportunity to 'play at being Canadian' as well as Amer-ican within the space of the American Other, while engaging in a sly mining of the semiotics of difference" (581)? We also wanted to frame *Crash* apropos Susan Lord's suggestion—underwritten by Mary Louise Pratt's formulation of a "contact zone"—that some films can be usefully viewed as examples of contact zones "where disparate cultures meet, clash [*crash?*], and grapple with each other, often in highly asymmetrical relations of domination and subordina-tion—like colonialism, slavery, or their aftermaths as they are lived out across the globe today" (qtd. in Lord 400). Paul Haggis's *Crash*, which follows the lives of a diverse set of characters who are literally crashing into one another, seemed to us ready-made to explore both Bodroghkozy's and Lord's theses.

To frame our project, we have had to draw upon Canadian media studies related to television and to Canadian audiences' reception of American television programs. This is because film studies tend not to focus their thinking on actual situated viewers. Rather, as Robert C. Allen argues, film studies treats film spectatorship from structuralist, feminist, and psychoanalytic perspectives (2006). While these sorts of approaches are useful for building "expert readings" of filmic texts, they are less useful for understanding how Canadians actually deploy *specific reading strategies* to make American cultural products their own. This knowledge seems important, especially in light of claims that "by engaging with the Other's popular media, inflected with the particularities of Canadian subjectivities during the process of reading, Canadians recode those texts as their own popular culture" (Bodroghkozy 574). Less clear is what these reading strategies actually look like on the ground. How do they operate, and in what and/or whose interests? In short, if "the beaver bites back," as some cultural studies scholars argue, how deep is that bite? Does it leave marks?

Frank E. Manning's concept of "reversible resistance," which he suggests defines Canadian popular culture, helps us think through possible answers to our above questions. In the anthology *The Beaver Bites Back? American Popular Culture in Canada*, Manning explains:

> Canadian popular culture is a relational phenomenon that assumes its significance vis à vis a particular Canadian conception of the United States ... Symbiotically, Canadian popular culture needs its American partner as an ambiguous and reversible opposite. Dialectically, Canadian popular culture imposes and redefines itself in terms of ambivalently held differences. That is why, from a Canadian perspective, the two popular cultures are a lode of contrasting stereotypes. (8–9)

Through the practice of reversible resistance, then, Canadians have acquired a capacity to reconstitute and recontextualize American cultural products in ways that consciously distinguish Canada from the United States (Manning 8). The border, it seems to us, plays an important if underestimated role in demarcating those two imagined spaces—Canadian and American—and the practices that produce them.

Aniko Bodroghkozy takes up Manning's concept of reversible resistance and draws on Linda Hutcheon's thoughts about Canadians' deployment of irony to theorize reading practices that Canadians might bring to bear on advertising and on television programs, especially Canadian programs that consciously take up American genres. First, Bodroghkozy asserts, "while meanings of 'Canadian' may need to be constantly inflected by region, language and ethnicity, I would argue there is one experience all residents of the True North Strong and Free share (if diversely): an ambivalent relationship to a fictive American Other" (572). She then suggests that Canadians can adopt a double spectatorship similar to that of female spectators, who can move between "masculine" and "feminine" viewing positions: Canadians can "play at being American" or "play at being Canadian." That is to say, Canadians are well trained to read television *as if* they are Americans. For Bodroghkozy, this fluidity is quite deliberate: "Canadians do know," she continues, "that 'here' is not the American 'there'" (574). Finally, she suggests that as a nation of "in-betweeners," Canadian television viewers have "managed to assert an ambivalent but ultimately affirming sense of national self ... using tactically deployed tools appropriated from the Other" (584–85). Again the Canada–US border is an important consideration here since it is a social construct that operates doubly—not only through legal and political discourses, including physical structures and practices such as border checks for passports and discussions with border guards, but also through a cultural imaginary produced through encounters with American cultural products.

In order to build on our previous findings where we discovered Canadian students engaging in forms of reversible resistance—at times identifying with American film "as if" they were part of the intended [white] American audience, and at other times denying their complicities (Easton and Hewson, "The Emergent," "Reflections")—we embarked on this project to explore further how Canadian viewers—in our case, post-secondary students—deploy their identity strategically when confronted with problematic aspects of racism. Our methodology embraces the goal of ethnography as outlined by Raymond Williams: that is, to capture a "structure of feeling" that differentiates "what is emergent in a setting from the interaction of well-defined dominant and residual formations with that which is not quite articulable to the subjects or analysts" (Marcus 66). Broadly positioned under the rubric of cultural studies, our approach is designed to address the erasure of the live viewing subject in film studies on one hand, and on the other, to underline how the assumption of the generic "first-year student" has elided the need to consider the multitude of sites and practices that have already worked to shape the undergraduate student who has elected to join our classrooms. As far back as the late 1980s and early 1990s, theorists of critical pedagogy were reminding educators of the folly of "ignoring the cultural and social forms that are authorized by youths and simultaneously empower or disempower them" (Giroux and Simon 3). We argue that just as educators in the public school system have done, pedagogues in higher education continue to refuse in any real sense to acknowledge— except perhaps to lament—"the importance of those sites and social practices outside of [education] that actively shape student experiences and through which students often define and construct their sense of identity, politics and culture" (Giroux and Simon 3). Our project attempts to take account of these sites and practices.

Case Study: Mount Royal—Canada's Oldest Newest University

Indeed, our educational location functions precisely to make us attuned to the important role that the geographic *and* educational contours of our institutional space play in influencing our students and ourselves. Mount Royal University is located in Calgary, considered in national parlance to be Canada's most Americanized city due to its large population of American expats, the many US oil company head offices located there, and the two daily flights between Calgary and Houston, Texas. One million or so Albertans live within 400 kilometres of the Montana border. Simultaneously, as a result of Treaty 7, the city sits on what were the traditional lands of the Blackfoot Confederacy: Siksika First Nation is to the east of Calgary, and the Peigan and Kainai First Nations to the south, while the southwest limit of the city itself borders directly on the T'suu Tina First Nation. Farther west, off the Trans-Canada Highway, are the Nakoda First Nations. Some of the city's expressways and subdivisions are named for the camping places, tribes, and leaders of the Treaty 7 nations— Shaganappi, Crowfoot, Stoney, and Sarcee Trails, Bearspaw—and are palimpsestuous reminders that before settler-invaders arrived and obliterated them, evolved borderlands existed between Indigenous peoples across the continent.

Our institution is attended by approximately 12,000 students. It offers applied degrees, university transfer, diplomas, certificates, and since 2008, bachelor's degrees. In recent years, Mount Royal has undergone the mandatory round of quality council and accreditation reviews, and in September 2010 the government granted it the right to call itself a "University." Mount Royal's student base is 63 percent female and predominantly white. It tends to attract students from the first-generation post-secondary learner group, and 65 percent of our students work while attending. Finally, our students, whose average age is 22.7, are older than many of their post-secondary institution counterparts, partly because of our professional degrees and partly due to our reputation as a supportive place to start or restart an educational journey.

The Respondent Group

We conducted two focus groups: one in November 2008, the other in April 2009. We received six volunteers in the fall semester and four in the winter; each person filled out a questionnaire about viewing habits, viewed *Crash* with the others, submitted written pre- and post-viewing responses, and participated in a taped focus group session, which we moderated. All the participants had taken at least one film studies course. For our purposes, we will be speaking about our respondents as a whole; however, there were some significant differences between the two focus groups, which we will delineate. The respondents self-identified as shown in Table 1 below.

Table 1   Focus group composition[a]

	Group 1	Group 2	Total
Gender identification	4 female, 2 male	1 female, 3 males	5 females, 5 males
Class identification	3 working class	2 working class, 1 upper-middle class, 1 middle class	5 working class, 3 middle class, 2 unknown
Sexual orientation	3 straight, 1 lesbian, 1 heterosexual	4 straight	7 straight, 1 lesbian, 1 heterosexual
Ethnicity	1 Hispanic, 4 Caucasian	1 "None," 1 white, 2 Caucasian	1 Hispanic, 1 white, 6 Caucasian

[a] Table shows the respondent group composition aligns with the broader demographics of our institution. The first group mirrors the university make-up precisely: predominantly female, working-class, white.

I. *Living the Border*

To begin our study, we asked the students to talk about their actual lived experiences of crossing the Canada–US border. We wanted to explore the extent to which their accounts aligned with some of the ways in which the border has been theorized. Six of our respondents had crossed the border, and these were their impressions:

- Canadian guards are assholes.
- I went to New York and had fun.
- A feeling of tenseness, like I had done something wrong.
- I've never had a problem crossing.
- It's stricter on the American side.
- Neutral ... as long as you obey border laws, it can be crossed efficiently.

Clearly these remarks suggest that crossing the border is a contradictory and individual experience. For some, it is about the physical experience of customs at border crossings; for others, it's America. Regarding the person who "never had a problem crossing," we are reminded that until recently, the border had generally been a line that many people freely and easily traversed. As one participant elaborated for us in her response to an initial draft of our findings: "For the record ... I hop across the border several times a year for pleasure and in recent years I have been conducting business in Portland, Oregon, with my aunt and have made a couple of trips for those purposes a year both by air and by car."

Many of our participants' experiences echo this respondent's sense of the border as a dotted line that can be crossed almost playfully. "I went to New York and had fun" highlights the simple lens through which many Canadians probably view the border—as America, as a place they can go and are entitled to go to unencumbered. Is this, we wonder, becoming a residual response, reflecting as it does the invisibility of the border and our naive, even complacent attitude to US sovereignty, which matches our own attitude to Canada's sovereignty? The comment characterized as coming from a neutral place, one that would make the US Secretary of State for Homeland Security proud, captures a decidedly pragmatic border/customs experience: "As long as you obey border laws, [the border] can be crossed efficiently." The other statements, however fleeting, are more indicative of an emerging post-9/11 border discourse: "It is stricter on the American side." With the Department of Homeland Security's construction of terrorists as "coming from without" as opposed to being homegrown, we recall the DEW Line,[1] the Cold War, and the Red Threat. It would seem that the DEW Line is being lowered and that Canada is the enemy. No longer a national park appended to the United States, we're the land of lenient immigration policies, the "back door" for terrorists to enter the States, and, as recently featured on numerous American televisions shows—specifically, *Lost* and *Law and Order*—the home and native land of the weird, the creepy, and the other. With passports required for cross-border travel and accords signed for the free flow of goods, if not people, the "interval of resonance" is morphing as we write.

II. *Imagining the Line: It's Neither Here nor There*

> The movie highlights L.A. [Los Angeles] over and over … [but] it could have been in any major city in America.

Without any sense of hypocrisy or of "crossing the line," eight of our group spoke authoritatively about American representations, with little accounting for the regional, economic, and historical differences that most Canadians insist be recognized in discourse about ourselves. The Los Angeles and America they were so fluently discussing, after all, were constructions founded on media representations—in this case, *Crash*—not on actual lived spaces, or, for that matter, actual experiences. These hyperrealities, we discovered, operate as powerful imaginaries that shape the felt lives of our students.

Not all the students had visited the States, yet they said that if they were transported there, they would certainly know the key signifiers that marked the landscape as "American." For half, the signature of America was the imagined commercialization of the culture: "McDonald's everywhere"; "stores that Canada doesn't have"; "different-colored Froot Loops"; "different Dorito labels"; "abundance of fast food chains." The latter comment was qualified thus: "However, I should mention my opinion is entirely based on what I've seen in film and television." When we pushed this question a little further in the focus group, we found the majority admitting that their cultural imaginings of America had been shaped by their frequent viewing of American television and film products. Our students had little personal experience with the United States or the border, yet they immediately linked America to consumerism while implicitly positioning Canada as the less commercial space, one with fewer choices and less emphasis on consumption. Does this reflect the stereotype of Canadian inferiority to America—the envious sibling syndrome? Or is there something else we might learn from our respondents?

Our students' familiarity with the United States drew to mind Roger Gibbins's contention with which we begin the paper, that the Canada–US border "penetrates the Canadian consciousness, identity, economy and polity." For instance, one respondent, who had never been to the States, articulated in considerable detail his perceived view of the differences in national personalities: "They [Americans] have stronger personalities than in Canada or perhaps not stronger, but more vibrant, more straightforward than us, more opinionated and much more comfortable with who they are. Most places don't have this independence or, for lack of a better word, 'brashness.'" Consistent with Bodroghkozy's theory of Canadians' viewing of American television programs, the students were also insistent about *Crash*'s American setting—they knew *Crash* was set *there*, in America, not *here*, in Canada—and circled back to emphasize how central Los Angeles was to *Crash's* stories of racism. Yet only one of them had ever been to LA. It would seem, from our admittedly limited view, that Canadian students' understandings of American race relations, geography, and history are often largely if not entirely mediated through film and television images—a point that came into focus in the second group's eagerness to "read" *Crash* through an association with *American History X*, a film about two brothers involved in the white supremacist movement set in, you guessed it, Los Angeles. Contrast this facility with American representations to how Canadian media—films in this case—figure as an *absence* in their imaginaries: nine of our participants acknowledged that they either never watched Canadian films or never deliberately did so. (One participant did mention that she made a point of viewing one Canadian film a month, as "a kind of homework assignment.") We weren't surprised by their assumptions about the Canadian film aesthetic being marked by a "low-budget look" and about Canadian films in general being "less accessible," not widely marketed, and independent. Yet one respondent declared when we asked the group to recode *Crash* in a Canadian setting: "Canadian films don't deal with such subject matter ... We think we're better than that." We certainly see here evidence of how reversible resistance enables our respondents to use the border as a way to position themselves and Canada paradoxically as both inferior and superior to America.

We do not want this point to be taken as simply a banal confirmation of what many Canadian post-secondary educators conclude to be the case—that our students are often wilfully ignorant of Canadian culture and possess mistaken media-driven views of the United States. We would like to suggest that our respondents' discussion substantiates how perceptions of the Canada–US border as benign, porous, and open to crossing and recrossing continue to reside in their imaginative and interpretive practices even when and while some respondents admit that the border has been hardened: "It's stricter on the American side." This dissonance might be explained as a kind of "interpretive lag," where the imaginary trails the lived experience but remains dominant. Furthermore, we hear evidence in their discourse that underlines the central tenet of reversible resistance—namely, that Anglo-Canadians appropriate American representations and talk about them *as if* they have a right to do so *irrespective* of the border. It seems that some of us freely play at "being American," talking as if we are them and they are all one; yet when necessary or convenient, we can withdraw and say "no, we're better than that …," or, more accurately—to repeat one of our student's trenchant observations—"we *think* we're better than that." This reflexivity points to the kind of ironic positioning that Bodroghkozy argues is emblematic of what Canadians "do" with American cultural products.

Perhaps another instance will illustrate the students' pick'n'choose viewing strategies. In our second focus group, which met after the Obama victory and directly on the heels of the dreary—by comparison—Canadian federal election campaign, several comments focused on Obamamania and the more vibrant political culture of the United States as markers of border crossing. In the focus group discussion, the students lamented the blandness of Canadian politics and expressed envy of the promise and hope that President Obama held out for a renewed political sphere. Interestingly, despite their being Canadians, they felt Obama was an energizing figure for them, much more so than our own prime minister. "Obamamania," then, seemed to be a resource for imagining a revived Canadian politics. A closer look, however, revealed that our respondents perceived the American political scene as something to be "watched" like a film—as something, that is, to take up "as if" we Canadians too could be part of the action; then, without taking measures to engage with our own political process, such as voting or getting involved, we could indulge our fallen status. Is this not again the trope of positing a "more vibrant, more comfortable with themselves … for lack of better word, 'brashness'" that makes Canadians seem the opposite of Americans? Our America-envy (and in the Bush era, our America-bashing) becomes a reason not to do anything about our own situation.

However, none of our respondents save one saw *Crash* as a vehicle for mining markers of semiotic difference between Canada and the States. When we asked whether the film's focus on health care and the dangers of firearms struck them as potentially "Canadian," they demurred. Nor did they feel that the figure of Peter Waters, the young African American carjacker who loves hockey, represented anything Canadian. One student did, however, indicate the rarity of snowfalls in Los Angeles at Christmas. When asked by us to elaborate on that point, he directed us to the film's conclusion and wryly drew on a Canadian stereotype: "It is snowing at the end, but in Calgary there would be snow in every segment." Perhaps this is an instance of semiotic mining, but we think it is better understood as a moment when the student recodes *Crash* as a Canadian film. The snow, a common enough trope in Canadian mythology, becomes the border between LA and Calgary. The beaver's bite, we posit, is less about finding pleasures in picking out markers of subtle national difference and more about using well-worn stereotypes about how Canada differs from its American neighbour.

III. *Transposing Racism: What Is a Border For, Anyway?*
What happens, then, when the focus shifts from the generalities to the specifics of race and racism as represented in *Crash*? How do Canadians recode American film when contentious issues are at stake? To get at this question, we asked how *Crash* would differ if the film were *transposed* to Canada or, specifically, Calgary. One respondent alluded to Calgary's racial mix, saying that "for starters, it'd be more white than anything. White's a minority in LA." (Curiously, our respondents' verbal awareness of "white" as a racial group was not evident in their written self-identifications: one identified as "white," while the others chose the more bureaucratic "Caucasian.") One female student stated that "there would be more native people and a higher Asian representation." Another female suggested that "Don Cheadle would be aboriginal [*sic*] and his brother would be a runaway from the reserve." We want to focus on this last comment because in our previous project on *Crash,* one respondent argued strenuously that it was precisely the *absence* of the Aboriginal that marked the film as Canadian (Easton and Hewson, "Emergent"). In this section, we explore how Aboriginal absence and presence structured these Western Canadian students' reception of *Crash* and the critical role that borders play in their recoding.

Let's start with the female student's comment that the main character would be Aboriginal and her allusion to the difficult conditions on reserves—conditions that often make the mainstream Canadian news media. Here she has transposed Haggis's focus on black/white race relations in America to settler-invader relations to Aboriginal peoples in Canada. What are we to make of this move? The student's casual comment that Detective Graham Waters and his brother would be Aboriginal and living on the reserve from which Peter escapes unconsciously references an entire history of colonial relations in western Canada that has been submerged, ignored, and repressed. Susan Lord's thinking proves fruitful here when she argues that in a western Canadian context, "the materialities of colonial history, such as the pass law and treaty processes, are more than context and are not merely of the past: they are the latent content of the present which becomes available to representation and/ or formal articulation due to particular triggers" (408–9). We would argue that this latent content is also available to western Canadian viewers as they recode American films such as *Crash*. Our respondent's hypothetical trans-position that sees Peter as a reserve runaway is an expression of these histor-ical materialities, albeit stripped of their accuracy.[2] It would seem to us that white Canadian identity, contra Manning and Bodroghkozy, is determined not only by our enmeshment with (white) American culture but also through our long-standing political, economic, and legal relations with Aboriginal peoples. Hence, we need to revise the concept of reversible resistance in order to accom-modate our students' responses. It's not so much that reversible resistance isn't working, as that reversible resistance requires an Aboriginal presence in order to shape a Canadian identity that resists American assimilation. The beaver needs the Aboriginal in order to bite back.

In the second focus group, another student stated that if the film were Can-adian, it might be set in Saskatchewan, which he described as "the racism cen-tre of Canada" between "non-native and native people." His evidence for this claim was testimony from his friends who hailed from that prairie province. His comment echoed that of a female student in the first focus group, who stated that "there are areas with more obvious cultural clashes [than Calgary]. Regina, for instance. Calgary doesn't have the same reputation for brutality. We all know how mean Regina police are to minorities. It's more plausible to stage it there." That Regina and Saskatchewan should surface in the students' imaginary was, for us, striking. We wonder if students in Halifax, Toronto, or (more pointedly) francophone Montreal, all with different histories of inter-cultural contact, race relations, and class structures, would choose Regina as the focal point for racialized Canadian conflicts. And what about students in Regina—native *and* non-native? Would they also pick their city as the metro-politan space where *Crash* would be set if in Canada?

One might conclude that the students think native/non-native racism is elsewhere because of the limited Aboriginal presence in their immediate environment, but this is hardly the case: Aboriginal students are present at Mount Royal University (albeit in small numbers—about 3 percent); there is an Aboriginal Education Project housed in the Iniskim Centre; and a very active and prominent Native Student Affairs Office runs regular events such as sweat lodges and powwows, to which it invites the university community. There is also significant visible evidence of the "touristification" of indigeneity—"Indian Village," for example, is an integral component of the city's premiere event, the Calgary Stampede.[3] Why, then, would Regina rather than Calgary become the space where it's more plausible to set a film like *Crash*? What would precipitate the "forgetting" of the racism between natives and non-natives here, in Calgary, and its displacement there, to Regina?

Certainly, the fact that so many Calgarians are emigrants from Saskatchewan, who come and tell their stories about racism, is at play here. Until Saskatchewan experienced its own oil boom in 2009, Calgary was a destination for many people from Saskatchewan, who brought both their expertise and their histories to the city. But this explanation takes us only so far in understanding the students' slip of the tongue or parapraxis. When it comes to policing on the prairies, most national and regional news reports focus not on Regina but on Saskatoon. Specifically, it is Saskatoon that was long associated with "starlight tours"—a term referring to allegations that some of that city's police officers would drive Aboriginal men and youth to the outskirts of town at night and in winter, leaving them out there to walk back. Some of these people were beaten en route, and some died of exposure.[4]

Yet three students selected Regina, a city whose number of insurance claims at one time earned it the title of "car theft capital of Canada," as the appropriate setting for a Canadian version of *Crash*. In fact, Regina did reign as Canada's car theft capital in 2001, but since instituting a number of programs aimed at reducing car theft, it now ranks sixteenth in the country (Regina Police Services 3). Are these responses indicative of an interpretive lag? Possibly. But there is more at work in this move. If we agree with Lord's observation that "the First Nations presence is more often than not a structuring absence in the field of Canadian identity ... [and] is a foundation upon which whiteness and Canadianness is made," then this parapraxis is an example of how such whiteness and Canadianness is achieved at Mount Royal University in Calgary. The students' displacement of racism onto Regina, Saskatchewan, effectively empties Calgary, Alberta, of any Aboriginal presence and of any trace of real racism that may exist in Calgary.

But it is also productive to think about borders in relation to what appears to us to be a process of disavowal and displacement. For example, one respondent referred to the Calgary bar scene as the site of racial problems, in that individuals were routinely being refused entrance on the basis of skin colour. The respondent felt that Calgarians/Canadians are "too polite to say horrible things" and suggested that here there was a "politically correct racism." We took this to mean that Calgary promotes an appearance of tolerance that masks the deeper problems of racism as manifested by the bars' "racial profiling." This acknowledges a qualified problem, to be sure, but interestingly, it is a problem of *Calgarians* and one whose denial gets enacted through a form of "politeness." "Politically correct racism" is contrasted with the inflammatory racism represented in *Crash* or imagined to exist "in Regina." Here again we need to nuance our understanding of how reversible resistance operates. The participants invoked borders to demarcate differences such that we have "polite" Canadian/Calgarian and "rude" American/Regina racists. Reversible resistance, then, is reversible racism; the Canada–US border protects a notion of white Canadianness, and when required, provincial borders can be called upon to perform the same function.

A close reading of one respondent's comments might substantiate this claim further: "I don't feel racial tension here. Calgarians do have racial problems, but don't admit [them]." The interesting shift from the speaker's personal perception of "no racial tension" to that of "Calgarians' problem" mirrors the characteristic othering of racism that we feel permeates Canadian identity. "*I* don't feel racial tension here. *Calgarians* do have racial problems, but don't admit [them]." The slip from the first-person "I" to the third-person "Calgarians" rehearses precisely the boundary-making we have described above.

Canada → USA   Alberta → "Regina," Saskatchewan   I → Calgary

In each case the othering occurs as a defence mechanism to acknowledge but disavow connection to the difficult problem of racial difference. John Doyle, the *Globe and Mail*'s television critic, noted a similar pattern in the responses to his criticism of Canadian television writers and Canadian television comedy: Doyle writes:

> [T]he journalism favoured by most Canadians is hectoring, finger-wagging disapproval of something or other ... This is reflected in our TV comedy, I think. *This Hour Has 22 Minutes* and *The Rick Mercer Report* tend towards the gentlest kinds of satire, and, in most instances, the comedy isn't aimed at Canadians anyway. It's aimed at politicians and other public figures. Thus, there's a distancing effect. It's not about us, it's about some big shots who are probably too big for their boots anyway.

Our students' responses therefore fit within a more general pattern of Canadians' tendency to use the border as a defensive line to protect their identity.

Concluding Thoughts

> So, in a way, they [the British imperialists] rewrote the surface mythology of Canada. You and I are still struggling with that.
>
> John Ralston Saul,
> *Globe and Mail* interview with Michael Valpy,
> September 2008

As we position ourselves in the "both/and space" of participant-observers, as ethnographers must do, what must our ears learn to hear? First, we must listen to the firmness with which these students expressed themselves in both writing and speaking about *Crash*. We cannot dismiss their insights as simply performative acts. Many students spoke about how their experiences in the film studies classroom provided them with other ways to think and talk about film beyond the "three thumbs up" consumerist model so prevalent in the mass media. Perhaps our curricular interventions have had some efficacy. As one of the students offered post-project: "I'm not sure that my own perceptions reflect the pedagogy of my instructors so much as my ability to articulate my own observations stems from their tutelage. I prefer to think so anyway!"

This comment draws us back to our original concern about the reading strategies deployed by students entering the Canadian film studies classroom. Reversible resistance *does* seem like a productive way to frame the process that many actually activate when they are viewing American films. However, we are not sure that our respondents' interpretations—save for one—showed much evidence of beaver bites that leave many marks. We wonder if the tendency to bite lightly has its roots in the kind of relationship our participants have with Canadian film. While they describe it—in easily availed-of stereotypical terms—they don't watch it. When viewing American television, Canadian viewers can "bite back" precisely because they have a rich repository of Canadian tropes from which to draw, resources that allow them to play at being Canadian or American. (For example, viewers might bring elements of an imagined Canadian identity inflected through Canadian television programming such as *Corner Gas, The Mercer Report*, and Canadian news programming.) However, our students bring no such Canadian counterweight to their viewing of American films. So, while they definitely deployed the border to differentiate between *here* in Calgary, Alberta, Canada, and *there*, the Los Angeles represented in *Crash*, they were unable to note the semiotic markers of difference that our "expert" eyes detected. Rather, they invoked an imaginary (white) Canada in contrast to a stereotypical America. The concept of reversible resistance, we contend, must be adapted for Canadian film viewing to take into careful account which "America" the Canadian viewer is mobilizing in his or her interpretation. In this case, the America our respondents imagined south of the 49th was captured by "LA"—urban, racially diverse, divided, and late capitalist—given that in our students' minds this "America" was so intimately linked to commercialization that it elided America's specific regional differences. The "as if" space the students seem so at ease with may have little to do with the way that race and racism works across the United States—there are, in other words, other Americas that Canadian spectators cannot know and perhaps wish not to know.

At a minimum, these students' responses suggest that reversible resistance is not only or centrally about our relationship to an imaginary America, however constructed. Reversible resistance founders on the fact of an Indigenous presence that refuses to be erased but that enables a reversible racism: it—the pronoun's ambiguity is deliberate—is always "over there." To theorize a Canadian film spectatorship, we need to be aware of the structuring role that Aboriginal absence and presence plays in the formation of whiteness and Canadianness in western Canada. Specific attention must also be paid to provincial borders and the ways they shape identities and influence reception practices. Based on our admittedly small sample size, we contend that provincial and regional differences may not just inflect a common Canadian identity but in fact may well construct a different identity position altogether. Certainly such a consideration complicates Bodroghkozy's assertion that the imagined American Other is the glue that binds Canadians together.

We want to end by reflecting on the implications and possibilities of our respondents' thoughts about the relations between settler-invader cultures and Indigenous peoples. In a preliminary way, we as researchers wonder how we might begin to organize a deeper exploration of John Ralston Saul's provocative formulation of Canada as a Métis nation. In his controversial book *A Fair Country: Telling Truths about Canada* (2008), Saul invites settler-invader readers to consider an alternative to the long-standing narrative of the Canadian nation that has held so many in its sway. Instead of the "two solitudes" model, which founds Canada on the plinth of Anglo-French relations, Saul offers a "tripod" foundation, thereby opening our eyes to the connections— often cooperative, not always conflictual—between Indigenous and settler-invader populations as the "plot" of Canada's story. He asks us to imagine ourselves as indigenized. Notwithstanding the lack of evidence Saul supplies for what he argues is a deeply rooted historical continuity with Aboriginal ways in Canada, his hypothesis suggests intriguing possibilities for identity (re)construction and for imagining the Canadian nation anew. What learning is required to consider one's settler-invader self indigenized? In pursuing this question, we are not positing an idealized subject that could elide the history of settlement. Rather, we are suggesting that Saul's approach might allow us to work through our complicities with settler histories and the legacies of colonial domination. His emphasis on the history of Canada before its entanglement with empire provides useful models of hybridization that we might profitably revisit. For instance, Joseph Boyden's *Three Day Road*, a story of Oji-Cree boys caught up in the maelstrom of the First World War, offers a potential starting point for how a Métis imagination might revise settler histories.

Still, how does one enter into a meaningful relationship with that Other, the one that settler-invader histories have rendered invisible? Jason Hazlett's film version of Drew Hayden Taylor's play, *In a World Created by a Drunken God* (2008), offers an interesting example for us to ponder. The film, which focuses on the story of a western Canadian Métis man who learns he has an American half-brother, may point us toward the kind of film studies curricular choices that would encourage an indigenized Métis/Canadian spectatorship. There are, of course, still questions about how such an indigenized curriculum would be thoughtfully imparted to students. The Province of Saskatchewan offers a possible model in its *School^Plus* approach, which mandates as one of its education system's curricular goals the promotion of "a harmonious and shared future with aboriginal peoples" (Government of Saskatchewan). Finally, we wonder what the borders would be in this reconfigured Métis/Canadian film studies curriculum. Which ones would count and why? Without our respondents' generous and frank comments we would not have these possibilities to explore. We thank them.

Notes

1   The Distance Early Warning radar system was constructed across Canada during the 1950s, as a defence system intended to provide the Canadian and American militaries with early warnings of Soviet nuclear attacks. A joint Canadian–American initiative, the DEW Line provided a Cold War version of a common security perimeter.

2   Until the legislative changes to the Indian Act in the 1950s, leaving the reserve required the permission of the Indian Agent. Without that permission, leaving the reserve was a criminal offence.

3   Hewson and Werier's investigation into the Calgary Stampede calls into question any simple narrative of the relationship between Indian Village, the Calgary Stampede, and the City of Calgary.

4   Neil Stonechild's death in 1990, which was ruled accidental, was reinvestigated by the provincial government in 2003, when, in 2000, two more Aboriginal men were found frozen to death on the outskirts of Saskatoon. No charges were laid against any officers. In 2005, Stonechild's family filed suits against the Saskatoon Police Force and the two officers involved in their son's death.

Works Cited

Allen, Robert C. "Relocating American Film History: The 'Problem' of the Empirical." *Cultural Studies* 20.1 (2006): 48–88.

Bodroghkozy, Aniko. "As Canadian as Possible … : Anglo-Canadian Popular Culture and the American Other." *Hop on Pop: The Pleasures and Politics of Popular Culture*. Ed. Henry Jenkins, Tara McPherson, and Jane Shattuc. Durham: Duke UP, 2002. 573–87.

Crash. Dir. Paul Haggis. Vancouver: Lions Gate Films, 2004.

Easton, Lee, and Kelly Hewson. "The Emergent and the Cosmopolitan: A Case Study of Student Responses." Delivered at the Film and Literature Association Conference, Tallahassee, Florida, 2007.

———. "Reflections on the Interplay of Race, Whiteness, and Canadian Identity in a Film Studies Classroom." *Reception: Texts, Readers, Audiences, History* 2 (2010): 116–46.

Gibbins, Roger. "Meaning and Significance of the Canadian–American Border." *Borders and Border Regions in Europe and North America*. Ed. Paul Ganster et al. San Diego: Institute for Regional Studies of the Californias: San Diego State UP, 1997. 315–31.

Giroux, Henry A., and Roger I. Simon. "Popular Culture as a Pedagogy of Pleasure and Meaning." *Popular Culture, Schooling and Everyday Life*. Ed. Henry A. Giroux and Roger I. Simon and contributors. London: Bergin & Garvey, 1989. 1–30.

Government of Saskatchewan. *School^(Plus) and the Effective Practices Framework.* http://ebookbrowse.com/schoolplus-and-the-effective-practices-framework -doc-d69016062. Accessed 20 June 2013.

Hewson, Kelly, and Cliff Werier. "Staging the West: Cowboys and Indians at the Calgary Stampede." Paper presented at the Under Western Skies Conference, Mount Royal University, October 2010.

In a World Created by a Drunken God. Dir. Jason Hazlett. Calgary: Pyramid Productions, 2008.

Lord, Susan. "Canadian Gothic: Multiculturalism, Indigenity, and Gender in Prairie Cinema." *Canadian Cultural Poesis: Essays on Canadian Culture.* Ed. Garry Sherbert, Annie Gerin, and Sheila Petty. Waterloo: Wilfrid Laurier UP, 2005. 399–419.

Manning, Frank E. "Reversible Resistance: Canadian Popular Culture and the American Other." *The Beaver Bites Back? American Popular Culture in Canada.* Ed. David H. Flaherty and Frank E. Manning. Montreal and Kingston: McGill–Queen's UP, 1993. 8–23.

Marchessault, Janine. *Marshall McLuhan.* London: Sage, 2005.

Marcus, George E. *Ethnography Through Thick and Thin.* Princeton: Princeton UP, 1998.

McLuhan, Marshall. "Canada: The Borderline Case." *The Canadian Imagination: Dimensions of a Literary Culture.* Ed. David Staines. Cambridge, MA: Harvard UP, 1977. 226–48.

Regina Police Service. "Regina Auto Theft Strategy." 2004. http://www.popcenter.org/ library/awards/goldstein/2004/04-33.pdf. Accessed 2 September 2010.

Saul, John Ralston. *A Fair Country: Telling Truths about Canada.* Toronto: Penguin Canada, 2008.

INDIGENOUS CULTURES
AND NORTH AMERICAN BORDERS

seven

Discursive Positioning
A Comparative Study of Postcolonialism in Native Studies Across
the US–Canada Border

Maggie Ann Bowers

IT MAY SEEM OBVIOUS that understandings of postcolonialism will differ
between nation-states with different histories of colonialism. So we can assume
that postcolonialism is viewed differently on either side of the Canada–US border. The contrasting idea that a tribal group split by the border may well have
a sense of solidarity and union with people of the same tribal group on the
other side of the border also seems self-evident. This idea has been applied
widely in a political manoeuvre by the American Indian Movement since the
1970s to create a shared sense of purposeful resistance to colonialism among
First Nations and Native American people in both nation-states. Thomas Biolsi
reiterates this attitude in his new edition of *Deadliest Enemies: Law and Race
Relations On and Off Rosebud Reservation* (2007), in which he indicates that in
order to examine localized racial inequalities, one must consider the broader
national context (xvi). I suggest that the broader context for examination could
usefully include comparative postcolonial studies from other parts of the globe.
This chapter reveals that the complexities created by the border, which has
divided North America's Native peoples between separate nation-states, and
thus between different experiences of colonialism, has also created a conflict
over the appropriateness of postcolonial theory in a Native North American
context. With this in mind, this chapter considers the First Nations of southern
Canada and the Native Americans of the geographical area of the United States
along the 49th parallel, which divides the nation-states. This is part of a larger
project that demands we also consider the Inuit and the Métis. The terminology this chapter employs deliberately avoids identifying Indigenous writers
as either Canadian or American, misleading as that may be when discussing
Indigenous sovereignty.

This chapter brings together consideration of the ontological plurality that
is created by the colonial imposition of the US–Canada border with various
attempts by critics to find a discursive position for Native North American
Studies to express the complexities of the Indigenous situation on the continent. I do not examine the specific details of these differences, for that would

demand research detail that is not available to me here, but I do propose to assert a broader point: that the different histories of postcolonialism in the distinct nation-states of Canada and the United States have influenced the debates about the acceptance or rejection of postcolonial theory in Native North American Studies. By bringing together the reactions of critics regarding Native North American cultural issues on both sides of the border in order to consider the reasons for rejecting or adopting postcolonialism, this chapter reveals the significant influence of the location of the critic in relation to the US–Canada border. This, I argue, has more influence over the acceptance or rejection of postcolonialism than whether the author/critic is Native North American and/or whether that author/critic is part of the Western academy. The analysis suggests that the complexities of Canada's postcolonial status have generated a marked resistance among some First Nations writers when it comes to engaging with postcolonial theory.

This is not to say that the adoption of postcolonial theory in Native Studies is unproblematic on either side of the border. The questions concerning its appropriateness are compounded by the complexities of "postcolonialism" as a term. I concur with Jace Weaver and Elizabeth Cook-Lynn, who conceive postcolonialism is applicable in Native American Studies in the United States when it refers to resistance to colonialism and to issues of transnationalism. Both Cook-Lynn (*New Indians* 215) and Weaver (*That the People Might Live* 43), although wary of postcolonial theory, find inspiration in the work of Edward Said and Homi K. Bhabha. Said's work as a commentator on Palestine is noted by both Cook-Lynn (*New Indians* 20) and Weaver (295), especially regarding the applicability of postcolonial ideas to issues of Indigeneity. Weaver, along with Kevin Bruyneel and Stuart Christie, is also interested in Bhabha's theories of transnationalism, through which Bhabha provides a framework for identifying elements of possible resistance in the spaces between categories, nations, and identities.

Weaver's approach stands in contrast to the rejection of postcolonial theory and its terms by American-born Cherokee Canadian writer and critic Thomas King in his 1990 essay "Godzilla vs. Post-Colonial." In that essay he sets out an alternative framework for considering the effects of colonization without relying on the vocabulary of the colonizer. In this sense, he rejects the implication that Native North American life is only understandable in relation to the colonial moment: "While postcolonialism purports to be a method by which we can begin to look at those literatures which are formed out of the struggle of the oppressed against the oppressor, the colonized and the colonizer, the term itself assumes that the starting point for that discussion is the advent of Europeans in North America" (11). King's impulse to reject postcolonialism is, as he explains, based on its "demands that I imagine myself as something I did not choose to be, as something I would not choose to become" (16). Moreover, he chooses to reject the postcolonial framework when other more culturally specific critical vocabularies are equally available. This is a seemingly sensible and straightforward response; however, it does not allow for transnational comparisons of colonial situations, suggestive of strategies for resistance, that are available through a postcolonial theoretical framework.

The point of Weaver's adoption of an anti-colonial postcolonialism is to negotiate a way out of being forced into "being colonized" individually and communally. Weaver, however, does not adopt postcolonial theory uncritically. His main contention regarding postcolonial theory is that it needs to be applied in actuality in order to be useful beyond the study of literature: "The problem is that at base postcolonialism is depoliticized ... It mistakes having deconstructed something theoretically for having displaced it politically" (*Other Words* 295). Cook-Lynn, too, identifies this as the main problem with postcolonial theory; she comments that it does not have "much to do with the actual deconstruction of colonial systems" ("Who Stole" 13). Few critics, in fact, venture to discuss the situation of Native North Americans in postcolonial terms without a sense of the possibility of moving into a Western academic perspective and thereby losing a self-critical position that seeks to avoid taking a singularly metropolitan view. Ella Shohat's "Notes on the 'Post-Colonial'" is often cited in Native North American criticism—notably by Jace Weaver—as a reminder to readers of the origins and predominant development of postcolonialism within the Western academy (*Other Words* 293). While King's objection to postcolonialism as a term remains, both Cook-Lynn and Weaver have cautiously moved toward an acceptance of the vocabulary and framework of postcolonialism where it indicates theoretical approaches to real problems. Cook-Lynn, for instance, cites attitudes toward the land, as well as use of the land, as the primary focus for concern (*New Indians* 199), where Weaver cites the legal position and sovereignty of Native Americans (*Other Words* 12). With this in mind, this chapter, written from a position outside the Native American context, suggests that the differences between the post/colonial states of the United States and Canada and the influences these differences have had on the Indigenous populations of these countries have not yet been fully explored, and that they need to be.

In *Other Words: American Indian Literature, Law, and Culture* (2001), Weaver discusses a strategy for developing a discourse suitable for countering the effects of the colonization of Native Americans based on what he calls "hermeneutical sovereignty." He explains: "What exactly a postcolonial we-hermeneutic will mean for Natives must emerge out of the community itself as we critically reflect upon our own communitist commitments. If, however, we are ever to dismantle the colonial paradigm and move to a place "after" and "beyond" colonialism, we must have hermeneutical sovereignty as well" (304). Most importantly, he sees the need for a hermeneutics based on Native American belief that simultaneously incorporates thinking that links this hermeneutics to their transnational situation. That is, if we regard Native Americans as participating in plural sovereignties (to use Stuart Christie's term)—that of a Native nation along with the imposed sovereignty of the United States/Canada—then the everyday existence of those with Native status moves between national contexts and across borders. For Native Americans to control their sovereignty, both legal and cultural, Weaver calls for the philosophical basis on which this sovereignty is defined and discussed to emanate from Native American systems of belief and transnational experience. For this purpose, he applies postcolonial theory to the situation of contemporary Native Americans, with notable reference to Bhabha's theories of migrancy and resistance and especial consideration of hybridity, community and language.

Weaver attempts, then, to use postcolonial discourse to create a Native American hermeneutics that is resistant to colonization; at the same time, he strategically makes comparisons to other colonized and Indigenous populations in the world. As such, the discourse he calls for requires a plural and inclusive ideological approach; it is both specific and comparative. The perspective he employs, encompassing both transnationalism and cultural specificity, has had currency in postcolonial studies for almost a decade. Gayatri Chakravorty Spivak, motivated by the move away from nation-based comparative literary studies, proposed a comparative postcolonial approach as long ago as 2003. While her concern is with the adoption of aspects of comparative literature within postcolonialism, she is clear that such an attempt cannot be a simple "splicing" (4); rather, the act of "reading closely in the original" (6) needs to include a "concern for the literary specificity of the autochthone" (15) while setting it in relation to and—I extrapolate—in allegiance with other Indigenous cultures.

Comparisons of the North American situation with those of other postcolonial nations are made by critics working on either side of the border. For instance, Canadian critic Laura Moss is keen to identify the differences between Canadian settler-invader postcolonialism and Nigerian postcolonialism (2), and Weaver, in the context of Native Americans in the United States, seeks to identify similarities with Palestinian and Kenyan postcolonialism (*Other Words* 12–14). Neither critic takes these respective comparisons far, but it is revealing that Weaver draws Native American Studies into a closer relationship with other studies of Indigenous colonized groups. Moss's comparison is an attempt to differentiate Canadian settler-invader postcolonialism from that of directly colonized nations such as Nigeria; she focuses on the specifics of the Canadian situation, while admitting that Nigeria and Canada share a responsibility to face the colonization of the Ogoni and First Nations, respectively (2).

For Spivak, the danger that needs to be avoided is taking up the positions either of the "native informant" or the "metropolitan" (10): those who speak as a token voice for the Indigenous and those who speak solely in an international and metropolitan context. For Native North Americans, the political unity of the Indigenous peoples of North America resides in the recognition of similarities across the border. However, the debates concerning the appropriate discursive position from which to create hermeneutical sovereignty reveal that there are subtle differences that need to be recognized between the differing colonial histories of the First Nations and Native American peoples. This debate is unpacked most effectively in the context of the borderlands, where Bhabha's theories of inbetweenness are useful.

The US–Canada border is a highly significant symbol and institution of colonialism, one that illustrates the difficulties of expressing sovereignty, in that the border is seen to appear and disappear according to whose sovereign position is being adopted. In this way the border functions similarly to the notion of sovereignty, which, as Peter D'Errico observes (243), can be withheld or enforced according to the whim of the US federal legal system. In legal terms, the border is an undeniable barrier to movement between the sovereign nation-states that police it. For those whose sovereignty resides in one of the First Nations or Native American tribal nations, the border is an imaginary line, yet it can have dividing power over the cultural integrity of the Indigenous nation. The problem is that the histories and cultural adaptations of the First Nations and Native American nations divided by the 49th parallel are inevitably different and influenced by the border, whether it is recognized as legitimate or not.

The significance of the Jay Treaty of 1794 cannot be overstated when considering the relationship of the First Nations of Canada and Native Americans to the colonially imposed border. The fact that the newly formed United States recognized the right of tribal bands such as the Mi'kmaq to cross the border freely indicates that during the earliest moments of the nation-state there was acknowledgement that Native Americans, although living on the same soil, were not a part of that same nation. In other words, Native Americans, from the very beginnings of the United States, have been legally treated as sovereign others belonging to recognizable other nations (even if this recognition is noted or rejected at will by the US government). As Christie notes in *Plural Sovereignties and Contemporary Indigenous Literature*, "the spirit of the Jay Treaty endorses—whereas regrettably it does not stipulate in practical terms—that members of Indigenous communities remain linked to the territorial integrity of their historical homelands … regardless of subsequent and artificial international boundaries dividing them" (16). The border is that of the nation-state and, by implication, according to the Jay Treaty, not that of the Native North Americans. In terms of Native American Studies, this provides a focal point for examining the relationship of First Nations/Native Americans (together referred to as Native North Americans) to their respective colonial nation-states, the United States and Canada.

The very fact that different terms are used on either side of the border (First Nations / Native Americans and American Indian; Tribal Groups / Bands) indicates that these groups are treated separately by the respective colonial powers, with ensuing differences in the development of tribal identity and in attitudes toward colonial circumstances. However arbitrary the border is, it has had consequences in terms of the differing experiences of colonization on either side. This has resulted in differences in how tribal bands organize and are organized through legal, social, and educational institutions, and in how individuals of respective tribal bands carry out resistance to colonizing institutions. These differences are often very subtle; yet, I would argue, they influence the discursive positions taken in relation to cultural debates. For instance, reservation land in the United States is "owned" by the federal government, whereas in the case of Canadian reserves, it is more often "owned" by the Crown (the British monarchy). In other words, the complexities of the (post) colonial status of the nation-state of Canada have created differences in how Native North Americans in Canada and the United States have been colonized. These actual political differences have influenced the discourse surrounding postcolonialism in Native Studies. This is most evident in the difference of opinion between King and Weaver, who is supported by the commentary of Canadian-born, US-based academic Kevin Bruyneel. Weaver and Bruyneel share the opinion that notwithstanding their cautious approach to applying postcolonial theory to Native American situations, there is something to be gained from attempting to understand the colonial circumstances of Native Americans through Bhabha's post-structuralist theories of identity. King, in contrast, is not alone in rejecting postcolonial theory on the grounds that it is a Western discourse that delimits his identity, political understanding, and discursive contribution to Native North American Studies.

King, I propose, strongly shares his suspicions of postcolonialism with non-Native Canadians. For instance, Moss posed the question "Is Canada Postcolonial?" in the title of an edited collection of articles by notable Canadian critics responding to that eponymous question. Among those critics is Diana Brydon, whose analysis of Canadian postcolonialism provides an illuminating background to our subject. Brydon, defining postcolonialism as "a hybrid and emergent discourse struggling with the legacies of Eurocentrism" (57), is clear about the need to differentiate the variants of postcolonialism that exist in the settler-invader population in contrast to the Indigenous population. Her analysis of Canadian postcolonialism proposes that Canada is a postmodern postcolonial nation; that is, it is "suspicious" of the nationalism that the independent Canadian nation-state embraces, "enabling a certain way of life ... along with its rhetoric of peace, order, and good government" (49). It is, she claims, a nation-state aware that its basis is a construct that "carries an unsavoury colonial history of theft and oppression" (49). Brydon's postmodern explanation of Canadian postcolonialism illuminates Canada's ambivalent relationship to its postcolonial status. She does not dismiss postcolonialism for its associations with the Western academy; rather, her definition subtly allows for the countering of any discourse of postcolonialism that appears to support the kind of Eurocentrism with which her idea of postcolonialism "struggles." The irony of the Canadian postcolonial state is that it is aware of its foundations in the colonization of Indigenous people and of the simultaneous dislocation of the settler identity. In the articles responding to this question it is clear that the postmodern irony with which Linda Hutcheon identifies the Canadian sensibility is equally applied to its recognition of its colonial past. In *Splitting Images: Contemporary Canadian Ironies*, Hutcheon provides a starting point for the further examination of the irony employed in Canadian literature to express the often covert acknowledgement of the uneasiness of settler Canadians on colonized ground (89). For Hutcheon, this is epitomized by the work of Robert Kroetsch, who examines colonial history through personal ironic postmodern narratives (Hutcheon, *The Canadian Postmodern* 168). Thus, Canada is acknowledged by Canadian postcolonial critics to have been a settler-invader colony that, having been a dominion of Great Britain (i.e., a semi-independent colony) is now, after independence, in a postcolonial state. However, there is widespread understanding that such postcolonialism is not straightforward. First, despite having achieved independence, Canada is still sovereign to the Queen of Canada (and the United Kingdom) and thus is linked clearly and strongly to its predominant colonizing nation. Second, the settler population continues to occupy a privileged position over the First Nations population. In fact, during much of Canada's postcolonial history the European settler-invader population has had governmental control and privilege over other non-European settlers, due to the influence of the past association of Europeans and colonial control.

Canada's role as a colonial power controlling the institutions and lives of First Nations is recognized but is often elided in debates about Canadian postcolonialism. Canada's ironic discomfort as a postcolonial nation is often based more upon its settler-invader past and on the associated "postcolonial anxiety" that accompanies its people's lack of Indigenous connection to the land they inhabit. In her book about the 1990 Oka Crisis, *National Identity and the Conflict at Oka*, Amelia Kalant points to postcolonial anxiety as one of the key characteristics of the dominant Canadian society. She notes that postcolonialism is a "moral mantle" sought by many groups in Canada, who seek to gain political influence by it (6–7). She proposes that the political capital in being a postcolonial nation only works within a framework where colonialism has been rejected and identified as morally wrong. Kalant notes that in addition to the First Nations and settler-invader Anglo-Canadians, Quebec and French Canada also have a claim to a different and morally indignant position. The

French Canadian argument links the early *voyageur* history to the creation of the Métis, with the added complication that, since Canada's head of state is still the monarch of the United Kingdom, French Canadians can claim to have been under continuous colonial rule from the time of General Wolfe.

For the settler-invader (post)colonial population there is an awareness that in the scramble for the moral high ground, those of British ancestry are tainted by colonial association. To add to this discomfort, settler-invader Canadians have long been identified with an ambivalent relationship to the land, strengthened by publications such as Margaret Atwood's analysis of Canadian identity in *Survival* (1972). One of the myths of Canadian national identity is that settler-invader Canadians are dislocated on Canadian ground; as Atwood's protagonist in *Surfacing* comments: "Now we're on my home ground, foreign territory" (5). Yet identification with the land, and particularly with the northern landscape, simultaneously provides a necessary contrast to differentiate Canada's national identity from that of the neighbouring United States. There is a tendency for this to coincide with the Canadian habit of portraying the United States as an aggressive and destructive neighbour, implying the opposite of Canada. Kalant argues that this is sometimes linked with attempts to compare the treatment of First Nations in Canada with that of Native Americans in the United States in order to shift the accusation of colonization (54). In this competition, Canada is often portrayed as a benevolent colonial power (Christie makes note of this in relation to John Collier, the Commissioner of the Bureau of Indian Affairs at the time of the US Indian Reorganisation Act of 1934 [24]).

The newest territory of Canada, Nunavut, has become the focus of such analysis. It is true that Nunavut stands for a new level of Indigenous autonomy within the confines of nation-state structures. However, it needs to be seen within the framework of colonialism and in relation to symbolic events that are more revealing of colonialism, such as the Oka Crisis, in which members of the Mohawk nation near the town of Oka, Quebec, clashed with government troops sent in to quell Mohawk protests over the misuse of sacred lands. Kalant's analysis of this situation points directly to attempts to shift blame onto the United States. She notes that the Oka Crisis revealed that "[i]n modern, developed Canada, sacred place has to be limited, not expansive, or it runs into the space of American economy and Canadian progress ... Mohawk protestors forced Canadians to confront this disjuncture between practice and desire, or between southern practice and the desire of the north/native" (220). Despite the passage of time, it seems that the resonance of Canada as a northern land still has influence. As Kalant further explains, "the metanarrative of Canadianness is 'Canadians lack a sense of place' or 'do not understand 'here'" (8), which leads to "the construction of a 'mainstream' Canada [that] is indebted to the mobility of the idea of 'native' as it circulates and passes from Indian to French

Canadian to Canadian through the relations of native/settler, colonized/not-quite-conqueror, nation/nation, nation/colony" (101).

While "postcolonial anxiety" can be understood as encompassing the anxiety of being the colonized disempowered on an imperial periphery, it can also be the anxiety of the lack of moral political position of the colonizer. The settler-invader Canadian has the combined anxiety of being both. In this way, Canada is a postmodern postcolonial country: aware of its postcoloniality even while recognizing its incompatability with such a sentiment. Thus, as Hutcheon identifies, Canada views its postcolonial status with a postmodern ironic self-awareness.

In contrast, awareness that the United States is a postcolonial settler-invader nation is very little acknowledged. Its settler colonization and brief dominion status more than two hundred years ago lead to questions about whether the United States is in fact in a postpostcolonial state, having left the remaining influences and anxieties of British colonization in the past. The political confidence of the United States, expressed through its Constitution and Bill of Rights, seems to reveal little if any postcolonial anxiety that we can last trace in the statements of the Declaration of Independence and the literature of the American Renaissance. Where postcolonial criticism finds voice most often in relation to the contemporary United States is in reference to its population of immigrant diasporas from previously colonized countries (such as seen in the work carried out by Amritjit Singh and Peter Schmidt; all but two of the essays in their collection *Postcolonial Theory and the United States* consider settler and immigrant postcolonialism).

Unlike in Canada, there is a lack of acknowledgement that the United States is a settler-invader nation (which implies the colonial taking control of a geographical area for the creation of prosperity) rather than an immigrant nation (implying a need for refuge, an escape from poverty, etc.). The narrative of the national identity of the United States as the "land of the free" is predicated on an ideal concept rather than on something tangible, even if idealized, such as the geographical North of Canadian identity. In that sense, the United States is based on concepts that can be interpreted and moulded as opposed to the already existing, intractable landscape of Canada. The narrative of the immigrant nation shifts attention away from the continuing colonization of Native Americans (and, for that matter, other instances of American colonization and neo-colonization throughout the latter half of the twentieth century). I suggest that ironically, this lack of colonial acknowledgement provides a fresh discursive arena for applying and discussing postcolonialism and its theories in relation to the United States, and most particularly Native Studies. It is the already crowded, ironized, and complex discursive arena of postcolonialism in Canada that makes its application in cultural studies of the First Nations so uncomfortable for writers and critics, as epitomized by King.

The rejection or adoption of postcolonial critical approaches in Native Studies in North America has led to splits between those who reject or adopt postcolonialism and between those with differing approaches to postcolonialism. This is most apparent to critics such as Weaver and Elvira Pulitano, who agree that Native Americans need to control their own cultural production and representation, founded upon a Native American communally based ideology. That is, the control that Native North Americans gain over their own cultural production and identification must be both inclusive of others' thinking and specifically Native American. This plurality, verging on paradox, is seen by Pulitano as innate in contemporary Native American tradition, and it finds a place in the "mixed blood" discourse of Louis Owens and Gerald Vizenor. It is Vizenor who is the most cited and influential of those Native American critics who seek to negotiate the ontological plurality of the Native American colonial position. Pulitano notes that "Vizenor intends to find his own path in theory, one that ultimately pushes back the boundaries of theory itself while subverting the monologic, totalitarian structure of western hermeneutics" (147).

The debate that Pulitano explores in her controversial *Towards a Native American Critical Theory* (2003) reveals a desire on the part of some writers to gain control over the discursive space of Native American Studies by applying criticism rooted solely in Native American thinking; she contends, however, that to do so is to miss the point that Native American literature is "itself the product of western and native cultural traditions" (189). She states that in this sense, Native traditions are "always-already mediated or hybridized states" (189). She takes her inspiration from a critical stance that appropriately incorporates a plural ontological position—that is, from a criticism of "Indigenous rhetoric(s) and world views incorporated into the strategies of Western critical discourse" (188).

At this point, the differences between postcolonial positions in Native American Studies become apparent. Weaver has written more than one attack on Pulitano's emphasis on hybridity in her application of postcolonial theory: first in *American Indian Literary Nationalism* with Robert Warrior and Craig Womack, and more recently in his *Notes from a Miner's Canary*. In these texts he articulates his fear that Pulitano's approach implies that "hybridity is all" (9). In other words, for Weaver, an overemphasis on hybridity negates the existence and promotion of what is distinctly Native American, making hermeneutical sovereignty an impossibility.

From my perspective, it is the subtleties of Bhabha's migrant theories with their related hybridity that are most useful in a Native American framework. Bhabha's analysis of living across borderlands does not imply that "hybridity is all" but rather that the migrant experience produces both hybridity and the identification of those "stubborn chunks" (219) of specific cultures that do not migrate and that thereby draw attention. There is a split between Weaver and

Pulitano in their understandings of hybridity; both, however, seek a critical framework that includes not only the specifically Native American but also the transnational postcolonial. While much has been made of their different approaches to hybridity, the subtle yet significant difference between them is found in their differing understandings of postcolonialism. Pulitano seeks to place Native American criticism within a postcolonial framework, which she defines in relation to transculturalism (10). Weaver, in contrast, seeks a balance between transnational postcolonialism and culturally specific Native American criticism so as to produce an anti-colonial "hermeneutical sovereignty" (*Other Words* 304). His critical approach, also influenced by Vizenor, adopts postcolonialism as a counternarrative, enabling comparative criticism that speaks to other colonized groups without being mediated through Western discourse (*Other Words* 12). For our purposes, the transnational anti-colonialism of Weaver is most useful in finding those common and specific cultural indicators of hermeneutical sovereignty across the US–Canada border, in opposition to the ideology of dominant American culture.

The treatment of the US–Canada border in Native North American literature reveals recognition of the existence of the border in nation-state ideology while plainly illustrating its non-existence in Indigenous thinking. Thomas King's novel *Truth & Bright Water* illustrates this point beautifully with the metaphor of an incomplete bridge crossing a river that denotes the border between the United States and Canada: "At a distance, the bridge between Truth and Bright Water looks whole and complete … But if you walk down into the coulees and stand in the shadows of the deserted columns and the concrete arches, you can look up through the open planking and the rusting webs of iron mesh, and see the sky" (1).

Initially the young Blackfoot character Lum is able to cross the bridge by running across its rafters, but they soon become too rotten, and he falls, presumably to his death. The metaphor illustrates the double-faceted nature of the border: it both exists and does not exist depending on the discursive position: that of the nation-state or the Native North American nation. Lum disappears because the nature of the border and its crossings is not consistent. Catherine Bates notes, in this collection, that the border illustrates the domination of one way of thinking over another—that even something imaginary can have fatal consequences. King's novel *Green Grass, Running Water* also plays with the dual nature of the border. In it he creates Indigenous characters with mythical characteristics, whom he names the Florida Indians, who are able to cross the border at will, in contrast to those characters more grounded in reality, who find themselves at the whim of the nation-state authorities. The Florida Indians are based on historical figures but are named after various mythical characters from American national mythology, including Fenimore Cooper's Hawkeye. Their ability to cross the border undetected and at will is linked to their mythological status. In contrast, Lionel Red Dog, a mundane character, finds himself caught in nation-state politics when he is arrested while travelling in the back of a van driven by members of the American Indian Movement (AIM). The members of AIM welcome Lionel despite his different national identity, although Lionel reaffirms his difference by stating his Canadian identity repeatedly. Gillian Roberts, in her chapter in this collection, makes it clear that Lionel's insistence on his Canadian identity represents his alignment with a white identity. Yet ultimately he finds himself disowned by the Canadian Department of Indian Affairs, and is unable to cross the border back to Canada. Instead he is arrested and held as a terrorist (59).

In terms of discourse, the border can be considered either as existing in terms of colonialism using a postcolonial theoretical framework, or as an imaginary concept lacking legitimacy in tribal thinking. But to express this paradox, a critical approach needs to be adopted that reflects this duality—both specifically Native American and postcolonial. Christie's study of contemporary Native American sovereignty, in which he cites Harold Cardinal and Vine Deloria, Jr., considers the effect of multiplicity created by the imposition on existing structures of new government, new languages, and so on through the processes of colonization. As Christie explains, the "contest between competing sovereignties and cultural values has produced a plurality in the contemporary indigenous imagining" (2). However, to heed Spivak's warning, the voice of the autochthone must be heard as well as that of the metropolitan; it must be a part of the process of creating a new discursive position. From a postcolonial perspective, Bhabha's study of the ambivalence of the in-between space of the borderlands (303–37) offers a clear critical vocabulary for examining this duality and for articulating a new discursive position. In his chapter "How Newness Enters the World" in *The Location of Culture*, Bhabha considers the notions of "in-between" and "third space" in relation to transnational migration. He explains that the process of migration and transnationalism is performed "in-between" categories, cultures and nations, creating "a cultural space—a third space—where the negotiation of incommensurable differences creates a tension peculiar to borderline existences" (218). For Bhabha, borderlands existences do not simply move between two realms but by the process of migration identify differences. The "third space" is crucially not simply where two realms meet but is the creation of something new that hesitates between the two, that maintains the differences, positing "an interstitial future, that emerges in-between the claims of the past and the needs of the present" (219). Such a focus extends the scope of Bruyneel's work on resistant Native sovereignty by which he finds that it can exist in the third space of "con-constitutive interaction" (xix) in the borderlands, in a way that "refuses to conform to the binaries and boundaries that frame dualistic choices for indigenous politics, such as assimilation-secession, inside-outside" (21). Weaver's hermeneutical sovereignty, too, can be sought in the "third space" that Bhabha proposes exists in the midst of such ambivalent cultural contexts. Bhabha's postcolonial theories may not have an actual political effect on the colonial situation of Native North Americans, but he provides a framework that moves beyond the oppositional structures of colonialism.

Despite King's rejection of postcolonialism in his critical work, Christie notes that King's fiction is highly illustrative of the transnational, plural identity of Native North Americans that is often associated with a postcolonial framework. Christie comments that King's writing is a "two-way portal" that forces the reader into "keeping an eye on both traditions at one and the same time— the sovereign and the colonial—and watching how and when they engage or turn away from each other" (214). Moreover, he sees King's work as "North American in scope" (179) in that he is "playing plural sovereignties off against one another" (181) as a form of anti-colonial resistance. Christie's analysis is best illustrated in relation to King's *Truth & Bright Water,* in which the protagonists move from Truth to Bright Water, crossing a river, delineating the border, in a bucket known as "the toilet" (42). This improvised border crossing is complex in transnational terms, for it is also a move from Canada to America, from rural reserve land to urban setting. The narrator Tecumseh takes another step toward maturity and understanding with every crossing he makes to the reserve and to his grandmother's house, although, as he comments, "except for Indian Days, there's no particular reason to go from the town to the reserve" (42). In other words, the rare crossing of the river is symbolic of the connection of the Native North American inhabitants of Truth to their traditions and to their extended families, indicating a compartmentalization of that part of their identity away from their everyday urban existence. King's novel thereby illustrates the uneasy balance of such plural sovereignty, which can accurately be described as ambivalent. The uncertainty created by the move from one national context to another creates a possibility for negotiating ideologies in both contexts. Tecumseh is able to reassess his life and grow toward maturity by the movement and distance created from one side of the border to the other.

In contrast, another "border writer," the American-born Chippewa Gerald Vizenor, embraces postcolonial (and other) theoretical writing. Vizenor's highly complex writing is particularly applicable when we consider the terms of Bhabha's discourse of the "third space" of "in-betweenness." Bhabha's analysis is based on the situation of migrant peoples; even so, the effect on Native North Americans of living on a borderland and in a transnational context of plural sovereignty (whether real or conceptual) makes his theories pertinent. In Vizenor's *The Heirs of Columbus,* the Santa Maria Casino boat moored on the international border between Canada and the United States becomes a "third space" of resistance between two states, with a status that is neither fully sovereign nor part of the larger nation-state. The local radio station finds a new audience when broadcasting shows from the boat, leading the local populace to conclude that the Santa Maria is a "new world" (9). In Bhabha's terms, it is a space in between two systems, one that has radical possibilities, where the new is made by creating a place that is neither one thing nor another but rather is a place of newness and negotiation. In terms of sovereignty, the dispute over the Santa Maria between state and federal governments reveals the problems generated by the inconsistencies of sovereignty recognized by the United States. When the state arrests Stone Columbus for running a casino on the boat, the federal judge deems it against his sovereign right as the inhabitant of a reservation—the boat itself has become a Native American nation of its own. As the novel declares, "sovereignty is neither fence nor feathers" but is "imaginative" (Vizenor 7). In this new third space that Stone Columbus creates, he begins to reinvent the world, adjusting and revealing all previously held assumptions. Stone Columbus begins by telling the people that Columbus was a Mayan who took all things civilized to Europe: "The Maya brought civilization to the savages of the Old World" (Vizenor 9).

Vizenor's novel is clearly based on the creation of casinos on Native American reservation land in the United States, which is encouraged by legal precedent in federal law. Bruyneel identifies this as a form of decolonization as set out in Deloria's *Custer Died for Your Sins* (1969), stating that "Deloria could not foresee that in the late twentieth century tribes would turn their 'knowledge of modern economic mores' and 'understanding of the strengths of tribal society' into, in some cases, vibrant casino-based political economies" (169). I would add that this can be interpreted as an enactment of an innovation created in the "third space" of plural sovereignty—in between a Native American nation sovereign to itself and the imposed sovereignty of the federal United States. It is only due to the unique political and legal situation of Native American nations, which allows such a different economic basis from other parts of the United States to develop.

In his analysis of Thomas King's resistance to postcolonialism, Gerry Turcotte underscores that postcolonialism must be wary of "speaking *for* indigenous peoples, for establishing its own empire, and perhaps even for scripting what it believes is *the* appropriate revolutionary strategy for the disempowered or the disenfranchised" (208). The point that Weaver, Christie, Pulitano and Bruyneel agree upon is that to base Native American hermeneutics on a Native American discourse that rejects international postcolonial (or other forms of) criticism and theory is to limit traditional Native American cultural inclusivity and useful transnational comparison. Turcotte's article, by taking the argument into the borderlands between the United States and Canada, reveals, in common with critics such as Weaver, Bruyneel, and Christie, the possibility of creating a discursive position to express and understand the dual-faceted ambivalence of the border, and thus reimagining strategies of decolonization and Native North American sovereignty, by bringing together specific Native American and international postcolonial discourses. Weaver (among others) does this with wariness of the threat to cultural specificity that he perceives in the discourse of hybridity, associated with Bhabha's theories of migrancy. However, the comparative study of the postcolonial situation on either side of the US–Canada border is necessary to provide a thorough understanding of the reasons for resisting postcolonial theory among some Native North American critics. It appears that due to the self-awareness of Canada as a nation of its postmodern postcolonial status, Native American writers in Canada have a more complex postcolonial field to negotiate, making the adoption of post-colonial theory more fraught but, I would counter, all the more useful where the very process of the interrogation of its applicability hones and adapts it to changing contexts.

Works Cited

Atwood, Margaret. *Surfacing*. 1972. London: Virago, 1979.

———. *Survival: A Thematic Guide to Canadian Literature*. 1972. Toronto: McClelland & Stewart, 1996.

Bhabha, Homi K. *The Location of Culture*. London: Routledge, 1994.

Biolsi, Thomas. *Deadliest Enemies: Law and Race Relations On and Off Rosebud Reservation*. 2nd ed. Minneapolis: U of Minnesota P, 2007.

Bruyneel, Kevin. *The Third Space of Sovereignty: The Postcolonial Politics of U.S.–Indigenous Relations*. Minneapolis: U of Minnesota P, 2007.

Christie, Stuart. *Plural Sovereignties and Contemporary Indigenous Literature*. New York: Palgrave Macmillan, 2009.

Cook-Lynn, Elizabeth. "Who Stole Native American Studies?" *Wicazo Sa Review* 12.1 (1997): 9–28.

———. *New Indians, Old Wars*. Urbana: U of Illinois P, 2007.

Deloria Jr., Vine. *Custer Died for Your Sins: An Indian Manifesto*. New York: Macmillan, 1969.

D'Errico, Peter. "American Indian Sovereignty: Now You See It, Now You Don't." *American Indian Rhetorics of Survivance: Word Medicine, Word Magic*. Ed. Ernest Stromberg. Pittsburgh: U of Pittsburgh P, 2006. 238–55.

Hutcheon, Linda. *The Canadian Postmodern: A Study of Contemporary English-Canadian Fiction*. Toronto: Oxford UP, 1988.

———. *Incredulity Toward Metanarrative: Negotiating Postmodernism and Feminisms*. Toronto: Second Story Press, 1994.

———. *Splitting Images: Contemporary Canadian Ironies*. Toronto: Oxford UP, 1991.

Jay, Gregory. *American Literature and the Culture Wars*. Ithaca: Cornell UP, 1997.

Kalant, Amelia. *National Identity and the Conflict at Oka: Native Belonging and Myths of Postcolonial Nationhood in Canada*. New York: Routledge, 2004.

Kroetsch, Robert. *Completed Field Notes: The Long Poems of Robert Kroetsch*, Edmonton: U Alberta P, 2000.

King, Thomas. "Godzilla vs. Post-Colonial." *World Literature Written in English* 30.2 (1990): 10–16.

———. *Green Grass, Running Water*. Toronto: HarperPerennial, 1993.

————. *Truth & Bright Water*. New York: Grove, 1999.

Moss, Laura, ed. *Is Canada Postcolonial? Unsettling Canadian Literature*. Waterloo: Wilfrid Laurier UP, 2003.

Owens, Louis. *Mixedblood Messages: Literature, Film, Family, Place*. Norman: U of Oklahoma P, 1998.

Pulitano, Elvira. *Toward a Native American Critical Theory*. Lincoln: U of Nebraska P, 2003.

Shohat, Ella. "Notes on the 'Post-Colonial.'" *Contemporary Postcolonial Theory: A Reader*. Ed. Padmini Mongia. London: Arnold, 1996. 321–34.

Singh, Amritjit, and Michael Schmidt, eds. *Postcolonial Theory and the United States: Race, Ethnicity, and Literature*. Jackson: U of Mississippi P, 2000.

Spivak, Gayatri Chakravorty. *Death of a Discipline*. New York: Columbia UP, 2003.

Turcotte, Gerry. "Re-Marking on History, or, Playing Basketball with Godzilla: Thomas King's Monstrous Post-Colonial Gesture." *Connections: Non-Native Responses to Native Canadian Literature*. Ed. H. Lutz and C. Vevaina. New Delhi: Creative Books, 2003. 205–35.

Weaver, Jace. *Notes from a Miner's Canary: Essays on the State of Native America*. Albuquerque: U of New Mexico P, 2010.

————. *Other Words: American Indian Literature, Law, and Culture*. Norman: U of Oklahoma P, 2001.

————. *That the People Might Live: Native American Literature and Native American Community*. New York: Oxford UP, 1997.

Weaver, Jace, Craig S. Womack, and Robert Warrior. *American Indian Literary Nationalism*. Albuquerque: U of New Mexico P, 2006.

Vizenor, Gerald. *The Heirs of Columbus*. Hanover: Wesleyan UP, 1991.

eight

Strategic Parallels

Invoking the Border in Thomas King's *Green Grass, Running Water* and Drew Hayden Taylor's *In a World Created by a Drunken God*

Gillian Roberts

IN "GRAY ZONE," EPISODE 2 of the first season of CBC's *The Border*, Canadian Immigration and Customs Security (ICS) agents clash with US Homeland Security's Bianca LaGarda over how to approach a case unfolding on Mohawk territory. "This stretch of the river is a black hole of border policing," LaGarda complains, only to have the Canadian Major Kessler inform her: "Jurisdiction is complicated. We're trespassing on Mohawk land now." "Gray Zone," a pivotal episode in the series, introduces a feminized, exoticized figure of US military might—"Mine's bigger than yours," LaGarda tells Kessler. "Get used to it"— and plays out its distinction between Canadian and American values against a Mohawk backdrop. Although Mohawk territory straddles the Canada–US border, Kessler and his crew have to educate the American LaGarda on how to treat the Mohawk respectfully. She claims, "It's bad enough the Natives run contraband with impunity," then finds herself speaking in the wrong discourse, and corrects herself in front of the Canadians: "OK ... exercise their cross-border treaty rights." That LaGarda should, albeit sarcastically, rearticulate Native cross-border activity in front of her Canadian company (none of whom are Indigenous) suggests that unlike its neighbour to the south, Canada respects the distinction between contraband and treaty rights. After all, Canadians have had to learn the hard way, Kessler intimates. The spectre of the Oka Crisis shadows his threat to LaGarda, after she announces that she will send US federal agents onto the Seaway Reserve: "If you wanna piss off the Mohawks," Kessler warns, "you do it on your side of the border. You can deal with the armed warriors and the blockaded expressway." During a telephone conversation, Mohawk policeman Frank Arthur, consenting to the presence of two undercover agents on the reserve, listens as LaGarda undermines Kessler concerning the agents' time of arrival. "Last I heard," Arthur comments, "this was Canada." LaGarda retorts, "Mohawks either recognize the border, or they don't. You can't have it both ways."

Although the Mohawk should not be taken as a kind of template for all Indigenous nations, and while there is much to debate about *The Border*'s representations of the Mohawk and of Canadian and US attitudes toward Indigenous peoples, LaGarda's statement regarding the border—"You can't have it both ways"—can be fruitfully assessed in relation to moments of multiple and (from some perspectives) incommensurate assertions of identity in cross-border texts by Thomas King and Drew Hayden Taylor. In *Green Grass, Running Water* (1993) and *In a World Created by a Drunken God* (2006), Native characters strategically deploy Canadian identities in order to resist various threats posed by American characters. These works thereby thematize debates in recent years regarding Canadian citizenship in relation to the First Nations, with some scholars arguing that nation-state citizenship is not desirable for Indigenous peoples and others indicating that, regardless of LaGarda's claim, it is indeed possible to "have it both ways." In King's and Taylor's texts, the border is physically crossed by individual characters, but it is also invoked at particular moments in order to distinguish between Canada and the United States. These distinctions need to be made meaningful, if only provisionally, for *Green Grass, Running Water*'s Latisha and *In a World Created by a Drunken God*'s Jason. Latisha's and Jason's complicated claims to Canadian identity navigate through the Euro-Canadian colonization of the First Nations and the US neo-colonization of Canada. If nation-state borders "figure as occasions to imagine, often aggressively, fixed and unrelenting standards of citizenship and belonging" (Castronovo 196), the implications of the Canada–US border and nation-state citizenship for Native North Americans arise in both King's and Taylor's narratives.

As Darlene Johnston writes, "The very word [citizenship] conjures up notions of freedom and autonomy, the right to participate, a sense of belonging"; but if "[t]he Western political tradition regards the evolution of citizenship as its crowning democratic achievement … for the First Nations over whom Canada asserts jurisdiction, the experience of Canadian citizenship has been somewhat less than ennobling" (349). The history of Canadian citizenship in relation to Indigenous peoples demonstrates how "citizenship can … function not only through the violence of exclusion, but by inclusion" as well (Chariandy and McCall 5). The Canadian state has long attempted to employ citizenship to strip Indigenous people of their culture and community through enfranchisement, beginning with the 1857 Act to Encourage the Gradual Civilization of the Indian Tribes in this Province, which stipulated that "all enactments making any distinction between the legal rights and abilities of the Indians and those of Her Majesty's other subjects, shall cease to apply to any Indian so declared to be enfranchised, who shall no longer be deemed an Indian within the meaning thereof" (qtd. in Johnston 354). Although "[t]his is hardly a decision that the province was entitled to make[,] [it] was the price to pay for the 'privilege' of British colonial citizenship" (Johnston 354). The next century saw a series of variations on the Canadian state's policy regarding criteria for the enfranchisement of First Nations people, as well as periods of time when enfranchisement was compulsory, especially for educated Native individuals such as doctors, lawyers, and clergymen. This reflected the government's assumption that most Indigenous people were "socially, linguistically, and economically incompetent to exercise full citizenship rights and duties" (Battiste and Semaganis 104); as Johnston writes, "it seems that, for the legislators, a well-educated Indian was a contradiction in terms" (361). The Canadian state attempted to make enfranchisement easier and more attractive for Native men, yet between 1857 and 1920 there were only 102 cases of enfranchisement, confounding the government's attempt to rid itself of what it called "the Indian problem." On the whole, enfranchisement would never be appealing to the vast majority of First Nations people, as "continued membership in their own communities was inconsistent with participation in Canadian society; ... they could only have a place in Canada if they renounced their heritage and denied their identity" (363).

Canadian citizenship, in this sense, represents an imposition of "the colonial paradigm" (Battiste and Semaganis 93) as well as an attack on First Nations sovereignty.[1] As Dale Turner notes, the colonial implications of Canadian citizenship continued as part of the liberal nation-state project through the Trudeau government's White Paper (1969), which sought to dismantle Indian status, reflecting the government's desire to "get out of the Indian business" (16) by absolving themselves of responsibility towards First Nations people. The White Paper envisioned that "Indians were to be 'welcomed' into mainstream Canadian society, complete with all its opportunities and benefits of citizenship, and the federal government would facilitate (and celebrate) the necessary institutional processes to make that happen" (16). That being so, the imperatives of the liberal nation-state with regard to equality represent a failure to account for group rights or to engage actively in decolonization. In "making individual citizenship the fundamental unit of political allegiance," the White Paper was an attempt to ensure that "the problem of recognizing special group rights [would] not arise" (31). It was also an attempt to erase distinctions between citizens in a way that would impede decolonization, for "[w]ithin liberal rights discourse, responsibility for historical injustices like those emerging from colonialism cannot be levelled at the beneficiaries of colonial history because all citizens are essentially equal and therefore blameless—neither victims nor victors" (McKegney 63).

The Canada–US border testifies to colonial history in that it cuts across tribal lands. It also acts as a reminder that nation-state citizenship is not simply a straightforward guarantee of rights, but also, in the context of Native peoples, part of an imposed colonial political system in which "Aboriginal people have been forced to accept the 'gift' of Canadian citizenship at the same time that they are expected to relinquish their Aboriginal rights" (Chariandy and McCall 7).

Where white Anglo-Canadians see a kind of cultural defence of the Canada–US border as paramount to their sovereignty, First Nations sovereignty does not depend on the border; indeed, the border represents the nation-states against which First Nations sovereignty must be exercised. As Donald A. Grinde, Jr., writes, "indigenous people's disregard for national borders expresses itself in their continuing attachment to a nation that is rooted in a particular place and in struggles for sovereignty from the nation-state and its political boundaries" (167). Thomas King's work often engages with the border and its irrelevance to Native North American peoples. In his short story "Borders" (1993), for instance, the protagonist and his mother become temporarily trapped in the border zone between Canada and the United States because the boy's mother, when asked by the border guard to designate her citizenship as either American or Canadian, responds that she is Blackfoot (137). As Arnold E. Davidson, Priscilla L. Walton, and Jennifer Andrews point out, in the late nineteenth century the border was used deliberately to divide the Blackfoot community: Commissioner Steele of the North-West Mounted Police believed that the "Canadian Blackfoot ... would be more manageable if they could not mingle freely with their American confederates, and so a strip of land on the southern side of the promised reserve ... was confiscated and made available for non-Native settlement" (124). The mother in King's story, therefore, refuses to be "manageable," and aligns herself with her own conception of nation, not with the Euro-North American nation-states that the border guards insists are her only legitimate options.

King returns to the border's capacity to divide a community in his novel *Truth & Bright Water* (1999). "Truth and Bright Water sit on opposite sides of the river, the railroad town on the American side, the reserve in Canada" (1), but as the novel's title suggests, the town and the reserve operate less in opposition with, and more in connection to, each other. The narrator Tecumseh and his mother live in Truth, but the implication in much of the novel is that these two locations cannot be separated from each other, even though the border runs between them. Indeed, King emphasizes a prehistoric coherence to this divided community when he states that "the whole area around Truth and Bright Water is full of dinosaur bones" (71). That more recent human history has ruptured this coherence becomes evident when the character Monroe Swimmer explicitly condemns the distinction drawn by the border. He "walks to the lip of the coulee and looks out across the river. 'There's Canada,' he says. Then he turns and spreads his arms. 'And this is the United States.' He spins around in a full circle, stumbles, and goes down in a heap. 'Ridiculous, isn't it?'" (131). Even more ridiculous is the description of the border running through Waterton Lake, as King illustrates the incongruity of a static nation-state marker bisecting a dynamic element:

> The cruise around the lake was interesting, and if I hadn't gone, I would never have known that the Canada/United States border ran right through the middle of the lake. When the guy driving the boat told us that, I expected to see a floating fence or inner tubes with barbed wire and lights, something to keep people from straying from one country into the other. There was a cutline in the trees along with border posts on opposite sides of the shore, and a small border station, to mark the line. (78)

There may not be a floating fence, but border crossing presents difficulties for this community. Tecumseh and his mother, without a car to drive to the Prairie View crossing, use "Charlie Ron's ferry, an old iron bucket suspended on a cable over the Shield" (42), bypassing the policed border altogether through direct crossing. There is also an unfinished bridge that was intended to connect Truth and Bright Water, although in its abandoned state, it is only a fractured link, as attested to by "the deserted columns" and "the open planking and the rusting webs of iron mesh" (1). As Davidson, Walton, and Andrews note, the bridge's description illustrates the border's "porousness" (142); but the bridge is also, as Robin Ridington points out, "a barrier" (290), and furthermore, a site of danger. When one child gets caught in the bridge, it requires Truth's fire department to rescue him. The bridge is also the site of Tecumseh's cousin Lum's suicide when he runs off the end of it. The bridge's abandonment brings physical, and fatal, danger to the divided community; it is "nothing more than a skeleton, the carcass of an enormous animal, picked to the bone" (256). Although this metaphor suggests an aesthetic alliance between the bridge and the prehistoric dinosaur bones of the region, the bridge's border location also signifies something more akin to the "open wound" of the US–Mexico border, as Gloria Anzaldúa has described it (25), than the standard image of peaceful, painless crossings at the 49th parallel.

But where *Truth & Bright Water* offers only a painful division between nation-states for the community it portrays, King's earlier novel *Green Grass, Running Water* (1993) offers a somewhat more complicated construction of the border. On the one hand, the sense of the border's irrelevance to Native North American peoples is clear when "Lionel Red Dog, Canadian citizen, government employee, and status Blackfoot Indian" (59), inadvertently gets caught up in American Indian Movement activities south of the border. His somewhat hapless protest, "I'm from Canada" (59), repeatedly falls on deaf ears when he is in the company of Native American members of AIM. Margery Fee and Jane Flick argue that the border is to blame for Lionel's ignorance: "Borders make us stupid and allow us to remain so if we let them"; Lionel's insistence that he is Canadian in response to AIM members' references to US history "is not so much an explanation of his ignorance as a defence of it" (132). Nation-state citizenship only matters to the white judge at Lionel's arraignment for his unpaid hotel bill (caused by his involuntary participation in AIM): "The judge gave Lionel thirty days ... 'Seeing as you're Canadian, I'll reduce it to ten days,' the judge told him" (63). Of course, Lionel, too, has used the border to distance himself from AIM, but much of Lionel's narrative focuses on his willingness to be co-opted by white society. Not only has he held a government position, but also, having lost his job after the mix-up with AIM, he works in a dead-end job for an ignorant white character who sells electronics. That his bosses in these two positions are named Duncan Scott (after Canadian poet and Deputy Superintendent of Indian Affairs Duncan Campbell Scott) and Bill Bursum (after the 1921 Bursum Bill in the United States), respectively, underscores his submission to Euro-North American governments and their attempts to legislate Native assimilation into the dominant culture and to facilitate the appropriation of Native lands by settler-invaders. Thus, Lionel's "defence" of himself as Canadian in the context of AIM comes across as part of his weakness and as suggesting that "he wants to be white" (Fee and Flick 132). The Canadian state itself is rendered suspect in the novel through references to the White Paper (*Green Grass* 271) and the narrative of Amos's family being mistreated by US border guards, followed by the hypocrisy of Canada's response regarding "the abuses that Canadian citizens had to suffer at the hands of Americans" and the insistence that "[t]he government of Canada has always had the greatest respect for our Aboriginal peoples and will continue to provide them with the same protections that every Canadian enjoys" (281).

On the other hand, the chapter focusing on the personal history of Lionel's sister, Latisha, articulates Canadianness in a very different and more complicated context, through her marriage to the white American George Morningstar. As Davidson, Walton, and Andrews note, the relationship between Latisha and George (himself an incarnation of Custer [*Green Grass* 384]) "encompasses both cultural imperialism and sexual dominance" (72). This imperialist and sexual dominance is seen in George's physical abuse of Latisha and in his insistence on American superiority over Canadians:

> "Americans are independent ... Canadians are dependent."
> Latisha told him she didn't think that he could make such a sweeping statement, that those kinds of generalizations were almost always false.
> "It's all observation, Country ... [T]he United States is an independent sovereign nation and Canada is a domestic dependent nation. Put fifty Canadians in a room with one American, and the American will be in charge in no time."
> George didn't say it with any pride, particularly. It was, for him, a statement of fact, an unassailable truth, a matter akin to genetics or instinct. (156)

"Country" is George's nickname for his wife, "a term of endearment that under-lines his perception of her as the embodiment of a land mass that needs to be dominated" (Davidson, Walton, and Andrews 165): for George, Latisha *becomes* Canada, the dependent, unconfident one in their "partnership." After the birth of their first child, George's comparisons accelerate, becoming increasingly "absurd": not only does the United States have "more" of everything (e.g., doc-tors, lawyers, motels, highways, universities, wars), but George also insists that

> Americans liked adventure and challenge. Canadians liked order and guarantees.
> "When a cop pulls a Canadian over for speeding on an open road with no other car in sight, the Canadian is happy. I've even seen them thank the cop for being so alert ..."
> In the end, simple avoidance proved to be the easiest course, and whenever George started to warm up, Latisha would take Christian into the bedroom and nurse him. There, in the warm darkness, she would stroke her son's head and whisper ferociously over and over again until it became a chant, a mantra, "You are a Canadian. You are a Canadian. You are a Canadian." (158)

In keeping with his own stereotype about Americans, George privileges con-flict by insisting on US dominance, while Latisha's tactic is "simple avoidance." But where George valorizes the qualities he identifies as American, Latisha insists on naming her child as a Canadian, thereby reversing George's infusion of Americanness with value and Canadianness with a lack thereof: "You are Canadian" acts as a soothing promise, a private comfort to counteract George's claims of dominance. As Davidson, Walton, and Andrews argue, however, "by situating her children within the recognized framework of the nation-state, Latisha may be in a better position to argue with George, but in doing so, she also systematically ignores a legitimate ... alternative: aligning herself and her children with a tribal community" (166). In this way, Latisha reinforces the Canada–US border in the context of her marriage, privileging the nation-state as the basis of identity. She does not claim that, as a Blackfoot, she stands outside the logic of the nation-states that her husband seeks to differentiate.

Drew Hayden Taylor's *In a World Created By a Drunken God* also presents a Native character based in Canada in opposition to a white American charac-ter. Jason Pierce, packing up his Toronto apartment in order to move home to his reserve, receives an unexpected guest in the form of Harry Dieter, a white man from Rhode Island claiming to be his half-brother, the son of a white father that Jason has never met. This father needs a kidney transplant, hence Harry's impromptu visit across the border. Much of the play's dramatic tension stems from the audacity of Harry's request (as Jason sees it) and Jason's refusal to entertain the possibility of saving his father's life (as Harry sees it). Jason articulates his opposition to Harry through a number of binaries, including legitimate versus illegitimate and Native versus white. Jason insists on their differences partly in response to Harry's ignorance and partly, no doubt, to make those differences seem resolutely unbridgeable in order to reduce Harry's claim on him. Jason says, "You've taken our language, our land, our culture, but I'm not letting you have my kidney. An Indian has to draw the line somewhere" (39). Here, the "you" surely refers to Euro-North Americans, that "line" drawn on the basis of race. But Jason also constructs the opposition between himself and his half-brother along national lines. The narrative of his parents' relationship reflects a kind of double colonization, wherein Canada features as a feminized, disempowered partner in relation to the United States. That Jason's father "met his mother when he was hunting up here in Ontario" (27) resonates with Edmund Wilson's description of Canada as "a kind of vast hunting preserve convenient to the United States" (qtd. in Atwood 16). Jason suggests his father was not merely hunting game north of the border.

In response to his half-brother's claims, Jason works to assert some Canadian cultural power. Attempting to prove his family credentials to Jason, Harry recites the following details: "Your mother's name is Harriet Pierce. She'd be almost sixty now. Your reservation is about three hours due north of here. And your father was not an Indian. He was an American." Jason responds, after a pause: "First of all, Harry, Harry Dieter, it's called a *reserve* up here in Canada. And we're called First Nations, not Indians" (17). In presenting a Canadian correction of Harry's terms, Jason is responding as a Native man *and* a Canadian, thus positioning himself as a Native Canadian by insisting that he is a First Nations person from a reserve. Harry's response, "That's all you have to say?" (17), both expresses his incredulity at Jason's failure or refusal to appreciate the significance of his visit and gestures toward the troubling status of the differences between Canada and the United States—that is, whether they are different *enough* to sustain Canadian distinctiveness. From Harry's perspective, "First Nations" and "reserve" are exasperating cases of what Lorraine Code has described as "mere variations in cultural *timbre*, inflection, intonation" (82) in distinctions between Canadian and US culture.

In his attempt to outmanoeuvre Harry, Jason quickly and quite literally changes the terms of the discussion:

> Jason: The thing is, I'm kinda partial to my bodily organs, and I don't just go around sharing them with strangers. I don't know anything about him. Or about you. Or about the wonderful state of Rhode Island. I'm just a poor Canadian Indian.
>
> Harry: I thought you said you were called First Nations up here.
>
> Jason: First thing to know about Canadian First Nations people is we hate being corrected. What I call myself is none of your business. (30)

Jason's rejoinder to Harry's attempt to correct him functions, on one level, as an attempted assertion of cultural power, one that emphasizes difference in order to diminish Harry's significance to him. But Harry also misses Jason's irony, and the extent to which Jason may be responding to Harry's interpellation of him, after the Harry hails him as "a poor Canadian Indian." Jason consents to this only ironically, by ventriloquizing his half-brother and naming himself as such.

Harry is not a wholly unsympathetic character, but the fact that he is a white American rather than a white Canadian is significant. Harry's national identity positions Jason, like Latisha, as doubly colonized. Taylor has certainly represented the ignorance of white *Canadian* characters before—for example, in *alterNatives* (2000), which indicts the lack of knowledge of a white Canadian professor of Native literature; and he has responded to white Canadian ignorance—and indeed, the problem of what constitutes Canada in the first place—in his essays. In reference to debates about residential schools in Canada, Taylor writes:

> David Frum, a columnist for the National Post [sic], is quoted as saying he has some difficulty believing that "teaching native children to speak English and adapt to Canadian ways constituted an act of 'cultural genocide.'" It is if you're not Canadian and speak a language far older and richer than English, and were here centuries before most columnist's [sic] immigrant ancestors got lost trying to find China looking for oregano, paprika and pepper, and ended up bastardizing an Iroquoian word meaning "a small village or group of huts" into a word called Canada which now has a popular ginger ale and beer named after it. (*Furious* 19)

Here, Canada is a debased concept, commodified, and irrelevant to Indigenous peoples. Elsewhere, Taylor insists that Native North Americans "don't recognize the imaginary dotted line that separates the Maple Leaf from the Stars and Stripes" (*Funny* 43). Yet Jason takes that imaginary dotted line and uses it to defend himself against the claims of his American half-brother. Harry gains some credibility by demonstrating knowledge of Canadian hockey history (identifying Tim Horton as a former Toronto Maple Leafs player rather than with the coffee and doughnuts of the franchise that bears his name: "You know that?" Jason asks. "How do you know that? Most Canadians don't remember that" [116]). But otherwise, Jason aligns Harry with aspects of the United States that most Canadians are determined to resist: "Manifest Destiny is your bag" (71). In response to Harry's presentation of himself as a decent person on the grounds that he raises money for hospitals, Jason counters: "You can keep your American hospitals because, from what I hear, only the rich can afford to use a hospital down there" (116). Here he invokes Canada's universal health care policy, which, as Jan Clarke's essay in this volume illustrates, is commonly identified within Canada as one of the most meaningful distinctions between us and our southern neighbour.

We might identify interpellation as integral to self-identification as Canadian for both Latisha and Jason. On the one hand, Latisha seems to distance herself from Canadianness in the context of the Dead Dog Cafe, where she and her co-workers identify the nationality of tourists through their stereotypical behaviour:

> As the people got off the bus, Latisha could see that they all had name tags neatly pasted to their chests. They filed off the bus in an orderly line and stood in front of the restaurant and waited until they were all together. Then, in unison, they walked two abreast to the front door, each couple keeping pace with the couple in front of them.
> "Canadian," Latisha shouted. (*Green Grass* 155)

But at the same time, the descriptions of the café and Latisha's interactions with customers (including "Polly" Johnson, who leaves Latisha a twenty-dollar tip under a copy of *The Shagganappi* [159]) are interspersed with the narrative of Latisha's marriage. Perhaps Latisha responds to George as a Canadian precisely because he *insists* she is Canadian, and his nickname for her, "Country," makes this "hailing" explicit: George does not allow her to conceive of herself outside the framework of the nation-state, and her resistance to his hailing of her is both to argue against his generalizations and to infuse Canadianness with value, even as Canadians appear as targets of ridicule at the Dead Dog Cafe. Similarly, Jason's self-identification fluctuates, but in relation to his American half-brother, he positions himself as a Canadian. To a certain extent, Latisha and Jason respond as Canadians *because of* their relationships to Americans, but also because these relationships, albeit for different reasons, pose threats to the Native characters. Latisha attempts to prove George wrong about his stereotypical generalizations (and tells her employee, Billy, "You sound like George," [159] when he expresses relief that not all their customers are Canadian), and Jason attempts to underscore a stereotypically American ignorance about Canada in his half-brother. For instance, Harry mistakes a parodic Canadian flag bearing a cannabis leaf as the actual Canadian flag; Jason also emphasizes the linguistic difference between Canada and the United States by saying, "*c'est la vie* ... That's French, we have two official languages in Canada." When Jason tries to offer a translation of "c'est la vie," Harry interrupts him: "I'm familiar with the term" (35), potentially embarrassing Jason by pointing out that he has overestimated Harry's ignorance, but, significantly, not indicating that he actually knows about Canada's official bilingualism.

Although Davidson, Walton, and Andrews argue that *Green Grass, Running Water*'s Latisha ultimately recalibrates her self-identification in favour of Blackfoot over nation-state affiliation when she stands up to George at the Sun Dance, supported by her relatives and a larger Blackfoot community (73), it is difficult to return all the elements of nation-state differentiation to the idea of the border's irrelevance to Native North American peoples. After all, Latisha could have had an abusive white *Canadian* husband; and Jason's white half-brother asking for a kidney could have been Canadian. Cultural dominance and colonial relationships would still be integral to the narratives. We might argue that the Americans George and Harry add another layer of dominance because of the United States' status as the world's only superpower; but their Americanness also inserts Canadianness as a point of identification for both Latisha and Jason.

It may be that Canadian readers and viewers of King's novel and Taylor's play are let off the hook to a certain extent, given that our recognition of US imperialism is indulged through Latisha's and Jason's resistance to George and Harry. Ultimately, however, neither text completely resolves the tension between nation-state and Indigenous identity. Rather, this lack of resolution may thematize debates about identity strategies, especially since Latisha and Jason's articulations of Canadianness seem to be strategic. In this sense, these texts invoke debates about citizenship—as represented explicitly in King's novel through through the abuse Amos suffers while he is crossing the border—through their questions about the imposition of identity versus the potential claims that might be made on the nation-state through the status of citizenship.

Many scholars have addressed the multiple affiliations that might be claimed by First Nations people, assessing the most effective strategies and most promising conceptions of citizenship. Since the rejection of the White Paper, Aboriginal rights (rights that Trudeau stated in 1969 "[t]he federal government [was] not prepared to guarantee" [qtd. in Cardinal 28]) have often been framed in terms of a nation-to-nation relationship. The Assembly of First Nations has argued that First Nations people "are, first and foremost, citizens in their First Nations. Their primary relationship with the federal government, with Canada, is as part of these First Nations" (Cassidy and Bish 56). The report of the Royal Commission on Aboriginal Peoples (1996) also deployed a nation-to-nation framework, one that has attracted the criticism of political scientist Alan C. Cairns: "the RCAP reiteration of nation-to-nation as the lens for viewing Aboriginal/non-Aboriginal relations inevitably conjures up images of a mini-international system and weakens the idea of a common citizenship" (7). Cairns views a common citizenship as a necessary link between Indigenous and non-Indigenous communities in Canada; he advocates a Citizens Plus status for Indigenous peoples along the lines of the Hawthorn Report (1966–67), of which Cairns was one of the authors. Rejected by Trudeau in favour of the White Paper's approach, the Hawthorn Report argued that a Citizens Plus status would encapsulate

> ongoing entitlements, some of which flowed from existing treaties, while others were to be worked out in the political processes of the future,

> which would identify the Indian peoples as deserving possessors of an
> additional category of rights based on a historical priority. In other words,
> we sought to preserve Indian "difference" while simultaneously support-
> ing a common citizenship as a basis for empathy and solidarity between
> the Indian people and the majority population. (Cairns 12)

Alarmed by the political capital of the nation-to-nation framework, while also
arguing against an assimilationist approach, Cairns argues that

> [w]hat is missing, or inadequately represented, is analysis of the middle
> ground that simultaneously recognizes both Aboriginal difference *and*
> the need for connection to, involvement with, and participation in the
> Canadian community. How can Aboriginal peoples be Canadian, and
> how can Canadians be Aboriginal? The task is to recognize two overlap-
> ping communities and identities. At base, the issue is citizenship. (85)

It is unclear how Cairns's concern for what Indigenous peoples and Canadians share as common citizens works effectively toward a just decolonization.
Cairns's argument implies that "common citizenship mysteriously trumps Canada's colonial past" (Turner 42), particularly given that Cairns's priority is to
leave the state intact, with limited Indigenous self-government embedded in
it, and with its rights and powers bestowed and protected by Canadian state.
In this way, "the Citizens Plus view remains committed to the White Paper liberalism's idea that the sovereignty of the Canadian state is non-negotiable,
and therefore would silence Aboriginal voices that defend various forms of
indigenous nationhood" (39). Cairns argues that although "Aboriginal peoples
seek nation-to-nation political relations [but] these cannot be achieved simply
by representation in Canadian political institutions" (144). But decolonization
is never simple, and Cairns limits his analysis to what is possible under current state configurations. Thus, Cairns's Citizens Plus solution not only fails to
address the question of "what is there in this polity that is supposed to attract
the attention and loyalty of those whose values and ideals as embodied in
culture it ruthlessly, relentlessly attacks?" (Kulchyski 250), but also, ultimately,
is "Eurocentric and unimaginative" (Warry 57). If Cairns blames "[t]he relative
unwillingness of many status Indians to identify themselves as Canadian citizens" on the state's "past policies when citizenship was equated with assimilation and the loss of Indian status" (87), suggesting that this resistance is now
outdated, his adherence to the Hawthorn Report's conception of citizenship
does not address the fact that Citizens Plus has "since been surpassed by a
more layered understanding of Aboriginal rights and citizenship" (Warry 46).
In relation to Indigenous self-government, Kulchyski writes that "the State can
be defined as a certain kind of writing. The State will not address Aboriginal
people until they learn this writing, this form. Negotiation, indeed discussion,
cannot proceed without it. But learning this form of writing means engaging

in the logic of the dominant order: a paradox. A precondition for playing the game is surrender" (17). In relation to the interpellation of Indigenous peoples as citizens, then, the state's writing, the writing that is the state, is predicated on their consent to the state and its power in the first place. If playing the game is always already to surrender, nation-state citizenship and Latisha's and Jason's strategies of identification with Canada may themselves be acts of surrender.

But although there are clear reasons for "the ambivalence and resistance that First Nations display toward Canadian citizenship" (Johnston 394), there is no clear consensus about the compatibility of Indigenous and Canadian allegiances. Taiaiake Alfred insists that nation-state citizenship is an example of "[t]he state's power ... [that] must be eradicated from politics in Native communities" (Peace 11); in the context of his own Kahnawake community, he argues that they are "citizens of another nation" (Heeding 104). However, Alfred acknowledges that not all Indigenous communities share this position, and that while in his view it is based on a false consciousness, "a lot of our Native people imagine themselves to be Canadians" (Peace 137–38, 19). In response to Cairns's advocation of Citizens Plus," Dale Turner argues: "No doubt, many if not most Aboriginal people see themselves as Canadian citizens, but many see themselves as citizens of an Indigenous nation in addition to (and often prior to) being citizens of Canada. In other words, Aboriginal political identities are multinational" (42). John Borrows, whom Cairns invokes for Indigenous support for Canadian citizenship, in fact envisions a very different kind of citizenship from what Cairns imagines. Borrows is less concerned about allegiances to nation-states "on both sides of the (comparatively newly created) U.S./Canadian border" (34), and sees Aboriginal citizenship as necessary for Aboriginal and non-Aboriginal peoples alike. Current citizenship frameworks are insufficient, with Indigenous peoples "struggl[ing] to fully identify themselves as citizens in Canada because they rarely see their primary perspectives and interests mirrored in the law, the expressed goals of the state, or the prevailing associations in society" (144). A new citizenship must be forged in order to remedy "[c]urrent conceptions of citizenship [that] are deficient both because they fail to give socio-cultural recognition to Aboriginal peoples' primary relationship and loyalties and because non-Aboriginal Canadians have not considered or made many of these allegiances, relationships, and obligations their own" (144). In contrast to the White Paper's attempt to "welcome" Indigenous peoples into Canadian citizenship and participation in mainstream Canadian society, Borrows seeks an Indigenous renovation of citizenship in which non-Indigenous Canadians will have to participate in order to bring about a decolonizing justice that emphasizes a "citizenship with the land" (138):

> [C]itizenship under Aboriginal influence may generate a greater attentiveness to the land uses and cultural practices preferred by many Aboriginal peoples. Canadian notions of citizenship might not only develop to

> include greater scope for people's involvement in sustenance activities, they might also reduce the tolerance for land uses that extirpate these pursuits. Recognition of the importance of these objectives could thus shield Aboriginal peoples from assimilation by ensuring sufficient space for the pursuit of preferred Aboriginal activities. Moreover, Canadian citizenship under Aboriginal influence may expand to recognize the land as citizen. (146)

Borrows thus proposes a radical revisioning of citizenship, one that would not only interpellate Indigenous peoples more successfully by addressing their communities' concerns, but also "welcome" Canadian citizens into a more effective relationship with Indigenous peoples and with the land.

   While it is clear that different thinkers conceive of both citizenship and the relationship between nation-state and Indigenous peoples in different ways, it is also clear that citizenship as a category does not signify in a straightforward manner for Indigenous peoples, even for those who have chosen to affiliate themselves with Canada as well as their Indigenous nations. Drew Hayden Taylor weighs up the options of nation-state citizenship on the one hand, and nation-to-nation negotiation on the other, in a discussion of the right to vote:

> Some have argued that, maybe, as Native people we should just sit this and all other elections out. Because participating in the Canadian electoral process might compromise our status as independent First Nations. Canada made its treaties with sovereign autonomous Aboriginal Nations and we shouldn't participate in their government anymore than they have a right to participate in ours. We are not Canadians. We are "insert your Nation here." Personally, I don't think it's as cut and dry as that. Granted there is a reasonable amount of logic to the argument but on the other hand, I've met too many Native war veterans who fought for and lost friends defending Canada. I'd feel uncomfortable telling them they didn't have the right to vote … Politics, like many things in life, is not always "all or nothing." I think you're allowed to fudge the boundary lines occasionally. (*Furious* 31)

"We are not Canadians," but "you're allowed to fudge the boundary lines occasionally": I would argue that both King and Taylor fudge boundary lines, by addressing them in the first place in their complication of nation-state and Native identifications, by making that nation-state border, "a figment of someone else's imagination" (King, "Introduction" 10), signify at all. King himself, originally from the United States, took out citizenship in Canada. He also ran as a candidate in the 2008 Canadian federal election for the New Democratic Party; he didn't win, but clearly he was willing to engage in nation-state politics. Similarly, in his essay on the vote, Taylor confesses to having voted NDP. Thus, even as their writing often advocates a disregard of a nation-state border, which is "artificial at best" (King, "Introduction" 10), these two authors have also engaged in political processes that depend on, and are generated by, the boundary they are so keen to fudge. In terms of their work, then, Latisha's and Jason's gestures toward Canadianness demonstrate that however arbitrarily drawn the Canada–US border may be, it has nevertheless produced political and cultural consequences and engendered provisional identifications, thereby offering a site of struggle over citizenship and its implications for Native North American peoples.

As indicated by *The Border*'s own "gray zone," the CBC imagines Canada to be hospitable to such struggles, displacing more combative attitudes toward Indigenous people onto the American character, the "cowboy" (as Kessler refers to LaGarda, before meeting her in person and discovering her gender) who seems eager to stomp all over Canadian sovereignty, never mind Mohawk sovereignty. *The Border* projects Canada's relationship to the Mohawk as a kinder, gentler, more respectful form of state power. Yet no retort is offered to LaGarda's insistence that "you can't have it both ways." Frank Arthur, the Mohawk policeman, simply states: "Two agents only. You work it out." The problem that requires solution is what time the agents will arrive on the reserve, not whether the Mohawk are entitled both to invoke the border in order to question US military interference and to disregard it in accordance with their treaty rights. Just because LaGarda acts as the mouthpiece for the negation of seemingly contradictory approaches to the border does not mean that the Canadian nation-state is any happier than its US counterpart to entertain this incommensurability, as the failure of "Gray Zone" to offer a response to LaGarda's assertion indicates. As the Idle No More movement powerfully reminds us, Canada is not a kinder, gentler state content to encourage Indigenous sovereignty; the kind of Canadian state projected by *The Border* is a fiction. Alan Cairns's hope that a Citizens Plus model will allow Canada to "have it both ways [in] that multiple identities are both possible and desirable, and that they can and should include one of several possible Aboriginal identities and an identity as a Canadian" (109), does not offer a break with the presupposition that the Canadian state's sovereignty takes precedence over Indigenous sovereignties. In other words, Cairns's "both ways" do not offer a radical challenge to LaGarda's rejection of what she views as an inconsistency in the Mohawk position. In contrast to both Cairns's and *The Border*'s framing of citizenship and nation-state affiliations, King's and Taylor's texts suggest that the multiple interpellations of Native individuals not only enable but perhaps also necessitate multiple, provisional, and strategic responses to the questions of whether, how, for whom, and when the border signifies.

Note

1 Note, however, that sovereignty is a point of debate among Indigenous scholars. For Taiaiake Alfred, sovereignty functions as "an exclusionary concept rooted in an adversarial and coercive Western notion of power" (*Peace* 59). But as Joanne Barker

notes, invoking sovereignty is one of the "discursive strategies" used by Indigenous peoples since the Second World War in order to "clai[m] a difference from minorities and a status akin to the status of nations" (19). Barker argues that we must attend to questions of "how and for whom sovereignty matters" through understanding of "the historical circumstances under which it is given meaning" (21). For Craig Womack, "Sovereignty, for all its problems and contradictions, is a reality in Indian country"; and while "[s]ome make strong cases that sovereignty does not work for their particular community," it does not follow "that it should be dismissed for all of Indian country" (74–75).

Works Cited

Alfred, Gerald R. [Taiaiake]. *Heeding the Voices of Our Ancestors: Kahnawake Mohawk Politics and the Rise of Native Nationalism*. Toronto: Oxford UP, 1995.

———. *Peace, Power, Righteousness: An Indigenous Manifesto*. 2nd ed. Toronto: Oxford UP, 2009.

Anzaldúa, Gloria. *Borderlands/La Frontera*. 2nd ed. San Francisco: Aunt Lute, 1999.

Atwood, Margaret. *Survival: A Thematic Guide to Canadian Literature*. 1972. Toronto: McClelland & Stewart, 1996.

Barker, Joanne. "For Whom Sovereignty Matters." *Sovereignty Matters: Locations of Contestation and Possibility in Indigenous Struggles for Self-Determination*. Ed. Joanne Barker. Lincoln: U of Nebraska P, 2005. 1–31.

Battiste, Marie, and Helen Semaganis. "First Thoughts on First Nations Citizenship: Issues in Education." *Citizenship in Transformation in Canada*. Ed. Yvonne Hébert. Toronto: U of Toronto P, 2002. 93–111.

Borrows, John. *Recovering Canada: The Resurgence of Indigenous Law*. Toronto: U of Toronto P, 2002.

Cairns, Alan C. *Citizens Plus: Aboriginal Peoples and the Canadian State*. Vancouver: UBC P, 2000.

Cardinal, Harold. *The Unjust Society*. Edmonton: Hurtig, 1969.

Cassidy, Frank, and Robert L. Bish. *Indian Government: Its Meaning in Practice*. Lantzville and Halifax: Oolichan and Institute for Research on Public Policy, 1989.

Castronovo, Russ. "Compromised Narratives Along the Border: The Mason-Dixon Line, Resistance, and Hegemony." *Border Theory: The Limits of Cultural Politics*. Ed. Scott Michaelsen and David E. Johnson. Minneapolis: U of Minnesota P, 1997. 195–220.

Chariandy, David, and Sophie McCall. "Introduction: Citizenship and Cultural Belonging." *West Coast Line* 59 (2008): 4–12.

Code, Lorraine. "How to Think Globally: Stretching the Limits of Imagination." *Hypatia* 13.2 (1998): 73–85.

Davidson, Arnold E., Priscilla L. Walton, and Jennifer Andrews. *Border Crossings: Thomas King's Comic Inversions*. Toronto: U of Toronto P, 2003.

Fee, Margery, and Jane Flick. "Coyote Pedagogy: Knowing Where the Borders Are in Thomas King's Green Grass, Running Water." *Canadian Literature* 161–62 (1999): 131–39.

"Gray Zone." *The Border: Season One*. CBC, 2007. DVD.

Grinde, Donald A., Jr. "Iroquois Border Crossings: Place, Politics, and the Jay Treaty." *Globalization on the Line: Culture, Capital, and Citizenship at U.S. Borders*. Ed. Claudia Sadowski-Smith. New York: Palgrave, 2002. 167–80.

Johnston, Darlene. "First Nations and Canadian Citizenship." *Belonging: The Meaning and Future of Canadian Citizenship.* Ed. William Kaplan. Montreal and Kingston: McGill–Queen's UP, 1993. 349–67.

King, Thomas. "Borders." *One Good Story, That One.* Toronto: HarperPerennial, 1993. 131–47.

———. *Green Grass, Running Water.* Toronto: HarperCollins, 1993.

———. "Introduction." *The Native in Literature.* Ed. Thomas King, Cheryl Calver, and Helen Hoy. Toronto: ECW, 1987. 7–14.

———. *Truth & Bright Water.* Toronto: HarperFlamingo, 1999.

Kulchyski, Peter. *Like the Sound of a Drum: Aboriginal Cultural Politics in Denendeh and Nunavut.* Winnipeg: U Manitoba P, 2005.

McKegney, Sam. "Tenuous Tolerance: The Politics of Inconvenience from Kanehsa-take to Caledonia." *West Coast Line* 59 (2008): 62–75.

Ridington, Robin. "Happy Trails to You: Contexted Discourse and Indian Removals in Thomas King's *Truth and Bright Water.*" *When You Sing It Now, Just Like New: First Nations Poetics, Voices, and Representations.* Robin Ridington and Jillian Ridington. Lincoln: U Nebraska P, 2006. 288–311.

Taylor, Drew Hayden. *In a World Created by a Drunken God.* Vancouver: Talonbooks, 2006.

———. *Funny, You Don't Look Like One: Observations from a Blue-Eyed Ojibway.* Penticton: Theytus, 1998.

———. *Furious Observations of a Blue-Eyed Ojibway: Funny, You Don't Look Like One Two Three.* Penticton: Theytus, 2002.

Turner, Dale. *This Is Not a Peace Pipe: Towards a Critical Indigenous Philosophy.* Toronto: U Toronto P, 2006.

Warry, Wayne. *Ending Denial: Understanding Aboriginal Issues.* Peterborough: Broadview, 2007.

Womack, Craig S. "A Single Decade: Book-Length Native Literary Criticism Between 1986 and 1997." *Reasoning Together: the Native Critics Collective.* Ed. Craig S. Womack, Daniel Heath Justice, and Christopher B. Teuton. Norman: U of Oklahoma P, 2008. 3–104.

nine

Waste-full Crossings in Thomas King's *Truth & Bright Water*

Catherine Bates

THOMAS KING'S *TRUTH & BRIGHT WATER* begins with an illusory image of a smooth border crossing that never takes place, anticipating the fatal, failed border crossing that constitutes the novel's tragic climax. King foregrounds the unfinished and wasted state of the only bridge "serving" the cross-border community:

> At a distance, the bridge between Truth and Bright Water looks whole and complete, a pale thin line, delicate and precise ... But if you ... stand in the shadows of the deserted columns and the concrete arches, you can look up through the open planking and the rusting webs of iron mesh, and see the sky. (1)

A distanced, ordering gaze creates the misleading, deceptively *coherent* perspective and perceives the bridge as complete. This gaze sees a version of the scene that is not dissimilar to the nineteenth-century landscape paintings that returning artist Monroe Swimmer later critiques. Swimmer tells Tecumseh, the novel's narrator and Swimmer's new employee and protégé: "They are all alike. Craggy mountains, foreboding trees ... Quiet ... Luminous clouds in the sky ... Blah, blah, blah" (129). These paintings present an idealized, ideologically suspect, imperial, and *tidy* package of the landscape that is unpeopled; they do not depict any of the people indigenous to the land. This distorting, ordering gaze facilitates what Judith Butler calls a "regime of regulatory production" (17); as she argues, "the symbolic is a register of regulatory ideality" (18). Both the paintings and the misleading idea of a completed bridge contribute to a reality constructed "according to rigid and generally falsifying borders and boundaries" (Sugars 179). The regulatory regime that provides this order involves a particularly forceful, damaging form of imagining that legitimizes particular identities and rejects others, at the same time as it sees what it wants to see and ignores the waste.

The Canada–US border as an imposed political boundary is significantly involved in this symbolic and physical control over bodies. King shows the border—what he calls "this line of someone else's imagination" (interview with Rooke 72)—to be a place of exposure where people are defined, judged, and policed by restricted, state-defined notions of culture, nation, and race. For him it becomes both an arbitrary line borne of the imperial imagination and a permanent sign of the continuing violence of colonization since it does not acknowledge the different spatial boundaries of cross-border tribal communities that live on either side. However, while King focuses on the border as a material place that, when policed, holds the Native peoples who cross it accountable to the nation-state, he also figures it as a place that *makes visible* the way lives and bodies are inscribed and constrained by the nation-state.

It is not only the political boundary but also the material presence of the river with the unfinished bridge that obstructs the people of Truth and Bright Water. King's narrator emphasizes the falsification produced by the original perspective that envisages a smooth border crossing; he then changes perspective, moves through the landscape, looks up from under the bridge, and finds it to be rusting and full of holes: it is wasting away, does not function safely, was never finished, and does not satisfactorily cross the border. In other words, the narrator asks us to look up and shows us that something is wrong. But this wasting away, while signifying neglect, also provides permeability, a way to see the sky. It is this precarious possibility offered up by the rusting webs of iron mesh—of experiencing the wasting while recognizing what it allows us to see—that brings to light for us the potentially productive messiness of King's border confusions. These ask us both to see and to hope for the *beyond* of falsifying bordered perspectives and the waste they create. In other words, the bridge does cross the border, but in its dilapidated state it shows us there is something wrong; and if treated as a monument to and metonymic symbol of the border, it signifies both an irrevocable *problem* with the border and a potential reimagining of it.

This reimagining involves a connection between the bridge, with its unfinished wasted gaps, and the river that both is and is beyond the political border. As Tecumseh's mother notes, the river predates them all (52). Despite this sense that it is beyond human construction, the river also has a strong connection with waste: figured as both boundary and bin, it is continually clogged with rubbish thrown in by passersby, and seeping in from the landfill on the reserve. Furthermore, both river and bridge must be connected to the paintings, which, in Monroe Swimmer's hands, problematize imperial ideology when "Indians" begin "bleeding" through (130). These collective seepings continually infiltrate King's novel, serving both as a persistent and multifarious reminder of the problems still facing Native communities, and as a way to emphasize the troubling temptation to see only coherence, to paint over the cracks, and to hide the waste. King shows that colonialism remains an open wound in need of addressing and in doing so provides two symbols that disrupt the narrative in ways that impel an alternative reading of Native communities and waste. First, the skull found in the river among the other waste functions as a disturbing disruption between body and waste, past and present. Moreover, as I will show, it refuses teleological explanation, necessitating alternative interpretative work. Second, the quilt that Tecumseh's mother is making throughout the novel, which she continues to sew even while it keeps a number of the characters warm, works as an alternative to the colonial painting. Rather than presenting a falsified perspective that necessarily seeps, it is covered in unexpected, potentially problematic objects, some of which could cause danger, such as razor blades, fish hooks, and porcupine quills. But these objects are, on the surface, clearly visible, which in turn suggests a need to pay attention to the problems Native communities face, rather than attempt to ignore the persistent seeping. The dialogue presented by skull and quilt, engaged in by Tecumseh and potentially by the reader, exposes the seeping but also raises the possibility for a more intimate, messy, and participatory relationship with wasted objects, people, communities.

King draws attention to the border by filling it with waste. Lum, Tecumseh, and Soldier find waste in the river; Elvin smuggles toxic waste across the border; and human sewage bubbles up on the reserve. The implications of the connection King makes so insistently between waste and the border enable a symbiotic interrogation of both. Waste is the product of a system, the material that needs to be discarded to make the system work; but for the system to work, waste should be out of sight. Within the symbolic order that King establishes, the border *is* the system. By clogging the border, the waste in King's novel remains a permanent reminder of the consequences of systematizing culture and identity restrictively. Drawing upon Mary Douglas's *Purity and Danger*, Jonathan Culler associates rubbish with dirt, arguing that "dirt is vital evidence for the total structure of thought in a culture because it is an omnibus category for everything that is out of place. To investigate what counts as dirt [and rubbish] helps to identify the categories of the system" (5). King uses his focus on the rubbish-filled border to expose the systems and inscribed boundaries that surround Native peoples' communities and bodies with rubbish and that figure them *as* waste. In this way, he brings to mind Gerald Vizenor's storytelling character Martin Bear Charme, who declares that "there was never refuse like this on the reservations ... On the old reservations the tribes were the refuse. We were the waste, solid and swill on the run, telling stories from a discarded culture to amuse the colonial refusers" (101). Charme's trickster analysis attempts to displace the notion of Indigenous people as waste onto the past; however, this process of discarding people as well as objects—and through the wasting of objects—constitutes a significant strain of other Indigenous works, such as Leslie Marmon Silko's *Almanac of the Dead* and Louise Erdrich's *The Antelope Wife*. *Truth & Bright Water* makes an important contribution to this body of work by suggesting possible ways that we can read, reconstruct, and re-story the waste productively, by affectively reimagining the border using approaches other than violent and systematizing logic.

"Indian" as Consumer Product

King's work has often been preoccupied with the way "Indianness" is packaged; his characters often have to choose between working within this system, and playing up to a preconceived notion of the "American Indian," or trying to expose the problems with this predetermined thinking. In *Truth & Bright Water*, Elvin—Tecumseh's father—clarifies the border's complicity with this packaging. When crossing the border with Tecumseh, Elvin puts on a routine "like the Indians" depicted on television westerns (86) for the border guards, afterwards telling Tecumseh, "They love that dumb Indian routine" (86). This movie version of "Indianness" allows them a smooth crossing, but it also perpetuates a limited, cartoon version of Native identity, one that works as an artifact—valued for its fixed state. Moreover, Elvin makes his living partly by crafting souvenirs designed to appeal to this reified and consumer-infused notion of Indianness. So it is inevitable that his little model coyotes get consigned to the rubbish bin by Skee, one of Truth's white inhabitants, who makes money from the Natives in his cafe. Elvin tells his son: "Everybody's going crazy over traditional Indian stuff. I figure I can sell these for fifty bucks [apiece]" (32). To authenticate the coyotes, Elvin plans not only to sign them but also to include his treaty number on an explanatory card to reinforce their Indianness (32). This reminds the reader of a further way in which Indigenous peoples are ordered according to external notions of value: the state puts a price on the treaty number, which is understood as authenticating the Indigenous person and by extension his or her art.[1] By this logic, Elvin's art is authentic; his inclusion of the treaty number demonstrates more clearly the problems with this form of valuing—more so than his opportunism in making money from a state compartmentalizing of identities. Paradoxically, as he turns them into consumable objects, Elvin overinvests the coyotes with meaning in order to sell them to people who, if they invest in this logic, reduce culture to the limited meaning of constructed "authentic" artifacts. Skee himself demonstrates this, first by inscribing *over* the cultural significance of the coyote to Tecumseh, ignoring the latter's protest that "[c]oyotes are sort of traditional" (35), and then by pushing the forgotten coyotes into the garbage with the leftover food. Again, it is not surprising that when tourists are around, on the reserve (the other side of the border), Elvin's business plan works. In Bright Water during the Indian Days festival, the coyotes sell like hotcakes to the German tourists, who seem to be trying to become a commercial version of "Indian" by buying as many objects as possible. This festival presents a kind of marketable veneer of "Indianness" that appeals to the tourists.. However, just as Swimmer describes the Indians "seeping" through the nineteenth-century landscape paintings, the waste seeps through the edges of the festival, signifying the inadequate performance.

We are told there has been a lingering smell of sewage in Bright Water since the time the tribal community tried to run a holiday camp only to find that the drainage system did not work. Furthermore, Elvin makes money transporting dangerous hospital waste across the border on his way to help with the festival. Tecumseh points out to Elvin the likelihood that this waste contains bodies (82)—a fear that is almost confirmed later, when Soldier the dog pulls a used hospital pad covered in junk out of the river; Tecumseh intitialy mistakes the pad for the body of the mystery woman. This incident presents us with a particularly bodily piece of waste, one that anticipates Lum's death. As Elvin points out when telling Tecumseh why the waste cannot be taken to the big dump at Prairie View, "they don't mind making the mess, but they don't want the job of cleaning it up" (141). Another way to think of this would be to say, "they want to still keep producing the rubbish and still keep forgetting its danger." The Assembly of First Nations (AFN) in Canada has produced a document that makes clear why landfills present a specific danger to people living on First Nations reserves (and Native American reservations) in particular. The problems they list include water contamination (many communities rely on well water), poor air quality, insufficient capacity, and insufficient funding for adequate management. This document emphasizes the challenges that dealing with their *own* waste presents for reserve communities. And the problem is compounded when these communities are pressured to deal with wastes produced by others (see Monague on the North Simcoe landfill). In *Truth & Bright Water* the border becomes a reminder of this disposable culture and of the deliberate efforts by the state to "forget": dangerous waste is made to "disappear" in Canada, and Indigenous identity is homogenized and made marketable to ensure a smooth crossing and a material living. But with Soldier's continual excavation of the border/river, the novel will not let its readers forget either the mess or the consequences for Indigenous communities of a system that depends on notions of inevitable obsolescence.

The Skull: Messing Up the Story

The presence of the skull does not allow us to forget the danger of the wasting process. It is the first object in the novel to jolt the reader—and Tecumseh—out of any comfortable reading of waste and of the border. King has argued that "we talk about our environmental ethic ... Sure, we don't like oil on our beaches ... but we do nothing to prevent such stories from happening again, because the stories we tell are about how they'll never happen again ... I think we're ethically lazy" (qtd. in Beauvais). He concludes that "if we change the stories we live by, we change our lives" (qtd. in Beauvais). This complicated process can begin with a rethinking of the focus of these stories. Gay Hawkins agrees, arguing that too often, our stories about waste become infected with lament, unhelpfully precluding a focus *on* the waste:

> Rather than rail against the effects of excessive consumption and a disposable culture ... or let my melancholy take over, I want to take notice of all those abandoned things. I want to think about the complexity of our relations with the material world that wasted things carry as traces on their scratched and broken surfaces. The minute you pay attention to waste a different relation with it is enacted. (*Ethics* 15)

From the beginning of *Truth & Bright Water* we are invited to pay attention to waste and the processes of wasting. After viewing the wasting bridge, we are introduced to Tecumseh and Lum, through a story that seems to be about the process of rubbishing. The teenagers *believe* they see a woman throwing garbage into the border river. Tecumseh tells us: "A lot of junk winds up in the river this way. Some of it gets washed out of the Bright Water landfill and some of it gets blown off the prairies ... But most of the garbage ... comes from people who figure that rolling an old washing machine down the side of a coulee ... isn't going to hurt anything" (8). The river becomes figured here as the place that is not seen (people throw stuff in so they won't have to see it any more). Tecumseh considers telling the woman to discard elsewhere. This kind of story about rubbish is very familiar: issues of "right and wrong" are clear-cut. The rubbish in the river should not be there; it is damaging to the environment; the people who put it there are unthinking and careless and should be reprimanded. However, Tecumseh's reaction raises a question: Where else could the garbage be put that would be less damaging? This garbage will hang around whether we want it to or not.[2] Moreover, we learn later that, however tempting Tecumseh's intended response was to rail at the woman, it would have been impossible and inappropriate. The story of waste being dumped changes to a less familiar narrative. The woman jumps in after the items she has thrown, and when the boys look for her, she has disappeared; all they find—with the help of Soldier the dog—is a soft, yellow, shiny, small, human skull. Lum's observation while he goads Soldier with the skull—that it "[m]akes you wonder what else she threw away" (13)—haunts the novel. A story of littering with a clear moral framework becomes a mystery that Tecumseh feels compelled to solve, but he fails in his attempt to do so.

Arguably, the familiar readings of waste we produce are imbued with the desire for it to disappear and remain hidden. As Shanks and colleagues assert, "to describe garbage, our discards, the artifacts that at some point are no longer wanted, we often use the truism 'out of sight, out of mind.' That indeed, seems to be a sincere goal—to totally eradicate our discards" (69). King, however, does not allow the waste to be "totally eradicated" or even hidden. He asks his characters and his readers to look at it, to read it, to make something of it. The skull the boys find is a troubling object. It is found as a thrown-away item and initially is treated as a reusable wasted object by Soldier and Lum: Soldier uses it as a toy, Lum as a football. But Tecumseh keeps it, and thus, its disturbing presence is felt throughout the novel as he develops his own theories about it. As Davidson, Walton, and Andrews argue, each theory is based on "formulaic (primarily romance-driven) scenarios that reinforce heterosexual and racial norms" (191). The skull disrupts each theory; importantly, however, so does the way Tecumseh tests those theories against his own situated experience within the community. His attempts to imagine what the woman was doing by the river reveal the structure of King's novel to be an important factor in his strategy to tell story differently: the ordered teleological narrative that can figure people as waste is disrupted by a persistent allowance for Tecumseh's life to surround and interrupt.

Tecumseh thinks through his first theory in the shower. He imagines the woman's husband has left her, so she throws his favourite belongings into the river out of revenge, jumping in after them, only to climb out afterwards and drive away. For Tecumseh, "this theory is simple and complete" but does not work: why did the woman choose to throw away the suitcase as well as its contents, and why was she dancing? Placing the woman in a melodramatic romance-gone-bad story explains too much away. Lum disturbs Tecumseh by sticking the skull in the shower, "letting it ... bob around in the soap suds for a moment and then settle to the bottom of the tub" (64). Tecumseh observes: "The skull looks funny sitting there, half-submerged, the soap slick floating in and out of the eye sockets" (64). The skull and Lum have impinged on Tecumseh's theorizing, punctuating his abstract thinking. Lum has made the skull a "thing," but a thing with eyes; its material presence as object-once-alive seems to confound the explanation.[3]

Tecumseh then theorizes that the woman could be mourning, throwing herself into the river with her late husband's belongings "as a gesture of love" (64) before driving away. To test this romantic cliché, Tecumseh compares it to his own experience: "When my father left Bright Water ... my mother didn't yell and throw things the way you see women do in the movies. She stayed ... worked on the quilt. I was pretty sure she was angry, but maybe she was sad at the same time" (65). Here, his life has helped interpret the skull, while the skull mystery has enabled Tecumseh to revisit an important part of his family's history and understand it to be not easily interpretable. When Tecumseh comes out of the shower to find Lum wearing the quilt (65), the quilt at this point seems to symbolize Tecumseh's parents' separation and his mother's anger and sadness. The quilt, here, as well as the skull, clearly function to disrupt Tecumseh's theories.

The following passage foregrounds Lum's preoccupation with their Indianness. He uses the suggestion in the newspaper "that Indians make up the largest of Canada's prison population" to conclude that the two of them "shouldn't be wasting ... time looking for jobs" (65). Tecumseh protests, but Lum disrupts the conversation by bouncing the skull. The skull remains a focus; while they decide to hide it in the rafters, Lum continues his tirade about what he understands to be their dead-end situation, concluding that "nobody comes back to Truth and Bright Water unless they're crazy or dying" (67). Lum's desperate frustration is emphasized in this interlude; as an unemployed Indian, he feels rubbished by a society in which he is statistically likely to remain impoverished or become imprisoned. Tecumseh tries to counter Lum's fatalism, but it is the hiding of the skull, which renders it an object pregnant with mystery lying in wait, that seems to offer a possibility beyond Lum's bleak outlook: the skull has the potential to tell a different story, an alternative to the one with a definite end (related to "Indian as obsolescent artifact") in which Lum feels trapped.

Tecumseh frames his third theory with doubt, thus making clearer that he is actually telling "likely" stories, drawing from popular culture: "The third theory is more melodramatic, and suicide sounds too much like a movie for me to like it much" (68). Here, the woman is mourning for a loved one by ceremonially jumping to her death with a suitcase of favourite possessions. After the explication of this final theory, Tecumseh's mother talks to Lum of another mystery (to the novel's readers), "the accident"—presumably a reference to his mother's death, with which the skull later becomes associated. The narrative then returns to this troubling object: the skull, which seems to have become infused with the boys' relationships, anxieties, and life problems, and with the secrets and mysteries that both hold them together and keep them apart. We find that the tempting moralizing story about littering does not hold up, with the skull-as-rubbish becoming the skull-as-possibility, but that neither do Tecumseh's theories. As he concludes himself: "the skull is the problem ... [it would be] easiest ... to forget it altogether" (69). However, Tecumseh cannot follow this "out of sight, out of mind" logic; the skull interrupts the theories that tempt him, but it also remains more significant than simply one of the many bones the two boys have a habit of finding.

The structure of King's writing encourages some connections to be made but does not allow for conclusions to be reached. The multiple-choice theories that come to nothing are a significant part of this structure, but so are the interruptions by Lum, the skull, and everyday living. Tecumseh is not left alone to theorize, because that is not how his life within a family and a community works. King identifies his own work as "associational literature," which he defines when discussing new ways to categorize First Nations writing. For King, associational literature connects narrative structure to narrative focus: "Associational literature, most often, describes a Native community ... concentrating ... on the daily activities and intricacies of Native life and organizing the elements of the plot along a rather flat narrative line that ignores the ubiquitous climaxes and resolutions that are so valued in non-Native literature. In addition to this flat narrative line, associational literature ... eschews judgements and conclusions" ("Godzilla" 13–14).

In *Truth & Bright Water*, Tecumseh's theories offer the potential for "climaxes," but none come to fruition; moreover, once Tecumseh does find out where the skull came from, it does not seem the explanatory revelation he sought. Monroe Swimmer's reburial project, of which the skull was a part, does not resolve the situation so much as perform the open wound of Native bone collection; this is highlighted by the skull's continually unburied nature. Moreover, Lum and Soldier change the shape of Tecumseh's story and storytelling, helping the reader "associate with [his] world" without becoming a part of it or being able to consume it (14). The significance of the skull, therefore, cannot be narrowed down to one essential factor; rather, the ways it disrupts otherwise neat theories reverberate throughout the novel. Just as with the wasting bridge beneath which it is found, there is something wrong to which we need to attend.

The Quilt: Refusing the Smooth Border Crossing, Re-Fusing the Story

The quilt that Tecumseh's mother is making throughout the novel also shows there is something wrong: like the skull, it does not fit into a normative, deterministic narrative. We are told by Tecumseh that his mother's quilt is not "the easy kind of quilt you can get at the Mennonite colony ... or one of the fancy ... quilts you could get in Prairie View" (61). In other words, it is not a recognizable artifact, for it does not follow a pre-existing pattern. Tecumseh continues: "Along with the squares and triangles and circles of cloth ... patterns with names like Harvest Star ... my mother has also fastened unexpected things to the quilt, such as the heavy metal washers that run along the outside edges and the clusters of needles that she has worked into the stitching just below the fish hooks and the chickens' feathers" (61).

Elvin interprets the quilt as having begun simply enough but having become a problem once she began sewing on "weird things"; he decides that ultimately, it is her way of dealing with frustration and disappointment. He adds somewhat dismissively that "finding all that weird stuff and wasting time sewing it on probably helps calm her down" (62). In an interview, King seems to substantiate this view, arguing that Tecumseh's mother is carrying on a feud with the quilt. Both point out the problem with the sharp objects, such as the razor blades and porcupine needles that had been sewn into the quilt. Elvin jokes that these could lead to castration, while King associates them with the mother's emotional guardedness, thus aligning her with the quilt: "you are alright, as long as you are underneath and not trying to get in" (interview with Andrews 170). The quilt represents a danger, then: it contains items that could penetrate the body; the surface presents a fraught border that is difficult to cross. However, tempting as it might be to read the quilt as a fixed symbol—as a physical manifestation of the way Tecumseh's mother deals with her problems and as a potential metaphor for the difficulties of border crossing—this reading does not account for the way Tecumseh and his family interact with the quilt.

First, it is not just that unexpected things get sewn onto the quilt; it is also that the quilt pops up as a thing to disrupt Tecumseh's skull theorizing and to provide comfort to unexpected people. At one point, thinking they are the only ones at home, Tecumseh warns a sniffing Soldier about the fish hooks. Appearing from underneath the quilt, Auntie Cassie denies any knowledge of the fish hooks; she then wraps the quilt around her, thereby denying its potential physical dangers (120). The more dangerous point of this scene, however, could be that Tecumseh's first reaction, when hearing the voice, is to say "Mom?" (120). This confusion is significant, considering the mystery surrounding his mother, his aunt, and a lost child—the quilt becomes imbricated with the possibility that Cassie could be Tecumseh's mother. But it does not resolve this issue, just as the objects on the quilt cannot be explained. The comfort and affection of the different people finding warmth from the quilt throughout the novel, despite Elvin's warnings, signifies a privileging of affect over a neatly solved mystery. King suggests that those who get underneath the quilt already occupy a place in Tecumseh's mother's affections; this reading, however, still points to the important role of the quilt as a place to reinscribe a processual and often difficult-to-express love.

A further complication is the quilt's relation to the nineteenth-century landscapes Swimmer attempts to "fix" (129). As mentioned, Swimmer recounts the focus of these paintings: sublime scenery, including trees, mountains, and valleys. Tecumseh points out that his mother's quilt depicts similar landscapes (129). He does not tell Swimmer about the other "unexpected things," but directly afterwards Swimmer describes the unexpected Indians who begin to bleed through the paintings; thus, the novel could be said to connect the "Indians" with the objects sewn into the quilt. My reading of the dialogue between Swimmer and Tecumseh—which, as with many of the conversations in the novel, reads as if they are having two conversations and not really listening to each other—is influenced by King's remark in an interview: "[T]hat's the way conversations go a lot of times: you have two people who are talking about the same thing but you'd never know it to listen to them, but in the end it all comes out alright" (qtd. in Ridington 357). This connection between quilt and paintings serves to recognize the Indians as rendered waste by the nineteenth-century paintings that are part of the project of disappearing them; it also emphasizes the limitations of viewing the objects on the quilt as mere signifiers of frustration rather than as important material entities in themselves. They push their way into the story to remind us that it is not as tidy as we might think; they might signify Tecumseh's mother's problems, which she does not articulate in any more direct way, but they also provide some comfort for Tecumseh, who reads them differently. He concludes his introduction to the quilt thus: "What I liked best were the needles. When you held the quilt up, they would tinkle like little bells and flash in the light like knives" (62).

The relationship that Tecumseh develops with the quilt refuses to hold it to account as a purely homogenous and functional item that should be finished by now. Rather, it allows the stuff on the quilt somehow to speak. This moment when Tecumseh looks at the quilt resists incorporation into a narrative of instrumentality; similarly, the things get appreciated in themselves—not just as part of the quilt. His reading practice involves engaging with the "thingness of things," rather than the systematization of "things" within capitalist narratives of function. For Bill Brown, objects become things when they demand our attention by not working in the way they have been designed. Once we cannot use an object, we are impelled to see and perhaps feel its materiality ("Thing" 4). The function of the quilt as a cover is denaturalized by the objects that cover it. Moreover, these objects are reanimated by their surprising presence on the quilt, but even more by Tecumseh's multisensory engagement with them. He hears the needles and appreciates their flashing physicality; he spends time being *with* the quilt. The objects that cover it become part of its constitution as a quilt that plays no straightforward instrumental role—their juxtaposition becomes a potential call for the reader to pay attention to these usually rejected "things" as matter that matters. By analogy, the connection between objects and Indians becomes a complicated call to understand that the Indigenous people *matter*.

These weird things on the quilt make its role a matter of debate; while it becomes a rich signifier that something has gone wrong for Tecumseh's mother, it also constitutes some kind of material evidence that she is paying attention to the rejected objects around her: if these are re-examined and recontextualized, they can become part of a larger project affiliated to Monroe Swimmer's restoration work. However, whereas Swimmer's projects are concerned with trying to re-place and re-story—the Indians back into the picture, the buffalo back into the landscape, the skull back into the burial ground—the quilt re-fuses the objects by placing them somewhere new. It is this—along with their potential to penetrate—that makes them disturbing but also gives them the potential to change the damaging narratives that lead to Lum's tragic death.

Bodies as Waste

The skull is a disturbing object; it does not allow for a neat separation between body and "thing." In fact, as I have been arguing, it signifies the danger of body-becoming-thing. As Michael Thompson notes, we make rubbish when "disregarded objects for some reason or other force their attention upon us (when we step in them perhaps)" (330). The skull in the border river forces its attention on Tecumseh and Lum: they step into the continuing story of the skull-as-waste-but-something-more. John Knechtel argues that "trash's malleability allows it to convert anything or anyone into garbage" (8). Moreover, in his discussions about the "order-building" of capitalist societies, Zygmunt Bauman—as if speaking to Lum's fears of becoming wasted—discusses the way that "to be declared redundant means to have been disposed of because of being disposable—just like the empty and non-refundable plastic bottle or once-used syringe … 'Redundancy' shares its semantic space with 'rejects,' 'wastrels,' 'garbage,' 'refuse'—with *waste*" (12). Furthermore, he discusses the settler-invasion process that rendered Native peoples in the US (and Canada) as rubbish:

> Ironically, the extermination of aborigines for the sake of clearing new sites for Europe's surplus population (that is, priming the sites for the role of dumping ground for the human waste which economic progress at home was turning out in quantities) was carried out in the name of the self-same progress that recycled the surplus of Europeans into "economic migrants." And so for instance, Theodore Roosevelt represented the extermination of American Indians as a selfless service to the cause of civilization: "The settler and pioneer have at bottom had justice on their side: this great continent could not have been kept as nothing but a game preserve for squalid savages." (38)

Bauman clearly articulates the way the ordering logic of colonialism rendered Indigenous peoples in North America as waste, "squalid savages" taking up space.

With his emphasis on the discarded skull itself, and his focus on its history as an object, King confuses the borders usually set up between bodies and waste to reveal the continuing legacy of damaging colonial practices. The consequence of treating people as objects is that their bodies and identities become part of a narrative of functionality in which they are read *through*; this precludes attention to the "daily intricacies" that constitute meaningful lives. Here we can see the political possibilities of "thing theory": Brown's attempt to remove objects from purely instrumental readings reveals the problem with capitalist logic, which potentially precludes the stories of materiality and affect that engage Tecumseh.[4] The status of the skull-as-wasted-object is made clear through the way *Truth & Bright Water* reminds readers of the attempted museumification of Indigenous cultures by Canadian and US governments. We learn that the skull was a Native Canadian child's, one of many dug up and removed from burial sites by anthropologists who presented them as collections to museums in Canada, the United States, and beyond. It is one of many that Monroe Swimmer found and "de-collected" (see Bruce 198) from museums, to rebury respectfully. By figuring the skull as waste at the beginning of the novel, King is highlighting the inevitable consequences of colonial collecting of bone for the purposes of museum display and scientific analysis. As Daniel Francis notes about Canada, just as "the government was trying to stamp out vestiges of traditional aboriginal culture in everyday life, it was creating a new institution [the ethnological museum] devoted to the preservation of the culture" (21). The museum allows the culture to be read in a contained, consumable form. Part of this practice involved digging up the bones of First Nations children to keep as artifacts, thereby creating "a museological construction of Natives as on the brink of extinction" (21). In this way, their bodies can be studied in a controlled context outside of their own, with no personal interaction or acknowledgement of the living culture necessary. The bones in this context show these museums and archives to be performative, not so much describing a culture as producing a version that solidifies a certain power relation: the curator defines the dying culture.[5]

While working as an artist "restoring" paintings, Monroe Swimmer gains access to many museums. Thus his mission becomes to retrieve as many skulls as possible (he finds them gathering dust in drawers in the back of museums). These skulls recall Theodor Adorno's anxieties about the decontextualization of objects in museums, which become *museal*, "a German word [that] describes objects to which the observer no longer has a vital relationship and which are in the process of dying" (173). While Adorno figures the museum as a place where objects go to die (so, advocating that we understand objects to have life), Tecumseh and Lum's engagement with the skull keeps it within a kind of living, changing narrative. In this way, it becomes related to the quilt: both disrupt the consumerist logic into which the treaty-stamped coyotes are designed to fit, and both are commensurate with Hawkins's analysis of Bill Keaggy's photo collection *50 Sad Chairs*. Hawkins writes: "[T]hese aren't obedient chairs clustered around a dining-room table ... Some have been dumped with other garbage or abandoned in the street and each one is accompanied by a comment from Keaggy which highlights both our moral attitude to trash ... and the subjectivity of the chair" ("Sad" 54). For Hawkins, the collection "animates things by putting them in new relations and classifications"; she observes that "by calling this collection of chairs 'sad,' he invites us to feel something for trash. He makes wasted things visible" (54). Similarly, the skull and the quilt re-fuse waste, showing it not to be a signifier of the past so much as a living entity with a present and a future. This idea is useful when considering those whose culture was effectively made waste within a colonial system that only figured them *as* the past. Indeed, it is important to note King's assertion that associational literature "reinforces the notion that, in addition to the usable past that the concurrence of oral literature and traditional history provide us with, we also have an active present marked by cultural tenacity and a viable future" ("Godzilla" 14). Swimmer takes the skull, which has been decontextualized and has become part of a process of reifying the past, and infuses it with present hopes and concerns to try to pave the way for a positive, viable future for the community. His project intends to refigure the skulls as part of a living culture, rather than use them to act as the mementos of a dying one. The skull, found in the margins of the museum, and then in the border, ultimately sits on the border between wasted artifact and body. Just as the skull stops Tecumseh's stories from working, it interrupts and exposes the imperial project that attempts to render Native peoples as artifacts and then, inevitably, as obsolete objects. And it reminds us of our body's relationship to waste by showing us that it can *become* waste.

Swimmer Restores, the Quilt Re-Stories

I have attempted to make comparisons between skull and quilt and glean hope from both. It is important, however, to note that they function differently. A closer examination of the relationship they have with Swimmer's ever-growing "restoration" work helps here. Arguably, Swimmer's art project is an attempt to challenge the attempted removal and marginalization of Indigenous culture by restoring or redoing what has been taken away, or by removing the symbolic presence of the imperial forces responsible for removal. As such, he paints the "Indians" back into the nineteenth-century landscapes that have attempted to unrepresent them; he tries (repeatedly) to rebury the skull; he installs signs to "teac[h] the Grass about Green" (43) and "Sky about Blue" (45); he replaces the buffalo with iron versions; and he tries to paint away the church. Arguably, however, this project does not work. The installed signs trip Tecumseh up more than they restore the colours of grass and sky; and the church never fully disappears (it can still be found at the end of the novel). Similarly, Swimmer laughs at the border at the same time that he reinscribes its importance by using it as a staging ground for his buffalo ceremony: "'There's Canada,' he says, '… and this is the United States.' He spins around in a full circle, stumbles … 'Ridiculous, isn't it?'" (132).[6]

Swimmer, then, is trying to reinstall the past through the imaginative potential of art: he wants to convince Tecumseh that the buffalo move and that the church is invisible. But Tecumseh, our worried narrator, presents the possibility that what is needed is not a restoration project, but a continual process of "re-storying." The skull, despite Tecumseh's theorizing, ultimately, in Lum's hands, and like Lum's body, remains fixed within damaging stories of the past. It will not be restored to the ground: first, it is retrieved by Soldier found among all the other waste; next, Lum overidentifies with it as it comes to signify his grief for his mother and his untenable position as an uncared for, wasted child; the border between skull and Lum blurs. The quilt, however, re-stories the rejected objects, keeping them sewn on and secure while ensuring that they serve as a dangerous reminder of the multifarious difficulties facing Tecumseh's community. In this way it relates to the new meaning that objects gain in Swimmer's giveaway: these become re-storied through the process of being passed on to be valued by a new person. They represent the continuing potential for objects to mean differently, rather than be delimited by the logic of planned obsolescence.

Indeed, it is clear that by attempting to become a successful runner, Lum was trying to put his own body within an alternative interpretative framework: to mean differently. His father's fists—which become metonyms for the material damage the continual displacement that Native peoples have experienced—have stopped him from running into a life with more potential; he finishes his story by running onto the wasting bordered bridge with the skull and exposing the larger processes of wasting: the bridge becomes complicit in Lum's death, a death that results in Lum's body becoming junk to be fished out of the river. This death becomes a kind of failed border crossing, as if to expose the problems with the bordered logic that asks bodies to be accountable at the same time as they fail to account for the lived reality *of* those bodies. The re-storied skull remains unburied, presumably to be retrieved from the river, again, as a reminder of the "Indian-as-artifact" mentality that haunts Tecumseh's community, and by analogy the existence of North American Indigenous peoples more widely. The quilt, however, refuses to become an artifact: it remains in process and displays its difficulties. It does not allow for the idea of the illusory smooth border crossing that the distanced view of the bridge suggests. Roland Barthes reminds us that "smoothness is always an attribute of perfection because its opposite reveals a technical and typically human operation of assembling" (88).[7] Within the imperfection of the quilt with its constituent weird things, as opposed to the uncanny cleanliness and shininess of the museumified skull, lies the possibility for Indigenous culture to become and mean differently. King's much-cited thoughts on the border could suggest a way a different relationship between border and body can be developed:

> Well, I guess I'm supposed to say that I believe in the line that exists between the US and Canada, but for me it's an imaginary line. It's a line from somebody else's imagination; it's not my imagination. It divides people like the Mohawk into the Canadian Mohawks and US Mohawks. They're the same people. It divides the Blackfoot who live in Browning from the Blackfoot who live at Standoff, for example. So the line is a political line, that border line … [T]hat kind of border and that kind of nationalism creates centres that I don't think do Indian people any good. It suggests things to us that we should become, things I'm not much interested in becoming. (interview with Rooke 72)

In identifying this difficulty—that the border signifies the dominance of one cultural imagination over another—King offers his strategy for dealing with this imposition: to identify the line *as* imaginary and to refuse to *become* the identity it asks him to be. By giving away the quilt to us, by impelling us to participate in its making through interpreting its unexpectedness, he potentially allows it to *become* differently: a different relation to both waste and the border starts to seem possible. The quilt signifies not a process of restoring so much as one of *re*-storying; the novel moves on from King's refusal, to invite us to become part of a re-fusing.

Acknowledgement

This chapter has developed from invaluable and continuing discussion about this ever-giving novel with Gillian Roberts and David Stirrup, and about waste with Susan Anderson, James Ward, and Milena Marinkova.

Notes

1 As David Stirrup notes, this also serves to comment on the Indian Arts and Crafts Act (1990), which prohibits art made by non-federally recognized Indians from being sold as Indian art.

2 While Gay Hawkins points out 'the material recalcitrance of trash, its lingering presence, its refusal to go away' ("Sad" 50), Mary Douglas tells us that "whenever a strict pattern of purity is imposed on our lives it is either highly uncomfortable or it leads into contradiction if closely followed, or it leads to hypocrisy. That which is negated is not thereby removed" (163). James Ward draws upon this idea that rubbish hangs around despite efforts to get rid of it with great effect, ultimately arguing that "what rubbish theory teaches us, however, is that fragmented, destabilized, decentred things—including selves, myths, and export industries—do not go away; they may seem invisible but they are durable" (91).

3 This recalls Merleau-Ponty's notion of the body as a "thing among things," further explored by Bill Brown ("Thing").

4 Brown's two more recent articles on things, about the artifacts of slavery ("Reification") and the way in which First Nations artist Robert Davidson recontextualizes iconic objects of late capitalist culture ("Objects"), clearly illustrate the political import of his thing theorizing.

5 See Bates (90–91) for further discussion about the performativity of the archive with particular reference to the postcolonial work in this area by Richards and Spivak.

6 Thanks to David Stirrup for his emphasis, in our continual conversations about the novel, upon the ambivalence of Swimmer's art project (see Stirrup).

7 Thanks to Olivia Rawes for reminding me of this helpful observation.

Works Cited

Adorno, Theodor W. *Prisms*. Trans. Samuel and Shierry Weber. 1967. Cambridge, MA: MIT P, 1983.

AFN (Assembly of First Nations). "Landfill Wastes." *AFN Environmental Stewardship: Respecting and Protecting Mother Earth*. http://64.26.129.156/article.asp?id =5011. Accessed 10 September 2012.

Bauman, Zygmunt. *Wasted Lives: Modernity and Its Outcasts*. Cambridge: Polity, 2004.

Bates, Catherine. "In the Hope of Making a Connection: Rereading Archival Bodies, Responses, and Love in Marian Engel's *Bear* and Alice Munro's 'Meneseteung.'" *Basements and Attics: Explorations in the Materiality and Ethics of Canadian Women's Archives*. Ed. Linda M. Morra and Jessica Schagerl. Waterloo: Wilfrid Laurier UP, 2012. 85–104.

Barthes, Roland. *Mythologies*. Trans. Annette Lavers. 1972. London: Vintage, 1993.

Beauvais, Ryan. "Thomas King Talks Ethics, Politics." *The Gateway* 18 November 2008. http://thegatewayonline.ca/articles/news/volume-xcix-number-20/thomas -king-talks-ethics-politics. Accessed 6 June 2009.

Brown, Bill. "Objects, Others, and Us (The Refabrication of Things)." *Critical Inquiry* 36.2 (2010): 183–206.

———. "Reification, Reanimation, and the American Uncanny." *Critical Inquiry* 32.2 (2006): 175–207.

———. "Thing Theory." *Critical Inquiry* 28.1 (2001): 1–22.

Bruce, Barbara S. "Figures of Collection and (Post)Colonial Processes in Major John Richardson's *Wacousta* and Thomas King's *Truth and Bright Water*." *Is Canada Postcolonial? Unsettling Canadian Literature*. Ed. Laura Moss. Waterloo: Wilfrid Laurier UP, 2003. 190–206.

Butler, Judith. *Bodies That Matter: On the Discursive Limits of Sex*. New York: Routledge, 1993.

Culler, Jonathan. "Review: Junk and Rubbish: A Semiotic Approach." *Diacritics* 15.3 (1985): 2–12.

Davidson, Arnold E., Priscilla L. Walton, and Jennifer Andrews. *Border Crossings: Thomas King's Cultural Inversions*. Toronto: U of Toronto P, 2003.

Douglas, Mary. *Purity and Danger: An Analysis of Concepts of Pollution and Taboo*. London: Routledge and Kegan Paul, 1966.

Francis, Daniel. *The Imaginary Indian: The Image of the Indian in Canadian Culture*. Vancouver: Arsenal Pulp, 1992.

Hawkins, Gay. *The Ethics of Waste: How We Relate to Rubbish*. Lanham: Rowman and Littlefield, 2006.

———. "Sad Chairs." Knechtel 50–61.

King, Thomas. "Godzilla vs. Postcolonial." *World Literature Written in English* 30.2 (1990): 10–16.

———. Interview with Jennifer Andrews. *Studies in Canadian Literature* 24.2 (1999): 161–85.

———. Interview with Constance Rooke. *World Literature Written in English* 30.2 (1990): 62–76.

———. *Truth & Bright Water*. New York: Grove, 1999.

Knechtel, John. "Introduction." Knechtel 8–10.

———, ed. *Trash*. Cambridge, MA: MIT Press/Alphabet City, 2007.

Monague, Vicki. "Aboriginal Women Protest Dumpsite 41." *Rabble.ca* 14 May 2009. http://rabble.ca/babble/aboriginal-issues-and-culture/aborginal-women -protes-dump-site-41. Accessed 10 September 2012.

Richards, Thomas. *The Imperial Archive and the Fantasy of Empire*. London: Verso, 1996.

Ridington, Robin. "Coyote's Cannon: Sharing Stories with Thomas King." *American Indian Quarterly* 22.3 (1998): 343–62.

Roosevelt, Theodore. *The Winning of the West: From the Alleghenies to the Mississippi, 1769–1776*. New York: Putnam, 1889.

Shanks, Michael, David Platt, William L. Rathje, and Scott Bukatman. "The Perfume of Garbage: Modernity and the Archaeological/Garbage: The Stuff That Dreams Are Made Of: Response to Michael Shanks, David Platt, and William L. Rathje." *Modernism/Modernity* 11.1 (2004): 61–87.

Spivak, Gayatri Chakravorty. *A Critique of Postcolonial Reason: Towards a History of the Vanishing Present*. Cambridge, MA: Harvard UP, 1999.

Stirrup, David. "Art, Borders, Citizenship: Containment and Flux in Selected Works by Eric Gansworth and Thomas King." British Association of Canadian Studies Conference, University of Birmingham, 5 April 2011.

Sugars, Cynthia. Review of *Border Crossings: Thomas King's Cultural Inversions*. *Journal of Canadian Studies* 38.2 (2004): 179–84.

Thompson, Michael. "Time's Square: Deriving Cultural Theory from Rubbish Theory." *Innovation* 16 (2003): 319–30.

Vizenor, Gerald. *Landfill Meditation: Crossblood Stories*. Hanover: Wesleyan UP, 1991.

Ward, James. "'London Is All Waste': Rubbish in Patrick Keiller's Robinson Films." *SubStance* 37.2 (2008): 78–93.

ten

Bridging the Third Bank

Indigeneity and Installation Art at the Canada–US Border

David Stirrup

Elders remind us to face the future with a computer in one hand and a drum in the other.

Douglas Cardinal, "Architecture"

As a phenomenological category, the border was something that people carried within themselves, in addition to being an external factor structuring their perceptions.

Claire F. Fox, "The Portable Border"

And the river, always the river, perpetually renewing itself. The river, always.

João Guimarães Rosa, "The Third Bank"

THIS CHAPTER CONSIDERS SIX NATIONS Mohawk artist Alan Michelson's *Third Bank of the River* (2009) and his earlier sound and video installation *TwoRow II* (2005), alongside non-Indigenous Canadian artist Alex McKay's *Treaty Canoe* and *Treaty of Niagara 1764* (1999) as examples of border art. Michelson's work clearly sits most comfortably within this art-historical category: *Third Bank* is sited at the Massena, NY, border post, while *TwoRowII* depicts the Grand River in southwestern Ontario, which separates the Six Nations Reserve from settler townships on land originally granted by the Crown to the Six Nations as part of the "Haldimand Tract" following the American War of Independence. Yet McKay's *Treaty Canoe* and its companion piece *Treaty of Niagara 1764* engage the border both conceptually and literally: through the treaty itself, so deeply evocative of that zone of contact and coexistence between settler-invader and Indigenous societies; and through the specificity of reference to Niagara, that most iconic of North American border sites.[1] Both Michelson's and McKay's works, then, expressly treat bordered states—referencing the border between Indigenous/colonial and (more literally in Michelson's case) between tribal

163

and colonial nations—and navigate the historical territory of the border as both passage and perimeter. My intention is not to compare qualitatively the intent behind these very different artworks but rather to consider the ways in which McKay's pieces initiate a critique of colonization that opens up a space for dialogue that is intrinsic to,[2] but reframed by, Michelson's emplaced evocation of Haudenosaunee values of reciprocity and responsibility. In many respects, the artworks call to each other (although neither is responsive to the other), each containing, utilizing, and inverting the others' symbolism: *Treaty Canoe* might thus be seen floating between the banks of *Third Bank*, the written treaties and beaded two-row in tension and, through that tension, dialogue. Similarly, the muted silence of *Treaty of Niagara 1764*'s megaphone is inverted in the cacophonous dual-track of *TwoRow II*, both voices, settler-invader and indigenous, reinserted into the river's narrative, superimposed, like the two-row itself, onto a particular space.

McKay calls on a familiar idiom, ironizing the dichotomy of settler-invader and displaced indigene by hybridizing recognizable cultural objects in order to critique assimilationist tropes. His pieces artfully participate in and interrogate that idiom, while the same relationship is reiterated in Michelson's work in a state of parallelism over opposition or merging. Michelson's artworks considered here both celebrate the border site of embodied sovereignty[3] and perform politically as examples of border art that, far from negotiating the "betwixt and between," presents the border site as what Kevin Bruyneel calls "the third space of sovereignty" while actively re-engaging the core values at stake in colonial agreements between the Six Nations Confederacy and the Crown. In both artists' work, then, document, object, and location cohere to scrutinize the logics of colonialism and sovereignty and the question of responsibility that inheres in both. "Sovereignty" is not a universally accepted concept in Indigenous Studies, and I am ever mindful of others' rejection of the term as it is currently (generally) used. Taiaiake Alfred, for instance, asserts that "in making a claim to sovereignty [indigenous politicians] are making a choice to accept the state as their model and to allow indigenous political goals to be framed and evaluated according to a 'statist' pattern" (80). It is worth remembering that the policies of colonial powers on both sides of the Canada–US border resulted in a process of enclosure, the cadastral boundaries of which were generally defined through treaties. Where lands were taken without provision, that land has often become a source of ongoing struggle between Native nations and the nation-state. As such, then, the question of borders and boundaries and territory-bound notions of nationhood and sovereignty are not easily dismissed. Although the art engages cross-border identification and unsettles the conventional border by emphasizing the ways in which Indigenous Nations in North America interrupt the normative boundaries of the nation-state, it also illuminates the significance of borders as an inevitable, if fiercely contested, constitutive element of indigenous sovereignty discourse—both as sites for erasure and as lines of demarcation of "national" cultural space—even as that discourse seeks to resist the models of containment implicit in its terms.

In 2009 a team of Mohawk construction workers, under Michelson's guidance, installed his monumental glass-and-light installation *Third Bank of the River* (Fig. 10.1) at the rebuilt US Land Port of Entry in Massena, NY. Commissioned by the US General Services Administration (GSA), *Third Bank*, whose title "reflects the unique geography of the international border-crossing at Massena" (Morris, "Art" 37), is "comprised of hundreds of photographs … shot from a boat and digitally joined into glowing, elegant bands depicting the Ontario and New York banks of the St. Lawrence" (38) incorporating the Cornwall Island shoreline. Sandblasted through a dot-matrix screen onto large sheets of glass (69 x 489 inches collectively), the images form two strips of purple separated by white bands of sky.

Their effect is of a photographic negative on the one hand, and a two-row wampum on the other, the overall composition "adapted from 19th-century panoramic maps" (Morris, "Art" 39), representing the collaging of a complex panorama that traverses Cornwall Island, sovereign territory of the Akwesasne Mohawk. While the delineation of the three separate shorelines conjures an image of cultural/national encounter and separation, the evocation of the wampum resists the obvious postcolonial reading by placing the Haudenosaunee document at the heart of the piece's aesthetic. The best-known two-row wampum, a double row of purple shell beads separated/spanned by white

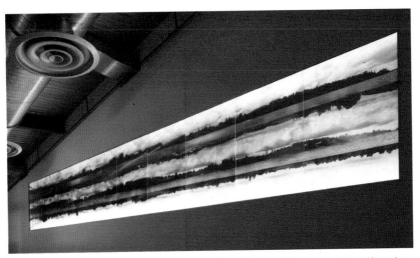

Fig. 10.1 Alan Michelson, *Third Bank of the River*, 2009 (Massena, NY). Ceramic glass melting colours on glass. Reproduced with the permission of the artist.

bands, was the *Kaswentha* (or *Guswehnta*), first delivered in diplomacy to the Dutch in 1613.

This document, signifying principles of peace, trust, and friendship, formed the basis for all subsequent treaties between the Haudenosaunee and European peoples. The parallel lines of purple wampum are commonly understood to represent a canoe and a ship travelling separate paths in the same direction, betokening the dignity and integrity of two coequal nations, neither impeding the other's progress or interfering in its affairs.

The video panorama and sound installation *TwoRow II* (Fig. 10.2) draws on much of the same imagery as the later *Third Bank*, although it depicts the Grand River in Ontario, which separates the Six Nations reserve from non-Native townships. Its soundtrack layers the English voiceover of a tourist river guide with the voices of Native elders talking about their experiences of the river.[4] First exhibited at the National Museum of the American Indian in New York, *TwoRowII* is now in the collection of the National Gallery of Canada.

While Michelson's works reassert the primary values at their heart (albeit carrying an implicit critique of Indigenous–colonial relations), McKay's two pieces, which also draw directly from treaty discourse, more immediately emphasize the "often fraught relationship between the Dominant Euro Settler Culture and First Nations here in North America" (McKay). *Treaty Canoe* (Fig. 10.3) is a canoe made from linen paper, glue, cedar, copper wire, ink, red ribbon, and birchbark. *Canoe* is made up of facsimiles of treaties, transcribed

Fig. 10.2 Alan Michelson, *TwoRowII*, 2005. Video and sound installation exhibited in *Stop (the) Gap*, 2011, at the Anne & Gordon Samstag Museum of Art, University of South Australia. Reproduced with the permission of the artist and with permission of the Anne & Gordon Samstag Museum of Art.

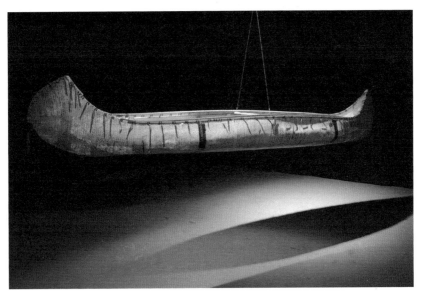

Fig. 10.3 Alex McKay, *Treaty Canoe*, 1999. Linen paper, glue, cedar, copper wire, ink, red ribbon, and birchbark. Photographers: Tory James and Alex McKay (University of Windsor, May 15, 2013). Reproduced with the permission of the artist.

Fig. 10.4 Alex McKay, *Treaty of Niagara 1764*, 1999. Birchbark, copper wire, red paint. Photographers: Tory James and Alex McKay (University of Windsor, May 15, 2013). Reproduced with the permission of the artist.

onto the linen paper by volunteers "using dip pen and ink, much as the originals would have been hand-written onto similar paper" (McKay). Installed in various locations to date, from the Niagara Artist's Company to the Canadian Canoe Museum, *Canoe* was first exhibited hanging from the ceiling: "Lit from above the craft becomes translucent; in casting a shadow it becomes two canoes, floating in the same current on separate but parallel courses" (McKay). This staging clearly evokes the same imagery of two-row wampum as Michelson's more literal representations.

McKay describes *Treaty Canoe* as "text" in contrast to its "sister piece, 'Treaty of Niagara 1764' (birch bark, copper wire, red paint)," which he describes as "mute" (Fig. 10.4). "Some say," he continues, "that the Treaty of Niagara is a 'lost treaty' reiterating and reinforcing the First Nations' understanding of The Royal Proclamation of 1763, that recognized the sovereignty of the First Nations. It is remembered and recorded by the First People as a Two Row Wampum" (McKay).

As John Borrows attests, "First Nations regarded the [Niagara] agreement, represented by the [Royal] Proclamation [of 1763] and the two-row wampum, as one that affirmed their powers of self-determination" (165). Equally significantly, he explains, "[t]he promises made at Niagara and echoed in the Royal Proclamation have never been abridged, repealed, or rendered nugatory" (168). The Treaty of Niagara and all it evokes, then, in terms of site specificity, negotiation, material product (treaty and two-row), and intrinsic value systems, provide key context here. McKay's pieces, however, suggest a material simplicity, invoking a historicized moment, that contrasts with the state-of-the-art technology of Michelson's installations. Similarly, McKay's pieces deal with the littoral subsumption and the literal appropriation of Aboriginal cultures, at once evoking and challenging the myth of the vanishing Indian wherein their abstraction emphasizes the shadows and silences of Native absence. In both *Treaty Canoe* and *Treaty of Niagara 1764*, the documents both reproduced and referred to, which recall a long history of political and legal exchange, simultaneously point to the absence of the bodies necessary to the canoe's and megaphone's uses, raising immediate questions of those treaties' status in the present. Michelson's site-specific *Third Bank*, meanwhile, is unequivocal in its demonstration of Mohawk presence, while through the two-row imagery, the dialogues it and *TwoRowII* enact with the geographies they portray demand acknowledgement of the system of ethics that underpins the treaty process.

From Border Art and Border Politics to Two-Row and Treaties

Where Wai Chee Dimock has noted that "'[g]lobalization' [has become] the familiar term to describe [an] unravelling of national sovereignty" (1), *Third Bank*, in the context of the continued Mohawk struggle for self-governance, intervenes in that narrative. As a piece of border art, it not only draws attention to the *fastness* of the border—and national territories—but also simultaneously addresses the ways in which sovereignty has been and continues to be negotiated. Or to put it another way, the presence of *Third Bank* at the border post provocatively alerts us both to the ways in which sovereignty defines and is defined by literal and figurative borders and to the importance of recognition of sovereignty—and its correlatives such as self-determination—in the mutual and open traversal of those borders. Using "sovereignty" and "nationhood" as interchangeable terms, Daniel Heath Justice argues that "Indigenous nationhood is a necessary ethical response to the assimilationist directive of imperialist nation states" (qtd. in Weaver 45). Perhaps ironically, then, *Third Bank* participates in the "transnational" conversation, illustrating the ways in which a community both straddles and transcends the border, and simultaneously illuminating its artificiality and invoking its legal–political paradigm. It does this by visually calling attention to the bifurcation the border enacts and by contextually calling attention to the ways in which border crossing for Indigenous peoples is often impeded by the failure to acknowledge the "presence and participation" of Indigenous Nations (Morris, "Art" 38). In other words, it "reimagines" the landscape not by refuting "the terms of territorial sovereignty" (Dimock 3) but by reframing them.

Border art has long been associated with the US–Mexico border, particularly since the foundation of The Border Art Workshop / Taller de Arte Fronterizo (BAW/TAF) by Michael Schnorr, David Avalos, and Victor Ochoa in 1984. Participants in the early Workshop events were not the first arts practitioners of/in the borderlands, of course. Chicano artists in the 1960s were producing politicized art in the region, for instance. However, it was Rupert García's 1973 painting "*¡Cesen Deportación!*" ("*Stop Deportation!*") that signalled the start of the border-as-motif (both political and aesthetic), and "[i]t was not [really] until the early eighties that art emerged at the borderlands that explicitly addressed border politics" (Prieto). Border art, then, has tended to be confrontational and often predicated on performance: embodiment at the border art-site is an explicit reminder of just what is at stake in nation-state politics. As developed by the acclaimed performance artist Guillermo Gómez-Peña, among a host of other Chicano/a, Mexican, and Anglo-American artists and performers, the tradition of site-specific border art on the US–Mexico border has focused on community engagement. Border art has, in the main, been predicated on radical, anti-neocolonial, anti-institutional values, although well-documented tensions around the institutional co-option of border art's popularity in the late 1980s generated splits and significant new directions in its movement (see Gómez-Peña, "Binational" 39–40).

But as Claire F. Fox asserts, "even though the U.S.–Mexico border retains a shadowy presence in the usage of these terms ["border" and "border crossing"], the border which is currently in vogue in the U.S., both among Chicano scholars and among those theorists working on other cultural differences, is rarely site-specific" (61). "Rather," she goes on to say, "it is invoked as a marker of hybrid or liminal subjectivities" (61). Indeed, in the introduction to their *La Frontera/The Border: Art About the Mexico/United States Border* Chávez, Grynsztejn, and Kanjo note:

> The border is not a physical boundary line separating two sovereign nations, but a place of its own, defined by a confluence of cultures that is not geographically bounded ... The border is a specific nexus of an authentic zone of hybridized cultural experience, reflecting the migration and cross-pollination of ideas and images between different cultures that arise from real and constant human, cultural, and sociopolitical movement. (xvii–xviii)

Having quoted this same passage, Neustadt explains its recontextualization of the border as "a zone, or stage, of cultural hybridism" (135). At one remove from the border's function as dividing line, he continues, "this account ... evokes the area's positive potential for cultural and political production," which "paradoxically resists the political construct of discrete nations" (135).

As several chapters in *Parallel Encounters* attest, cultural production at the Canada–US border and theorizing around that site have tended, almost like the border itself, to be far less visible than their counterparts at the southern border of the United States. Perceived to be benign, the 49th parallel is caught up, where it is invoked at all, in Canada's politico-economic relationship with the United States in particular. This includes concerns over neo-imperial attitudes and anxieties about the impact of the 1989 Free Trade Agreement between the United States and Canada, and the later 1994 North American Free Trade Agreement (NAFTA). The instances of site-specific work and work that invokes particular places under consideration here return this discussion to the border site itself, asking what it is that these Canada–US border examples bring to the conversation, retaining, as I think they do, both their dependence on site-specific context and the broader reflection outlined above on what Fox calls "liminal subjectivities," becoming or resisting "space[s] of fantasy and sociopolitical allegory" (61).

For Fox, then, the "border" is always already synecdochic (62); insofar as it is symbolic within the discourse of border studies, it has taken on the double weight of disenfranchisement *and* resistance. But we must remember the specific contexts of that border before simply transposing it, as semiotic coda, to other border sites. In "The New World Border," Gómez-Peña characterizes encountering the US–Mexico border as "a common yet dangerous experience ... crossing from the Third to the First World, from the past to the future" (138). Clearly, this is one aspect of the southern US border that does not stretch north, while Fox's assertion that "institutional support for local artists and writers [in border cities] remains very modest" (75) contrasts with Michelson's $200,000 GSA grant. By no means indicative of a common establishment gift to the arts, this particular production scenario nevertheless differs markedly from the "guerrilla" activities and anti-establishment productions most clearly associated with border art as we know it.

Notwithstanding these caveats, the Canada–US border *has* figured as a site of dissent and resistance in Indigenous North Americans' struggles for the securing of rights and freedoms, and for the sovereign status of Indigenous nations, particularly those that straddle the border. Article III of the 1794 Jay Treaty (the Treaty of Amity, Commerce, and Navigation between Great Britain and the United States) recognized the pre-existing rights of Indigenous peoples to pass freely between the "recently formed United States and Canadian nations" (qtd. in Bruyneel 119) and to transport "their own proper goods and effects" (Jay Treaty) without taxation. Although reconfirmed in the 1814 Treaty of Ghent, neither document was a treaty *with* Native peoples, yet the Canada–US border imposed a perimeter around, and in some cases directly through, the traditional territories of several tribal groups. As such, it has provided the focus for a number of localized acts of resistance and transgression, as well as for a more general stand in favour of Indigenous rights. Ironically, perhaps, the border itself presents an obstacle to the interpretation of the very clauses intended to erase it for Native peoples, since successive court systems in the United States and Canada have been unable to interpret the treaty in the same way. It has been codified in the United States in Section 289 of the Immigration and Nationality Act, which allows Native people to cross into the United States to live and work without a work permit on the production of evidence that they have 50 percent Aboriginal blood; its sanction in Canada, meanwhile, is far less clear and has generated numerous court cases, particularly over payment of duty. Arrests of Akwesasne women in 2008 for "border running" seriously undermined tribal jurisdiction and affronted the sovereign claims of the Mohawk, yet their story, magnified in the context of tensions on Six Nations land, is not uncommon for Native peoples along the length of the border. The Haudenosaunee, who do not formally recognize the United States and Canada as independent nation-states, are collectively perhaps the single best example, with well-known, decades-long controversies over bootlegging, and recent international news stories about the issuing of Haudenosaunee passports (see our introduction to this volume), border policing (in 2009 in particular), and the controversial evictions of non-Mohawk residents from Kahnawake in Quebec (2010). Such irregularities *are* frequently contested and protested.

The Indian Defense League of America (IDLA), for instance, was formed by Chief Clinton Rickard (Tuscarora) on 1 December 1926 in the wake of the Immigration Act (1924), "to guarantee unrestricted passage on the continent of North America for Indian people" (qtd. in Bruyneel 118). Rickard, Bruyneel notes, had been instructed by Chief Deskaheh (Levi General), "the official speaker and international spokesman for the Grand River Council of the Six Nations residing within Canada," to "fight for the line" shortly before the former's death (117). The IDLA's success in securing an amendment to the Immigration Act that guaranteed the rights of Indigenous peoples born in Canada to cross freely into the United States was celebrated with a parade across the Niagara Falls bridge, from Ontario to upper New York State, on 14 July 1928, an event repeated annually to this day (Bruyneel 199; for a description of other major gatherings at the border, see Northrup). What Rickard sought to redress in 1926, then, dubbed by Bruyneel "the postcolonial boundary politics of indigenous people" (119), is very much a live issue.

But it is not "merely" politics at stake in this shift of focus from the southern to the northern US border. While for "BAW/TAF members, the border was always much more than a line demarcating national space" (Fox 63), in *Third Bank* it is precisely that line of demarcation that we are invited to consider—partly through its imagery, partly through its placement. And where BAW/TAF members emphasized "the social and cultural dimensions of the U.S.–Mexico border over topographical ones" (Fox 63), Michelson emphatically returns us to topography, literally overlaying the political and cultural with that double evocation of a specific locale and a panoramic map; the photographic "witness" merges with cartographic (and commodifying) document, signifying the controlling mechanisms of land ownership (including surveying, surveillance, and commerce) and evoking the frontier as trade route. Where Rickard's endeavours broadly address a general principle in the free movement of Indigenous peoples in North America, Michelson's two pieces speak much more specifically to the act of *living on and in* that border region, indeed, in actively participating in its maintenance, where the "figment of someone else's imagination" (King 102) is a very clear and present geographical and political reality. In other words, although the borderlands themselves represent a space of social and cultural confluence, signified most directly in the title of Michelson's *Third Bank of the River*, the overlaying of the two-row wampum onto the border's topography returns the viewer to the ways in which the border-as-official narrative, whether national, social, or cultural, cuts across human interactions and interrupts the treaty's explicit acknowledgement of respect and reciprocity. Meanwhile, thinking about McKay's pieces as border art that speaks to the boundaried nature of Native experience, can, to borrow from Bruyneel's methodology, "demonstrate the complex and perennially contested way in which [North] American and Indigenous political actors map their people's claims to belong and therefore their authority in time and space" (xvi–xvii). The invocation of the border site in McKay's *Treaty of Niagara 1764*, for instance, oblique though it is, speaks directly to this doubled image, wherein the Niagara region itself represents both confluence (of cultures, nations, languages in trade and diplomacy) and barrier, both natural and artificial.

In the contexts described above, and in the contexts outlined by Maggie Bowers in chapter 7 of this book, the siting and nature of Michelson's art would seem to invite a postcolonial paradigm. Yet despite its location in the tri-nations border zone, and despite its blend of traditional imagery and contemporary media, the third bank metaphor in the context outlined here resists an all-subsuming rhetoric of hybridity implicated in border theory. Indeed, the piece's title invokes Homi Bhabha's "third space" and, in many ways, works away in the interstices (where better than a border post?). However, I emphasize here, and I believe the imagery itself stresses, the legal-political demarcation and the centralizing of Mohawk ethics and aesthetics in the transnational conversation. This is not to reassert a binary of pre- and postcolonial, or pure and corrupted notions of the authentic, but rather to look outside of the "conditions of colonial antagonism and inequity" (Meredith 2) that define postcolonial theory's hybridities.

From reductive assumptions about the syncretic nature of "mixed blood" identities, through the often pejorative notion of "cultural/colonial encounter" to designate a binary of conflict or assimilation, to the theoretical self-referentiality of postcolonialism's "third space," this discourse harbours assumptions about culture that risk forgetting the local, the topological, and the transcultural, in favour of the universal, cartographic, and transnational. That forgetting is ironic, given the emphasis on the local in postcolonial theory and the iconic placement of hybridity both at and as the border site in Gloria Anzaldúa's theorizing of the new *mestiza*. But as Laura Smyth Groening points out, all too often in a Native context, hybridity has become a code word for assimilation, lacking a truly "reciprocal" application to Native Canadian contexts (143 and *passim*). Although the language of postcolonial theory is broadly applicable to aspects of settler-invader/Native relations in the United States and Canada, Michelson's artwork and the fundamental premise of this chapter—the treaty itself—begin with an agreement between sovereign powers (see Borrows, Stark), which reminds us, first, of that nation-to-nation accord that belies the subsequent colonial narrative, and second, of the occlusion of Indigenous histories rendered by the postcolonial: "There is a troubling temporal aspect to most postcolonial discourse," writes Jace Weaver. "'Postcolonial' truly means a time *after* colonialism, and for the indigenes of the Anglo-colonial settler colonies that time has not yet come" (39). This contrasts dramatically with the image of colonial oppression/absorption and the consequent psychic resistance implicit in postcolonial discourse, albeit that resistance *has* frequently been an attendant consequence of the breaking of treaties.

For many Indigenous commentators, decolonization in North America begins and ends with the recognition and reassertion of pre-existing

Indigenous sovereignty (expressed predominantly through land, language, and self-governance). The power to "inhabit" one's hybridity, then, is by necessity also the power to resist it as an imposed category that prioritizes colonial contact over and above self-determination. Jace Weaver, in an essay in which he embraces the notion of pluralist separatism as a concept that both adequately defines the nature of American Indian (literary) nationalism and admits of the diversity and disagreement that more conventional notions of nationalism tend to preclude, notes simply that "to press everyone into a hybrid or mixed-blood mold is to consummate finally the as yet uncompleted enterprise of colonialism ... By accepting the label 'hybrid' ... Indigenous people relinquish the power to name themselves" (29). If one result of the postcolonial taxonomy is, ironically, to deprioritize the right to self-determination, an Indigenous response, according to Kanien'kehaka anthropologist Audra Simpson, is a "self-conscious traditionalism" in which the assertion of difference through performance becomes bound up with assertions of sovereignty: "Our very sovereignty," she writes, "in the European sense—depends on [that traditionalism], as we must continually prove our difference in order to have our rights respected ... This traditionalism is, therefore, very important in the context of the neo-colonial present, because it is the basis of our claim to difference, and difference is tied to sovereignty" (qtd. in Alfred 90). In this respect, indigeneity is so deeply implicated in colonialism and anthropology as, according to Simpson, the means by which Indigenous peoples have been known (Simpson 67), that its mechanisms of "resistance" and "subversion" through difference tend, ironically, to perpetuate the power imbalance. In the long run, "we might lose who we really are in order to perfect a dance that looks great, feels good at the time, but is done largely for the benefit of others—to meet someone else's standards of Indianness" (Simpson, qtd. in Alfred 90). She points, instead, to a Kahnawakero:non tradition of "refusal," in particular, "how refusal worked in everyday encounters to enunciate repeatedly to ourselves and to outsiders that 'this is who we are, this who you are, these are my rights'" (Simpson 73).

Fellow Kanien'kehaka Taiaiake Alfred, sympathetic to Simpson's concerns, nevertheless moderates them: "Working within a traditional framework, we must acknowledge the fact that cultures change and that any particular notion of what constitutes tradition will be contested. Nevertheless, we can identify certain common beliefs, values, and principles that form the persistent core of a community's culture" (16). He cites the two-row as the epitome of that commonality. All of this, in itself, is under scrutiny in *Third Bank*, whose aesthetic invites the "traditional" but resists the static museological compresses of "Indian art." In its evocation of the two-row wampum, *Third Bank* draws heavily on ideas of tradition and its representative practices, not least where, as Dale Turner notes in *This Is Not a Peace Pipe*, "indigenous philosophy is rooted in the oral tradition" (47). He continues: "The main political significance of wampum was to represent—materially—the morally binding nature of an agreement or promise ... Wampum belts served as the 'text' in the sense that they materialized the agreement itself. What made the wampum belts valuable was that each had a story attached to it" (47). Alfred helpfully notes that "[t]he meanings of our traditional teachings are embedded in the structure of the narrative as much as in any words one might write to explain them" (15). But the state-of-the-art techniques Michelson employs evoke an equally postmodern vernacular—one that negates any notional "pastness" associated with "tradition" through the logic of currency, presence, contemporaneity. If we view the wampum and Third Bank as narrative, then the values they impart are arguably intrinsic to their form, both in the parallel strips of purple and (literally in the former, figuratively in the latter) in the weft and weave of thread and bead. The story they tell is of ongoing dynamic exchange—of sovereign entities at once evolving and resisting subordination to the other—within a third space of contact. In this space, theoretical, legal, and political, citizenship may be multiple, national identity mutable, and cultural identity a rich and textured fabric that admits of both change and continuity.

This separation of form and content inheres in the distinction Craig S. Womack draws between the specific (value within community) and the abstract ("authenticity"): "A more astute model for tradition would acknowledge its meanings in a community rather than expending so much energy on point of origin. It would acknowledge other possibilities than hybridity by recognizing traditions that are fluid yet still retain some kind of continuity with the community that claims them and perceives them as part of its own culture" (140). Whether or not the Mohawk community claims Michelson's art,[5] the imagery it conveys is deeply rooted in the values and history shared by the Haudenosaunee directly and shared (strategically) with First Nations peoples more generally in the two-row principle, which encompasses the wampum, the territory of the river and its shoreline itself, and treaty-recognized sovereignty. "Hybrid" it may be in the strictest sense of its materials, but philosophically, aesthetically, and ethically it is well grounded in a centuries-long tradition that includes adaptation and exchange among its core constituents.

Birchbark, Treaties, and Two-Row Wampum

Alex McKay's *Treaty Canoe* and *Treaty of Niagara 1764* maintain a quietly insistent interrogation of historic treaty relations and their ongoing legacy, while Michelson's installation at Massena, considered within this framework, engenders a number of additional questions of serious import for Native art and politics in both the United States and Canada. His exploration of the triple representation of national "territory," landscape, and the colonial relationship, and the political significance of siting *Third Bank* not just at the border but at a port of entry into the United States, cannot be seen outside the many claims to and arguments over the political and cultural sovereignty of Native peoples. What does it mean to recognize the complex "balance" the border site represents, both straddled in this fashion and "centred" by Akwesasne sovereign territory? In what kind of discourse does the artwork engage the public communities that pass through the site? How important is the official sanctioning of this kind of artwork, by a Native artist, particularly in relation to the "guerrilla" art, unofficial installations, and artistic protests long associated with the US–Mexico border? And finally, as pieces of artwork, how do *Third Bank* and *TwoRow II* succeed in representing the complex cultural and political nexus of the borderlands of New York and Ontario?

McKay's two pieces, responding clearly to many of the same issues and sources as Michelson, do so, at first, in more apparently museological terms. *Canoe* merges two seemingly dichotomous cultural "vehicles," one of which engenders something fixed while the other recalls the flux and contingency of the river, the hunt, and so on. In doing so, it emphasizes agreement and cooperation between Aboriginal and Euro-Canadian peoples in a form that also actualizes the appropriative mechanisms of colonial dominance that ultimately absorb the indigenous vessel into "a central place in the life and culture of Canada" (qtd. in Canadian Canoe Museum). Thus, *Canoe* imagines the respectful and mutual relationship reflected by the treaties themselves, critiques their undoing, and, in the contexts engendered by Michelson's work, enacts their figurative mapping onto Indigenous cultures as both a sustaining *and* vanishing force. Paradox is also at the heart of *Niagara* in the shape of the megaphone that is "mute." Again, signifying the treaty as means of both communication and occlusion, the sister piece to *Canoe* also speaks of "mutual, sacred bonds of honour" (McKay) in the recognition of Indigenous sovereignty, while implicitly addressing the repeated failures of those bonds, such as promises made in the Royal Proclamation of 1763, the Treaty of Fort Niagara in 1764, and the Treaty of Fort Stanwix in 1768, which were then ignored by the border-establishing 1783 Treaty of Paris. Taking much of the same imagery as Michelson's work, placing a similar emphasis on the river and on matters of "landscape, place, and identity," McKay's works ask perhaps more generally what it means to be Canadian—or, more specifically, what it means to be part of this historic and ongoing treaty relationship, which includes, of course, Great Britain, the implications of which are once more under the spotlight with the development of the Idle No More movement (see our Introduction to this volume). Questions of citizenship and sovereignty lie at the heart of both, as well as a dialectic of absence and presence, whereby the dissolve between landscape and two-row figures Native presence in the landscape in Michelson's work. In McKay's, this is arguably inverted, the canoe—that most "indigenous" of symbols—cast in treaty facsimiles signifying a spectral absence, echoing the muteness of *Niagara*.

Both *Canoe* and *Niagara* make simple but powerful gestures to defamiliarize the media of their construction. The birchbark megaphone inscribed with the piece's title at once evokes the scrolls (*wiigwaasabakoon*) long used by Anishinaabeg (among others) for geometric patterns, mnemonic writing systems, and sacred maps, and of course a simple but effective technology most commonly associated with political protest and/or crowd control. Inverting assumptions (about Indigenous writing systems, European orature), the piece both unsettles the comfortable dichotomy of Native and settler-invader while ironically emphasizing the historical amnesia that the metaphor of the silent megaphone represents. *Canoe*, meanwhile, plays with the juxtaposition of technologies and economies by replacing the traditional birchbark skin of the canoe with transcribed treaties. That the piece evokes the two-row wampum when it casts its shadow invokes the further juxtaposition of mnemonics and writing, the two forms of treaty or accord, and the specifics of the value systems brought into tension by the artwork. Explicitly blurring the boundaries between text and speech, tradition and "progress," through technological intervention, McKay's work both reminds its viewers of the core values inherent in these moments of cultural and political exchange, and of the implicit betrayals they have come to signify.

Figuring bordered experience as a series of "borrowings" and "mergings," McKay's pieces commemorate the cultural encounter as a problematic site of good intention and betrayal. *Canoe*, in particular, celebrates diplomacy and memorializes the act of collaboration in one of Canada's most recognizable—and recognizably Indigenous—symbols. That in doing so the piece risks eliding the problematic aspect of that collaboration, effectively re-enacting the appropriative nature of the relationship, is then acknowledged explicitly in *Niagara*. *Niagara* not only addresses the process of elision implicit in the colonial endeavour but also re-places both artworks as site-specific (both geographically and historically) at the borders of First Nations and European experience, thereby grounding the more ubiquitous symbolism of *Canoe* in a localized context of the Great Lakes.[6] So the two pieces together simultaneously address *and* embody the silencing of Native voices and the smothering of Native sovereignty through several levels of political, economic, and cultural co-option. In doing so they force conversation about the impact of those processes—particularly as they articulate connections between apparently benign "borrowings" such as the canoe itself and the wholesale land grab of colonization—as well as reflection on the ongoing obligations, including historical culpability, of present-day Canadian society. Recent events around the Idle No More movement in Canada make such recognition ever more potent, such conversations ever more urgent.

At the darker end of this interpretation, then, the canoe becomes a metonym for First Nations autonomy, smothered by the smoke and mirrors of

Western sovereignty, an example of the assimilative bureaucracy identified by Alfred and others. And of course, the legal jurisdictions of treaty-making, including their metes and bounds provisions, are easily trammelled when the rules—and the type—are established by one side with the good faith of the other. Heidi Kiiwetinepinesiik Stark, for instance, notes that "the written document rarely represented the vast expressions of Indigenous sovereignty, nationhood, and land tenure articulated within the council" (149): the treaty, or the various gifts involved such as wampum, in other words, confirmed but did not represent or articulate the decisions made at council negotiations. Here, then, *Niagara* reminds us of the silencing action of treaties, literally parcelling up that good faith, while the shadow of the *Treaty Canoe* cast on the gallery wall raises *Kaswehnta* as a vaporous spectre, a resonant trace of the neither fully realizable nor fully escapable ideal of Indigenous–white political relations.

Both artists' work, however, reminds us that the intent behind the treaty—in spirit if not in fine print—needs to be kept very much alive. In their very different evocations of the dynamics of interpersonal and intercultural relations, the border between the ship and the canoe (both perimeter and bridge) remains clear and crisp yet: the tangled relations between settler and Native societies inhere in this symbolic invocation of rivers, vessels, and covenants. If *Treaty Canoe* begins (and I stress the word *begins*) with a notion of failure, with the absented "Indian" absorbed into a national icon comprised of the very documentation that justified settlement and removal, then it ends in reflection and demands conversation as to the role of the viewer in its ongoing journey. In *Third Bank*, meanwhile, the treaty, rather than standing as synecdoche for diplomatic failures, takes on the presence of the river itself, that ever-changing yet ever-present force. When visitors encounter Michelson's monumental glass-and-light installation at the border post, they witness a reassertion of the principles inherent in that original accord. In that respect, *Third Bank* is a demonstration of aesthetic and political sovereignty—or, more appropriately, *tewatatowie* ("we take care of ourselves" [Alfred 135])—that also effects a bridge across the border, visually joining its three banks while mapping the border zone itself. Although the piece combines its elements—and although *TwoRow II* becomes the sum of its opposing shorelines and juxtaposed audio—those elements remain separate, *plural*, brought together but never merged. In the spirit of the two-row, the artwork renegotiates cooperation with independence. As Kanien'Kehaka spokesman Atsenhaienton notes of that principle, "I do believe that we can coexist with the Canadian and American governments without violating our own constitution. They have to understand that we don't intend to destroy Canada or the United States, but that we have a right to determine for ourselves our relationships" (qtd. in Alfred 138–9). That right, underpinned by the key principles of peace, responsibility, and reciprocity, is explicit in the ethical foundation of the two-row accord.

The aesthetic dimension of the work, which reflects that ethics, similarly re-places First Nations self-determination in the foreground. Michelson draws subtly on a picturesque tradition, complicating and interrogating its (and our) assumptions about land and landscape, transition and deep belonging to place. On one level, the colonial narrative of the national border, along with its attendant narratives of nationhood, territorial possession, and sovereignty, is interrupted, displaced even, by the presence of Cornwall Island (both literally and in the artwork). As Alfred reminds us:

> You need your space; each person and every nation shares the proper allotment in the circle, and that's how our nationhood was expressed. Part of the problem now is that our space hasn't been respected, that we've had structures and ideas imposed on us. We need to reclaim our intellectual, political, and geographical space. (19; Alfred's italics)

On another level, the picturesque tradition is itself disrupted. Intervening in those cultural narratives described above, Michelson draws the political out of the scenic: an image of the Alcoa brick factory at Massena, for instance, undercuts the Romantic, while in the similarly evocative *TwoRow II* the voices of elders telling stories about the river interfere with and juxtapose that touristic spiel that posits the river as source of leisure and commerce. It is precisely through these interruptions that *Third Bank* actively reframes, rather than rejects, the multiple histories of hybridity discourse and, negating that commodified image of land-as-leisure, reconstitutes the landscape *as* ethical framework. Although neither artwork includes people (notwithstanding the human interaction that is clearly supplied by individuals in the museum/border post, actualizing the ethical interaction with the landscape in the act of viewing the art), *Third Bank* in particular figures those multiple histories in the spatial-temporal relationship between the river (diachronic), the brick factory (synchronic), and the Seaway International Bridge (chronotopic).

TwoRowII arguably places far greater weight on cultural "clash." Morris notes: "In the gallery, the two [audiovisual loops] run simultaneously, competing and conflicting as narratives, but never quite canceling one another out. As if to further underscore the degree to which the two cultures—the two sides of the river—are at odds, Michelson set the two video tracks moving in opposite directions; the Native and the non-Native worlds literally run at cross purposes" (Morris, "Art" 39). Running parallel but separate, the discordant sense of sound and sight in *TwoRow II* emphasizes cultural and political separateness, figured in the shared space of the borderland but not absorbed by it, while *Third Bank* more forcefully reasserts the significance of accord.

Like McKay's two pieces, "*TwoRow II* reminds viewers that the treaties and agreements made between Native and European Nations have not been honored." An example is the loss of "nearly 90 percent of the [Six Nations]

Reserve's land base promised by the [1784] Haldimand Deed," as noted in the soundtrack (Morris, "Art" 39). But *Third Bank* shifts the emphasis of those ear- lier pieces away from the disruption/refraction of the colonial text (already challenged in *TwoRow II* by the dominant two-row motif). In other words, it does not perform in quite the same way, as an anti-(neo)colonial critique. The danger is that *Third Bank*'s bold statement suggests that Native nations are equal participants in the tri-nation relationship, rendering them complicit in the mechanisms of state policing enacted at the border. But again, *Third Bank*'s location simultaneously invites and deflates such a reading. The thirty-seven newly built and/or renovated border posts on the US side of the border have all been established with a dual purpose: the first is that of surveillance and containment in the wake of 9/11; the second is with the specific remit of pre- senting a positive face for federal operations to new arrivals in the United States (Morris, "Art" 38). The potential for a vaguely troubling kind of institutional endorsement in this context is self-consciously acknowledged by Smith-Miller and Hawkinson, the architects of the Massena Land Port, who incorporated Michelson's artwork. According to publicity for a 2009 exhibition at the Van Alen Institute in New York, which included two of their land ports and Michel- son's installation, "as both ceremonial gateways and sites of surveillance and regulation, the ports must convey a sense of openness as well as security. The architects use aesthetics—particularly material effects of transparency, trans- lucency, and opacity—to negotiate the contradictions of the program and to gesture towards the buildings' equivocal, post-9/11 geopolitical landscape" (Van Alen Institute).

An ironic footnote to this balance between aesthetic openness and security is that a 180-foot supergraphic "United States" banner situated on the Can- adian face of the port building was dismantled in August 2009 due to mainten- ance and security concerns. In this context, Michelson's artwork, then, arguably echoes the architects' remit (and is certainly used in that way by them), offering itself as a "ceremonial gateway" even while drawing attention to the border as a site of "surveillance and regulation." Again, where better than the border with Akwesasne territory to engage this paradox? It literally welcomes transient travellers *as guests* onto Mohawk land but somewhat subversively refuses the kind of cultural bridging one might anticipate in such a dominant, publicly funded (and public) artwork, converting barrier to bridge by way of permission to pass, perhaps more than by licence to remain. Rather, it powerfully reminds/ alerts its viewers of/to the longer history of Haudenosaunee presence in the region, prioritizing Native peoples' deep belonging to this land and this river and this island. It literally inhabits the border as a site of Indigenous presence that unsettles coherent narratives of the nation-state. As Tuscarora artist, pho- tographer, and art historian Jolene Rickard has argued, "the cultural arena is a viable site to enact and witness art that probes Indigenous experience in the ongoing struggle to have a presence in the global cultural space" (qtd. in Ginsberg 28). *Third Bank*, then, intervenes in the transnational discourse of border crossing in surprising and subtly provocative ways.

Conclusion

Both McKay and Michelson draw on concrete motifs that ground their works in geographical and figurative borderlands. But *Third Bank* steps away from the synecdochic sense of the border or boundary as assumption of difference and damage—the dishonoured treaty, the unbridgeable divide between self and other—or the borderland as contact zone, to reimagine all of these things (difference, divide, encounter) in terms of the original two-row wampum and as an explicit foregrounding of the sovereignty of the Akwesasne Mohawk: separate but equal. If this seems an optimistic reading, it is perhaps because of its very location, within the public domain of the US border post. Writing about the US–Mexico border, Anzaldúa insists on the ambiguity of bordered identity; *Third Bank*, in contrast, invokes emplaced citizenship at the border. It imagines a state not of ambiguity but of certainty, neither hybridity nor some unreachable notion of "purity," but primacy of the dual concerns and values implicit in the two-row treaty. If the southern US border is an open wound (Anzaldúa 25), at the northern border we see gestures toward healing by the refusal to compromise those earlier accords and timeless values. That it raises difficult questions about the nature of citizenship at precisely this juncture—about Alan Cairns's reiteration of "Citizens Plus" at one end of the political spectrum, and about Seneca scholar Robert Porter's assertion that dual citizenship is a "zero-sum game of political participation" (qtd. in Biolsi 253) at the other; about the hospitality of the Mohawk, who play host to border crossers on a daily basis yet whose own right to host is still a matter of urgent struggle; and about the temporal and spatial span of US and Canadian history as reflected through this purple and white lens—speaks to its timeliness.

The distinction I have made here is in reading *Third Bank* particularly not just as a work that reflects a political reality or hope, but also as one that both enacts and demands an ethical engagement into the future. Its viewers are not asked to search their consciences; rather, they are reminded that as they cross to Cornwall Island they are participating in a long-standing mutual agreement between representatives of their nation and another. The artwork's position at the physical border post is crucial here, for politics *and* art, particularly in light of Fisher's claim that Western (art) institutions tend "to position 'ethnic' artists outside the discourses of modern experience" (44). In the wake of 9/11, what could be more "modern" than a state-of-the-art border post?

Third Bank becomes an example of Native art that stands for a "means of worldly intervention … that can simultaneously strengthen [Native artists'] own communities while assisting in, and insisting on, the broader presence of Indigenous perspectives in a variety of arenas" (Ginsberg 28–29). Here, the Canada–US relationship is a negotiation with and through a third self-defining sovereign nation. That placement forces the transnational dialogue to be refigured through another lens, with the Mohawk at the centre rather than on the periphery. That the primary vehicle for this refiguring (unlike the treaty scripts of McKay's *Canoe*, despite its evocative shadow) is the highly culturally specific wampum belt adds one further important element to the mix. As Gough notes, "the use of alternative visual/vocal language forms may help in offering other interpretations of stories without the inherent historical/cultural boundaries of the English language … If used within these possibilities the English language will appear the interloper rather than the omniscient inventor" (94).

Bruyneel describes the persistent imposition of boundaries on tribal nations, noting, however, that "indigenous tribes straddle the temporal and spatial boundaries of American politics, exposing the incoherence of these boundaries" (xv). Cornwall Island, sitting as it does mid-stream, disrupts the spatial boundary of the US–Canada border and floats (literally) outside its temporal parameters, biding its moment. If, as McKay's works subtly but provocatively remind us, successive colonial governments have failed to live up to their side of the bargain, Michelson's installation at the Massena border post is a timely reminder that the accord is a vital—in every sense—aspect of the geopolitical landscape. Neither *Third Bank* nor *TwoRow II* idealize the geographies of the St. Lawrence and Grand rivers; neither romanticizes the present-day relationship between Native and non-Native communities or governments. Both, however, force their viewers (and listeners) to look and keep looking as the familiar changes; as new features of the landscape resolve; and as the significance of the artworks emerges.

Notes

1 *Treaty Canoe* has, since its first installation, always been exhibited with *Treaty of Niagara 1764*.

2 This "space" is not uncomplicated, and McKay's work represents a fraught politics, since he is a non-Native artist utilizing and engaging with motifs and concerns so central to First Nations identities and resistance. It is clear, though, that the intent behind the piece is to both recognize occlusive processes and, through their self-conscious articulation, to generate a kind of collective self-reflection that can ultimately inform change in Canadian–First Nations relations. Misao Dean, for instance, describes the work as an act of decolonization (of the canoe, specifically).

3 For a useful summary of key issues (that partly reflects the differences in the relationships between tribal nations and the US and Canadian governments), see Dobson 113–21, and Roberts in this volume, as well as Barker and Weaver.

4 An excerpt of the installation can be viewed on the artist's website: http://alan michelson.com/work.

5 Michelson has noted that at the time of the piece's installation, and despite "long-simmering border issues (Canada's decision to arm its border agents on Cornwall Island) and land claims issues (Six Nations land reclamation in Caledonia,

Ontario)," he was not aware of any community response to his *TwoRowII*, which had largely been restricted to a museum audience, and the community at Akwesasne had not yet had a chance to interact with *Third Bank* (personal correspondence, 19 March 2011).

6   Significantly, Indigenous protestors from Michigan and Ontario commemorated the Jay Treaty / protested the failures to uphold its spirit by paddling canoes across the Detroit river (and thus across the border) in August 2010 (see Welker).

Works Cited

Alfred, Taiaiake. *Peace, Power, Righteousness: An Indigenous Manifesto*. Toronto: Oxford UP, 2009.

Anzaldúa, Gloria. *Borderlands/La Frontera: The New Mestiza*. 2nd ed. San Francisco: Aunt Lute, 1999.

Barker, Joanne. "For Whom Sovereignty Matters." *Sovereignty Matters: Locations of Contestation and Possibility in Indigenous Struggles for Self-Determination*. Ed. Joanne Barker. Lincoln: U of Nebraska P, 2005. 1–31.

Bhabha, Homi K. *The Location of Culture*. London: Routledge, 1994.

Biolsi, Thomas. "Imagined Geographies: Sovereignty, Indigenous Space, and American Indian Struggle." *American Ethnologist* 32.2 (2005): 239–59.

Borrows, John. "Wampum at Niagara: The Royal Proclamation, Canadian Legal History, and Self-Government." *Aboriginal Treaty Rights in Canada: Essays on Law, Equity, and Respect for Difference*. Ed. Michael Asch. Vancouver: UBC P, 1997. 155–72.

Bruyneel, Kevin. *The Third Space of Sovereignty: The Postcolonial Politics of U.S.–Indigenous Relations*. Minneapolis: U of Minnesota P, 2007.

Canadian Canoe Museum. "Treaty Canoe Exhibit." 2009. http://www.canoemuseum .ca/index.php/20090227171/collections-exhibits/treaty-canoe-exhibit/treaty -canoe.html. Accessed 15 September 2010.

Cardinal, Douglas J. "Architecture as a Living Process." *Canadian Journal of Native Education* 22.1 (1998): 3–9.

Chávez, Patricio, Madelein Grynsztejn, and Kathryn Kanjo, eds. *La Frontera/The Border: Art about the Mexican/United States Border Experience*. San Diego: Centro Cultural de la Raza, 1993.

Dean, Misao. *Inheriting a Canoe Paddle: The Canoe in Discourses of English-Canadian Nationalism*. Toronto: U of Toronto P, 2013.

Dimock, Wai Chee. "Introduction: Planet and America, Set and Subset." *Shades of the Planet: American Literature as World Literature*. Ed. Wai Chee Dimock and Lawrence Buell. Princeton: Princeton UP, 2007. 1–16.

Dobson, Kit. *Transnational Canadas: Anglo-Canadian Literature and Globalization*. Waterloo: Wilfrid Laurier UP, 2009.

Fisher, Jean. "In Search of the 'Inauthentic': Disturbing Signs in Contemporary Native American Art." *Art Journal* 51.3 (1992): 44–50.

Fox, Claire F. "The Portable Border: Site-Specificity, Art, and the U.S.–Mexico Frontier." *Social Text* 41 (1994): 61–82.

Ginsberg, Faye. "Resources of Hope: Learning from the Local in a Transnational Era." Smith and Ward 27–47.

Gómez-Peña, Guillermo. "A Binational Performance Pilgrimage." *Drama Review (TDR)* 35.3 (1991): 22–45.

———. "The New World Border: Prophecies for the End of the Century." *TDR* 38.1 (1994): 119–42.

Gough, Julie. "History, Representation, Globalisation and Indigenous Cultures: A Tasmanian Perspective." Smith and Ward 89–108.

Groening, Laura Smyth. *Listening to Old Woman Speak: Natives and alterNatives in Canadian Literature.* Montreal and Kingston: McGill–Queen's UP, 2004.

Guimarães Rosa, João. "The Third Bank of the River." Trans. William L. Grossman. *The Oxford Book of Latin American Short Stories.* Ed. Roberto González Echevarría. New York: Oxford UP, 1997. 256–60.

Jay's Treaty. *Treaty of Amity, Commerce, and Navigation.* 1794. Internet. http://www.earlyamerica.com/earlyamerica/milestonesjaytreaty/text.html. Accessed 11 September 2010.

King, Thomas. *The Truth about Stories: A Native Narrative.* Minneapolis: U of Minnesota P, 2005.

McKay, Alex. *A. MCKAY: PROJECTS, 1988–1999.* http://www.alexmckay.ca/alexmckay.ca/Past_Projects.html. Accessed 11 September 2010.

Meredith, Paul. "Hybridity in the Third Space: Rethinking Bi-cultural Politics in Aotearoa/New Zealand." Paper presented to Te Oru Rangahau Maori Research and Development Conference. 1998. http://lianz.waikato.ac.nz/PAPERS/paul/hybridity.pdf. Accessed 7 September 2010.

Michelson, Alan. *Alan Michelson.* http://alanmichelson.com. Accessed 7 September 2010.

Morris, Kate. "Art on the River: Alan Michelson Highlights Border-Crossing Issues." *American Indian* (Winter 2009): 37–40.

———. 2011. "Running the 'Medicine Line': Images of the Border in Contemporary Native American Art." *American Indian Quarterly* 35.4 (2011): 549–78.

Neustadt, Robert Alan. *(Con)fusing Signs and Postmodern Positions: Spanish American Performance: Spanish American Performance, Experimental Writing, and the Critique of Political Confusion.* New York: Garland, 1999.

Northrup, Jim. *Rez Road Follies: Canoes, Casinos, Computers, and Birch Bark Baskets.* Minneapolis: U of Minnesota P, 1999.

Prieto, Antonio. "Border Art as a Political Strategy." 1999. *Information Services Latin America.* http://isla.igc.org/Features/Border/mex6.html. Accessed 8 September 10.

Simpson, Audra. "On Ethnographic Refusal: Indigeneity, 'Voice,' and Colonial Citizenship." *Junctures: The Journal for Thematic Dialogue* 9 (2007): 67–80.

Smith, Claire, and Graham K. Ward, eds. *Indigenous Cultures in an Interconnected World.* Vancouver: UBC P, 2000.

Stark, Heidi Kiiwetinepinesiik. "Respect, Responsibility, and Renewal: The Foundations of Anishinaabe Treaty Making with the United States and Canada." *American Indian Culture and Research Journal* 34.2 (2010): 145–64.

Turner, Dale. *This Is Not a Peace Pipe: Towards a Critical Indigenous Philosophy.* Toronto: U of Toronto P, 2006.

Van Alen Institute. "Aesthetics of Crossing: Land Ports of Entry / Citizenship by Design." *Projects in Public Architecture* 1–31 July 2009. http://www.vanalen.org/projects/exhibitions/AestheticsOfCrossing. Accessed 12 January 2011.

Weaver, Jace. "Splitting the Earth: First Utterances and Pluralist Separatism." Weaver, Womack, and Warrior 1–90.

Weaver, Jace, Craig S. Womack, and Robert Warrior. *American Indian Literary Nationalism*. Albuquerque: U of New Mexico P, 2006.

Welker, Glenn. "Jay Treaty Crossing: Michigan Asserts Sovereignty Rights in Canoe Crossing." *Indigenous People's Literature Weblog.* http://indiglit.wordpress.com/2010/08/31/jay-treaty-crossing-michigan-asserts-sovereignty-rights-in-canoe-crossing.html. Accessed 6 May 2011.

Womack, Craig S. "The Integrity of American Indian Claims: or How I Learned to Stop Worrying and Love My Hybridity." Weaver, Womack, and Warrior 91–178.

eleven

Cross-Border Identifications and Dislocations
Visual Art and the Construction of Identity in North America

Sarah E.K. Smith

My America is a continent (not a country) that is not described by the outlines on any of the standard maps. In my America, "West" and "North" are mere nostalgic abstraction—the South and the East have slipped into their mythical space.

Guillermo Gómez-Peña, 1996

Geography as an epistemic category is in turn grounded in issues of positionality, in questions of who has the power and authority to name, of who has the power and authority to subsume others into its hegemonic identity.

Irit Rogoff, 2001

CONTEMPORARY PERFORMANCE ARTIST AND WRITER Guillermo Gómez-Peña suggests the possibility of redefining America in terms of hemispheric unity, as a North American continent where national boundaries are irrelevant. Ironically, his utopian vision is seemingly legitimized by processes of neoliberal globalization that have led to increasing North American integration under free trade agreements implemented since the late 1980s. At the same time, Gómez-Peña draws attention to the constructed nature of our understanding of geography, with each direction a changing construct charged with racial and political stereotypes. The naturalization of these geographic categories is also critiqued by visual culture historian Irit Rogoff, who exposes the significant amount of power accorded to geographic methods of organization, which she notes are rarely critically examined (21). Links among terrain, identity, and power are seen in the state's capacity to employ art in the service of national/ist projects.[1] Visual art has long been harnessed to create and disseminate national myths. In the post-national context, in which the naturalization of the nation-state as an organizing structure has been revealed, visual art is being employed in new ways to shore up the nation; in doing so, it is playing a key role in defining and sustaining state borders in North America.

In this chapter, I examine the border between Canada and the United States in relation to the visual arts, for the purpose of revealing the role that exhibitions and artworks play in defining borders in the "new" North America. My focus will be on the historical context of the North American Free Trade Agreement (NAFTA). Conventionally, Border Studies scholars have focused in North America on the US–Mexico border, perceiving it as highly charged compared to the Canada–US border. The same emphasis is found in art history, where scholarship about border art has foregrounded the US–Mexico border as a locus of artistic energy. This focus is exemplified by artistic collectives such as the Border Arts Workshop/Taller de Arte Fronterizo, established in San Diego in 1984 with the mandate to produce art addressing issues along the US–Mexico border ("Border Art"). While the significance of the US–Mexico border as both a site and an impetus for cultural production is undeniable, this focus has overshadowed the study of the Canada–US border in relation to the visual arts. Specifically, it has marginalized the study of the Canada–US border's relation to the US–Mexico border, as well as the larger North American context of both borders.

This chapter addresses the lack of attention paid to the Canada–US border. I connect that border to North American exhibitions of modern art employed to promote hemispheric continental integration in the post-NAFTA era. I begin by investigating the online exhibition "Panoramas: The North American Landscape in Art" as a venue for the three North American governments to advance continental parity.[2] Here, my discussion extends beyond the physical Canada–US border to focus on how visual art has been employed in public education about the border and in the formation of new relationships across borders in North America. After that, I investigate Canadian Aboriginal artist Rebecca Belmore's installation *Awasinake: On the Other Side* (1997), recontextualizing her work as part of a more expansive discussion of Indigeneity in North America. Subsequently, I contrast her work with the continent's visual culture as it has been promoted by the modern art exhibitions that have proliferated since the signing of NAFTA.

Picturing the "New" North America

The "new" North America heralded during the 1990s grew slowly out of North American economic integration, which began in the late 1980s. Historian and anthropologist Herman W. Konrad suggests that this integration dates back even earlier to the late nineteenth century (15). Integration is neither a permanent process nor a static one; to date, Canada continues to negotiate free trade agreements with nations outside of North America ("Foreign Affairs and International Trade Canada"). North American integration has been characterized as a gradual movement, one that links states at the regional and binational levels and that leads in turn to global agreements such the World Trade Organization (WTO) (Grinspun and Shamsie 3). The trade agreement regulating North

America is NAFTA, implemented on 1 January 1994. NAFTA is both evidence of ongoing continental integration and a result of that integration. It is also significant for being the first agreement to unite the three North American nations and to assert their neoliberal approaches to trade.

This integration has not been without resistance. The alter-globalization movement has questioned the dominance of economic neoliberalism, which has been promoted and expanded largely through free trade agreements and entities such as the WTO.[3] In Canada, free trade with the United States, under the FTA (the Canada–United States Free Trade Agreement, the predecessor of NAFTA), was the dominant issue in the 1988 federal election. NAFTA was similarly controversial across the continent, both before and after its implementation. In the United States in the early 1990s, the public grew increasingly wary the closer the agreement came to being ratified (Orme xiv). NAFTA's implementation was also marred by the Zapatista rebellion in Chiapas. More recently, in the wake of the 9/11 terrorist attacks on New York and Washington, security issues have become prominent at North American borders. The events of 9/11 have led to a "thickened" Canada–US border: the number of guards increased more than threefold between 2001 and 2008, and trade across the border has dropped significantly since 2001 (Grady). Such developments underscore the need for trilateral cultural initiatives, including visual art exhibitions, since NAFTA.

"The relationship among nations and societies cannot be understood," Stephen J. Randall and Herman W. Konrad argue, "let alone legitimately defined, solely in economic terms" (11). Events in Canada during the 1990s encouraged trilateral relations outside NAFTA's parameters. Canada hosted the XIII Pan American Games, the Conference of the Spouses of Heads of State and Government of the Americas, the American Business Forum (in Toronto), the Free Trade Area of the Americas Trade Ministers Meeting, the Organization of American States General Assembly, and the Third Summit of the Americas in Quebec City (NGCA [Pappas]). It is not a coincidence that these events were held while exhibitions promoting a unified North America were being conceptualized and developed. Clearly, then, NAFTA can be read as a marker of change in North American representation, signifying the creation and promotion of a new North American landscape characterized by increasing economic and cultural ties across the three states. As a result of this reconceptualization of the continent and its borders, we can understand the period following NAFTA as rife with societal and national/ist changes that were mediated by visual art exhibitions. In fact, cultural theorist George Yúdice argues that free trade has intensified changes in national culture in the North American states (*Expediency* 230).

All of this has had an impact on North America's borders. The neoliberal approach to trade taken by Canada, Mexico, and the United States emphasized the permeability of North America's borders, even if this was not extended to all the people who were attempting to cross them. Significantly, public understandings of the border changed with NAFTA, in the sense that the continent was increasingly viewed as an integrated unit. As José Manuel Valenzuela Arce suggests, borders need to be understood as spaces of dynamic interaction and as "spheres of changing social relations" (79). These social relations changed after NAFTA's implementation in ways that affected the identity of individual nations as well as the relations among the three North American nations. Furthermore, national myths are strongly linked to a nation's borders, for states draw upon or resist these boundaries to create narratives. As Amelia Kalant puts it, "myths normalize and create boundaries (territorial, cultural, racial, linguistic) of the nation" (14). With NAFTA, new relationships were created—for instance, a strengthened partnership between Canada and Mexico. NAFTA also changed the Canada–US border, not only by increasing commerce between the two states but also by reconceptualizing the continent's bilateral and trilateral relationships. This integration was tempered, however, by tensions between cultural distinctiveness and the need for cultural parity. Kalant describes this ambiguous relationship as Canada's "double life within the U.S. shadow," a bond characterized by certain privileges but simultaneously by fears of marginalization (5).

Notwithstanding the rise of post-national rhetoric, national/ist projects have retained their importance in a globalizing world. "The state itself has been a key agent in the implementation of global processes," Saskia Sassen explains, "and it emerged quite altered by this participation" (28). Culture has done much to reaffirm national/ist projects in the wake of increased neoliberal globalization. A framework for understanding the changing role of culture during times of neoliberal globalization is provided by Yúdice, who writes that culture has become entrenched in economic and political spheres (*Expediency* 9). He proposes a process of transnational cultural brokering as a structure from which to understand new uses of culture. Yúdice posits that this process of meditating national/ist projects between states is different from the traditional employment of art in the service of the nation due to its reliance on transnational relationships (*Expediency* 239; "Transnational" 199). Transnational cultural brokering entails using culture to deploy national/ist projects in order to further a nation's global interests—for example, within trade partnerships (*Expediency* 93). One prominent case of such brokering in North America was "Mexico: Splendors of Thirty Centuries" (Canclini 102), an exhibition shown in New York City, San Antonio, and Los Angeles in 1990 to 1991, and in revised form in Monterrey, Mexico, in 1992. However, this exhibition's prominence is unusual; many other exhibitions have been invisible as vehicles for cultural diplomacy.

The turn of the millennium saw several large exhibitions, mainly of modern art, that promoted North American artists and circulated in Canada, Mexico, and the United States. These included "Mexican Modern Art, 1900–1950"; "Panoramas: The North American Landscape in Art"; "Carr, O'Keeffe, Kahlo: Places of Their Own"; and "Perspectives: Women Artists in North America." Two trends are evidenced by these exhibitions. The first is the strong promotion of Mexican art in Canada, notable because Canadian museums had paid little attention before to Mexican art. The second trend, and the focus of this chapter, has been the rise of exhibitions that celebrate North American cultural parity, promoting a new regional identity that bonds artists and artworks together from the three North American national canons. Exhibitions exemplifying this trend include "Panoramas" and "Perspectives," online exhibitions launched in 2001 and 2002 respectively; and "Carr, O'Keeffe, Kahlo," a touring exhibition shown in Canada and the United States in 2001 and 2002. "Panoramas" and "Perspectives" attracted large and diverse audiences, partly because they were online and were available in English, French, and Spanish. "Carr, O'Keeffe, Kahlo" was widely shown in Canada and the United States. This accessibility cannot be understated. As Judith Huggins Balfe suggests, "artworks are intended to 'win the hearts and minds of the people,' who may never even attend their domestic exhibition but know of it only through media coverage" (213).

Each of these exhibition had its own distinct focus, but all of them also had much in common—in particular, they involved using artworks identified with specific nations to deploy a new understanding of the North American continent. As such, these exhibitions constructed a public vision of the future that embodied the Canadian, Mexican, and United States governments' aspirations for an economically integrated North America, one that would be united by free trade and economic prosperity. I read these exhibitions as a form of cultural diplomacy serving to mediate the changes that have resulted from the new trade alliances, thereby reconciling national/ist identities with the future of an integrated continent.

Cross-Border Identifications: Heritage, Landscape, and State

"Panoramas" exemplified the aforementioned dynamics of manipulation of national symbols. A large-scale online exhibition, "Panoramas" featured an extensive range of artworks, most of which were paintings. Geographically, it was representative of artists across North America; historically, it featured pieces dating in production from 1800 to 2000. Analysis of the project's history demonstrates the role that politics played in this exhibition and, at the same time, the role that art played in North American politics.

Archival research reveals that "Panoramas" was driven from the start by senior bureaucrats in Canada and the United States. It was conceived in January 2000 and presented at a meeting between Canada's Deputy Minister of Heritage Alexander Himelfarb and the United States' Undersecretary of State for Public Diplomacy and Public Affairs Evelyn Lieberman (CH [Gelinas]).

Himelfarb and Lieberman met to launch discussions, supported by both national governments, about the bilateral exchange of cultural information. Lieberman suggested a cultural project, in the form of an online art exhibition, that would reflect the importance of the bilateral relationship between Canada and the United States. She also raised the idea of expanding the project to include Mexico in the context of NAFTA. Pointedly, documents reflect that Lieberman was not interested in "areas of trade and culture" (Gelinas). Culture had long been a controversial area in free trade agreements between the two nations and had been ambiguously treated within NAFTA (Thompson 408). Historically, Canadians had been defensive about cultural exchanges with the United States, fearing that they would be overwhelmed by American cultural products (Thompson 394). As historian John Herd Thompson explains, the "NAFTA accord left the provisions of the Canada–U.S. FTA—the agreement to disagree about Canada's cultural policies—unchanged" (408).

In a memorandum following the meeting, the project was characterized as an initiative supporting "cooperative Canada–U.S. activities in non-irritant domains such as heritage" (CH [Himelfarb]). What is interesting here is how heritage was identified as a "non-irritant"—that is, as an uncontentious means for the two countries to promote their bilateral relationship and to convey to the public their shared goals as trade partners. By February 2000 the project was firmly situated within the Canadian government as part of a new program to "better manage bilateral cultural relations" with the United States, organized by the International Relations Directorate of the Department of Canadian Heritage and by the United States Bureau of the Canadian Department of Foreign Affairs and International Trade (CH [D'Auray]). This program had several objectives, including the creation of "a positive brand for Canada." It was also an attempt to "forestall trade action on cultural issues" (CH [D'Auray]). Government memoranda reveal that as the project expanded to include Mexico, this online exhibition came to be seen as part of a broader effort to develop North American trilateral relationships. There are several references in the documents to this "broader framework," which located the project as only one part of a larger foreign affairs plan to invigorate relations between Canada and Mexico (CH [Himelfarb]). Other documents point to the significance of maintaining a synchronized plan to "ensure a coordinated [Canadian] governmental approach" between the Department of Foreign Affairs and International Trade and the Canada Council (CH [Himelfarb]).

It is worth examining how the theme of landscape—expressly the "social interpretation of landscape art"—was chosen for this project (CH ["Trilateral"]). With the selection of such an open theme, the project lost the support of the National Gallery of Canada (NGC), which had been approached early on to be the Canadian institutional partner. In what could be read as the gallery asserting a measure of independence from the state, the NGC later withdrew its support for the project. It explained its refusal to participate as stemming from the list of conditions set by the United States State Department. This list included a provision specifying the inclusion of Mexico as a partner in the exhibition, as well as a requirement that the project have a "socio-historical focus rather than aesthetic or solely visual" (CH [Sarkar]). But American politicians were insisting on this approach, and United States State Department funding was contingent upon it. In the end, the Winnipeg Art Gallery replaced the NGC as Canadian partner (CH [Sarkar]).

The theme of landscape was being considered as early as February 2000, while preliminary discussions for the project were taking place between senior government officials (CH ["North American"]). "The theme would need to be elaborated by the partners," a memorandum states, "but, as a starting point, we would propose something that would permit an exploration of the differences and similarities in the creative perspective of artists in the three countries (e.g. relationship with the land)" (CH [Himelfarb]). Only one other theme was mentioned briefly, that of family portraits (CH ["North American"]). Thus, it appears that the museum partners involved did not have a choice in the theme; rather, it had been chosen by high-level bureaucrats in the Canadian and American governments, which highlights the importance the exhibition was being given as a means of cultural diplomacy. This unusual level of political involvement was acknowledged; as one government employee commented on a draft press release for the exhibition, "It is not the first world collaboration—but the first that is 'ordered' or backed … by the State [and] … politically supported … [O]thers … have always been at the level of the Institution" (CH [Ross]). The explicit political purpose of "Panoramas" helps explain the bureaucrats' choice of landscape as the exhibition's theme, for it is a subject with historic importance to constructions of national identity, which were in flux at the time as a consequence of neoliberal globalization. "From the land we derive … a sense of who we are as individuals, communities, and nations," an online exhibition text would later state, the implication being that the exhibition was intended to be a platform for re-educating the public about the place of the nation in the new, integrated North America. By asserting the primacy of the nation-state, this statement was also denying each state's origins and marginalizing Indigenous claims to the land.

The exhibition's pedagogical role was established from the outset. A memorandum states that in the initial meeting between Himelfarb and Lieberman, "Ms. Lieberman indicated that she was particularly struck by the deputy's references about the importance of ensuring that children see their society, history, and values reflected in their stories, movies, and books" (CH [Gelinas]). This seems to suggest that the governments read North American society as uniform across all three nation-states, again reinforcing the marginalization of other communities within each state. In initial proposals for the project, education was a priority, and there were references to the need to appeal to youth (CH [Educational Component]). One proposal stated that the objective of the exhibition was to "develop a resource which will include educational material and will have long term use-value" (CH ["North American"]).

In the end, this emphasis on education took the form of separate "Education" pages linked to each of the exhibition's four main themes. These pages provided additional activities and topics related to the exhibition—not limited to aesthetic issues—for those exploring the website. This was augmented by a list of textual sources. The use of "Panoramas" for educational purposes was also visible in the "Panoramas Education Project," described as "a series of online education activities structured as a global classroom within a virtual community hosted by the Smithsonian American Art Museum" (CH [Educational Component]). This initiative connected teachers and students from each of the three North American nations to trained docents who would work with students and teachers to facilitate the project (CH [Educational Component]). All of this suggests that the exhibition was seen as a platform for educating the public about new ways to understand national borders in North America—in particular, as a message of cultural parity and integration across the continent.

While it was supported by all three nations, the project was grounded in Canada, which made the NGC's refusal to participate even more noticeable. The project was based in the Canadian Heritage Information Network (CHIN), an operating agency of the Department of Canadian Heritage, which took a lead role in its development. CHIN had been creating virtual exhibitions since 1996, but "Panoramas" was the first project launched under the recently established Virtual Museum of Canada (VMC) and was a significant international exhibition (CH [Himelfarb]). CHIN took responsibility for bringing together museum partners in all three nations. Eventually, several large institutional partners participated in the project, including, in Canada, the Winnipeg Art Gallery and the Canadian Museum of Civilization; in the United States, the Smithsonian American Art Museum; and in Mexico, the Instituto Nacional de Bellas Artes. Government departments in all three states were also involved, including the Department of Canadian Heritage (specifically, CHIN), the United States Department of State, and Mexico's National Council for Arts and Culture. Each institutional partner was free to make its own choices of artworks to express the exhibition theme as it saw fit. Thus, the partners did not interfere in one another's choices. All of this suggests that each country was responsible for the labels that accompanied each piece, although these texts were not credited (Bauer 109).

Bureaucratic involvement continued for the duration of the project. "Panoramas" was officially launched on 3 April 2001, inaugurated by lavish opening events held simultaneously in Canada, Mexico, and the United States, all of them linked by video conferencing ("Launching"). Shelia Copps, then

Minister of Canadian Heritage, officiated at the Ottawa ceremony, against the backdrop of the Canadian Museum of Civilization. Emphasizing unity and a shared identity among North American citizens, she stated: "The art in this exhibit reflects not only our natural environments, but also our histories, our industries, our cultures and our belief systems." She also declared that "this project will make our cultural heritage more accessible to the citizens of the three participating countries and to the entire world"—a statement that highlighted the exhibition's presentation of culture as a universally valued and understood tool through which the public would be able to gain a better understanding of North America. Key representatives from Mexico and the United States joined Copps in celebrating the project, including Gordon D. Giffin, the American Ambassador to Canada, and Sari Bermudez, President of Mexico's National Council for Culture and the Arts ("Launching"). The presence of these politicians, and the wide media coverage in each country, demonstrates that this event was an important stage for transnational cultural brokering. Those present, and the governments and organizations they represented, all had a vested interest in promoting North American integration and viewed this exhibition as a sturdy platform from which to promote these aims to the public. The political involvement in the exhibition from conception to launch reinforces the fact that it was an exercise in cultural relations. I would argue that the opening and the exhibition functioned to promote ties among the NAFTA states, as much as the artworks on display. In fact, the art played a key role in enabling cultural diplomacy.

The exhibition's virtual location enabled viewers to interact individually with it. "Panoramas" provided an initial structure for viewing the artworks, which were grouped around four major themes—the Evolving Landscape, the Mythic Landscape, the Social Landscape, and the Personal Landscape— with subthemes within these larger categories. Viewers could bypass this structure entirely, however; search options allowed them to view artworks by concept, subject, country, chronological era, and region as well as through an unrestricted text search option. Ultimately, viewers controlled the amount of information they received about each piece, as each work was hyperlinked to a larger digital image that was displayed with a didactic text, written to contextualize that individual artwork. They could also choose to interact with "Panoramas" via the "Media" section of the exhibition, which offered virtual tours of the exhibition, movies and music about the landscape of North America, and virtual panoramic views. This non-linear structure, and the encyclopedic quantity of art presented, worked against the conventional narrative conveyed through large, survey-format exhibitions of visual art. "Panoramas" allowed for new readings of artworks by prioritizing social and cultural associations— for instance, an approach based on east-to-west associations, as opposed to national boundaries that lie to the north and south. As such, despite the appearance that only arbitrary meanings were generated through the self-directed structure of the exhibition, I argue that "Panoramas" clearly conveyed a message supporting a unified North American culture. Regardless of the order in which viewers encountered the images, the artworks were positioned in a manner that reinforced the state ideology, leaving no space for alternative readings by the viewer.

Further analysis of the curatorial approach employed in "Panoramas" reveals the two intertwined messages conveyed by "Panoramas": the first affirmed nationalism within globalization, and the second promoted a new unified North American identity.[4] The chosen theme being landscape, many of the artists featured and artworks presented have historical ties to national/ist projects, from Diego Rivera to Winslow Homer to Tom Thomson. Each artist's national origin was identified by a tiny flag visible alongside each work, placed above the artist's name. Accompanying each work was a hyperlink to a map, which identified a specific geographic region within the nation associated with the artwork. The same map featured a smaller-scale map of North America, cleverly reinforcing the broader continental context of the artwork and a message of unity in North American cultural production. In this way, nationalism was placed in the service of North American unity, echoing the neoliberal agendas of each state (even though within this neoliberal framework, each state sought different benefits from NAFTA). However, the larger message of the exhibition was cultural parity across the continent; that message was expressed through the celebratory language promoting artistic production in all three North American countries.

This is evident when we examine how "Panoramas" dealt with works by Tom Thomson and the Group of Seven, who have long been associated with Canada's landscape and national identity. Indeed, state organizations market their artworks as distinctly Canadian. Art historian Peter White argues that these portrayals are contradictory:

> While the strongly romantic vision of the Canadian landscape epitomized by Tom Thomson [and] the Group of Seven ... may be acknowledged to be a dated and limited vehicle for the representation of national identity and feeling, emotionally this perception nonetheless continues to retain a powerful hold on the national imagination ... [and] the association of this image of landscape with national spirit and meaning is deeply ingrained in Canada's national psyche. (11)

"Panoramas" featured artworks by three members of the Group of Seven—Lawren Harris, Frederick Horsman Varley, and Frank H. Johnson—in addition to that of Tom Thomson, who was closely associated with the group. Conspicuously, these works were positioned in the exhibition in a manner that emphasized their universal social and cultural values—values that could be widely applied to North America. As such, these artworks no longer operated as national/ist symbols of a distinct Canadian identity located in wilderness. Rather, the larger project of constructing North American values took priority. In "Panoramas" they were grouped with paintings by artists who are national icons in other countries, in a manner that promoted them as part of a larger group of artists emblematic of the greater project of a united North America. In this way, "Panoramas" drew parallels between various artists' depictions of the North American landscape, promoting North American cultural parity despite inevitable diversity. Thus, the exhibition created and promoted a unified North American identity and a reconceptualized North American landscape in accordance with NAFTA.

Cross-Border Dislocations: Contemporary Art as a Means to Negotiate the "Other Side"

At a time when cultural initiatives, including art exhibitions, were increasingly promoting canonical national/ist projects to further North American integration, contemporary artists were considering the same topic. Relative to the state-sponsored exhibitions predominantly featuring modern art, contemporary artworks and exhibitions emphasized a different agenda, questioning the national as a dominant category of organization. The most prominent exhibition of this kind in North America was inSite, which commissioned artistic interventions by an international group of contemporary artists in the San Diego–Tijuana border region between 1992 and 2005. In particular, inSite celebrated artistic interventions that revealed the diversity of the border as a site for multiple readings and relationships. Each of the five versions of inSite took the form of a large-scale event, with exhibited commissioned public artworks augmented by public programs and publications, which took place over the course of several months. With its mandate to address this specific border zone's conflicting barriers and permeability, inSite was an important locus of transnational contemporary artistic production and part of the art world's larger fascination with "border art" at the end of the twentieth century.

Political philosopher and social theorist Susan Buck-Morss lends support to the potential of contemporary artistic production as critical practice, explaining that contemporary art has the potential to "contribute to a general reactivation of social imagination ... [and provide a] critical counter-culture" (72). Such possibilities are exemplified by many of the artworks featured in inSite. Of particular relevance to discussions of North American integration is the work of contemporary artist Rebecca Belmore, who is renowned for her performance pieces. Belmore's Anishnabe heritage has greatly shaped her artistic practice, and she has also sought to address transnational Indigenous issues, especially in the Americas (Rickard 68). Artist, curator, and historian Jolene Rickard describes her position: "As a First Nations or aboriginal person,

Belmore's homeland is now the modern nation of Canada; yet, there is reluctance by the art world to recognizing this condition as a continuous form of cultural and political exile ... I think of her as an Anishnabe living in the continuously colonial space of the Americas" (68).

Belmore participated in "inSite97," where she created the installation *Awasinake* (Fig. 11.1), comprised of backlit photographs displayed on the marquee of the Casino Theatre, an abandoned cinema in downtown San Diego (Tuer; Pincus). This work explored Belmore's identity as an Aboriginal woman in North America, foregrounding the numerous borders that she crossed to take part in inSite97. The piece highlighted the US–Mexico border but also touched on divisions based on cultures, languages, and economies. Throughout the creation of this piece, Belmore overtly played with the concept of traversing these different borders. To produce the work, she explored Tijuana to find an appropriate subject for her portraiture (Tuer). She selected a young Indigenous woman from Oaxaca waiting to cross the border; notably, the woman bore a strong resemblance to the artist (Pincus; Tuer). After exchanging money with her sitter, Belmore arranged for her to be photographed in front of the US–Mexico border fence, as well as against solid primary-coloured backgrounds found in Tijuana: red, blue, green, yellow, and white. Jessica Bradley, one of a team of four international curators who organized inSite97, describes the portraiture

Fig. 11.1 Rebecca Belmore, *Awasinake: On the Other Side*, 1997 (installation view, San Diego). Installation: backlit photographs, movie theatre marquee. Photographers: Michael Beynon and Philipp Scholz Rittermann. Reproduced with the permission of the artist and with permission of the inSite Archives, Mandeville Special Collections Library, UC San Diego.

session, explaining that Belmore arranged for her sitter "to be photographed by one of the many photographers who roam Tijuana with donkeys and sombreros for tourists to pose with" (43). By incorporating this aspect of Tijuana's tourist industry and by partly inverting the standard relationship by paying the sitter, Belmore foregrounds typical economic transactions on the border.

In the final installation, six distinct portraits featuring the woman in different poses were mounted horizontally on the marquee, and two of the photographs were oriented in the opposing direction to the others. Both aspects challenged viewers' conventional expectations of portraiture (Figure 11.2). When reviewing inSite97, Dot Tuer read this positioning as a reference to a film strip, playing into the work's location at the vacant theatre. Belmore's portraits, as well as the way in which she selected her subject, also made reference to the charged historical practice of anthropological photography. In the exhibition catalogue, Belmore detailed her process in her artist statement: "I cross over to the other side. I recognize history in indigenous women standing at the edge of a place. I imagine their stories and give them a few American dollars. I cross back to a faraway place" (133). This explanation highlights the ambiguity of

Fig. 11.2   Rebecca Belmore, *Awasinake: On the Other Side*, 1997 (detail). Installation: backlit photographs, movie theatre marquee. Photographers: Michael Beynon and Philipp Scholz Rittermann. Reproduced with the permission of the artist and with permission of the inSite Archives, Mandeville Special Collections Library, UC San Diego.

the border space, referenced only as "the other side" in relation to "a faraway place," thus allowing for a reading of the piece outside of the US–Mexico border. This further affirms the disconnect between Belmore and her subject; at no point is the sitter's name referenced, and the artist confirms that her stories are "imagined"—that is, they were not a site of exchange during the portrait session. *Awasinake* has been described as "incongruous" (Tuer) and can also be read as complicit in reproducing these historic processes of marginalization. Inequality was again emphasized by the display of these images across the border in San Diego—a site that Belmore's sitter, based in Tijuana, could not access (Bradley 43).

This work, aided by its association with inSite, is often considered solely within its relation to the US–Mexico border zone. While this border is indisputably relevant, I argue that it does not provide the only context from which to understand this work. Instead, I see the benefits of reading this piece as part of a larger movement of visual art questioning identities in North America. Within this structure, Belmore's identity as Anishnabe and Canadian must also be taken into account in order for us to understand her portraits of an Indigenous Mexican woman subsequently installed in San Diego. This reframing of *Awasinake* works against the primacy of national borders. The artist discussed her own experiences traversing numerous borders, in addition to the demarcation of the American and Mexican states, when creating this project. Bradley explains: "Belmore was taken as one of the locals [in Tijuana], but could speak neither Spanish nor the indigenous Native languages ... when in San Diego, she could communicate easily but was mistaken for a Latina" (43). The work also functions as a means of displacement, in that the artist deals with her own border crossing by employing an Indigenous woman who resembles her at another border site, evoking the absent United States as a "faraway place" that divides the artist from her subject geographically, economically, politically, culturally, and linguistically.

Awasinake is a multilayered piece that brings into question transnational issues of colonialism, identity, and access to land, as well as gender, nationality, and Indigenous heritage. These dislocations and connections are at the heart of *Awasinake:* "Race and history linked Belmore and her subject. Language, history, geography and politics isolated them from each other" (Bradley 43). While making specific references to the US–Mexico border, the piece also connects these themes to a larger North American context. Tuer describes a "collective vision" created by the inSite97 works, which served to bridge the "North/South divide of the Americas." Indeed, Belmore seems to hint at a more open reading of her work. Several years after participating in inSite, when discussing the complicated relations between Indigenous and colonial national identities, she elucidated her thoughts on being associated with the Canadian state—in particular, on being called upon to represent Canada as an artist at the 2005

Venice Biennale. "I cannot ignore that North America was cut into three pieces and not very gently. Is that not a long, wide, load of history to bear? I hope I do it justice" (Watson and Belmore 28). Significantly, *Awasinake* focuses on the tensions among the various identities at play across all three North American states. Belmore has spoken about the difficulty of negotiating the identities assigned to her, especially in light of her work internationally. "My work is really happening at the intersection of many identities," she explains. "It is seeing how these sit together, often through my own body and the power relations that affect it, and this is what my work is about" (28).

This exploration of Indigenous cross-border identification is especially relevant given the tenuous relationship between Indigenous culture and colonial national/ist projects. Across North America, indigenous histories have been largely obscured by myths of the nation, although when convenient, aspects of Indigenous cultures are appropriated by such narratives. Kalant explains this ambiguous relationship: "the post-colonial settler's quandary [is that] of 'belatedness'—the condition of having to become native in an already inhabited country where the 'pre-colonial population' disturbs the pretension of settlers to an authentic belonging" (87). This dynamic is very much a part of Belmore's approach in *Awasinake* and in her broader practice. She explains: "I think this process of negotiating space and occupying it shows up in the other work that I make: the installations, the photographs" (Watson and Belmore 24). *Awasinake*, through its investigation of the diversity of border zones and complex relationships across these boundaries, operates in opposition to state-sponsored blockbuster exhibitions such as "Panoramas." This context can also be extended to many of the other works at inSite97, which transcended the US–Mexico border and addressed changing identities and associations across North America.

Visual Art and the Construction of Identity

Through discussion of "Panoramas" and *Awasinake*, my aim has been to reveal the importance of visual art in continually negotiating representations of North America and thereby altering perceptions of its borders. Both case studies illustrate distinct moments in the construction of North America and point to the links between artistic production, national/ist projects, landscape, and the state. As such, further consideration of the history of representations of North America in exhibitions will be necessary in order for us to move beyond national frameworks and contextualize exhibitions within transnational developments. Through such studies, the Canada–US border will be better understood in relation to its larger hemispheric context, including neoliberal trade agreements such as NAFTA. The Canada–US border also needs to be examined in the context of North American visual histories—specifically, cultural projects surrounding North American integration.

202 Sarah E.K. Smith

I read "Panoramas" as part of a larger movement at the turn of the millennium: NAFTA states were utilizing culture to project new versions of national identity in order to publicly endorse and legitimize recent transnational economic connections. Research that critically examines these constructions is necessary because the complex political nature of these exhibitions is not widely apparent. Instead, the political messages associated with such projects are concealed by the aura of neutrality associated with the artworks (Wallis 272). In contrast to these top-down representations, *Awasinake* offers a lens through which the Canada–US border can be considered in relation to questions of indigeneity. Contemporary art provides a means of resisting and challenging North American representations—in particular, state-sponsored visions of North American borders—as well as a means to draw attention to those aspects obscured by national/ist projects, namely Indigenous histories.

Studies of artworks and exhibitions help us discern which representations, identities, and alliances are being mined to write national/ist narratives. National/ist projects are affected by many things, not only by the deployment of artworks, but also by a combination of different forces, including national governments, transnational corporations, free trade agreements, and processes of globalization. However, I want to emphasize the importance of recognizing how art and culture work their way into this mix. Critical examination of exhibitions and artworks in relation to these aspects is essential to understanding constructions of national culture as they are continuously created, promoted, and managed to educate the public (both within and outside of a specific state) about state politics, current alliances, and borders.

Acknowledgements

I would like to express my thanks to Rebecca Belmore for kindly granting me permission to reproduce two images of *Awasinake* in this book. I would also like to extend my gratitude to the inSite Archives, Mandeville Special Collections Library, UC San Diego.

Notes

1   In this essay I rely on the term "national identity," while recognizing the problematic nature of this concept. I use this term to refer to the official national identities promoted by each North American state government, including the narratives written, supported, reproduced and sanctioned by these states. I also employ the term "national/ist" to signal the constructed nature of such projects.

2   All subsequent description of "Panoramas" is taken from the online exhibition.

3   I employ the term "alter-globalization" because it more accurately reflects the aims of these protesters than the label "anti-globalization." As scholars have noted, those participating in this movement were not entirely against globalization, instead they united to advocate for a different form of globalization. See Robertson and Cronin 17, 21.

4   For further analysis of the curatorial approach employed in "Panoramas," see Sarah E.K. Smith, "Visualizing the 'New' North American Landscape" in *Negotiations in a Vacant Lot: Studying the Visual in Canada*. Ed. Lynda Jessup, Erin Morton and Kirsty Robertson. Montreal and Kingston: McGill-Queen's UP, forthcoming 2014.

Works Cited

Balfe, Judith Huggins. "Artworks as Symbols in International Politics." *International Journal of Politics, Culture, and Society* 1.2 (1987): 195–217.

Bauer, Kimberly A. "The Virtual Museum of Canada: Evaluating the Potential of the Digital Environment For the Display of Art." MA thesis. Carleton University, 2002.

Belmore, Rebecca. "Rebecca Belmore: Awasinake (On the Other Side)." *inSite97: Private Time in Public Space*. San Diego: Installation Gallery, 1998. 132–33.

"Border Art Workshop Mission Statement." Border Art Workshop / Taller de Arte Fronterizo. http://www.borderartworkshop.com/Statement/statement.html. Accessed 25 March 2011.

Bradley, Jessica. "Rebecca Belmore: Art and the Object of Performance." *Rebecca Belmore: Fountain*. Vancouver: Morris and Helen Belkin Art Gallery, 2005. 42–48.

Buck-Morss, Susan. *Thinking Past Terror: Islamism and Critical Theory on the Left*. London: Verso, 2003.

CH (Canadian Heritage. Virtual Museum of Canada). [Gelinas]. Executive Produced Exhibitions—Panoramas: The North American Landscape in Art. 80 B 4220–P1. Vol. 1. Denny Gelinas to Michelle d'Auray. 12 January 2000.

———. [Himelfarb]. Executive Produced Exhibitions—Panoramas: The North American Landscape in Art. 80 B 4220–P1. Vol. 1. Memorandum to Alex Himelfarb. 28 January 2000.

———. [D'Auray]. Executive Produced Exhibitions—Panoramas: The North American Landscape in Art. 80 B 4220–P1. Vol. 1. Memorandum to Michelle D'Auray. 11 February 2000.

———. ["Trilateral"]. Executive Produced Exhibitions—Panoramas: The North American Landscape in Art. 80 B 4220–P1. Vol. 2. "Trilateral Senior Officials Meeting." 14 July 2000.

———. [Sarkar]. Executive Produced Exhibitions—Panoramas: The North American Landscape in Art. Memorandum to Madame Eileen Sarkar. Canada–US–Mexico Trilateral Landscape Exhibit. n.d.

———. ["North American"]. Executive Produced Exhibitions—Panoramas: The North American Landscape in Art. 80 B 4220–P1. Vol. 1. "North American Virtual Exhibition Project Canada–US–Mexico." Draft. 9 February 2000.

———. [Ross]. Executive Produced Exhibitions—Panoramas: The North American Landscape in Art. Cara Ross to Danielle Boily et al. 15 August 2000.

———. [Educational Component]. Executive Produced Exhibitions—Panoramas: The North American Landscape in Art. 80 B 4220–P3. Vol. 1. Educational Component. n.d.

Canclini, Néstor García. "A Re-Imagined Public Art on the Border." *Intromisiones Compartidas: Arte y Sociedad en la Frontera Mexico/Estados Unidos*. Ed. Néstor García Canclini and José Manuel Valenzuela Arce. San Diego and Tijuana: Fondo Nacional para la Cultural y las Artes; inSite97, 2000. 101–10.

Foreign Affairs and International Trade Canada. "Negotiations and Agreements." 2011. http://www.internationalgc.ca/trade-agreements-accords-commerciaux/agr-acc/index.aspx?lang=en#free. Accessed 13 January 2011.

Gómez-Peña, Guillermo. *The New World Border: Prophecies, Poems, and Loqueras for the End of the Century*. San Francisco: City Lights Books, 1996.

Grady, Patrick. "Mr. Obama, Tear Down That Border." Financial Post Comment. *National Post* 19 January 2009.

Grinspun, Ricardo, and Yasmine Shamsie. "Canada, Free Trade, and 'Deep Integration' in North America: Context, Problems, and Challenges." *Whose Canada? Continental Integration, Fortress North America, and the Corporate Agenda*. Ed. Ricardo Grinspun and Yasmine Shamsie. Montreal and Kingston: McGill–Queen's UP, 2007. 3–53.

Kalant, Amelia. *National Identity and the Conflict at Oka*. New York: Routledge, 2004.

Konrad, Herman W. "North American Continental Relationships: Historical Trends and Antecedents. *NAFTA in Transition*. Ed. Stephen J. Randal and Herman W. Konrad. Calgary: U of Calgary P, 1995. 15–35.

"Launching of the Virtual Exhibit Panoramas: The North American Landscape in Art." Virtual Museum of Canada. Canadian Heritage Information Network. 2001. http://www.virtualmuseum.ca/English/Pressroom/p-04-01-1.html. Accessed 20 August 2008.

NGCA (National Gallery of Canada Archives). [Springer]. National Gallery of Canada Fonds. Exhibitions—Mexican Modern Art, 1998. 7398-008-19. Vol. 1. "Clippings." José M. Springer. "A Tale of Cultural Exchange."

———. [Pappas]. Exhibitions—Mexican Modern Art, 1998. "Sponsorship." Christine Pappas to Mayo Graham. 8 February 1999.

Orme, William A., Jr. *Understanding NAFTA: Mexico, Free Trade, and the New North America*. Austin: U of Texas P, 1996.

Pincus, Robert L. "Public Spectacles Grand-Scale Exhibition Reflects Border Region." *San Diego Union-Tribune* 21 September 1997: E1.

Randall, Stephen J., and Herman W. Konrad, eds. *NAFTA in Transition*. Calgary: U of Calgary P, 1995.

Rickard, Jolene. "Rebecca Belmore: Performing Power." *Rebecca Belmore: Fountain*. Vancouver: Morris and Helen Belkin Art Gallery, 2005. 68–76.

Robertson, Kirsty, and J. Keri Cronin. "Imagining Resistance: An Introduction." *Imagining Resistance: Visual Culture and Activism in Canada*. Ed. J. Keri Cronin and Kirsty Robertson. Waterloo: Wilfrid Laurier UP, 2011. 1–22.

Rogoff, Irit. *Terra Infirma: Geography's Visual Culture*. London: Routledge, 2000.

Sassen, Saskia. *Losing Control? Sovereignty in an Age of Globalization*. New York: Columbia UP, 1996.

Thompson, John Herd. "Canada's Quest for Cultural Sovereignty: Protection, Promotion, and Popular Culture." Randall and Konrad 393–410.

Tuer, Dot. "At the Gates: Steel and Barbwire Cut a Swath Between the US and Mexico. The Art of Insite97 Takes the Border as Its Subject." *Canadian Art* 15.1 (1998): 72–78.

Valenzuela Arce, José Manuel. "Forms of Resistance, Corridors of Power: Public Art on the Mexico–U.S. Border." *Intromisiones Compartidas: Arte y Sociedad en la Frontera Mexico/Estados Unidos*. Ed. Néstor García Canclini and José Manuel Valenzuela Arce. San Diego and Tijuana: Fondo Nacional para la Cultural y las Artes; inSite97, 2000. 79–100.

Wallis, Brian. "Selling Nations." *Museum Culture*. Ed. Daniel J. Sherman and Irit Rogoff. Minneapolis: U of Minnesota P, 1994. 265–81.

Watson, Scott, and Rebecca Belmore. "Interview." *Rebecca Belmore: Fountain*. Vancouver: Morris and Helen Belkin Art Gallery, 2005. 24–28.

White, Peter. "Out of the Woods." *Beyond Wilderness: The Group of Seven, Canadian Identity, and Contemporary Art.* Ed. John O'Brian and Peter White. Montreal and Kingston: McGill–Queen's UP, 2007. 11–20.

Yúdice, George. *The Expediency of Culture: Uses of Culture in the Global Era.* Durham: Duke UP, 2003.

———. "Transnational Cultural Brokering of Art." *Beyond the Fantastic: Contemporary Art Criticism From Latin America.* Ed. Gerardo Mosquera. London: Institute of International Visual Arts, 1995. 198–215.

twelve

Conversations That Never Happened

The Writing and Activism of Gloria Anzaldúa, Maria Campbell, and Howard Adams

Zalfa Feghali

> I am a nomadic Mexican artist/writer in the process of Chicanization, which means I am slowly heading North.
>
> Guillermo Gómez-Peña, *The New World Border*

OVER THE PAST THREE DECADES an entire field of study has emerged from the US–Mexico border. The discipline of border studies congratulates itself on its inter- and cross-disciplinary nature: encompassing the fields of history, politics, economics, anthropology, and literature, it concerns itself with a variety of themes, which include identity, immigration, hybridity, and the myriad complexities of the cross-border exchange. However, because it originated in the US–Mexico border region, border studies does not always address the many other boundaries to which its name lays claim. Only recently has border studies expanded to consider the US–Mexico border's counterpart to the north, the Canada–US border. In this chapter, to appropriate Guillermo Gómez-Peña's comments from the epigraph above, I intend to track border studies as it *slowly heads north*.

To that end, I listen in on conversations that might have taken place had Gloria Anzaldúa, Maria Campbell, and Howard Adams collaborated on their work. Writing from the US–Mexico borderlands, self-defined "Chicana *tejana*-lesbian-feminist poet and fiction writer" (253) Gloria Anzaldúa is best known for formulating the "new *mestiza* consciousness" set out in her *Borderlands/La Frontera* and for her involvement in the Chicano civil rights movement. Maria Campbell, the Canadian Métis author of *Halfbreed*, has played a pivotal role in Métis politics and culture and was one of the first to bring the status of the Métis to a mainstream literary audience. Howard Adams, a prominent Canadian Métis academic, was one of the first intellectuals to theorize and articulate the Métis political, cultural, and social positions from an academic perspective. Bringing these writers together could be fruitful, as they wrote—for the most part contemporaneously—on the same or similar themes. Because, as I hope to show, the histories of the Chicano and Métis struggles bear striking similarities to each other, resolutions to these struggles may also be similar; thus, studying writers from each side of each of the US borders could be extremely beneficial.

Focusing primarily on Anzaldúa's *Borderlands/La Frontera*, Campbell's *Halfbreed*, and Adams's *Prison of Grass* and *A Tortured People*, I will be analyzing essential sites of both convergence and divergence within their thought: their personal understanding, revisiting, and reclamation of history; their analysis of the internalized mindset of colonization; their engagement with and relationship to language; and, finally, their approaches to activism and Indigenous politics. I contend that synthesizing these writers' positions on these issues will generate important connections and parallels. Ultimately, each of these writers presents a different version of the same hope for community and coalition building across minority groups. The seeds of this hope exist and are easy to see: for example, Howard Adams suggests that the Métis struggle can be usefully compared to that of the Mayans in Chiapas, Mexico, yet in the rest of his writing he does not consider the similarities between the Métis and Chicano movements. Crucial to this consideration is the fact that the Métis political actions of the 1960s in Saskatchewan, nicknamed Flour Power, coincided almost exactly with the founding of the National Farm Workers Association in Texas, a pivotal moment in the Chicano civil rights movement. For her part, Anzaldúa presents her compelling theory of the new *mestiza* but does not write with a concrete political application in mind. Campbell, in contrast, provides an excellent first-hand account of the tensions experienced by the Métis—who tread the fine line between "white" and "Native" in Canada, and for whom political considerations cannot be separated from personal narrative—but is unable to resolve this tension in her writing. Given these linkages, I show how these writers complement and at the same time supplement one another.

When listening to the conversation between the work and thought of Campbell, Anzaldúa, and Adams, I explore the following questions: To what extent can work done on one specific border (in this case, the US–Mexico border) be transposed to other borders? Where does a Métis woman like Campbell stand in relation to Anzaldúa's new *mestiza*, and to what extent can we use these terms interchangeably? How can we explain the distinct parallels between the histories of the *mestizo/a* populations in Mexico and the United States and that of the Métis population of Canada? Following on from this, how can we account for the similarities between the Chicano and the Métis as politically engaged populations born from the processes of *mestizaje* and *métissage*? What lessons can be learned from these groups?

There are important and productive parallels to be made between the Chicano and Métis struggles. For example, there are immediate similarities in the status of these two groups within the United States and Canada respectively. In the United States, Chicanos are Mexican Americans who view themselves as politically aware and, to some degree, politically active. *Chicanismo* originated in the same US–Mexico borderlands that Gloria Anzaldúa writes from and about. Chicanos have not been taken seriously by the US state, either as a political group or as an identification or as a self-identified ethnic group. The Métis, an Indigenous group within Canada, report similar experiences of marginalization in the legal, social, or political realms.

My choice to begin with an analysis of Anzaldúa's work rather than that of Campbell or Adams, who chronologically precede her, is deliberate. I am reluctant to reinforce the common practice in border studies of engaging with a text that does not originate at the US–Mexico border, reading it almost taxonomically and comparing it with a "seminal" text of border studies, but I must do so here in order to contextualize US–Mexico border studies before I follow it on its travels to the north.

As noted earlier, border studies is most often associated with the US–Mexico border. In turn, that particular border is inseparable from Chicano/a studies and the Chicano civil rights movement of the 1960s, which lasted well into the 1980s. In this chapter, Chicano/a will refer to a political and cultural identification within the United States. In terms of its political significance and geohistorical origins, it is closely related to the Spanish term *mestizo/a*, which refers to the offspring born of the mixing of racial groups. The term *mestizaje* refers to one's *mestizo/a* character—one's *mestiza*-ness. It can also refer to the process of becoming *mestizo/a*. Both terms form the basis of Anzaldúa's work and refer historically to the human products of interracial mixing, and specifically, the interracial mixing that took place during the Spanish invasion of the Americas. This new hybrid people, living on the borders of different racial groups, were to be the ancestors of those who today live on either side of the physical political border between the United States and Mexico. The term "Chicano/a" refers specifically to a politically engaged individual, most often of Mexican descent, and is adapted from the terms "Mexicano," "Meschicano," and "Xicano." Chicanos generally identify as "Latino," which means that their ancestors were of Hispanic/Indigenous ancestry as opposed to Anglo-American/white European descent. The aim of the Chicano civil rights movement was to achieve equal rights for Chicanos as a minority group in the United States. The Chicano movement, or *El Movimiento Chicano*, is considered to have officially begun in 1965, when Cesar Chavez helped found the National Farm Workers Association. It is significant that the movement's first event involved the unionizing of farm workers. This reflected the position of

Chicanos at that time: most of them either worked in agriculture or came from families that did. As sharecroppers or migrant workers who moved around the United States, these Chicanos did not have civil or labour rights, and they were often discriminated against and exploited by white landowners or factory owners. With the formation of *La Raza Unida* political party in 1970, what began as a farm workers' movement developed into a full-fledged political movement for civil, social, and economic rights.

In the 1960s, in a clear parallel with the Chicano civil rights movement in the United States, the Métis in Canada launched what some describe as their own civil rights movement. Its main focus "was on ethnicity, race, and nationalism" (Adams, *Tortured* 85). In the 1970s and 1980s, the movement's focus shifted to broader, class-based concerns, which opened the doors to coalitions and alliances with non-Native poor and working-class people. During one such action, "Operation Flour Power," the Métis worked together with white mill owners in the face of government neglect. This action, which took place in 1970 in Saskatchewan, was a pivotal moment in Métis history. That same year, in a pivotal moment in the Chicano civil rights movement, the United Farm Workers Party was founded in Texas.

Gloria Anzaldúa was heavily involved in the Chicano movement, having grown up in the Texas borderlands and come to terms with her own hybrid identity or *mestizaje*. Her writing reflects her unique understanding of borderlands and the identities that emerge from them. According to her, "the Borderlands are physically present wherever two or more cultures edge each other, where people of different races occupy the same territory, where under, lower, middle and upper classes touch, where the space between two individuals shrinks with intimacy" (20). In this vein, it may be useful to consider Renato Rosaldo's characterization of borders as "sites where identities and cultures intersect" and are "always in motion" (149, 217). This is significant, for Anzaldúa does not limit her conception of borders to physical locations, and neither does Rosaldo. Consequently, borders could be, for example, internal to one individual—as in the case of hybrid identities.

According to Anzaldúa, the *mestiza* exists in borderlands and is "neither *hispana india negra española / ni gabacha*" [neither Hispanic, Indian, Black, Spanish / nor white]"; rather, she is "*mestiza, mulata,* half-breed / caught in the crossfire between camps / while carrying all five races on [her] back / not knowing which side to turn to, run from" (216). Thus, her *mestizaje* does not allow her to fit in with any of her constituent groups. She exists on the fringes of those groups, always reminded that she is the embodiment of the "other" and therefore not pure enough to be admitted entry. As such, her *mestizaje* is a double-edged sword. Anzaldúa writes from personal experience: as a seventh-generation native of the borderlands, she is well aware not only of her own many layers of *mestizaje* but also of the impact of *mestizaje* on her life.

For example, she is "too Mexican" in the United States and "too American" in Mexico, and her Indigenous past is often denied on both sides of the border. Anzaldúa's treatment of *mestizaje* (in a culturally specific sense rather than a larger framework) has been applied in parallel with other processes of racial mixture, such as *métissage* in the case of Canada and other former French colonies. On a broader level, the *mestizo/a* as a figure of resistance is also used in conjunction with the *métis(se)* and the *mulatto/a*. Critics such as Rafael Pérez-Torres, José David Saldívar, and Françoise Lionnet insist that the *mestiza*, as both a literal figure and a conceptual tool, has the potential to instigate change. For the purposes of this chapter, I consider both the theoretical figure of the *mestizo/a* and the Chicano/as (as a group very much comprised of *mestizo/a* constituents) to have their counterparts in the Canadian Métis.

According to the Canadian Métis National Council, when "written with a small '"m', métis is a racial term for anyone of mixed Indian and European ancestry. When written with a capital 'M', Métis is a sociocultural or political term for those originally of mixed ancestry who evolved into a distinct Indigenous people during a certain historical period in a certain region in Canada" (Peterson and Brown 6). Crucial to understanding this difference is appreciating the nuances of "mixed ancestry"; historically, the distinction between métis and "half-breed" groups has been found in differences in their mixed ancestry. Half-breed groups had Native and English or Scottish roots, while métis groups could trace their non-Native ancestry to French fur traders. As such, the group appellations either were Anglicized or used adaptations of French, depending on group ancestry. This has become complicated, however, with the emergence of the Métis as a distinct entity with political aspirations to nationhood. As a consequence of those aspirations, the Métis now comprise both half-breeds and groups that were formerly called métis. The Métis consider themselves a distinct Aboriginal group, although debate still rages as to whether the Métis should be included as "First Nations"—the designation given to other Aboriginal groups in Canada—given that they are far younger than the other nations.[1] On 8 January 2013, a Canadian Federal Court ruled that Métis groups should indeed be included in the definition of "Indian" under the s.91(24) of the Constitution Act of 1867 (*Daniels v. Canada*). This landmark ruling may yet be overturned on appeal; even so, Métis advocacy groups such as the Métis National Council and the Congress of Aboriginal Peoples are likely to resort to it as a legal precedent as they continue to challenge the legal system that for almost two centuries has systematically excluded them from "status." After the Canadian federal government appealed the Federal Court ruling, Clément Chartier, Head of the Métis National Council, said that the ruling "should signal to all governments that the time has come for them to move forward on Metis rights and self-government or the courts will continue to force their hands in order to ensure Canada's constitution is respected" (qtd.

in Métis Nation of Ontario). The Métis National Council is now seeking land rights in areas of "what is considered the Métis Homeland" (Métis National Council, "Métis Rights").

The term "Indian" is no longer considered "politically correct," yet it continues to be used as part of the legal framework when it comes to Native matters. Similarly, the term "half-breed" is pejorative. This is linked to an issue of translation: there is no English equivalent for "*mestizaje*" or "*métissage*," concepts that refer to the genetic, cultural, and linguistic intermingling that takes place at sites where various groups are exposed to one another. In fact, in English, only the products of such mixing or intermingling are named: "half-breed," "mixed-blood," "mixed-race," and so on. There is no word for the process itself. As Lionnet puts it: "these expressions always carry a negative connotation, precisely because they imply biological abnormality and reduce human reproduction to the level of animal breeding" (13). As processes, then, both *mestizaje* and *métissage* remain unrepresented (or at least *under*represented) in English. However, contemporary Métis artists and critics such as Gregory Scofield and Marilyn Dumont use the term "half-breed" ironically and strategically. Jennifer Andrews suggests that this allows them "to reclaim the word for themselves" (4).

An important implication here is linked to the Métis not being recognized as a distinct group, notwithstanding *Daniels v. Canada*. Indeed, as Robert K. Thomas has put it: "In Canada, the legal definition and status of the métis are ambiguous, at best. In the United States, the courts do not at present even recognize the existence of métis in law. Moreover, most North Americans do not have a conceptual place for the métis in their view of the world" (247). The very idea that the Métis lack *a conceptual place* is troubling, not least because they clearly comprise a group that at this moment *exists*. Obviously, it is far simpler to call something into question in legal terms than to introduce a conceptual place in the mind of the mainstream. However, the Métis have long considered themselves "not merely biracial, multilingual and bicultural, but the proud owners of a new language; of syncretic cosmology and religious repertoire; of distinctive modes of dress, cuisine, architecture, vehicles of transport, music, and dance; and after 1815 of a quasi-military political organization, a flag, a bardic tradition, a rich folklore and a natural history" (Peterson and Brown 64).

This need on the part of the Métis to establish themselves as a legitimate nation is linked in part to their displacement not just within Canada but also across the Canada–US border to North Dakota and Montana.

This impetus is reflected in Métis writer Maria Campbell's work. *Halfbreed* is widely viewed as a foundational text in Canadian Métis literature. First published in 1973, *Halfbreed* sheds light on the daily lives and struggles of the Métis in Canada during the 1940s. Many have described the work as a classic, vital account of a young Métis woman's struggle to come to terms with the realities of her northern Saskatchewan childhood. Maria is a strong and sensitive child who lives in a community deprived of its pride and dignity by the dominant culture. At the age of fifteen, she tries to escape by marrying a white man, only to find herself trapped in the slums of Vancouver, addicted to drugs, tempted by suicide, and close to death. But her Cree great-grandmother, Cheechum, gives her confidence in herself and in her people, confidence that she needs to survive. *Halfbreed* offers a unique understanding of the Métis people and of the racism they face on a daily basis. As she relates her story, Campbell reveals how personal identity and personal space were heavily politicized in 1940s Métis society. She lived this reality first-hand: her family, being Métis or half-breed, was considered part of the "landless, non-status native peoples without aboriginal rights" (Kaup 198). As Métis people whose identities lay on the borders of "native" and "settler," her family was only permitted to exist within specific spaces. The only space for home, then, was on a border—on either side of rail lines and roads. Historically, many Métis lived on Crown lands—that is, on unused lands belonging to and administered by the provincial government. Their lack of legal "status" precluded their being granted reserve territory. This literalized the Métis border experience.

Campbell makes the personal political by writing a first-hand account of the social and political challenges of being Métis. Her themes of drug and alcohol addiction and sexual exploitation shed light on difficulties faced by all Native groups; however, her focus on the Métis is clear. That said, *Halfbreed* makes only scant references to political movements and actions associated with the Métis civil rights movement. It is Howard Adams who chronicles those, in both *Prison of Grass* and *The Tortured People*. Adams writes in a more academic tone, and argues the Métis case using the political tools and discourse of what he would call the dominant colonizer. His writing takes a clear polemic stance. Both of his books under study in this chapter begin with a recounting of personal experiences; from these, he extrapolates broader themes and arguments. Widely viewed as an alternative account to mainstream ones of Métis history, *Prison of Grass: Canada From a Native Point of View* was considered groundbreaking in its uncompromising depiction of what its author describes as colonization and institutionalized racism in Canada. His second book, *A Tortured People: The Politics of Colonization,* brings to light the Aboriginal perspective on the effects of colonization while also introducing his thoughts on the challenge of decolonization. Both texts are important because they provide the historical backdrop to the Métis struggle as well as a critique of the status quo, besides highlighting areas where practical progress can be made.

Inasmuch as Anzaldúa, Campbell, and Adams can be viewed as border-landers and as "representing" their respective marginalized groups (at least in terms of critical reception), how far do their similarities go? I suggest that the connections we can make between their writings are manifold. The most immediate of these has to do with how they relate to history. Anzaldúa and Campbell begin their books by relating their versions of their respective peoples' histories. Campbell clearly has little regard for establishment history, for as she puts it, "the history books say that Halfbreeds were defeated at Batoche in 1884" (11)—a clear reference to Louis Riel (whom I discuss in greater detail below), viewed from a perspective she clearly does not share. For her part, Anzaldúa focuses on relating the history of how the US–Mexico border came to exist, and begins this history from "the original peopling of the Americas" (26). Adams's principal aim over the course of *Prison of Grass* and *The Tortured People* is to reclaim what he views as a hijacked history of Native–white relations by applying "a theoretical framework for analyzing Aboriginal history and culture" (*Tortured* 3). All three writers express their dissatisfaction with white historians' versions of Native events.

This focus on history is rooted in what they see as the silencing of and disregard for alternative versions of history. As they bring those alternative histories back to light, each writer reconfigures his or her people as having played a significant part in the history of the country of which they are now a part—a clear sign of resistance to the dominant group. Anzaldúa, for example, believes that it is not enough to reclaim and retell history; for her, it must also be passed on: "To the immigrant *mexicano* and the recent arrivals we must teach our history" (109). Adams shares this opinion, asserting the potential of the reclaiming and retelling of history to change the injustice of the status quo: "Honesty for Indian and Métis history and culture is more than a quest for decolonization and a national identity; it is a pursuit to transform imperial structures of the state. History, as told by authentic Aboriginal historians, does more than retell establishment history. It explains the struggles for self-determination and promotes efforts to overcome present colonization" (*Tortured* 1). These revisions also remind their peoples of their history, which has been silenced for so long that it has sometimes been forgotten. As Anzaldúa notes: "I have so internalized the borderland conflict that sometimes I feel like one cancels out the other and we are zero, nothing, no one" (85). Her writing thus aims to remind Chicanos that they are a people with an identity, a history, and a future.

Similarly, from Campbell: "I write this for all of you [Canadians, "white" or otherwise], to tell you what it is like to be a Halfbreed woman in our country. I want to tell you about the joys and sorrows, the oppressing poverty, the frustrations and the dreams" (*Halfbreed* 8). Not only does Campbell want to tell her story, but she also wants her readers to know that although her personal situation has changed, life is still the same for many others. As she puts it: "I only want to say: this is what it was like; this is what it is still like. I know that poverty is not ours alone. Your people have it too, but in those earlier days you at least had dreams, you had a tomorrow. My parents and I never shared any aspirations for a future" (13). Indeed, Métis people were systematically convinced that they were nothing but "no good Halfbreeds" (90), a process Adams picks up on in the opening pages of *Prison of Grass:* from a young age, Native children are "conditioned to accept inferiority as a natural way of life" (9). And from a personal perspective, Adams recalls actively working to dissociate himself from his "half-breed" community because in his mind, to be half-breed was to be "ugly and shameful" (9). The authoritative white gaze looked at half-breeds/Métis only through racial stereotypes, which Adams internalized until he too "began to see [himself] as a stupid, dirty breed, drunken and irresponsible" (11). This is linked to perceptions of Louis Riel, a towering figure in Métis history. Critics like Adams suggest that Riel has been represented in Canadian history education as a madman and a traitor and that this has instilled shame and embarrassment in those who identify as Métis. The consequence, as both Adams and Campbell see it, is that the Métis have been excluded from mainstream Canadian history. As Adams notes: "The segregation of Aboriginal peoples from white mainstream society was a deliberate strategy employed by the state. This separation tended to reinforce stereotypical images of Indigenous Peoples who were cast aside as being dirty, lazy, vulgar, and unsuitable to live amongst so-called civilized and clean white society" (*Tortured* 125). This was most certainly the case with Riel, who led the Métis in the Red River Rebellion of 1869, went into exile in the United States, then returned to join the North West Rebellion of 1885 before being hanged for treason the same year by the Canadian government. Setting aside allegations that he was mentally ill, Riel's significance as a Métis leader cannot be underestimated, particularly with regard to issues of Métis identity as hybrid, which will be addressed later in this chapter; in fact, as Albert Braz notes, Riel "envisaged the Métis as 'a transracial nationality,'" suggesting that "both Natives and Newcomers were destined to fuse into a new nationality, the Métis Nation" (83). However, this aspect of Riel's thought has been largely ignored in mainstream Canadian historiography and history education. As the Métis poet Gregory Scofield asserts: "I'm the history lesson / you flunked at school" (31).

Closely linked to the issue of silenced histories within the Canadian education system is the colonial experience shared by Anzaldúa and Campbell. That experience, which extends to their struggles with the colonial system of education, marks another point of convergence between the two groups: language. In the same way that some US–Mexico borderlanders (characterized by their *mestizaje*) speak a patois of English, Spanish, and Nahuatl (known as both *pachuco* or *caló*), some Métis speak Michif. With its unique syntax and grammar, Michif reflects the hybrid character of the Métis themselves. According to the Métis National Council, Michif is "a combination of French nouns and Cree verbs" (Métis National Council, "Michif"). Many Métis, especially those who grew up in more isolated Métis communities, speak Michif far more fluently than they do English or French but must learn to silence their tongue in order to gain entry into mainstream society. Campbell remembers: "We weren't allowed to speak Cree, only French and English, and for disobeying this, I was pushed into a small closet with no windows or light, and locked in for what seemed like hours" (44). And Anzaldúa remembers being punished for speaking Spanish in school. One schoolteacher told her: "If you want to be American, speak 'American.' If you don't like it, go back to Mexico where you belong" (75). Adams does not engage with Michif, but he does bring to light another facet of the same debate: the superior command of language and discourse wielded by whites. As he puts it, he "hated talking to whites because it was such an agonizing experience—their attitudes and the tone of their conversation left no doubt about white supremacy" (*Prison* 11). This impression was in line with his having been taught that his Native ancestors were "cruel, sadistic savages who had not even reached the early stages of civilization" (12).

These denials of the right to speak their own language can be linked to the many different oppressions experienced by Anzaldúa, Campbell, and Adams. Anzaldúa notes that she suffers multiple oppressions, as a Mexican/Chicana/Latina in the Anglo United States, and as a queer woman. Campbell, too, recognizes the colonial legacy of oppression in her life: "I realize now that the system that fucked me up fucked up our men even worse. The missionaries had impressed upon us the feeling that women were a source of evil. This belief, combined with the ancient Indian recognition of the power of women, is still holding back the progress of our people today" (144). Adams theorizes these points with a view to how colonization works: "As colonized peoples, we internalize much of the state ideology and its ethnic, class and race dynamics which perpetuate our subjugation and repression" (*Tortured* 41).

Anzaldúa, Campbell, and Adams also identify the denial of land rights as an central factor in the oppressions their groups face. As a US–Mexico *tejana* borderlander, Anzaldúa identifies with land that has been stolen from her people by white colonizers. Her relationship to land is also tied to Indigenous and Mexican cultural practices relating to food and harvesting—essentially, to survival. Similarly, Campbell's relationship with land reflects the Métis predicament, as does Adams's. Since the state had not recognized them as "real" Native people, the Métis were not present when, as Campbell puts it, "the treaty-makers came" (15). Without Indian status, they had no rights to the land they had been living on, nor were they provided for when reserves were being created. Nor were provisions made for them when the state wrote the homesteading laws. Adams's references to the "ghetto" (*Prison* 3) in which he grew up signal the implications of this denial of land rights.

What, then, is the relationship between Anzaldúa's, Campbell's, and Adams's revisionist histories and their activism? Perhaps the best strategy here is to return to the purpose of their writing. All three state clearly that one of the aims of their work is to bring to light the experiences of a specific group of marginalized people (whether Chicano or Métis) and to remind that group of their own stories and histories. While this is an important similarity, there are also important differences with regard to how far each goes to stake a claim in the overtly political. Anzaldúa clearly intends for a community characterized by its *mestizaje* to be formed, one that challenges all borders and that thinks with a logic of "and" rather than "or." Adams feels a responsibility to tell the Métis story: "Since I am a Métis, I have developed the historical discussion as much as possible from a Native viewpoint" (*Prison* x). Campbell does not write solely or overtly to advocate a specific political standpoint. In fact, as already mentioned, she barely refers to the political meetings that have long been part of the Métis civil rights movement (*Halfbreed* 151). Perhaps her most significant political contribution is that she has recuperated and reclaimed the term "halfbreed." As noted earlier, that term was most often derogatory, reflecting as it did the low social, economic, and political standing of the person to whom it was assigned. In using it for the title of her autobiography, Campbell reclaimed it for the Métis, who by extension can now stake a claim on the colonizer's language. At the very end of *Halfbreed*, however, Campbell's political views rise to the surface: "I realize that an armed revolution of Native people will never come about; even if such a thing were possible what would we achieve? We would only end up oppressing someone else. I believe that one day, very soon, people will set aside their differences and come together as one. Not because we love one another, but because we will need each other to survive" (156). Campbell's comment has significant implications for what I have been trying to do in this chapter. She recognizes that "us-versus-them" binary thinking will only lead to a people's demise, something with which Anzaldúa most certainly agrees. Indeed, of the *mestiza*, Anzaldúa writes: "The work of *mestiza* consciousness is to break down the subject-object duality that keeps her a prisoner and to show ... how duality is transcended ... A massive uprooting of dualistic thinking in the individual and collective consciousness is the beginning of a long struggle, but one that could, in our best hopes, bring us to the end of rape, of violence, of war" (102). The difference here is that Anzaldúa believes that the *mestiza* can (and has begun to) trigger this change; in contrast, Campbell sees the change happening but does not readily identify a trigger. This important difference is most evident in the way Anzaldúa, Campbell, and Adams frame their books: Anzaldúa intends *Borderlands/La Frontera* as "an invitation" (20) to the dominant culture from the new *mestizas* to join together in a movement that she sees as already happening. Campbell's prediction that "people will come together as one" is hopeful but vague in the sense that it involves no time frame or structure. Adams is less optimistic, observing that there is very little awareness of the exploitation of Métis and that whenever such political consciousness has arisen—which is rarely—it has failed to mobilize the people.

With the situation as it is, Adams's hope, expressed in the closing lines of *A Tortured People*, is that all Natives in Canada will "shatter the bureaucracy and structures of capitalism that imprison [them] under colonialism" (204) and achieve liberation.

Given the many similarities and concurrent differences found in each, appropriating Anzaldúa's strategy (as that of "mainstream" "border studies") and transposing it onto a reading of the work of Campbell and Adams is a useful exercise and may be indicative of how far US–Mexico border studies can travel. For her part, Anzaldúa presents a series of steps the *mestiza* must take as she moves toward her new consciousness and begins her life of action. It is important here to note that Anzaldúa sees herself as this new *mestiza* figure and that she feels she has already completed these steps.

As I similarly note in another essay on Anzaldúa ("Border Studies"), the first step she lists is to "take inventory" by looking at who she is and separating out which parts of her come from which of her disparate ancestors (Anzaldúa 104). This step is important, for she makes a point of exposing and reiterating her Spanish *and* her Indigenous blood—the latter being something the Chicano movement has often tended to downplay and deny. The *new mestiza* must continue by "putting history through a sieve" (step two), enacting a reminder that her own *mestizaje* has its history in conquest, rape, violence, and occupation (104). After scrutinizing history—in this case, Western accounts of and justifications for Spanish conquest in the Americas—she "communicates the rupture" (step three) with oppressive traditions (104). In doing so, the new *mestiza* articulates her own feminist agenda, refusing to remain silent. As she "documents the struggle" by writing it down (the fourth step), she "reinterprets history" (step five), reclaiming it as her own narrative and, finally, "using new symbols, shapes new myths" (step six) that move away from "Greek myths and the Western Cartesian split point of view" (104). In so doing, the new *mestiza* is able to "root" herself "in the mythological soil and soul of this continent" and thereby attain a consciousness that does not adhere to traditional "Western" modes of thought (104). Indeed, Anzaldúa's intention in *Borderlands/La Frontera* is to mirror this process. The structure of the book makes it clear that her own work reflects the process she prescribes to aspiring new *mestizas*, which in turn suggests that she sees herself as a vanguard of this movement. If the first steps toward her new *mestiza* consciousness are to "take inventory" and "put history through a sieve," in the same vein, the first two chapters of *Borderlands/La Frontera* revisit the history of the US–Mexico border region and enact a reminder of Anzaldúa's own ancestry.

Over the next five chapters, Anzaldúa proceeds to "document the struggle" of Chicano men and women, as well as her own particular struggle as a queer woman of colour in the United States. Her reclaiming of the story of *La Malinche* can only be described as a "reinterpret[ation] of history," and her creation of "a new culture—*una cultura mestiza*—with [her] own lumber, own bricks and mortar, and own feminist architecture" constitutes the shaping of new myths with new symbols (44). Indeed, Anzaldúa views *Borderlands/La Frontera* as an "invitation from the new *mestizas*"—of which she clearly considers herself a member—to anyone interested in joining this new community characterized by mutual dialogue (20). As such, she sees the new *mestiza* as capable of joining forces with any other group of people whose interests lie in building a community using an architecture and language of multiplicity and plurality rather than dualistic thinking and what she calls the "Western Cartesian split point of view" (104).

The question is, can these steps be identified in Campbell's and Adams's work also? I suggest that they can be to a certain degree, as their engagement with their own personal histories—and, on a broader level, with Métis history—certainly qualifies as "taking inventory" and "putting history through a sieve." In their critiques of a system that oppresses Native and Métis men and women by various means, including education, land rights, and civil rights, Campbell and Adams "communicate the rupture" and "document the struggle." And in their adamant reclamations of Métis history, with a particular focus on Louis Riel, both "reinterpret history." Finally, Campbell's reclamation of the word "half-breed" qualifies as "using new symbols [and] shaping new myths." However, Anzaldúa's steps to achieving the new *mestiza* consciousness are not intended to serve as a monolithic model, nor do they succeed in doing so, as is evident here. What emerges from this discussion is the need for various components from the writings of Anzaldúa, Campbell, and Adams to be brought together to articulate a new guide or set of steps, one in which border studies' roots on the US–Mexico border are neither denied nor considered sacrosanct. Perhaps by using Adams's historical acumen and in-depth scholarly analysis of exactly how imperialism and colonization operate, alongside Anzaldúa's focus on the porous and flexible nature of all borders and boundaries, physical or otherwise, and tempering both with Campbell's highly effective reclamation of language through humble narrative, we will be able to reach a new understanding of the commonalities of the *mestizo/a* and Métis experience.

Note

1   Yet the issue of First Nationhood is debatable as it is linked to a history of treaties made between Indigenous peoples and what is now the Canadian government. This history is skewed in the sense that not all groups entitled to treaty "rights" were present at the treaty signing. As a result, there is a litany of names that Indigenous peoples in Canada can be identified by, including but not limited to the following: status Indian, non-status Indian, mixed-breed, or half-breed (the latter two describe a very specific kind of Native without status but outside the legal bounds of non-status-hood). Here, the term "status" refers to legal status. In this framework, an individual can only be considered an "Indian" if the state recognizes her/him as an Indian in legal terms in accordance with the Indian Act and Bill C-31.

Works Cited

Adams, Howard. *Prison of Grass: Canada from a Native Point of View.* Toronto: New Press, 1975.

———. *A Tortured People: The Politics of Colonization.* Penticton: Theytus, 1995.

Andrews, Jennifer. "Irony, Métis Style: Reading the Poetry of Marilyn Dumont and Gregory Scofield." *Canadian Poetry* 50 (2002). http://canadianpoetry.org/ volumes/vol50/andrews.html. Accessed 22 February 2013.

Anzaldúa, Gloria. *Borderlands/La Frontera: The New Mestiza.* 2nd ed. San Francisco: Aunt Lute, 1999.

Braz, Albert. "North of America: Racial Hybridity and Canada's (Non)place in Inter-American Discourse." *Comparative American Studies* 3.1 (2005): 79–88.

Campbell, Maria. *Halfbreed.* Lincoln: U of Nebraska P, 1982.

Daniels v. Canada (Minister of Indian Affairs and Northern Development) (T.D.), 2002 FCT 295, [2002] 4 F.C. 550. http://reports.fja.gc.ca/eng/2002/2002fct295.html. Accessed 20 February 2013.

Feghali, Zalfa. "Border Studies and Indigenous Peoples: Reconsidering our Approach." *Beyond the Border: Tensions across the 49th Parallel in the Great Plains and Prairies.* Ed. Kyle Conway and Timothy Pasch. Montreal and Kingston: McGill–Queen's UP, 2013. 153–69.

Gómez-Peña, Guillermo. *The New World Border: Prophecies, Poems, and Loqueras for the End of the Century.* San Francisco: City Lights Books, 1996.

Kaup, Monika. "Constituting Hybridity as Hybrid: Métis Canadian and Mexican American Formations." *Mixing Race, Mixing Culture: Inter-American Literary Dialogues.* Ed. Monika Kaup and Debra J. Rosenthal. Austin: U of Texas P, 2002. 185–210.

Lionnet, Françoise. *Postcolonial Representations: Women, Literature, Identity.* Ithaca: Cornell UP, 1995.

Métis Nation of Ontario. "Métis Rights in the Courts Again." http://www.metisnation .org/news--media/news/metis-rights-in-the-courts-again. Accessed 7 February 2013.

Métis National Council. "Métis Rights and Self-Government." http://www .albertametis.com/MNAHome/MNA2/MNA-RightsGovernment.aspx. Accessed 15 February 2011.

———. "Michif: The Language of the Métis." http://www.albertametis.com/ MNAHome/MNA-Culture2/Michif.aspx. Accessed 15 June 2013.

Pérez-Torres, Rafael. *Mestizaje: Critical Uses of Race in Chicano Culture.* Minneapolis: Minnesota University Press, 2005.

Peterson, Jacqueline, and Jennifer S.H. Brown. "Introduction." Peterson and Brown 3–16.

———, eds. *The New Peoples: Being and Becoming Métis in North America.* Winnipeg: U of Manitoba P, 1985.

Rosaldo, Renato. *Culture and Truth: The Remaking of Social Analysis.* 1989. London: Routledge, 1993.

Saldívar, José David. *Border Matters: Remapping American Cultural Studies.* Berkeley: University of California Press, 1997.

Scofield, Gregory. "When It Come to Your Turn." *The Gathering: Stones for the Medicine Wheel.* Vancouver: Polestar, 1993. 31.

Thomas, Robert K. "Afterword." Peterson and Brown 243–51.

THEORIZING THE BORDER:
LITERATURE, PERFORMANCE, TRANSLATION

thirteen

"Some Borders Are More Easily Crossed Than Others"

Negotiating Guillermo Verdecchia's *Fronteras Americanas*

Maureen Kincaid Speller

> Where and what exactly is the border? Is it this line in the dirt, stretching for 3,000 kilometres? Is the border more accurately described as a zone which includes the towns of El Paso and Ciudad Juárez? Or is the border—is the border the whole country, the whole continent?
>
> (Verdecchia 21)

"VERDECCHIA" POSES THIS QUESTION in the opening scene of Guillermo Verdecchia's *Fronteras Americanas/American Borders* (1997). "Verdecchia" is "lost and trying to figure out where I took that wrong turn ... I suspect we got lost while crossing the border" (20). At this stage, "Verdecchia" is no clearer than his audience as to which border he has got lost on; and although he has "hired a translator who will meet us on the other side" (21), he likewise seems to have little idea of what the "other side" will look like, or indeed what one actually crosses in order to reach the other side. As he muses about the border, it rapidly expands from a line in the dirt to something far more abstract. In asking how a whole country—a whole continent, even—can be a border, "Verdecchia" the character and the playwright, Verdecchia, point toward a concept of a border as something more than a physical division between two countries. Yet the "line in the dirt" is how most people first experience the border.

At the beginning of the twenty-first century, national borders represent perhaps the greatest anxiety in contemporary life, for governments and for individuals alike. On the one hand, and particularly in the wake of the 9/11 terrorist attacks, many governments are increasingly concerned about monitoring who precisely is entering their country. On the other hand, for many individuals, crossing a border has become a necessity in order to gain political asylum or to achieve economic stability, and they are willing to place themselves in extraordinary danger to make that crossing, often with the assistance of human traffickers. Moreover, tourists and other supposedly legitimate travellers are increasingly subject to levels of regulation that are little more than "security theatre,"[1] or they are treated as suspects for no better reason than that they happen to share a name with an alleged terrorist or because their superficial appearance matches an equally superficial profile of what an unacceptable border crosser might look like. Thus a physical border generates a complex set of relationships between those who seek to cross it and those who seek to maintain its integrity.

The nature of the physical border between two countries is often obscure. When I fly to the United States from England, as I leave the ground I am transported from English to international airspace, but it is not clear when I actually *enter* the United States. The passage through Canadian airspace and the transfer into US airspace are not formally acknowledged. Unless I happen to be looking out the window, I do not see the plane cross into Canadian airspace, and if I am not familiar with the geography of the US–Canada border, I do not recognize when the plane has moved into US airspace. When I land at Chicago O'Hare airport and leave the plane, I am on US soil, but my formal entry into the country does not occur until I enter the immigration hall and cross a coloured line marked on the floor. Each immigration booth has its own coloured line: does each of those lines constitute a separate border, or should they be viewed as the visible fragments of a contiguous whole running through the hall? No charted national border runs through O'Hare Airport, so to all intents and purposes I queue at an imagined fragment of border until I am invited to step into the United States of America by an immigration official, and I only formally enter the country when my passport is stamped. The journey from the plane to acquiring the passport stamp, while it leads the passenger through an entrance ritual, also demonstrates that even a clearly delineated "border" is really only a scuffed line on a floor until someone invests it with territorial significance. With the border transformed from an actual line in the dirt to a conceptual marker in a building physically detached from any territorial border, its nature becomes more mysterious. Each person standing at the coloured line is engaging with a border that exists only for them.

In *Fronteras Americanas*, "Verdecchia" negotiates the US–Canada border in what, from the context offered, appears to be Los Angeles airport. We hear only his answers to the questions asked by the Customs agent, but one is invited to suppose that he is being questioned on the basis of received notions arising from his name rather than where he has actually come from. His Canadian citizenship is no proof against this. "[W]e're supposed to be friends," he says at one point. "You know, Free Trade, the longest undefended border in the world … all that?" (57). Instead, "Verdecchia" is forced to state three times that he is travelling for pleasure as well as to explain the nature of his employment in some detail. The unspoken assumption is, clearly, that someone with a Latin American name cannot possibly be on holiday or employed, and must therefore be trying to find their way into the United States for other, presumably illegal, purposes. This consideration totally overrides the passport's statement of "Verdecchia's" Canadian citizenship. It becomes easier, then, to see what "Verdecchia" means about taking a wrong turn and about needing a translator on the other side.

This suggests in turn that we may need to find new ways of describing the border. "Verdecchia" proposes "line," "zone," and "the whole country, the whole continent," expanding the physical dimensions of the border as he goes, but these words cannot fully describe the nature of the border, nor indeed how it functions for each individual. As *Fronteras Americanas* progresses, "Verdecchia" will endeavour to create a new definition of "border," one that reflects his own experience of it and that will perhaps enable him to live more comfortably with the concept of the border. Other Latin American and US Latino/a writers, such as Carlos Fuentes, Guillermo Gómez-Peña, and Gloria Anzaldúa, have also sought to articulate their often troubling experience of the border and to find ways of incorporating this experience into their daily lives. For them, as for "Verdecchia," a difficulty arises when they attempt to reconcile the physical elements of the border with its metaphysical aspects.

Michel Foucault's text "Des Espace Autres" ("Of Other Spaces") may offer a way of negotiating this difficulty while developing the notion of the border as a conceptual space that offers each individual the chance to negotiate with his/her personal line in the dirt. Foucault defines the modern experience of the world as "less that of a long life developing through time than that of a network that connects points and intersects with its own skein" (22). He further notes that "the anxiety of our era has to do fundamentally with space, no doubt a great deal more than with time" (23), that is, with history. This anxiety is clearly reflected in contemporary worries about maintaining the integrity of a country's borders.

Foucault proposes "an hierarchic ensemble of places" (22), including "places where things had been put because they had been violently displaced, and then on the contrary places where things found their natural ground and stability" (22). He describes this "intersection of places that constituted what could very roughly be described as medieval space" as the space of "emplacement" or localization. The notion of a long life developing through time points toward remaining in one place (historically, or pre-historically), putting down deep roots and remaining connected to the land, and indeed knowing one's place. The network, however, points toward movement, which becomes necessary in order to make those connections and intersections actively. Foucault's hierarchy of space replaces localization with extension, a shift brought about by Galileo's "constitution of an infinite and infinitely open space," which is substituted for localization (23). Foucault argues that the closed space of emplacement is dissolved and that "a thing's place was no longer anything but a point in its movement, just as the stability of a thing was only its movement indefinitely slowed down" (23). In turn, in modern times, the "site" is substituted for "extension." Although Foucault is, throughout the text, somewhat vague in his definition of "site" by comparison with his descriptions of "place" or "space," such examples as he does give suggest that he envisages the "site" as a collection of items rather than as a specific geographical location. The term, as he applies it, appears to be sufficiently capacious to allow for a multiplying of ideas. For example, when he talks about "sites of temporary relaxation" (23), he is considering "cafés, cinemas, beaches" (24). When he speaks of "sites of transportation" (23), he identifies them as "streets, trains" (23); by extension, one can include airport, airplane, and other areas distinctively associated with transportation. Foucault's vagueness in constructing a definition for "site" suggests that the concept is constantly shifting.

However, these "clusters of relations" can also take on a more abstract character. Foucault envisages the site as being "defined by relations of proximity between points and elements" (23), though he is also vague about what these "points and elements" might be. On the one hand, he notes the importance of the site "as a problem in contemporary technical work" (23) (i.e., in the storage of data, a problem which has become even greater since the advent of the Internet); on the other, he notes also that "the problem of siting or placement arises for mankind in terms of demography," in particular, "knowing what relations of propinquity, what time of storage, circulation, marking and classification of human elements should be adopted in a given situation in order to achieve a given end. Our epoch is one in which space takes for us the form of relations among sites" (23). This suggests to me that it may be possible to view the border as a "site," comprising border markers, crossing points, adjacent dwellings and towns, and indeed the local population on either side of the official territorial boundary. Alternatively, one might argue that the border is a series of sites, which are in turn related to one another. According to Foucault, "we are in the epoch of simultaneity: we are in the epoch of juxtaposition, the epoch of the near and far, of the side-by-side, of the dispersed" (22). "Simultaneity" and "juxtaposition" both point not only to the proximity of relations, but also to the possibility of being more than one thing at a time, and being in more than one "place." This will become significant in considering people such as "Verdecchia," who describes himself as a hyphenated person, an Argentinean-Canadian, who is uncertain of his identity as a result of that conjunction, as well as border crossers such as Guillermo Gómez-Peña, who commutes between San Diego and Tijuana and finds himself caught on the border fence of the oblique. Here the hyphen and the oblique are borders as real as the territorial borders both men have to negotiate. Possibly, a sense of connection between two places, two national identities, might be created as a result of this simultaneity. Equally, the possibility of the emergence of a totally new kind of identity might emerge.

Foucault concentrates on "certain [sites] that have the curious property of being in relation to all the other sites, but in such a way as to suspect, neutralize, or invert the set or relations that they happen to designate, mirror, or reflect" (24). He goes on to define the certain sites as being of two kinds. The first he calls utopias, "sites with no real place" (24), while the second type he calls "heterotopias," because "these places are so absolutely different from all the sites that they reflect and speak about" (24). He goes on to say:

> There are ... probably in every culture, in every civilization, real places—places that do exist and that are formed in the very founding of society—which are something like counter-sites, a kind of effectively enacted utopia in which the real sites, all the other real sites that can be found within the culture, are simultaneously represented, contested, and inverted. Places of this kind are outside of all places, even though it may be possible to indicate their location in reality. (24)

If we view the border as a site, it may also be possible to view it as a heterotopic space, insofar as it engages with the cultures it divides and/or encloses in a variety of conflicting ways. When Foucault talks of heterotopias as being "so absolutely different from all the sites that they reflect and speak about," the border site fits this definition, given that it is both the end and the beginning of a territory, depending on where it is viewed from, but it is also a space in which people are forced to make sometimes unwelcome decisions about identity and allegiance.

However, in advancing the idea of the heterotopia, Foucault also speculates that between it and the utopia, "there might be a sort of mixed, joint experience, which would be the mirror ... In the mirror, I see myself there where I am not, in an unreal, virtual space that opens up behind the surface; I am over there, there where I am not, a sort of shadow that gives my own visibility to myself, that enables me to see myself there, where I am absent" (24). Foucault in fact seems to be arguing for the mirror as utopia, and also as heterotopia: "it makes this place that I occupy at the moment when I look at myself in the glass at once absolutely real, connected with all the space that surrounds it, and absolutely unreal, since in order to be perceived it has to pass through this virtual point which is over there" (24). This dual image points to a possibility that the border can also have some sort of double function, first as a heterotopic space but second in generating a commentary on the existence of the heterotopic space. This suggests in turn that there are two levels of commentary in play. The existence of the heterotopic space enables its occupants to stand outside time (or history) and assess their position, but in turn the joint experience of the real and unreal spaces, and the virtual point represented by Foucault's mirror, obliges them to engage further with their own response to the original situation.

"Verdecchia" seems inadvertently to create such a space when he tries to move between countries. Crossing into the United States from Canada at a point that is far removed from the physical boundary between the two countries appears to confuse the Customs agent; "Verdecchia's" attempt to return "home," to the country he left as a small child and does not actually remember, is similarly marked by an unorthodox approach, in that this time he is flying from Canada to Chile, then crossing the Argentinean border by bus. Although he claims that this is to avoid detection by the Argentinean military authorities, who may wish to detain him for not carrying out his military service, it is as though "Verdecchia" is incapable of directly negotiating with the borders embodied in his birth and citizenship statuses.

In the first of his 1984 CBC Massey Lectures, Carlos Fuentes says that "our faces see themselves across this frontier, which then becomes the frontier each of us carries within him" (8). To interpret this comment in the context of Foucault's heterotopic mirror is to realize that while he recognizes that each person carries that frontier within, Fuentes nonetheless wishes it to remain a division or a barrier rather than something that can be crossed or explored. In Foucault's terms, Fuentes is arguing persistently for localization, for emplacement, and for the security that this historically represents. One might also argue that "Verdecchia" subconsciously is seeking something similar—to secure his sense of his own identity—but that his efforts misfire, placing him in ridiculous situations because he does not understand that such localization has become historically defunct. While Fuentes explores the notion of the border purely in theoretical terms, enabling him effectively to ignore its changing reality, "Verdecchia" directly confronts the "real" border and finds himself unable to negotiate it easily.

Fuentes begins his first lecture with what he describes as one of his "earliest photographic memories": his "father, a young man of twenty-five with horn-rimmed glasses and a straw boater, straddling the Mexican–American border at towns with hot, dusty names: Laredo/Nuevo Laredo; El Paso/Ciudad Juarez; Nogales, Arizona/Nogales, Sonora" (7). Fuentes's father was a lawyer who had just started work for the Mexican–American Border Claims Commission after the Mexican Revolution, dealing with the complaints of Mexicans and US citizens who had suffered because of alleged border incursions by Pershing and Pancho Villa, respectively. Consequently, much of his work would have been focused on the precise position of the border vis-à-vis the alleged incursions.

It is easy enough to imagine that for Fuentes's father, it was a matter of pure amusement, an escape from his day's work, or perhaps even an ironic comment on his situation, to have himself photographed with each foot in a different country, rather as modern tourists at the Greenwich Observatory like to be photographed with a foot on either side of the Greenwich Meridian. The straw boater, an unlikely piece of border apparel, seems to underline the sense of playfulness in the man's action; he would not seem out of place in a vaudeville show, yet the reparations work he is engaged in directly addresses the losses of those caught up in the Mexican Revolution.[2]

However, Fuentes's recollection also raises a number of difficult questions. He includes no illustrations in the published version of what were originally radio lectures, and he seems not to consider it necessary to explain the exact physical nature of the border that his father was supposedly straddling. The physical barriers that now mark the path of the border in places such as Tijuana are a more recent innovation. One could speculate that the path of the border might have been marked in places with some sort of barbed wire fence (although much of the border is marked by the course of the Rio Grande), but given that Fuentes's father has apparently been photographed performing this act of border crossing in one of the twin border towns, the reasonable assumption might be that he is at a crossing point, in which case the border is presumably delineated not by a barrier but by an opening, in which Fuentes's father is standing. In other words, unless someone has actually drawn a line on the ground, Fuentes's father is more than likely straddling a completely intangible border. And even if there is a painted mark, one might reasonably ask how that makes the idea of the border any more real. Assuming that Fuentes himself is not being fanciful in his description, his father goes on to document this act of border crossing in a number of different places, as if needing to reinforce a belief that he has genuinely had a foot in two different countries.

The image is also personally significant for Fuentes in that it "became a picture of my own self, a symbol of my own imagination" (7). Fuentes casts the Mexico–US border not only as "the border between the United States and all of Latin America" (8) but also as a border "between the industrialized and the developing worlds" (8), and a boundary between cultures, "the Protestant, capitalist, Nordic culture, and the southern Indo-Mediterranean, Catholic culture of syncretism and the baroque" (8). What does not figure in Fuentes's perception of North America is Canada. The Massey lectures are presented annually under the auspices of CBC Radio, but throughout the entire series of five lectures, Fuentes mentions Canada just once, in the first lecture, and at another point in the same lecture he specifically defines North Americans as the citizens of the United States of America (9). While "Norteamericano" does mean "US American" in Spanish, suggesting that some confusion may have arisen in translation, Fuentes nonetheless seems quite clear that he refers only to US Americans; for him, Canada seems to have no existence whatsoever. Fuentes does not acknowledge the existence of another country above the 49th parallel, or if he does, he cannot see any way that Mexico and Canada can engage with each other directly because they have no physical border. This in turn might prompt us to re-examine the Customs agent's exchange with "Verdecchia" as being less about his supposed Latin American heritage and rather more about his coming from a place that means nothing at all to the agent simply because he is not accustomed to dealing with the concept of a US–Canada border in California.

While Fuentes's father represents the border as either a place of personal entertainment or as a line with which to construct or refute legal claims, Fuentes himself seems to be much more troubled by what it represents. He recognizes that the border is an internal as well as an abstract concept: "Every Latin American has a personal frontier with the United States. And every North American, before this century, [sic] is over, will find that he or she has a personal frontier with Latin America" (8). But even as he recognizes this fact, he places restrictions on it. "Verdecchia" responds directly to this, and indirectly criticizes Fuentes, when he says: "And when I say AMERICA I don't mean the country, I mean the continent. Somos todos Americanos. We are all Americans" (20). Later he asks: "Where does the U.S. end and Canada begin? Does the U.S. end at the 49th parallel or does the U.S. only end at your living room when you switch on the CBC?" (21). Both character and playwright perceive North America very differently from Fuentes, yet Verdecchia and "Verdecchia" seem ambivalent about their country's relationship with the United States. The production of *Fronteras Americanas* includes a map of the Mexico–US border projected as a slide, but no corresponding map of the US–Canada border. It is not clear whether Verdecchia assumes that his Canadian audience will know where the border is or whether he is, consciously or not, reflecting an assumption that Canada and the United States *are* more or less the same thing. Alternatively, rather as "Verdecchia" seems to be trying to circumvent his country's own border, it may be that Verdecchia is doing the same in writing the play. In the final moments before "Verdecchia" leads the audience across the border, it is no longer apparent which border is being crossed. "I myself will walk backwards so that it looks as though I am heading north" (21), he says. If he were crossing the border from the United States into Mexico, why would he want to appear to be moving northwards *into* the United States when a border patrol is less likely to worry about someone heading *out of* the country? But if one instead thinks of "Verdecchia" crossing the 49th parallel, it makes more sense to think of him trying to cover his tracks and appear to be leaving *for* Canada rather than entering the United States and rejecting his Canadian identity—in which case, he really is lost.

"Verdecchia's" aspirations are greater than simply wanting to engage with the United States, the country with which Canada shares a border. "Somos todos Americanos" indicates that he wants to engage with the entire continent, something that Fuentes seems unable to accept. Fuentes can say that "[t]his is a living frontier, which can be nourished by information but, above all, by knowledge, by understanding, by the pursuit of enlightened self-interest on both parts" (8), echoing Foucault's perception of the "site" as a cluster of relations, and as a network, as well as "Verdecchia's" exclamation: "Here we are. All together. At long last. Very exciting" (19). However, Fuentes follows his comment almost immediately by quoting a conversation with the Mexican writer and diplomat Octavio Paz, in which the latter observed that the problems between the two countries would persist "because the two cultures are so different, so dissimilar in their origins, so strange to each other and therefore so challenging to the comprehension of the other side" (9). Fuentes amplifies this comment: "We are different, we are other: North Americans (by which I mean only the citizens of the United States) and Latin Americans. But we cannot impose our vision of the world on the United States, nor can they on us. We must try to bridge our differences without denying them" (9).

Yet even as he says this, Fuentes is guilty of a further geographical elision. On the one hand he has completely erased the presence of Canada on the North American continent, while on the other he has erased the territorial identities of the countries of Central and South America, collapsing them into a non-existent entity called "Latin America." The complexity of Mexico's own situation is shown here. While it is regarded geographically as part of North America, although more often politically linked to the countries of Central and South America, Fuentes here separates it from the United States while on occasion allowing "Mexico" itself to stand as a metonym for "Latin America" in constructing his continental binary. At the same time, were it not for that specific identification of the United States with "North America," one might argue that Fuentes is doing only what other commentators have done, and indeed what "Verdecchia" has done for himself in trying to create a vision of "home" in Latin America. His Latin American home, as the character acknowledges, is constructed out of "newspapers, novels and every Amnesty International report on South America" (37); it cannot possibly provide him with a sense of the reality of living in Argentina. Instead, "Verdecchia" has effectively constructed another heterotopic space in which to explore his sense of himself as being from Latin America. But it is a version of Latin America that is a fantasy.

Fuentes appears to be suggesting that the personal frontier he claims every Latin American has with the United States should *remain* a barrier rather than become an opening, while for North Americans, the fact of having a personal frontier with Latin America seems to carry an implicit notion of "whether they want it or not" without suggesting what this might mean in terms of an engagement between cultures on either side of the border. What is striking about Fuentes's comments is the way in which he emphasizes difference and how, in laying out the differences between the two Americas, Latin America is invariably presented in negative terms while North American aspirations are always more positive. To take a few examples:

We represent the abundance of poverty.
They, the poverty of abundance.

They want to live better.
We want to die better.

North Americans are accustomed to success.
Latin Americans, to failure. (9)

Most significantly, Fuentes appears to be positioning the whole of Latin America as the exoticized "other" in relation to North America. The use of the pronoun "we" might be taken to be ambiguous; Fuentes might be endeavouring to suggest that the two "countries" are different from each other, are "other" to each other, but the ways in which he tabulates difference tend to point consistently toward Latin America as the poor and needy relation in the dynamic. If the two Americas are strange to each other, Fuentes seems to be suggesting that Latin America has a much clearer idea of what is on offer in North America than the other way round.

This perhaps enables us to make greater sense of the photograph of Fuentes's father. Not only is he portrayed as having each foot in a different country, but each foot is also in an entirely different culture, at least according to Fuentes's own representation of the situation. The question then is which country is his father leaving, which culture is he entering, or is he perpetually caught between the two in real life, much as he has been captured in Fuentes's "photographic memory"? His Massey Lectures suggest that Fuentes believes that Mexico, and by extension the whole of "Latin" America, should turn its back on North America—that is, the United States of America—and establish itself without cross-border interference, although he subsequently contradicts himself by also suggesting that cross-border economic aid, with no strings attached, would be nonetheless welcome to help the Latin American countries establish themselves. This re-emphasizes Fuentes's own apparent confusion about his relationship with the border, and hints at a sense of embarrassment at the disparity between Mexico and the United States.

Fuentes seems to want to retain the border, in order to preserve a sense of Mexico's own cultural identity (although as already noted, this is frequently conflated with a wider, non-specific "Latin" American identity). Yet he also seems to recognize that the border is, to some extent at least, porous. While it is a barrier, it is still a "living frontier," and he is aware of those faces on the other side, looking back, which suggests that he finds it difficult to adhere to the idea of the border as a rigid division between countries and cultures, but neither can he accept what would happen if it were to be more easily crossed. While his father can stand artlessly with one foot either side of a contested barrier—indeed, a barrier whose position he may himself be contesting—Fuentes sees the frontier purely as a means by which to maintain the integrity of his own culture by keeping out the cultures of others. For him, the existence of the border always represents a threat insofar as it means there may be something, and someone, beyond it.

Gloria Anzaldúa, writing within a couple of years of Fuentes's delivery of the Massey Lectures (although there is no indication that she is responding directly to them), proposes a reading of the border that differs greatly from the light-hearted approach of Fuentes's father. Nonetheless, her reading makes a connection with Fuentes, Sr.'s perception of himself as having a foot in two camps even as it struggles with the younger Fuentes's dark vision of the border as a necessary barrier. Anzaldúa's account of the border positions it as a heterotopic site of contention, which recognizes yet also rejects Fuentes's "us and them" dichotomy. For Anzaldúa, while the border is still a barrier to be straddled, it is also made physical, transformed into *una herida abierta* [an open wound] where the Third World grates against the first and bleeds" (25). This image is echoed in *Fronteras Americanas* when "Verdecchia" is told by El Brujo, in Toronto, that "you have a very bad border wound" (71). El Brujo goes on to say that "here in Mexico any border wounds or afflictions are easily aggravated" (71). Putting aside El Brujo's perception of himself as being in Mexico despite being in Canada, one might also speculate whether "Verdecchia's" border wound arises as much from his inability to negotiate the US–Canada border in Los Angeles as from the significance he invests in the border between himself as Canadian and himself as Argentinean. Mayte Gómez argues that "[t]he individual who experiences two cultures defies acculturation, as he searches for a place where two cultures interact with one another equally." However, in the case of "Verdecchia" the process of acculturation is based on a flawed assumption, that he can construct for himself a "Latin American" culture where none existed before. If Gomez's argument admits the notion of a constructed culture existing alongside a lived culture, then it might be argued that "Verdecchia" can exploit his "border wound" in order to find "Home." However, as "Verdecchia" himself suggests, his constructed culture consistently fails him: "All sides of the border have claimed and rejected me. On all sides I have been asked: How long have you been …? How old were you when …? When did you leave? When did you arrive?" (51). On this basis, there is no reason to assume that "Verdecchia" can at this stage conduct a successful interaction with his "personal border."

Like Fuentes, Anzaldúa has a memory of an old photograph: "I am six years old. I stand between my father and mother, head cocked to the right, the toes of my flat feet gripping the ground. I hold my mother's hand" (37). Anzaldúa goes on to say: "To this day I'm not sure where I found the strength to leave the source, the mother, disengage from my family, *mi tierra, mi gente*, and all that picture stood for. I had to leave home so that I could find myself, find my own intrinsic nature buried under the personality that had been imposed on me" (38). As the first person in six generations of her family actually to leave "home"—and here she seems to be referring to house, town, and region— Anzaldúa can be seen as emerging from a community with a strong sense of emplacement, of physical ties to the land. Anzaldúa's argument, however, is that "I didn't leave all the parts of me: I kept the ground of my own being. On it I walked away, taking with me the land, the Valley, Texas" (38). She has internalized and personalized her relationship to the place where she sees herself as coming from, a geographical point but also a cultural position. While the physical borderland that she engages with is, as she notes, the "Texas–U.S Southwest/Mexican border" (19), she is also dealing with other borders. As she puts it, "the Borderlands are physically present wherever two or more cultures edge each other, where people of different races occupy the same territory, where under, lower, middle and upper classes touch, where the space between two individuals shrinks with intimacy" (19).

Foucault's third principle of heterotopias proposes that "the heterotopia is capable of juxtaposing in a single real place, several spaces, several sites that are in themselves incompatible" (25), and Anzaldúa has superimposed other meta-phorical borderlands on this physical spot, having already proposed that the Borderlands are physically present "*wherever* two or more cultures edge each other," which suggests ties that are other than geographically based. Whereas Fuentes refuses the commonality of people looking at one another across a frontier, Anzaldúa evokes a commonality of people linked by ethnic identity, gender, sexual orientation, or experience, but not tied to a specific geograph-ical area, nor divided by conventional borders. While Anzaldúa recognizes that "hatred, anger and exploitation are the prominent features of this landscape" (19), there are positive aspects: "keeping intact one's shifting and multiple iden-tity and integrity, is like trying to swim in a new element, an 'alien' element. There is an exhilaration in being a participant in the further evolution of human-kind, in being 'worked' on" (19). In effect, as a heterotopic space, the border-land, having become a place in which different sites of contention have been superimposed, is then transformed into a place in which Anzaldúa can experi-ment with her various identities. Fuentes uses the border to maintain identity, whereas for Anzaldúa, the border can also collapse one identity into another, offering an opportunity to forge something new, in her case, "the new *mestiza*."

While Fuentes's father is forever suspended between two countries, and his son has argued in favour of turning one's back on the country and people beyond the border, Anzaldúa specifically asks to remain by choice within the borderland: "if going home is denied me, then I will have to stand and claim my space, making a new culture—*una cultura mestiza*—with my own lumber, my own bricks and mortar, and my own feminist architecture" (44). Anzaldúa argues that as a *mestiza* she has no country and that her lesbianism and fem-inism have cut her off from her people and culture; thus, the heterotopic conditions of the border provide her with a space in which to participate in "the creation of another culture," and by extension a new country in which, as a "new *mestiza*," she can live, and that provides her with a base from which to operate. If, as Foucault argues, it is possible, within a heterotopia, for us to contest sites of activity even as they are represented, then this is clearly what Anzaldúa has set out to do in constructing a distinctively *mestiza* identity for herself: "Cradled in one culture, sandwiched between two cultures, straddling all three cultures and their value systems, *la mestiza* undergoes a struggle of flesh, a struggle of borders, an inner war ... The coming together of two self-consistent but habitually incompatible frames of reference causes *un choque*, a cultural collision" (100). To counteract this, she envisages a point where cultural combatants need to find themselves on "both shores at once" (100), or else make decisions to "cross the border into a wholly new and separate territory" (101). The new *mestiza* brings tolerance to bear upon her experience by examining it through the heterotopic mirror.

If Anzaldúa searches for ways to articulate physically the idea of border dwelling, the experience of the modern border dweller or crosser, such as the performance artist Guillermo Gómez-Peña, is more focused on how to live beyond physical borders. In *Fronteras Americanas*, Verdecchia addresses the difficulty of being a hyphenated person, torn between two countries, with no real sense of belonging to either one, and explores how he might reconcile himself to this often unwelcome conjoined existence. Similarly, Gómez-Peña finds himself caught among different points of existence: what he describes as his now "mythical home" in Mexico, the place where he grew up; his *casa*, the current place that he leaves and to which he returns; and *la jornado*, his life on the road, which he calls his conceptual home. Both artists might all too easily find themselves impaled on the oblique that separates Tijuana from San Diego, or fall into the space created by a hyphenated identity. Their problem, then, is how to account for being a border crosser even when not physically in the border country. Fuentes's notion of the "personal frontier" is particularly useful at this point.

To return to Foucault's principles of the heterotopia, his fifth principle suggests that "[h]eterotopias always presuppose a system of opening and closing that both isolates them and makes them penetrable. In general, the heterotopic site is not freely accessible" (26). Foucault goes on to suggest that "the individual has to submit to rites and purifications" (26) in order to enter, but he does not clarify who is in control of the heterotopic site. In the case of a frontier, one might suggest that border guards or a border authority would be, but Foucault remains silent on this. If, then, Anzaldúa has staked out a personal border territory, both Gómez-Peña and Verdecchia explore what it might mean to internalize that territory and render it completely portable by carrying the frontier within one.

Throughout the play, Verdecchia's character, "Verdecchia," has been searching for a stable identity for himself as a hyphenated person. He was taken to Canada from Argentina as a child and has spent years endeavouring to construct a memory of his former country, his home, through films, books, and music, and most importantly, through talking to Latin American exiles. His perception of his original country is thus mediated by the recollections of those who are also distant from it, and of those who never lived there, and their memories are shaped as much as anything by the manner of their leaving South America. In effect, "Verdecchia" has become doubly exiled, from a country he barely knew, and from the Latin America that he has created in his own mind but that he cannot fully experience because it does not actually exist.

He is not clear where his personal frontier with his country actually lies, or indeed which country is foremost in the construction of that frontier. Context suggests that "Verdecchia" has been an Argentinean-Canadian far longer than he has been purely Argentinean, but his identity as a Canadian is constantly deconstructed when people see his name, and he has deconstructed his own identity as an Argentinean by manufacturing a more general but spurious Latin American identity. It is surely significant that when he finally decides to return to Argentina, he takes out a Canadian passport in order to erase the fact that he is Argentinean by birth, as if tacitly admitting that his entire Latin American identity is already insecure. Rather than finding that he can "claim my place in the universe when I Go Home," he walks into a situation that is identical to his imagined experience of his "country"—a man, believed to be a criminal, is shot outside his hotel in Santiago de Chile, and dies because the police show little interest in getting him to hospital. "Verdecchia" becomes convinced that he has willed this event into being, because it mirrors the "Latin America" he has manufactured for himself in his obsessive reading and conversations about the country. This suggests that his "country," his "home," is entirely subject to his own ability to construct or destroy it, and in truth he has no emotional ties to this place and cannot accept how it works, any more than he truly belongs to Canada.

The encounter with El Brujo, who moves through time and space seemingly without leaving his consulting room (incidentally giving the lie to Foucault's claim that "it is not possible to disregard the fatal intersection of time with space [22]), prompts Verdecchia to recognize how he might live, and this leads him to make a statement that directly echoes Anzaldúa's declaration about making space for herself: "I am learning to live the border. I have called off the Border Patrol. I am a hyphenated person but I am not falling apart, I am putting together. I am building a house on the border" (78).

In terms of heterotopic space, it might be argued that Verdecchia's is a heterotopia of compensation (Foucault 27), poised somewhere between Argentina and Canada but also specific to Verdecchia and contained within him. Verdecchia may be building a house on the border, but he specifically *lives* the border, which suggests that he has internalized it and created a heterotopic space within himself, to which he has access because he acknowledges himself as a border crosser and shapes his life specifically around that understanding. However, the deeper question might be, what would an Argentinean-Canadian border look like? If Verdecchia cannot physically stand with a foot in two countries, how can he know when he has crossed from one to the other? Can that crossing ever successfully be made, or must one inevitably, as Verdecchia appears to have done, get lost on the way?

Gómez-Peña extends this idea even further in that he constantly enacts anew the process of crossing the border in his work as a performance artist. In his video performance diary, *Borderstasis* (1998), he comments: "I make art about the ongoing misunderstandings that take place in the zone. But to me, the border is no longer located in a geopolitical site. I carry the border wherever I go" (Gómez-Peña, *Dangerous* 147). Foucault suggests that in order to enter the heterotopic space, "one must have a certain permission and make certain gestures" (26), and Gómez-Peña appears to facilitate this by granting himself that permission and using his performances to create those "certain gestures." This suggests in turn that Gómez-Peña is able to reinvent constantly the heterotopic space he inhabits, superimposing identities on one another and collapsing them into one another to suit the specific moment and location: "I think that what we are trying to do is to open up spaces of ambiguity where there are contradictory voices and contradictory ideas clashing in front of the audience—spaces of ambiguity in which audience members can undergo multiple emotional and intellectual journeys that lead to different responses and different political positionalities" (Gómez-Peña, *Dangerous* 177). Foucault recognizes the theatre as a heterotopia, "capable of juxtaposing in a single real place several spaces, several sites that are in themselves incompatible" (25), and it is this form of heterotopia that Gómez-Peña exploits in order to transform the border into pure concept: "Performance art is a conceptual "territory" with fluctuating weather and borders, a place where contradiction, ambiguity and paradox are not only tolerated but encouraged. Every territory a performance artist stakes (including this text) is slightly different from that of their neighbor. We converge in this overlapping terrain precisely because it grants us special freedoms often denied to us in other monocultural/unidisciplinary realms" (Gómez-Peña, *Ethno-techno* 22).

This comment recognizes that the border as conceptual territory needs to be constantly reinvented and kept moving in order to avoid its ossification, which in turn means it must be entirely cut loose from the fixed geographical border. Among the freedoms Gómez-Peña mentions must be that of adopting the role of the heterotopic mirror, intended to exert the counteraction on the position occupied by those who have not, for whatever reason, crossed the fixed border into the conceptual territory occupied by Gómez-Peña and his fellow performers. Gómez-Peña represents himself and fellow performers as "interstitial creatures and border citizens by nature—insiders/outsiders at the same time—and we rejoice in this paradoxical condition. In fact, in the act of crossing a border, we find temporary emancipation" (23).

What remains unclear is what happens to those who cannot, for whatever reason, cross the physical or conceptual border. Foucault's concept of a heterotopia seems to suggest that for everyone who either seeks or needs one, a heterotopic space of some kind can be discovered. The individual experiences of Fuentes and Anzaldúa suggest that the choice lies with the individual to either turn away from or else bridge the border, while Gómez-Peña opts to become an insider/outsider, embracing the oblique rather than becoming caught on it. Each finds a space that satisfies them. The implication is that if one is aware of the border's existence, one cannot fail to interact with it in one way or another, and that this interaction will reach a satisfactory conclusion. Yet for "Verdecchia" not only does the nature of that interaction remain unresolved, but also it is unclear which borders he is attempting to interact with. His claim that he is "learning to live the border" echoes Anzaldúa's claiming of a space and culture, but his previous efforts to construct a culture for himself have consisted of recycling elements of other people's cultures rather than creating something that is distinctively new. Moreover, Anzaldúa knows clearly which border she is living, but for "Verdecchia" there are many possibilities, perhaps too many, and he lacks the facility to narrow them down. His journey through the play may be viewed as an attempt to discover a border that he can actively live, but at the end of the play, although he is "learning to live the border," the nature of that border remains unclear. Instead, there is a strong sense that he is expressing what seems to be an appropriate stance in his situation, proclaiming himself as a hyphenated person, and reaching back to the earlier failed construction of himself as a Latin American person, which is itself built on an earlier failed attempt to become "Willy" (33), the wholly Canadian boy. "Verdecchia" still hasn't identified what it is that makes him specifically "Verdecchia" and instead fractures and reconstructs himself within the heterotopic space of the drama itself, experimenting with the idea of being "Wideload" or else "Verdecchia" as others see him rather than finding an identity that is fully portable or a border that he can carry with him. Appropriately for an actor, "Verdecchia" enacts identities without fully embracing any of them. Until he can determine what is different about him he cannot fully develop that identity. Until then, his border is a performance but not in the way that Gomez-Peña performs it. "Verdecchia's" personal border remains at a distance from him because he cannot bring himself properly to delineate it, or even to refuse it; instead he half-heartedly negotiates with a series of potential borders, trying to find one that he can cross.

Anne F. Nothof notes, "Only in his dreams can ["Verdecchia"] imaginatively experience the landscape of South America," and she goes on to suggest that through the naming process that he carries out in those dreams, "Verdecchia" "reinscribes the landscape with personal cultural value." Nothof's argument seems to be that "Verdecchia" is reclaiming a part of his own history through such dreams and such naming processes. However, rather than representing this as "Verdecchia" being made whole by reabsorbing the Latin American component of his identity, it is also possible to interpret the dreams as showing a way forward for "Verdecchia." In searching for something distinctive about himself he has so far failed to notice his own ability to employ language in a deeply evocative way, conveying the emotional elements of border crossing. "Verdecchia's" meditation on the tango as the soundtrack of exile is a case in point. His representation of the emotional experience of exile in fact transcends any need to tie it to the reference point of a particular Latin American dance, suggesting that "Verdecchia's" own experience of the border moves away from the specifics of geographical location to the border as a state of mind, but a state of mind that transcends the continent. "Verdecchia's" border is personal in that he is able to articulate the feelings that others cannot. His art, once he recognizes it, will collapse borders in ways that his physical journeys and his attempts to reclaim or construct history cannot, at which point he will truly carry the border within himself.

Notes

1 A term coined by security expert Bruce Schneier, who defines it thus: "Security theater refers to security measures that make people feel more secure without doing anything to actually improve their security."
2 It has also been pointed out to me that a straw boater was typical headgear for American men of a certain class at this time. It was also primarily urban wear, further emphasizing Fuentes's father's association with the population on the northern side of the border.

Works Cited

Anzaldúa, Gloria. *Borderlands/La Frontera: The New Mestiza*. 3rd ed. San Francisco: Aunt Lute, 2007.

Foucault, Michel. "Of Other Spaces." *Diacritics* 16.1 (1986): 22–27.

Fuentes, Carlos. *Latin America: At War with the Past*. CBC Massey Lectures. Toronto: House of Anansi, 1985.

Gómez, Mayte. "Healing the Border Wound: *Fronteras Americanas* and the Future of Canadian Multiculturalism." *Theatre Research in Canada* 16.1–2 (1995). http://www.lib.unb.ca/Texts/TRIC/bin/get.cgi?directory=vol16_1_2/&filename=Gomez.htm. Accessed 15 May 2011.

Gómez-Peña, Guillermo. *Dangerous Border Crossers: The Artist Talks Back*. London and New York: Routledge, 2000.

———. *Ethno-techno: Writings on Performance, Activism, and Pedagogy*. Ed. Elaine Peña. New York and London: Routledge, 2005.

Nothof, Anne F. "The Construction and Deconstruction of Border Zones in *Fronteras Americanas* by Guillermo Verdecchia and *Amigo's Blue Guitar* by Joan Macleod." *Theatre Research in Canada* 20.1 (1999). http://journals.hil.unb.ca/index.php/TRIC/article/view/7094. Accessed 15 May 2011.

Schneier, Bruce. "Beyond Security Theater." *Schneier on Security*. http://www.schneier.com/blog/archives/2009/11/beyond_security.html. Accessed 15 May 2011.

Verdecchia, Guillermo. *Fronteras Americanas (American Borders)*. 1993. Vancouver: Talonbooks, 1997.

fourteen

Discounting Slavery

The Currency Wars, Minstrelsy, and "The White Nigger" in Thomas Chandler Haliburton's *The Clockmaker*

Jade Ferguson

> So, as for our declaration of independence, I guess you need'nt twitt me with our slave-sales, for we deal only in blacks; but Blue Nose approbates no distinction in colours, and when reduced to poverty, is reduced to slavery, and is sold—*a White Nigger.*
>
> Thomas Chandler Haliburton, *The Clockmaker* (1836)

> "If they don't fit the other one's mouth, he ain't the white nigger that was in the lean-to."
>
> Mark Twain, "Tom Sawyer's Conspiracy" (1897)

IN THE LAST DECADE, New World slavery has been one of the central grounds of comparative analysis in Hemispheric American Studies. Examinations of slavery and its legacy in the Americas have for the most part employed the "plantation as a New World paradigm": "the plantation—more than anything else—ties the South both to the rest of the United States and to the rest of the New World," write Jon Smith and Deborah Cohn (8, 6). Significantly, the absence of the plantation economy in Canada has meant the frequent omission of Canada's history of slavery in studies of slavery in the Americas. Drawing attention to this history north of the US–Canada border, Rachel Adams and Sarah Phillips Casteel write that "Canada's status as the Promised Land of slave narratives and oral history has given rise to the myth that Canada did not have its own history of slavery, when in fact slavery lasted in New France for 71 years and was legal in British North America until 1834" (8). In order to contest the pervasive discounting of slavery in Canada, it is paramount that scholars explore how Canada's investment in slavery, while it did not manifest itself in the plantation system, shared cultural, literary, and historical commonalities with the rest of the Americas.

The popular writings of nineteenth-century Nova Scotian historian and humorist Thomas Chandler Haliburton often engage the arguments, rhetoric, and imagery informing debates about slavery in the Americas. While Haliburton "often discusses the 'peculiar institution' in his histories and in his humorous *Clockmaker* and *Attaché* sketches," George Elliott Clarke observes that "scholars have seldom addressed Haliburton's views of slavery" and have "scarcely noted his treatment of New World Africans, mainly African-Americans and Africadians" ("White Niggers" 13). According to Clarke, the "conception of Canada as a racial Utopia" has meant that "the racism of *ur*-Canadian figures such as Thomas Chandler Haliburton, a defender of slavery, inspires scant interrogation" (*Odysseys* 315). This chapter interrogates Haliburton's views of slavery by exploring the ways in which he deploys the metaphor of slavery in his examination of race and money. Following the critical work of Michael O'Malley and Michael Germana on the convergence of the language of money and the language of race in nineteenth-century American literature and culture, I argue that the hotly debated issue of monetary policy in the United States provided an ideology of value, one that Haliburton used in *The Clockmaker* to mobilize Nova Scotians for economic reform. In my reading of Haliburton's 1836 sketch "The White Nigger," I examine Haliburton's deployment of the analogy between money and race, employed in early blackface minstrelsy, to critique paper money and the dispossession of white privilege it represents. The circulation of the figure of "the white nigger" across the US–Canada border suggests the need to explore constructions of whiteness and white supremacy in hemispheric contexts.

Between September 1835 and February 1836, Haliburton published a series of comic sketches titled "Recollections of Nova Scotia" in *The Novascotian*, a Halifax newspaper published by Joseph Howe. In these sketches, a gentleman narrator known simply as "the Squire" records the adventures and antics of a Yankee clock peddler named Sam Slick. Upon the series' immediate success, Howe in late 1836 published the twenty-one sketches, supplemented with twelve unpublished or new sketches, in book form under the title *The Clockmaker; or, the Sayings and Doings of Samuel Slick of Slickville*. Throughout these sketches, Slick editorializes on Nova Scotia's money problems; in this, he serves as Haliburton's mouthpiece for hard money legislation. In "The Clockmaker," the Squire is astonished by Slick's ability "to sell such an immense number of clocks, (which certainly cannot be called necessary articles,) among a people with whom there seems to be so great a scarcity of money" (11). Slick surmises that his success among the Blue Noses is due to the fact they do not know "*the value of money*," for "they'd have more cash, and fewer clocks and tin reflectors" if they did (90, my emphasis). In the United States, "popular discussions of the nature and value of money filled newspapers, magazines, textbooks, and the *Congressional Record* throughout the century" (O'Malley 370). Germana argues that at stake in the debates on monetary policy that appeared on the pages and stages of American popular culture "was the very definition of value, including the nature of its production and the sources of its authenticity" (6). If Haliburton believed that Nova Scotia "had nothing to learn politically from the States but it had a lot to learn economically," as Northrop Frye contends (319), then it seems that Slick's lessons on the value and form of money in *The Clockmaker* are fundamental to any understanding of what Clarke describes as Haliburton's "racist *philosophy*" ("Must" 29).

In *A General Description of Nova Scotia* (1823), Haliburton describes the province's economy as possessing no "legal tender" (183). He lists the various kinds of precious metal coins that function as the ultimate means of settlements of accounts:

> The current coin is any coin which reaches the country. — doubloons and their parts, dollars and their fractions, copper coin of every description, American eagles, English sovereigns and guineas, French, Spanish, and Portugal Gold, Silver, and provincial papers. A doubloon passes for four pounds; although by statute it is not worth more than £ 3 17 6. — This jumble and mixture of money although apparently absurd and troublesome, answers very well in practice; and occasions no serious inconvenience whatever. (183)

While Haliburton claims that this specie economy presented "no serious inconvenience" (183), "the bewildering array of coins from different countries" meant that "the value of each individual coin could be determined only by weight, such had been the extent of clipping and 'sweating'" (Schull and Gibson 5). And while "provincial papers"—the Treasury notes of the province of Nova Scotia—did circulate as money, they were not universally acceptable. For a young and expanding colony, a specie economy resulted in a chronic shortage of cash, and the mechanics of storage and transfer of coins made for a burdensome business. In September 1825, two years after the publication of Haliburton's *General Description*, Nova Scotia's first bank, the Halifax Banking Company, opened its doors. Its founders wanted to establish a "public bank," but members of the House of Assembly, "particularly from the rural areas, could not stomach the thought of a single commercial group in Halifax controlling money and credit for the entire province" (6). A private corporation, the Halifax Banking Company "accepted deposits, made loans, discounted merchants' notes and bills of exchange, and bought and sold specie" (7). The new bank issued its own bank notes, backed by the founders' own credit; this flow of "new money" helped increase trade in the province (7).

One of the earliest critics of the Halifax Banking Company's monopoly of credit was a young Joseph Howe, who was to become prominent in Halifax as the publisher of *The Novascotian*. Bank customers believed that because banknotes could be redeemed in "gold, or silver, or Province papers," they could receive whatever form of money they wished; however, "it was a rare man who received gold at the wicket when he presented the bank notes for redemption" (8). Howe believed that the private bank was creating, in his own words, "one currency for the rich and another for the poor" (qtd. in Schull and Gibson 8). In January 1832, 184 citizens—including Howe—signed a petition to the House of Assembly, arguing that "the establishment of a Public Bank at Halifax is greatly and generally desired" (10). With both houses in agreement, Royal Assent was given to the bill incorporating "The President, Directors and Company of the Bank of Nova Scotia" in March 1832. In the Bank of Nova Scotia's charter was the provision requiring it to redeem all banknotes in specie; unlike the Halifax Banking Company, the Bank of Nova Scotia could not redeem banknotes with provincial notes. Howe became a customer of the new institution. "Believing as he did the checks and balances theory," Howe "strongly supported setting up a second bank, hoping that it would create rival interests" (Beck 116). However, in *The Clockmaker*, Sam Slick describes the disastrous outcome of these two rival banks for Nova Scotians: "they have been running back so fast lately, that they have tumbled over a *Bank* or two, and nearly broke their necks; and now they've got up and shook themselves, they swear their dirty clothes and bloody noses are all owing to the *Banks*" (32). A neck-snapping change of direction in the form of money redemption contributed to a financial panic and eventual economic depression in 1834.

As early as January 1833, the columns of *The Novascotian* were filled with letters bewailing the depreciated state of paper money. The Bank of Nova Scotia had issued very few banknotes because it was required to redeem them in specie. But while the bank only accepted its own notes and its specie at its counters, it took notes of the Halifax Banking Company from its shareholders. The bank accumulated £23,000 worth of notes, and with malicious intent, it demanded specie for them. The Halifax Banking Company met these demands in part, before suspending payments in specie, and subsequently redeemed its own notes in Treasury notes. By 1833, provincial notes were "no longer the equivalent of specie at the old bank, irredeemable since 1828 in their own right [and] after August 1832, unacceptable at the new bank" (Beck 114). Because each bank was hoarding its specie and declining provincial notes whenever possible, commercial loans were restricted and the price of gold and silver rose. Working-class Nova Scotians were significantly affected by the war between the banks and by the overabundance of paper money; in *The Clockmaker*, Slick says that "if a man ... has no money, why he says its all owin to the banks, they wont discount, there's no money, they've ruined the Province" (81). By the time the banks agreed to a clearing system for notes in 1834, "the Treasury notes were now in grave danger of depreciating to the point of being worthless" (Beck 114). In the context of depreciating paper money, and a deteriorating economic condition partly caused by the currency wars, Howe launched a legislative review on the currency question. Over the next two years, he denounced "the impropriety of allowing, in any country, an inundation of Paper Currency, which is not responded in the precious metals" (114). Interestingly, Howe's call for a specie economy reiterated the argument made by Jacksonian Democrats that only hard money, gold and silver specie, was sound money.

In his introduction to *The Clockmaker*, George L. Parker asserts that Jacksonian policies such as "its handling of land grants, its refusal to renew the charter of the Bank of the United States, its imposition of tariffs against the will of certain states, and its distribution of patronage appointments all worried the Nova Scotian" (xxviii). Soon after his inauguration in 1829, Jackson expressed his desire to dismantle the Second Bank of the United States. His position against the Bank was, Germana argues, "at bottom an expression of his belief about the form that money should take" (29). Paper money was "the tool of the privileged and the bane of the laboring classes when in over-abundance" (29). When the Bank applied to Congress for the renewal of its charter four years early, in 1832, Jackson vowed to oppose its renewal. Much like Howe, who accused the Bank of Nova Scotia of creating "one currency for the rich and another for the poor" through its monopoly on credit and by flooding the market with paper money, Jackson in his veto message to the bill passed by Congress accused the Second Bank of the United States of creating "artificial distinctions" that were making "the rich richer and the potent more powerful": "the humble members of society—the farmers, mechanics, and laborers—who have neither time nor the means of securing like favors to themselves, have a right to complain of the injustice of the Government," he argued (qtd. in Germana 30). Deeming the bank to be unconstitutional because it had failed to provide the nation with a sound currency, Jackson dismantled it, removed federal deposits from its vaults, and placed the government's money in state "pet" banks.

At the core of Jacksonian monetary policy lay the belief that replacing paper money with hard money could remedy the class antagonisms that threatened the republic's artisanal way of life. Jackson proposed various ways of removing paper money from the market. These included eliminating all banknotes under twenty dollars and bringing gold coins bank into circulation. In an attempt to regulate the value of coin money, Congress passed the Coinage Act of 1834, also known as the Gold Coin Act, which adjusted gold's value relative to silver from 15:1 to 16:1. Sixteen times as many grains of silver as grains of gold would now be needed to make a dollar. Gold coin's value was regulated within the market at the expense of the diving silver dollar, which became more valuable as bullion than as specie. In *The Clockmaker*, Slick tells the Squire of the various lessons he learned from his father as a young boy, including one about the importance of hard money: "They may talk of independence, says father, but Sam, I'll tell you what independence is, and he gave his hands a slap agin his trowses, pocket, and made the gold eagles he won at the race all the jin again" (87). If "independence" is in some sense the possession of oneself, Slick learns from his father that the working classes can only possess themselves as long as American money possesses its own value. Slick's father advises him to "line the pocket well first" with gold coins, for paper money often proves itself to be the agent of dispossession within the new market economy (88). Slick's father's object lesson in hard money insists on the essential, non-negotiable, value of specie.

Germana argues that Jackson's hard-money policy was a class-inflected monetary ideology that sought to "assuage fears of those attached to or associated with the old republican order" by securing the inherent value of money (31). Subjected to new forms of labour discipline, white workers were made anxious by fear of dependency. For male artisans, "the rise of a small sector of full-fledged factory production symbolized threats to independence, and offered the possibility to experiment with application of the slavery metaphor to white (often child and female) factory workers without necessarily applying it to themselves" (Roediger 70). In *The Clockmaker*, Slick talks enthusiastically about New England factories and the Lowell system. And he praises the efficiency and productivity of factory work: "In our ship yards, our factories, our mills, and even in our vessels, there's no talk—a man can't work and talk too. I guess if you were at the factories of Lowell we'd show you a wonder—*five hundred galls at work together all in silence*" (17). Ironically, the women of Lowell were far from being the "The Silent Girls" of the sketch's title. In 1834, Lowell's female "strikers cast themselves as virtually in 'bondage' as threatened with *future* slavery by the 'oppressing hand of avarice'" (Roediger 69). Two years later, Lowell women sang:

> Oh! I cannot be a slave;
> I will not be a slave.
> For I'm so fond of liberty
> That I cannot be a slave. (qtd. in Roediger 69)

The factory system confined and disciplined white workers in unprecedented ways; Lowell's factory women "described themselves as slaves to long hours, as slaves to the 'powers that be' and as 'slaves in every sense of the word'" (Roediger 71). While seemingly oblivious to the Lowell women's protests against "factory slavery," Slick uses the metaphor of slavery to describe the working conditions of the white working class in the sketch immediately following "The Silent Girls."

In "Conversations at the River Philip," the Squire narrates an encounter between Sam Slick and an Irishman, Pat Lannigan, who protests the exploitation of white workers in the United States: "Upon my soul, Mr. Slick, said he, the poor laborer does not last long in your country ... You'll see the graves of the Irish each side of the canals" (22). Hoping to earn more money for his work in the United States, Pat soon discovers that he is "no better off in pocket than in Nova Scotia": "Faith, I soon found out my two days' pay in one, I had to do two days' work in one and pay two weeks' board in one" (22). Lannigan's image of Irish graves lining the sides of canals echoes the images of coffins featured on handbills of New York City journeymen tailors in 1836. Distributed throughout the city, the coffin handbills read: "The Rich against the Poor! ... Mechanics and Workingmen! A deadly blow has been struck at your liberty! The prize for which your fathers fought has been robbed from you! The Freemen of the North are now on a level with the slaves of the South!—with no other privileges than laboring that drones may fatten on your life-blood!" (qtd. in Tomlins 163). References to slavery shaped the language of nascent labour movements in the antebellum United States, with labour activists cautiously comparing white workers to black slaves. If white workers were cast as slaves, the coffin handbills made it clear that they were slaves not "because they were hirelings but because the state had deprived them of the freedoms necessary for defending their rights" (Roediger 65). The coffin handbills made a comparison with slaves but also suggested that white workers remained beyond comparison with slaves.

Employing the metaphor of slavery in his description of "hard work" in the United States, Slick surmises: "We have two kinds of slaves, the niggers and the white slaves. All European laborers and blacks, who come out to us, do our hard bodily work, while we direct it to a profitable end; neither rich nor poor, high nor low with us, eat the bread of idleness" (22). Slick describes a new market economy that is remaking the meaning of racial difference, such that "bodily" investments are to be understood in terms of exchange value rather than racial value. Comparing the slave to the wage labourer in *Grundisse*, Karl Marx writes: "As a slave, the worker has exchange value, a value; as a free wage-worker he has no value; it is rather his power of disposing of his labor, effected by exchange with him which has value" (288–89). In this new economy, the white workers' "valuelessness and devaluation is the presupposition of capital precondition of free labor in general" (289). In "Whiteness as Property," Cheryl Harris argues that whiteness has been so tied to the right to own property as to constitute in itself a legally recognizable, usable, and cherished form of property, possessed by all whites. The attempted reduction of blacks, but not whites, to "objects of property" in slavery "established whiteness as a prerequisite to the enforceable property rights," and created, she argues, an enduring set of expectations that whiteness had a value as property (1721, 1724). Whiteness not only became associated with owning property, but also became "status property" (1729). The status property of whiteness guaranteed its wages, and these wages provided the legal protection of class privilege and the right to expect upward social mobility (1759).

Early minstrelsy songs and sketches critiqued an emergent economic system that was dispossessing whites of their status property, thereby turning white workers into white slaves. Born when T.D. Rice first "jumped Jim Crow" in or around 1830, blackface minstrelsy flourished during the years of Jackson's presidency. Early minstrelsy compositions often appealed to audiences of Jacksonian persuasion. In an early version of "Jim Crow," published in 1833, the narrator describes poor whites' monetary misfortunes and their envy of blacks, who, unlike them, have retained the "privileges" of their "colour":

> Now my brudder niggars,
> I do not think it right,
> Dat you should laught at dem
> Who happen to be white.
>
> Kase it dar misfortune,
> An' dey'd spend ebery dollar,
> If dey only could be
> Gentlemen ob colour. (qtd. in Lott 260n17)

Antebellum labour activists who compared white wage labour with chattel slavery often found the latter less oppressive. They argued "on shreds of evidence, that Southern masters worked their Black slaves far fewer hours per day—perhaps only half the number required by Northern employers" (Roediger 76). When computing rates of exploitation, they found "that a much greater proportion of the value produced by a Black slave was returned to him or her than was returned to the white slaves in the North" (76). To the degree that black–white relations in this new economy involved devaluation of the white worker, it was fitting that early minstrelsy grafted the language of money—and its ideology of value—onto black–white relations. Examining the symbolism of the silver dollar in "Zip Coon"—published the same year as the Coinage Act of 1834—Germana argues that money was a "productive mirror in the text for minstrel performers who wore the mask of the dispossessed slave to express a belief in the inherent value of white bodies" (33). Like the silver dollar, whiteness was "more than just skin color, transcending face value to script social standing and even moral superiority" (34). For early minstrelsy, the money question—What form should money take?—was germane to the race question—What form should black–white relations take?

In "White Niggers, Black Slaves," Clarke describes Haliburton's work as "the literary equivalent of black-face minstrelsy" (31): "From time to time, the voice of white supremacy and Anglo-Saxon unity is uttered through a Black mask" (31). In the sketch "Slavery," from the second series of *The Clockmaker* (1838), the Squire describes a meeting between Slick and Scip, a black livery stable hand and former slave. When he takes the Squire and Slick's horses at the inn, Scip immediately recognizes Slick as his former master's brother. The Squire describes the reunion between the two men: Scip "suddenly pulled off his hat, and throwing it up in the air, uttered one of the most piercing yells I think I ever heard" (266). The prospect of being captured by slave catchers produced much fear among fugitive slaves in the North and Canada. In this regard, Scip's recognition of his master's brother and his subsequent screams, followed by expressions of gratitude, are noteworthy: Scip "throw[s] himself upon the ground, seiz[ing] Mr. Slick round the legs with his arms. Oh, Massa Sammy! Massy Sammy! Oh, my Gor!—only tink old Scippy see you once more! How you do, Massa Sammy? Gor Ormighty bless you! How you do?" (266–67). A sobbing Scip "blames himself for leaving so good a master and so comfortable a home" (267). Lamenting the loss of his southern plantation home and master, Scip begs Slick to "receive him as a servant" (268). Scip's exaggerated bodily gestures and distorted dialect reflect his minstrel show origins. Andrew Silver argues that minstrel shows played an integral role in recasting black terror as a comic trope for white audiences. "Especially popular," writes Silver, "was the virulently racist convention of minstrel fright, which delighted white audiences by depicting African-American declarations of impossible bravery consistently undercut by white fantasies of their sudden and irrefutable cowardice" (10). In "Slavery," Haliburton makes this moment of black fright—a fugitive slave's capture—comical, for any notion of black equality with white is thereby undercut through black self-subjugation.

For Clarke, the depiction of an "unhappy" Scip yearning for his former servitude reflects Haliburton's staunch belief that slavery was "a benign, communitarian institution" ("White Niggers" 29). However, the "Slavery" sketch is not merely a pro-slavery argument; its pro-slavery affinities and denunciation of white slavery must be understood in relation to each other. Reiterating labour's comparison of the exploitation of black and white workers, Slick contends that blacks enjoy more leisure time and liberty and fare quite well: "Every critter must work in this world, and a labourer is a slave; but the labourer only gets enough to live on from day to day, while the slave is tended in infancy, sickness, and old age, and has spare time enough given him to airn a good deal too" (272). In a comparison that finds chattel slavery less oppressive than wage slavery, Slick likens white workers to black slaves, but he does not extend abolition on the black slave's behalf. "Notwithstanding all the sweets attending a state of liberty," Scip was "unhappy under the influence of a cold climate, hard labour, and the absence of all that real sympathy, which, notwithstanding the rod of the master, exists nowhere but where there is a community of interests" (267). Slick's argument carries a pro-slavery implication, in that its representation of chattel slavery as a benevolent institution supports the continued subjugation of blacks. But also significant in his depiction of the South as an "idealized" community is the idea that it appropriately values and protects its economic "interests."

Throughout *The Clockmaker*, Slick's response to black–white equality is informed by his opinions on paper money and the debts it represents. In "Cumberland Oysters Produce Melancholy Forebodings," Slick lists the racial and economic conflicts that are threatening the nation's stability:

> *The Blacks and the Whites* in the States show their teeth and snarl, they are jist ready to fall to. *The Protestants and Catholics* begin to lay back their ears, and turn tail for kickin. *The Abolitionists and Planters* are at it like two bulls in a pastur. *Mob law and Lynch law* are working like yeast in a barrel, and frothing at the bung hole. *Nullification and Tariff* are like a charcoal pit, all covered up, but burning inside, and sending out smoke at every crack, enough to stifle a horse. *General Government and State Government* every now and then square off and sparr, and the first blow given will bring a genuine set-to. *Surplus Revenue* is another bone of contention; like a shin of beef thrown among a pack of dogs it will set the whole on 'em by the ears. (56)

Significantly, Slick's description of the turmoil in the United States begins with the race problem and ends with the money problem. For Slick, "the elements of spontaneous combustion among us in abundance" is paper money (56). Jackson's decision to remove the federal government's deposits from the Second Bank of the United States was in anticipation of federal surplus revenue, which would have gone into the bank and from there found its way into the hated paper economy. Examining the merging of the language of money with the language of race in nineteenth-century American literature and culture, O'Malley writes that "the essential value of specie, like the essential character of certain races or occupations, helped resolve the ambiguity of identity in public by a resort to 'natural facts'" (370). Slick follows his father's belief that money should take the form of specie because of its inherent value and fixed identity. Like his father's opinions on specie, Slick's opinions on race focus on the essential or inherent character of species determined by natural laws: "*All critters in natur are better in their own element,*" says Slick (80), who posits a similarity between political economy and biological taxonomy.

For Slick, economic incompetence as well as genius can be explained by intrinsic racial or genetic character. He contends that Nova Scotians do not understand the value of their "natural privileges" (16). To illustrate his point, he compares Nova Scotians to blacks: "A little nigger boy in New York found a diamond worth 2,000 dollars; well, he sold it to a watchmaker for 50 cents—the little critter did'nt know no better. *You people are just like the nigger boy, they don't know the value of their diamond*" (17). Slick's comparison of Nova Scotians to blacks underscores what he sees to be Nova Scotia's misunderstanding of monetary value. In contrast to Nova Scotian economic incompetence,

Yankee economic genius is the result of a "spirit of enterprise that will beget other useful improvements" (34). In *White*, Richard Dyer describes the ways in which the idea of progress is deeply informed by a central value of whiteness that he calls "spirit" or "enterprise." According to Dyer, enterprise is often presented as the sign of white spirit—that is, as "energy, will, ambition, the ability to do things, and see things through—and its effect—discovery, science, business, wealth creation, the building of nations, the organization of labour (carried out by racially lesser humans)" (31). American "enterprise" is reflected, Slick contends, in the ways in which "we improve on every thing and we have improved on our species" (91). Indifferent to wealth creation and apathetic to the organization of labour, Slick finds there to be "neither spirit, enterprise, nor patriotism here" (92). The hotly debated issue of monetary policy in the United States is absent here, which leaves Nova Scotians, Slick reckons, "much behind the intelligence of the age" (16). Slick teaches Nova Scotians the "value of money," what he sees as the essential or inherent character of specie and species (90).

Slick's lesson about the nature and value of money is perhaps most evident in "The White Nigger." The sketch begins with the Squire critiquing Slick's use of the word "free" to describe the conditions of Americans: "Excuse me, said I, Mr. Slick, but really you appropriate the word 'free' to your countrymen, as if you thought no other people in the world were entitled to it but yourself" (172). Citing the sentence, "We hold this truth to be self-evident, that all men are created equal," Slick praises the "declaration of independence," and challenges the Squire to find fault in such "a beautiful piece of penmanship" (172). The Squire responds to the challenge: "Jefferson forgot to insert—one little word, said I, he should have said 'all white men'; for, as it now stands, it is a practical untruth, in a country which tolerates domestic slavery in its worst and most forbidding form. It is a declaration of *shame*, and not of *independence*" (172; italics in text). The Squire praises the Slavery Abolition Act, that abolished slavery throughout most of the British Empire in 1834: "Thank God, said I, slavery does not exist in any part of his Majesty's dominions now, we have at last wiped off that national stain" (173). Slick does not allow the Squire to feel triumphant for long, immediately suggesting that slavery has not in fact been abolished in Nova Scotia and using as an example the sale of poor whites. Slick's example here is a consequence of an act passed in Nova Scotia in 1763 that enabled "the Inhabitants of the several Townships within the Province, to maintain their Poor" through an annual meeting held "on the first Monday in January," where the "freeholders" of a township would "vote such sums of money as they shall judge necessary for the current year to support and maintain their poor" (Parker, "Explanatory" 691–92). Twelve townspeople were chosen to "'assess' their fellow townsmen for the money, which was to be distributed to the needy by 'overseers of the poor'" (692). For Slick, the material and discursive conditions constituting this sale of poor whites is like that of chattel slavery, which renders poor whites, in Slick's assessment, "white slaves" (173).

In abolitionist discourses, chattel slavery was staged in such a way that the "the crime of the trade was seen as the crime of the heart—'the outrages of feelings and affection'"—and was reproduced in the style of the "melo-dramatic tableau" (Hartman 27). Saidiya Hartman argues that these staged accounts of whippings, rape, mutilation, and suicide functioned to assault the barrier of indifference, and that these scenes of terror, ranging from the coffle to the whipping post, were used to give rise to a shared sentience between those formerly indifferent and those suffering (18). Early minstrelsy appro-priated scenes of the slave auction in their articulations of white workers' fear of dependency in the new market economy. In "The White Nigger," Slick describes seeing the "trade in white slaves"—"I have seed these human cattle sales with my own eyes" (173)—and provides an account of "the pageantry of the trade, the unabashed display of the market's brutality, the juxtaposition of sorrow and mirth, and the separation of families" that dominated anti-slavery writers' accounts of "the most horrible feature of the institution of slavery" (Hartman 32). Slick describes encountering this annual sale of poor whites on his way to Partridge Island. Hearing festivities and seeing "an amazin crowd of folks" at Old Furlong's house, Slick enters the house and finds Deacon Westfall, at the centre of the crowd's attention, selling Jerry Oaks:

> I see but deacon Westfall, a smooth faced, slick haired, meechin lookin chap as you'd see in a hundred, a standin on a stool, with an auctioneer's hammer in his hand; and afore him was one Jerry Oaks and his wife, and two little orphan children, the prettiest little toads I ever beheld in all my born days. Gentleman, said he, I will begin the sale by putting up Jerry Oaks, of Apple Rivers, he's a considerable of a smart man yet, and can do many little chores besides feedin the children and pigs, I guess he's near about worth his keep. (173)

Following abolitionists' accounts of slave auctions, Slick's descriptions of the auction's festivities are juxtaposed to the cruelty of the practice, in which mirth is accompanied by sorrow. Jerry begs Deacon Westfall not to separate him from his wife: "Fifty years have we lived together as man and wife, and a good wife has she been to me … do sell us together" (174). The Deacon ignores Jerry's pleas and sells him, causing "the poor critter to give one long loud deep groan" (174). Jerry's wife begs, prays, and cries, and when she faints in exhaustion, she is carried onto the auction block and "sold in that condition" (174). Within this minstrel scene of whites cast as blacks at a slave auction, Haliburton appropri-ates the rhetorical strategies of abolitionist discourse to produce empathy for the poor and newly dispossessed whites.

Haliburton's slave auction depicts the plight of poor whites in a paper money economy. Hartman describes the slave auction as the "theatre of the marketplace," wherein "the simulation of good times and the to-and-fro of half-naked bodies on display all acted to incite the flow of capital" (37–38). One slaveholder advised that "the best stock, in which he can invest Capital, is, I think, negro Stock ... Negroes will yield a much larger income than any Bank dividend" (qtd. in Clarke, "White Niggers" 35). In "The White Nigger," poor whites find themselves discounted during their sale. Jerry is ascribed an initial monetary value by the Deacon—"he's cheap at 7s. 6d"—but rather than increasing in value during the auction, Jerry is purchased for much less, sold for "six shillings a week" (174). Confused by this "calculatin'" of value, Slick asks John Porter why the "misfortunate wretch" should be sold in this particular way. Porter replies: "[W]e always sell the poor for the year, to the lowest bidder. Them that will keep them for the lowest sum, gets them" (175). These poor whites mirror the depreciated value of the province's Treasury notes. Unlike gold or silver coins, which have inherent value, Nova Scotia's Treasury notes and poor whites have "no distinction in colour" (176). At the mercy of the bank's pricing, provincial notes are depreciated to the point of being worthless; at the mercy of the "freeholders'" assessments, poor whites are similarly reduced to a discounted price. In this theatre of the marketplace, Slick observes the development of two currencies. Poor white Nova Scotians "will keep" paper money and accept the "lowest sum" for it (175). Noting that it is poor whites who purchase poor whites at the auction, Slick says: "Why, says I, that feller that bought him is a pauper himself, to my sartan knowledge. If you were to take him up by the heels and shake him for a week, you could'nt shake sixpence out of him" (175). Haliburton's critique of the dispossession of poor whites in "The White Nigger" reiterates Howe's argument that banks were creating "one currency for the rich and another for the poor" (qtd. in Shull and Gibson 8). Slick surmises that the "rich man" in the room is Deacon Westfall, the capitalist who responds to Jerry's appeals to be sold with his wife with "such a smile as a November sun gives" (174). Deacon Westfall's riches ("Can't afford it, Jerry—can't afford it"), like those of the bank shareholders, come from the discounted paper money (Jerry) redeemed by poor whites and from the shiny gold specie ("November sun") retained within the walls of the banks (174).

In "The White Nigger," Haliburton uses Slick's description of the poor white slave auction to suggest that a government must protect its citizens' independence and that it can do so by regulating money. Slick's hatred of paper money follows from his father's counsel that paper money is the agent of dispossession in the new market economy. Slick concludes that when "Blue Nose approbates no distinction in colours, and when reduced to poverty," he "is reduced to slavery, and is sold—*a White Nigger*" (176). For Clarke, "Haliburton's invention of the 'white nigger' suggests, radically, that class determines race: as the white falls in social status, the blacker he or she becomes" ("White Niggers" 35). Rather than class determining race, however, I suggest that for Haliburton it is *money* that determines race. That is, a market that negotiates the nature and value of money is a market that also negotiates the meaning of racial difference. Slick advocates a hard-money policy that articulates an ideology of value that "is essential, irreducible, non-negotiable, and intrinsic difference" (O'Malley 370). Slick expresses this ideology of value when he describes the sale of black slaves in the United States: "we deal only in niggers,—and those thick skulled, crooked shanked, flat footed, long heeled, wooly heady gentlemen, don't seem fir for much else but slavery" (172). For Slick, the form that black–white relations takes in the United States, where "blacks" and "whites" are fixed in their proper and stable places, is the form that money should take, too. For Slick, money must have a fixed identity, with its inherent value intrinsic to its distinctions in colour. In *The Clockmaker*, Haliburton uses debates about the form of black-white relations across the border to awaken Nova Scotians to the province's economic instability and to agitate them into legislative reforms that would fix the nature and value of its money.

Roediger argues that the new and negative term "white nigger" entered American English at the same time as "white slavery" became prominent in the 1830s: "*white nigger* (that is, 'drudge') and *work like a nigger* (that is, 'to do hard drudging work')" were seen "to indicate the performance of work in ways unbecoming to whites" (68). Arguing that Haliburton's racism was in keeping with that of his contemporaries, Greg Marquis counters Clarke's assessment of Haliburton's unique racial terminology: "Racial terminology had varied and evolving meanings in the nineteenth century and was part of the language of everyday life. The term 'white nigger,' like 'white slave,' was not, as Clarke seems to imply, invented by Haliburton as a critique of colonial society, but well-established in artisanal and republic rhetoric by the early nineteenth century if not earlier" (199). In *The Clockmaker*, Haliburton's appropriation of artisanal discourses of white slavery, and his use of the popular cultural form of blackface minstrelsy, which was linked in its early manifestations with the nascent working-class movements, inform his use of the phrase "white nigger." But as Roediger explains, rather than symbolizing forms of work, the term "white nigger" in Haliburton's sketch symbolizes forms of money that are unbecoming to whites. Haliburton may not have invented "the white nigger," but he gave the term a new meaning as he applied it in a Nova Scotian context.

In the United States, the term continued to circulate with a seemingly new meaning; Barbara Ladd writes that "beginning in the 1890s, the expression 'white nigger' could be used not only to designate the mulatto, but also refer to the white man morally compromised by associations with blacks" (136n80). The term "white nigger" appears in Mark Twain's 1897 short story "Tom Sawyer's Conspiracy" (1897), an attempted sequel to *Adventures of Huckleberry Finn* (1884). In his biography of Twain, Cyril Clemens describes the purchase of *The Clockmaker* by a young Twain in Hannibal, Missouri, from a "Yankee pack-pedler": "For weeks after that," says Mrs. Frazer, "every chance he got—even in church on one occasion!—he was reading that old book and laughing aloud" (38). In "Sam Slick and American Popular Humour," Daniel Royot notes that Deacon Westfall's "Can't afford it Jerry, can't afford it" response to the pleas of the white slave Jerry Oakes in "The White Nigger" is "exactly what Miss Watson says when she wants to sell Jim down the River in *Huckleberry Finn*" (131).

In "Tom Sawyer's Conspiracy," the term "white nigger" is ascribed to Tom, who "blackens up" in hopes of profiting by selling and stealing himself as a slave. At the slave trader's cabin, Tom recognizes the Duke as another "white nigger"; the Duke has also been passing himself off as a slave in order to be sold for profit by the King. Twain's "white nigger" does not fit the 1830s definition of the term (in Roediger) or the 1890s definition (in Ladd). Stephanie LeMenager's explication of its meaning and function for Twain is similar to my own understanding of "white nigger" in Haliburton's sketch. "Twain breaks whiteness away from the constellation of mobility, property, and nature, the constellation of Euro-American virtues that had underwritten U.S. manifest destiny and conferred a national-racial character," writes LeMenager. "Tom Sawyer's race [is] unnatural [as it is] caught up in a proliferation of the commodity-form that threatens to cancel even the most apparently essential human values" (415). O'Malley notes that the debates about the nature and value of money in the United States in the 1830s were also prominent in the 1890s. These anxieties about the form that money should take arose simultaneously with African American renegotiations of the meaning of race, which involved assertions of their own claims to economic self-determination (394). "The height of the nineteenth-century gold and silver debate—1896—came as southern whites were establishing formal racial segregation and disenfranchisement," writes O'Malley (394). It seems that Twain's "white nigger" signified in much the same way as Haliburton's; through the minstrelsy of "the white nigger," both writers were meditating on black enslavement (a central theme of *Huckleberry Finn*) and protesting the social death of the "natural" privileges of whiteness in a paper economy.

This chapter's examination of Haliburton's *The Clockmaker* has foregrounded the ways in which the discourse of slavery in the United States informed Canadian economic policy debates, and also the ways in which this "US" discourse transcended national boundaries and evolved in particular social contexts across North America. A reading of Haliburton's use of the slavery metaphor in his examination of the dispossession of white privilege in a new paper-money economy maps a series of literary, cultural, and historical commonalities between early Canada and the United States. The figure of "the white nigger" as it crossed the US–Canada border in the writings of Haliburton and Twain suggests the need to further explore the hemispheric scope and scale of constructions of whiteness. I am not suggesting that the only way to include slavery in Canada with slavery in the rest of the Americas is through reading it figuratively. In fact, scholarship on the significance of the institution of slavery in early Canada is paramount in order to counter what Katherine McKittrick has described as "the anticipated and unexpected denials" (94): "Slavery in Canada (British North America and New France), for example, is either forthrightly denied or deemed too brief and too small to warrant intellectual and political consideration" (97). My interrogation of Haliburton's comparison of poor whites in Nova Scotia with black slaves in the United States rejects such discounting of intellectual and political considerations of slavery in Canada. While the institution of slavery may not have been vital to the organization of economic activities in Nova Scotia, Haliburton's sketches suggest that the discourse of slavery was central to economic debates and reforms and vital to the construction of the privileges of whiteness and the idea of white solidarity.

Works Cited

Adams, Rachel, and Sarah Casteel. "Introduction: Canada and the Americas." *Comparative American Studies* 3.1 (2005): 5–13.

Beck, J. Murray. *Joseph Howe*. Montreal and Kingston: McGill–Queen's UP, 1982.

Clarke, George Elliott. "Must We Burn Haliburton?" *The Haliburton Bi-Centenary Chaplet*. Ed. Richard A. Davies. Wolfville: Gaspereau, 1997. 1–35.

———. *Odysseys Home: Mapping African-Canadian Literature*. Toronto: U of Toronto P, 2002.

———. "White Niggers, Black Slaves: Slavery, Race, and Class in T.C. Haliburton's the Clockmaker." *Nova Scotia Historical Review* 14.1 (1994): 13–40.

Clemens, Cyril. *Young Sam Clemens*. Portland: Leon Tebbetts Editions, 1942.

Dyer, Richard. *White*. London and New York: Routledge, 1997.

Frye, Northrop. "Haliburton: Mask and Ego." *Northrop Frye on Canada*. Ed. Jean O'Grady and David Staines. Toronto: U of Toronto P, 2003. 316–20.

Germana, Michael. *Standards of Value: Money, Race, and Literature in America*. Iowa City: U of Iowa P, 2009.

Haliburton, Thomas Chandler. *The Clockmaker; or, the Sayings and Doings of Samuel Slick, of Slickville*. Toronto: McClelland & Stewart, 2007.

———. *A General Description of Nova Scotia: Illustrated by a New and Correct Map*. Halifax: Royal Acadian School, 1823.

———. "Slavery." *The Clockmaker: Series One, Two, and Three*. Ed. George L. Parker. Ottawa: Carleton UP, 1995. 266–76.

Harris, Cheryl. "Whiteness as Property." *Harvard Law Review* 106 (1993): 1709–91.

Hartman, Saidiya. *Scenes of Subjection: Terror, Slavery, and Self-Making in Nineteenth-Century America*. Oxford: Oxford UP, 1997.

Ladd, Barbara. *Nationalism and the Color Line in George W. Cable, Mark Twain, and William Faulkner*. Baton Rouge: Louisiana State UP, 1996.

LeMenager, Stephanie. "Floating Capital: The Trouble with Whiteness on Twain's Mississippi." *ELH* 70.2 (2004): 405–31.

Lott, Eric. *Love and Theft: Blackface Minstrelsy and the American Working Class*. New York: Oxford UP, 1993.

Marquis, Greg. "Haliburton, Maritime Intellectuals, and 'The Problem of Freedom.'" *The Haliburton Bi-Centenary Chaplet.* Ed. Richard A. Davies. Wolfville: Gaspereau, 1997. 195–235.

Marx, Karl. *Grundisse: Foundations of the Critique of Political Economy.* London: Penguin Classics, 1993.

McKittrick, Katherine. *Demonic Grounds: Black Women and the Cartographies of Struggles.* Minneapolis: U of Minnesota P, 2006.

O'Malley, Michael. "Specie and Species: Race and the Money Question in Nineteenth-Century America." *American Historical Review* 99 (1994): 369–95.

Parker, George L. "Editor's Introduction." *The Clockmaker: Series One, Two, and Three.* Ed. George L. Parker. Ottawa: Carleton UP, 1994. xvii–ci.

———. "Explanatory Notes." *The Clockmaker: Series One, Two, and Three.* Ed. George L. Parker. Ottawa: Carleton UP, 1994. 657–750.

Roediger, David. *The Wages of Whiteness: Race and the Making of the American Working Class.* London: Verso, 1991.

Royot, Daniel. "Sam Slick and American Popular Humor." *The Thomas Chandler Haliburton Symposium.* Ed. Frank M. Tierney. Ottawa: U of Ottawa P, 1985. 123–34.

Schull, Joseph, and J. Douglas Gibson. *The Scotiabank Story: A History of the Bank of Nova Scotia, 1832–1982.* Toronto: Macmillan of Canada, 1982.

Silver, Andrew. *Minstrelsy and Murder: The Crisis of Southern Humor, 1835–1925.* Baton Rouge: Louisiana State UP, 2006.

Smith, Jon, and Deborah Cohn. "Introduction: Uncanny Hybridities." *Look Away!: The U.S. South in New World Studies.* Ed. Jon Smith and Deborah Cohn. Durham: Duke UP, 2004. 1–23.

Tomlins, Christopher L. *Law, Labor, and Ideology in the Early American Republic.* Cambridge: Cambridge UP, 1993.

Twain, Mark. "Tom Sawyer's Conspiracy." *Huck Finn and Tom Sawyer among the Indians and Other Unfinished Stories.* Berkeley: U of California P, 1989. 134–213.

fifteen

Detained at Customs
Jane Rule, Censorship, and the Politics of Crossing the Canada– US Border

Susan Billingham

> Conventions, like clichés, have a way of surviving their own usefulness ... For everyone, foreign by birth or by nature, convention is a mark of fluency.
>
> Jane Rule, *Desert of the Heart*

> For Canada, the United States remains our significant Other.
>
> Reg Whitaker

THIS CHAPTER ANALYZES THE OPERATIONS of the Canada–US border as an instrument of "bio-power" in the regulation of citizens' lives, taking the literal and figurative border crossings in the life and work of Jane Rule as its principal case study. In *The History of Sexuality*, Michel Foucault identifies two forms of power over life, one focused on the body as machine and the other on the "species body." Bio-power is Foucault's term for the diverse techniques employed in the subjugation of bodies and control of populations, power invested throughout life in a series of regulatory interventions (139). National boundaries in general, and the Canada–US border in particular, function as sites where bio-power is implemented and where its effects become visible. As an American Canadian who chose to make Canada her permanent intellectual home, Rule occupied an ambivalent insider/outsider status with respect to both nations; this sharpened her observation of the perpetual fluctuation between cultural sameness and difference. My discussion focuses on three linked aspects of Rule's career: her decision to move from the United States to Canada in 1956; her critique of America's "discredited institutions" (*Young* 120) in fictions from the 1970s; and her involvement in the Little Sister's constitutional challenge to Canada Customs' seizure of books and magazines imported across the Canada– US border in the 1980s and 1990s. My reading is informed by Gary Kinsman's extensive analyses of Canada's "culture of regulation"—specifically, "the deep roots of heterosexism in Canadian state and social formation" and "the anti-queer history which continues to shape our present" ("Canadian Cold War"

112). Rule rejected the United States' "super-patriotism" in favour of Canada's more self-reflexive forms of allegiance; nevertheless, she remained subject to the institutional biases and cultural mechanisms of the Canadian nation-state that served to reinforce heteronormativity. At the same time, Rule consistently resisted the conventions—be they literary, social, or legal—that formed the idiom of daily existence and that sought to censor her person, her work, and her community.

Rule occupies a curious place in Canadian literary history, in part because her oeuvre resists easy categorization. Born and raised in the United States but a Canadian citizen by choice, she fails to slot neatly into nationalist canons. Much of her fiction was written and published at a time when the Canadian academy was seeking to legitimate itself and establish a distinctive voice; anti-Americanism played a prominent part in these cultural developments, which may be one factor explaining Rule's oblique relationship to the canon. Furthermore, Rule simultaneously anticipated feminist and lesbian movements and stood apart from them. When she published *Desert of the Heart* in 1964, five years before amendments to the Criminal Code that would partly decriminalize homosexual acts,[1] she became Canada's most visible lesbian, a sometimes reluctant role model and spokesperson for her communities. That she nearly lost her teaching position at the University of British Columbia and was often viewed as a sexual deviant rather than reviewed for the quality of her writing are salutary reminders of how recently public attitudes have changed and how fragile these victories remain (see "Labels"). Rule was political by practical example in the early 1970s, as a teacher of nascent Women's Studies courses, a participant in consciousness-raising groups, and a feminist advocating equal treatment and pay for women working on university campuses. Yet her writing has frequently been castigated as apolitical, or perhaps as not political in the correct ways: her texts have been regarded (variously) as too humanist, too assimilationist, and too realist at a time when (lesbian) literary trends favoured separatism, utopian role models, or postmodern linguistic experimentation. Rule was an out lesbian all her adult life, yet she did not participate actively in the 1950s bar scene or in more recent lesbian subcultures. (She also understood and felt compassion toward individuals who chose to remain closeted.) At the same time, she retained her links to the gay male community during the turbulent period in the late 1970s to early 1980s when the conservative backlash against the increasing visibility of queer communities led to police harassment—a time when the "woman-identified" version of lesbian feminist identity politics polarized debates over censorship and pornography along gender lines. Most notably, Rule wrote regularly for the controversial gay liberationist magazine *The Body Politic* as a gesture of support in the face of police raids and obscenity charges; *The Body Politic* was reviled by some anti-porn feminists as condoning man–boy relationships.

Rule lived with Helen Sonthoff from 1956 until the latter's death in 2000, yet she expressed reservations about the gay marriage lobby, suggesting that "[t]o be forced back into the heterosexual cage of coupledom is not a step forward but a step back into state-imposed definitions of relationships" ("Heterosexual Cage"). In short, Rule was a nonconformist with a marked tendency to refuse to toe the political line, regardless of which party or interest group happened to draw it. The fascinating cross-currents revealed by her work, combined with her willingness to engage in public debates on contentious subjects, make her oeuvre as pertinent today as when it was first released.

Rule moved to Vancouver in 1956 at the age of twenty-five. In an essay written just before Ronald Reagan's re-election in 1984, she explains why "1954 was the last year I celebrated the 4th of July" (*Hot-Eyed* 198). Following her graduation from Mills College in Oakland, California, Rule lived in England while she completed her first (unpublished) book manuscript. Travel and distance, as well as European responses to Americans in the years following the Second World War, sharpened certain cultural questions for her, so that she no longer felt at home on her return: "The patriotism which required citizens to be proudly, blindly loyal seemed a peculiar American vice which I no longer shared" (9). The figure who symbolized this disenchantment for Rule was Senator Joseph McCarthy, who zealously pursued Communists and homosexuals (clearly interchangeable in his view). Rule was perturbed to find that a majority of people apparently believed that "McCarthy was doing the country an essential service in ridding it of dangerous subversion" (199). The conflation of (homo)sexual "perversion" with political subversion in Cold War rhetoric and politics—both viewed as threats to national security—placed Rule in a precarious position at the beginning of her career. As a college graduate and teacher, Rule would have to find work in one of the institutions McCarthy was targeting; she might be required to take a loyalty oath or face dismissal for "moral turpitude." Also around this period, Rule spent a short time at the Stanford Graduate School of Writing, where she became aware of "the unreality of [her] ambition to write about and as [she] pleased and also be published" (199). Her "4th of July" essay closes: "I left the country, and for thirty years I have not marked the date" (204).

In Rule's life and in her fictions, Canada performs the function ascribed by W.H. New to "the American-paradigm-'next-door'" within Canadian culture: that is, "generator ... of the principle of *choice*" (40–41). Today, Vancouver is one of Canada's most populous and cosmopolitan cities, but when Rule first arrived she discovered a community of "human scale" on the verge of a period of rapid development (*Hot-Eyed* 9). Perceiving herself as one immigrant among many, she found in Canada a perspective from which to critique America's "discredited institutions." But many of those institutions straddle the border, and Canada had a Cold War of its own. The main distinction between US and

Canadian manifestations of the Cold War lay in a combination of anti-Americanism with anti-Communism and "the greater control which Canada's centralized power structure had over its effects" (Cavell, "Introduction" 5). As Richard Cavell asserts, "the cultural processes associated with the Cold War in Canada *preceded* the fall of the Iron Curtain and *survived* the collapse of the Berlin Wall ... [I]n Canada, the cultural Cold War was waged as an extension of state regulatory power ... for nothing less than control of national self-representation, including norms of gender and sexuality" ("Introduction" 4, 7; see also Kinsman and Whitaker in the same volume). Crossing the border did not render Rule immune to the effects of bio-power, even if they sometimes took a more mundane guise than McCarthy's flamboyant hearings. Close analysis of Rule's fictions from the 1970s and the fate of her work at the hands of Canada Customs reveal various forms of cultural regulation that discourage dissent and enforce heteronormativity. My discussion focuses particularly on the family as site of contestation. A key trope in myths of nation-building—myths from which queer subjects are generally excluded—family is often employed as metaphor in feminist and lesbigay discourses of the period.

"My Country Wrong," the penultimate story in *Theme for Diverse Instruments* (1975), was first published in the lesbian periodical *The Ladder* in 1968. As the title implies, Rule disputes the old American adage "my country right or wrong." The story is set in late-1960s San Francisco during the Christmas season. The unnamed first-person narrator has not travelled home for Christmas for fifteen years (only for deaths or marriages), but finds herself there on 23 December because of an unexplained "hole in a blasted schedule" (159, 149). As Marilyn R. Schuster comments, "the story thus begins with a gap, a negative space created by a conventional calendar the narrator doesn't observe but that continues to shape her plans," and the narrative as a whole "explores gaps left by fragmenting systems of meaning that once created coherence but are no longer adequate" (124). Indeed, the opening paragraph is full of negatives, absences, and qualifications. The first sentence begins, "There should always be a reason for going somewhere," whereas the explanation for her arrival in this instance would be "nothing but a list of nonreasons" (149). The remark that "even a business trip provides excuse for discomfort, focuses discontent," implies the speaker experiences both discomfort and discontent in this return to the parental home, to the United States, and (to a lesser extent) to San Francisco itself, described as "familiar *enough*, home city as much as I ever had one, growing up American" (149, emphasis added). The narrator continues, "I don't want to talk about the death of friends, failures of domestic courage, the negative guilt of an ex-patriot" (149). The spelling of this last word appears significant: not just an expatriate, the more neutral expression for someone living abroad, but an ex-patriot, suggesting an active rejection of allegiance to the country of origin. The narrator's plans for the three days she must fill prove equally unfixed and uncertain. Significantly, on arrival she does not go directly to the family home but stays at the Hilton. A hotel room offers anonymous, neutral, and transient space and signals the protagonist's desire to distance herself emotionally or politically from her situation, to sustain her role as traveller or tourist for as long as possible. The story juxtaposes a series of encounters with friends and acquaintances, culminating in Christmas dinner at home. These episodes explore different constructs of urban and domestic space, which in turn imply shifting or alternative definitions of family and home.

The narrator finds a city full of uniforms once again, but the present conflict differs from the one in which her father served. The moral and social certainties that underpinned notions of valour and patriotism during the Second World War have come under siege. Three of the narrator's friends are on their way to jail:

> Lawrence was pleading not guilty to disturbing the peace in an anti-draft demonstration. He was trying to disturb the war, he said. Last time I came home my mother said ... "You're not going to get involved in any of these marches, are you, darling? You really don't have time to go to jail." It would have been unseemly of me, surely, having given up my citizenship years ago for positive social reasons, for wanting a vote where I lived. (150)

This suggests simultaneously the narrator's sympathy with these political views and her diffidence to involve herself in direct action now that she has formed civic attachments elsewhere. Indeed, at the time when this story was written and set, the terms of Section 349 of the Immigration and Nationality Act meant that an adult over the age of eighteen who became a naturalized citizen of another country would automatically be deemed to have forfeited her US citizenship. Consequently, the narrator inhabits an ambiguous insider/outsider status with respect to her birthplace.

The first social encounter evokes the anti-establishment, countercultural debates of the period, anticipating the kind of voluntary community that Rule explores more extensively in *The Young in One Another's Arms*. At the home of artist friend Michael, the younger people engage in earnest conversation about going to jail, draft resistance, and race riots. Charlie, a college student who plans to leave for Canada as soon as he finishes his degree, accuses the children of being "uncool": "The country's a jail already. You don't have to go anywhere" (155). Rule also alludes in passing to the McCarthy purges in connection with Michael's wife Jessica, who went to jail on principle in a slightly earlier era (155). This reference is developed in the narrator's second social engagement with her friend Lynn. Asked whether she would work in war industries, Lynn retorts that "moral choice is a theoretical exercise": "The point is I can't work in war industry. I can't get security clearance ... When the security people come to ask me about friends I had in graduate school, they ask two questions: is he homosexual and has he ever been to a psychiatrist" (158). The friends' excursion to a lesbian bar in Haight-Ashbury contrasts with the conventional Christmas meal in the home of the narrator's parents, one hundred miles south of San Francisco. The ambience of this final gathering is conveyed through disjointed snippets of conversation, unattributed to any individual speaker. While Rule often writes dialogue without identifying characters by name, leaving readers to deduce who is speaking from the context, the lack of attribution is more striking in this section than in the passages describing the other occasions. Sample remarks include "Aren't you proud of your brother going off to Vietnam? They'll only send him where it's safe, of course, just where the President goes," and "People with long hair want to go to jail" (167). This strategy tends to reduce the utterances to the rote observance of well-worn platitudes. The story closes with the narrator's realization that she has come home "to say goodbye to the children" (169).

If in "My Country Wrong" Canada appears fleetingly as a potential escape route, to be chosen by young draft resisters like Charlie or rejected by closeted professionals like Lynn, the perspective shifts in *The Young in One Another's Arms* (1977), Rule's fourth novel but her first to be set explicitly in Canada. The year of its publication coincided with an anti-gay backlash that was gathering momentum across North America, exemplified by Anita Bryant's "Save Our Children" campaign to repeal anti-discrimination laws in Dade County, Florida. In Canada as well, homosexuals increasingly became targets of heightened police attention. Gary Kinsman documents how the police attempted moral regulation of the gay male community by enforcing bawdy-house laws and overcrowding regulations against gay baths and bars (*Regulation* 338–41); Lynne Fernie similarly notes the harassment or intimidation of lesbian women by charging them with petty offences such as jaywalking, or being indigent if they did not have a stipulated amount of money with them (Goldie 60). The early 1970s, when the novel was composed, mark a period when Rule and Sonthoff became increasingly active in local feminist politics, a time of economic recession, energy crisis, and rising awareness of environmental degradation. Winner of the Canadian Author's Association Award for best novel (1978), *The Young in One Another's Arms* was held at the border by Canada Customs officials in 1990—during Freedom to Read week, as Cavell notes sardonically ("Jane Rule" 164). Rule's books often cross borders not just in content but literally, she typically sought international publishers as well as or instead of Canadian houses; *The Young in One Another's Arms* was first published by Doubleday New York in 1977 and subsequently reissued by Naiad in Tallahassee (1984). Both the novel's subject matter and its subsequent history of detention are worth further scrutiny.

The Young in One Another's Arms revolves around Ruth Wheeler, the one-armed, fifty-year-old proprietor of a Vancouver boarding house, and the assortment of lodgers she draws into her voluntary family. These include Willard Steele, a "three-quarter witted" shoe salesman (20); Tom Petross, landed immigrant and first of the American draft resisters to find sanctuary with Ruth; Gladys Ledger, a countercultural street radical who cares for disabled children; Mavis Collingwood, the conservative repressed lesbian writing a PhD thesis on Dickens; and Arthur, the latest American hiding out in the basement. Partway through the novel these characters are joined by a young black gay man from Detroit who calls himself Boy Wonder. The plot unfolds over approximately eighteen months, and its events are consistent with the late 1960s or early 1970s. The story is punctuated by a number of violent accidents, losses, and deaths. The boarding house has been expropriated by the local council and is scheduled for demolition to pave the way for the approach to a new bridge. In the course of the narrative, Arthur is deported; Willard barricades himself in the house, shoots Tom in the shoulder, and is himself shot dead by police; Gladys gives birth to a stillborn son; and Ruth's estranged husband Hal has a heart attack while driving his road grader and later dies on the operating table. As in much of Rule's fiction, however, plot and action appear subordinate to the relationships between the characters. *The Young in One Another's Arms* is a study in loss and compensation, survival and risk, capturing the 1970s mood of economic uncertainty and public insecurity in the face of the twin Cold War threats of nuclear annihilation and environmental degradation.

If the text bears traces of the seasonal rhythms of ancient vegetation myths and the epic cycles of birth, death, and resurrection, Rule also engages with the social order imposed by the Western Christian calendar. As in "My Country Wrong," her treatment of Christmas in *The Young in One Another's Arms* is intensely parodic, serving to illuminate simultaneously the waning of religious festivals and the failings of the family as an institution. Indeed, this novel features not one but two Christmases. The first occurs about one-third of the way into the text and constitutes a focal point for Rule's anatomy of various discredited institutions, including marriage, the family, and Christmas itself. Hal Wheeler arrives unexpectedly the week before Christmas to put his mother Clara into a retirement home, initiating the "dispersion" or "diaspora" of the boarding house's first configuration (Schuster 210). Clearly, that Christmas does not symbolize peace, goodwill, and unity. Having deprived Ruth of her long-time companion and alienated all the young people in the house, Hal departs before the holiday. Left to her own devices, Ruth would not celebrate Christmas; "I don't keep birthdays of the dead" she informs Tom (74), implicitly linking the sacrificial Christ figure with her dead daughter Claire. Even so, Tom seeks to organize Christmas to distract Ruth from her stiff loss and to repay her assistance and support: "All right, it's obscene, barbaric, commercial, and all things unholy, but it happens to be the only thing we've got" (74). Of equal significance with the timing of Hal's irruption is Boy's appearance and disappearance in the text: he arrives just before the first Christmas celebration (98) and departs just before the second (195). Symbolically, however, the novel closes not on Christmas day, but on April Fool's Day—the day Gladys feels is most appropriate for her to return home from her genealogical family in Toronto to her adoptive family on Galiano Island (217), where some of the lodgers resettle following their displacement from Vancouver.

There can be little doubt that one of the discredited institutions that Rule exposes in her text is Christianity—if not faith per se, then certainly the effects produced by centuries of religious discourse in North American society. This is signalled from the text's opening page, in the image of Ruth's dead daughter "falling like a sparrow out of the sky" (18)—the notion that God sees every sparrow that falls is proverbial. The vulnerability of the young to forces beyond their control (whether "acts of God," natural disasters, or government agents and officials) is underlined by Ruth's reflections on the succession of fugitive Americans who have sought her out by word of mouth: "Legality for them was such a frail security that you couldn't read it in their behavior. The police, cooperating with American authorities, weren't always concerned with such niceties. In a world where even God, never mind Abraham, killed his only son as a loving gesture, how could the police understand a young Isaac or Jesus who wouldn't offer himself up to the slaughter?" (32). This telling passage from the end of Chapter 1 metaphorically links repressive state apparatuses (the Canadian police and US military) with ideological ones (the Christian church) in a context that implicitly rejects the sacrifice endorsed by these regimes as senseless. Many of the text's other biblical allusions originate in Boy's signifyin' impersonation of a succession of black stereotypes. Rule links the histories of draft resisters and slaves escaping into Canada through Boy's allusion to entering the country via the "underground railroad" (102). Just as spirituals were used to pass coded messages of resistance among slaves, Boy uses religious rhetoric to deflect questions he does not wish to answer, anticipating racial or homophobic slurs. For instance, when Tom asks Boy where he comes from, instead of replying directly, he answers, "I come from walking to and fro upon the earth, making out a report on Job's daughters" (100). To cite another example, the café on Galiano Island—bought as a communal business venture in the aftermath of Willard's death and Tom's injury—is renamed Jonah's following Boy's remark on their safe emergence from the ferry, "spat out of the belly of the whale at last" (160). But perhaps the most pervasive biblical allusion is encoded in Ruth's own name. Her many griefs and losses recall her namesake amid the alien corn; they also link her to her biblical counterpart through her deep affection for her mother-in-law Clara—an attachment that is reciprocated. Ruth wonders whether many women marry because they love their mothers-in-law (21), while Clara muses that the only important thing she ever did that she really did not want to do was leave Ruth when Hal returned from his war service (94). When an interfering landlady pronounces coming between husband and wife "unnatural," Clara retorts: "I don't come between. I come before and after. He says he doesn't want her. I do" (94). As Marilyn Schuster notes, "The Ruth and Naomi story is one of the biblical stories that gay and lesbian activists turned to in the 1970s because of the positive valuing of same sex relationships" (206). Although not overtly sexual, the bond between Ruth and Clara, more intimate than that between Ruth and her husband, forms the matrilineal core for the unorthodox family that develops around them.

Ruth's unconventional marriage and boarding house are indicative of Rule's reconfiguration of notions of family and home on both domestic and national fronts. At regular intervals throughout, various characters allude to reasons why they cannot or will not go "home," with reference either to the nuclear family or to the United States, and often both. Once again, Christmas provides the occasion for many of these reflections. By definition, the boarding house represents a space that straddles private and public domains. Converted from a suburban family dwelling, the boarding house contains communal areas and (semi-)private bedrooms; the occupants inhabit the house on a temporary basis and may choose to move on at any time; the house is simultaneously a business and a home. The residents have been brought together by chance in the first instance, and as Christmas approaches some lodgers depart for their own families. Arthur has already been deported, and Clara has been removed to the nursing home. This leaves a fraction of the original community, on the brink of the final dissolution that must occur by March, when the house will be razed. The conventions of buying and trimming a tree, preparing a feast, and singing carols can thus be seen as ritual gestures warding off an uncertain future. But some of the lodgers are about to embark on an intentional as opposed to an aleatory collective. Gladys, Mavis, and Tom inform Ruth that they wish to start a commune with a dictator (75); Ruth calls it a conspiracy, Gladys calls it a peaceful revolution, and Tom calls it "a family solution to a family problem" (81). This plan forms the basis for the eventual move to Galiano, with the additions of Clara and Boy. Ruth observes that Tom is the most resolute about Christmas because as a draft evader, he is the only one who cannot choose to go home (79). As Boy integrates himself into the group, he similarly invokes family, leading Ruth to reflect: "Boy had adopted Tom's vocabulary. Was it their shared nationality and their being deprived of it that made them sentimental about its discredited institutions?" (120). The rifts produced within the concept of family by changes in national, political, or ethical allegiances are widened further by the inflections of queer desire. Mavis's family lives in Vancouver, yet she has not seen them for five years, since "[t]hey threw her out because they discovered she had a crush on one of her female teachers and wouldn't go to a psychiatrist about it" (125). Clara's question, "What kind of a family is that?" (125), is more than rhetorical. The text stages further debates about the nature of family through Gladys's view of marriage as a prison (130) and her iconoclastic ideas concerning children. Perceiving child-birth and -rearing as a "trumped-up destiny" demanded of women, she proposes it might be better to raise other people's children rather than one's own, to make it clear that it is "just a job"; children should never be conceived as their parents' salvation or reason for living (129). When Gladys does finally agree to marry Tom, the wedding itself occurs offstage and is summarized in a single sentence (165). Indeed, in the aftermath of Willard's shooting, Gladys wonders who coined the term "nuclear family" (144)—a phrase that resonates with apocalyptic Cold War fears, given their embattled state.

The figure of Hal Wheeler provides the hinge between family and repressive state apparatuses. A stock representation of the unreconstructed patriarch, Hal is perhaps the most two-dimensional of Rule's characters, bullying, bigoted, and intolerant. His occupation as a road builder makes him complicit in the economic and government forces that displace Ruth and her boarders from their residence. Rule parodies the iconic image of the cowboy or frontiersman, describing Hal as "a hero on the road gang, riding tall on his great earth-moving machines" (61), literally paving the way for the exploitation of British Columbia's natural resources and figuratively taming the wilderness. Yet Ruth is not without sympathy for her husband's situation as a man deprived by time and circumstance of the role he has been taught to fulfil by the combined weight of North America's heteronormative institutions. The establishment that trained Hal to fight and kill in the Second World War now struggles to contain the effects of the civil rights, feminist, and gay liberation movements.

Apart from Hal, Rule represents the power of state repression chiefly through the military and the police, whose pursuit, surveillance, and ultimate violence toward the boarders serve to contain and harass the community. Initially, Ruth's politeness, missing arm, and middle-class home appear to temper the authority of the officers searching for draft dodgers (31), but this proves illusory. When the police return to remove Arthur, they do not arrest or charge him formally; they simply transport him to the US military police across the border at Blaine, which is "cheaper than a deportation order" (53). Those left behind organize protests and media publicity, but they cannot save Arthur. While Canadian public opinion increasingly sympathized with draft resisters as the Vietnam War dragged on, official government policy remained ambivalent, and Canada supplied arms and intelligence to the United States during this period. War resisters were not actively deterred, but neither were they granted political asylum; rather, Americans of service age had to apply for landed immigrant status by the usual channels. Rule's portrait captures the expedience typical of Canada's relations with its powerful neighbour.

The most extreme exercise of force occurs with Willard's shooting death. As the stretchers are carried away, Ruth yells at the authorities, "What have you done with Arthur? ... What have you done? They're *my* children, *all* of them, *mine*. You kill everything. Bastards! Bastards!" (133). Schuster's archival research indicates that this scene was originally projected as the novel's tragic climax. Rule's realization that the incident should instead be positioned at the midpoint marked a breakthrough in her composition: "Rather than end the novel in urban violence and defeat with her main characters fighting against 'the system,' she would have them regroup and attempt to fight *for* something—a redefined family in the community of Galiano" (205). Although Rule is skeptical about communes, she clearly wishes to frame the effort of building and sustaining a voluntary community as positive action. Ruth's unorthodox family also reaches out to the other islanders; they use Jonah's as a soup kitchen and as a base for meals-on-wheels during the winter months, offer to do Christmas shopping for shut-ins, and run a day care centre for the children. Reciprocating these gestures, the whole island turns out to bring gifts for Gladys's newborn daughter. But this tentative rapprochement among the island's diverse residents is destabilized when the police search for Boy. Threatened with discovery during the Christmas roadblocks to detect drunk drivers, Boy chooses to disappear to safeguard the others. In the wake of his departure, Ruth's home is once again subjected to unwelcome scrutiny, as a police helicopter hovers over the farmhouse day after day. This harassment causes trouble with the other islanders, and the landlady plans to evict them. Boy's observation concerning official papers and (il)legality sums up the tenuous position of Rule's band of nonconformists: "White folks is always wantin' to be legal. No piece of paper ever goin' to make me legal 'less somebody wants it to, and somebody don't'" (116). In theory, all citizens share the same constitutional rights before the law; in practice, enforcement and interpretation of that law can be highly selective.

Rule's exposition of the workings of bio-power in *The Young in One Another's Arms* finds its counterpart in the text's own fate at the hands of Canada Customs and its author's resistance to censorship. The legal battles between Vancouver's Little Sister's Book and Art Emporium and the Canadian government, battles that lasted twenty years, have become almost legendary. The conflict dates from December 1986, when Canada Customs stopped the first of many shipments destined for the bookstore at the Canada–US border on suspicion that their contents violated obscenity laws. The Customs Act empowers officials to exercise "prior restraint" by seizing any item believed to be obscene as defined by Criminal Code's Section 163(8). Tariff Code 9956 entitles customs agents to stop representations of any kind deemed to be obscene, treasonable, seditious, or hate propaganda. The repeated seizure of materials bound for specialty bookstores (as opposed to other outlets) can be viewed as reflecting a broad shift to the right in North American politics and government as well as an intensifying backlash against feminist and gay movements. In June 1990 the owners of Little Sister's, along with the B.C. Civil Liberties Association, filed a Statement of Claim in the provincial Supreme Court. They had decided to mount a constitutional challenge based on the Charter of Rights and Freedoms, instead of fighting each detention on a case-by-case basis (a strategy they had previously tried, using issues of *The Advocate*, but had found ineffective).[2] Little Sister's argued that the prior restraint clause, which placed the onus on businesses to prove that the confiscated material was not obscene, violated the right to freedom of expression guaranteed by Section 2(b) of the Charter. They also maintained that Customs agents' routine targeting of gay and lesbian businesses violated the owners' rights to equal treatment under the law (Section 15).

Jane Rule was one of many well-known figures who testified on behalf of Little Sister's in October 1994, when the case finally was heard. Rule's works had been detained and released by Customs officials more than once; these detentions had included *The Young in One Another's Arms* in 1990 and *Contract with the World* (1980) in 1993. Bizarrely, the realities of the Canadian publishing and book distribution industries are such that works published *in Canada* are vulnerable to regulation by the Canada Border Services Agency (CBSA).[3] Rule's books often have to be imported from the United States when Canadian editions are out of print or when certain titles are published by small lesbian presses, notably Naiad in Florida. In 2000, the Canadian Supreme Court ruled that "it is fundamentally unacceptable that expression which is free within the country can become stigmatized and harassed by government officials simply because it crosses an international boundary, and is thereby brought within the bailiwick of the Customs department. The appellants' constitutional right to … freedom of expression does not stop at the border" (7). While this ruling refers specifically to gay and lesbian erotica, the point holds true for other literature. As a result of the anomaly just described, the entirely incidental action of importing certain works rather than purchasing them domestically is exposing marginalized groups—LBGTQ artists in this case—to scrutiny and policing they would not otherwise be subjected to.

As it happens, there is little explicit sexual content, straight or queer, in *The Young in One Another's Arms*. Boy talks openly about going to the steam baths, and Tom, Gladys, and Mavis engage in what might be termed a *ménage à trois*, but no sexual acts are described. One is left to speculate: either the book was stopped purely because of its destination, or the Customs officers were remarkably squeamish—if they read the book at all. The entire episode stands as an object lesson in how the border can function as an instrument of bio-power regulating citizens' texts and bodies.

In light of her professional standing, Rule was asked to give evidence concerning the artistic merit of various lesbian works and the harm caused by such detentions. According to the legal precedent set by *R. v. Butler* (1992), artistic merit and educational, scientific, or medical purposes were mitigating factors in determining whether a work violated the Criminal Code. Rule noted the potential alienation of the wider audience for whom she was seeking to write, as well as the damaging attitude toward the lesbian and gay communities in the inference that lesbian writing must be pornographic by definition:

> I have to carry a reputation created by this charge from which I have no way of defending myself ... I bitterly resent the attempt to marginalize, trivialize and even criminalize what I have to say because I happen to be a lesbian ... The assumption is that there must be something pornographic [in my writing] because of my sexual orientation ... a shocking way to deal with my community. ("Detained" 18)

Rule was fully aware that her opinion was being accorded respect mainly because she was a prominent award-winning author. When *The Young in One Another's Arms* was impounded, the media quickly contacted her for a reaction. Rule chastised the media for failing to address the real political import of this episode:

> [I]t is not important that *this* book is stopped. It is important that you hear that these books are stopped every week and not make a fuss simply because this book got the Canadian Author's Association Best Novel of the Year for 1978. They're not exactly a radical, porn-supporting organization, so you can pretty well guess that this book is not going to offend your grandmother. But what you should be offended about is the harassment of the gay bookstores. And you should be headlining *that* every week. ("Interview" 31)

Rule was also aware that her person as well as her texts might be "censored" crossing the border. Historical experience suggests that such instances tend to rise in times of national insecurity.

The point at issue both in Rule's lived experience and in the Little Sister's constitutional challenge is that censorship of explicit representations of sexuality is applied unevenly. In their account of the trial, Janine Fuller and Stuart Blackley point out that *Desert Hearts*, the 1985 movie based on Rule's first novel, circulated freely in Canadian cinemas and video stores before being detained by Customs in 1993—and that "Rule's books sat peacefully in almost every mainstream Canadian bookstore and library, yet had the occasional dust-up at the border, especially when ordered by a gay bookstore" (76). During the first forty-day hearing, the plaintiffs produced an impressive array of evidence to support the allegation that queer businesses were being singled out for discriminatory treatment. High-ranking Customs officials confirmed that most mainstream bookstores never experienced detentions or delays—indeed, they never had any communication with Canada Customs at all (26). Furthermore, John Shearer, the Director General of the Tariff Division, admitted there had been a "lookout" in the Vancouver mail area for importations by Little Sister's (134). This distinction in procedure was graphically demonstrated in May 1993 when one American book distributor, frustrated by the increasing rate of detention and consequent damage to goods, adopted a new tactic: the consolidation of *all* books headed for Canada into one massive shipment. Unable to distinguish which items were going where, Customs agents "stripped the shipment" of every suspect title—many of which were bound for thirty-six different bookstores, including mainstream and university shops that had never encountered problems before. The seizure of nearly half a ton of books worth an estimated $10,000 attracted hostile editorials from across the political spectrum (27–28). The crowning irony, however, emerged through the testimony of Celia Duthie, owner of what was at that time the largest independent book chain in western Canada. The prosecution had requested multiple copies of several books due to be discussed during the trial. Realizing that anything sent to Little Sister's was likely to be stopped at the border, Janine Fuller approached Duthie for help, and she successfully imported the banned books without difficulty. Evidently the significance of this manoeuvre was entirely lost on the Crown (30–31). The same merchandise that was passing freely across the border when destined for library shelves or mainstream outlets was being intercepted, scrutinized, and held indefinitely when addressed to Little Sister's.

If the goal of this exercise in power is to cause inconvenience and perhaps even bankruptcy, the application of Tariff Code 9956 is particularly effective. The process for challenging Canada Customs seizures is bureaucratic and confusing; it has several stages, any of which can generate extended delays and lead to costly litigation. Every detention must be fought individually, and previous court decisions have no effect on the subsequent behaviour of Customs officers—they just stop another consignment. (Indeed, there is evidence that if anything, the odds *increase* that a shipment will be stopped if either the importer or the publication has come under suspicion before.) By the time the courts overturn the ruling and declare the work not obscene (as they have done increasingly over time), the material has often been defaced, "lost," or incinerated. Or, in the case of periodicals, the work is so out of date as to be unmarketable. In B.C. between 1989 and 1992, only fourteen obscenity cases were prosecuted under the Criminal Code, whereas Canada Customs used Tariff 9956 to prohibit 34,748 shipments during that same time—and a shipment generally comprises more than one item (Fuller and Blackley 165). But highly trained police officers are bound by strict codes of conduct, whereas Customs officials receive minimal instruction and rarely have expertise in obscenity laws:

> The tasks of determining artistic merit and substantial risk of harm to society, as well as the meaning of the notoriously vague concepts of degrading and dehumanizing, befuddle even our most intelligent judges who have had the benefit of days of expert testimony. Legislation that asks Customs officers to make the same determinations on a routine basis with no assistance places everyone, including those officers, in an absurd situation. (Cossman and Ryder 110)

While government agencies have virtually unlimited resources at their disposal, small marginal businesses can ill afford the loss of revenue, let alone the legal costs to mount an adequate defence against such harassment. Thus in 2002 Little Sister's applied to the courts for "Advance Costs" to continue their resistance. Few precedents exist for such awards; the case must be deemed sufficiently important to all Canadian citizens, and the recipients must be in such financial straits that the case could not be argued without assistance. When the appeal was denied in January 2007, the bookstore finally conceded defeat. The message seems clear: conservative opponents to LBGTQ existence hope to close down such businesses either through censorship, bankruptcy or sheer exhaustion—as indeed happened in the instance of *The Body Politic* in the 1980s—but the ramifications of such proceedings are not considered "important" to all Canadian citizens.

Throughout their resistance to the institutional forces arrayed against them, Little Sister's and their supporters have sought official recognition of the lack of accountability and systemic homophobia inherent in the administration and legislation as currently framed. The various decisions handed down represent only partial victories. Following the initial case, Justice Kenneth Smith reserved judgment for over a year before upholding Customs' rights of detention, despite criticizing the "arbitrary and improper manner" in which their powers were frequently exercised. Smith determined the inevitable violations of freedom of expression in the application of the code qualified as a reasonable limit under Section 1 of the Charter. After two further appeals, the Supreme Court's decision in 2000 represents a limited improvement at best. The majority decision (six to three) acknowledges, "The Customs treatment was high-handed and dismissive of the appellants' right to receive lawful expressive material which they had every right to import" and recognizes that other "vulnerable groups" might equally be "at risk from overzealous censorship" (7). But, like Justice Smith, the majority criticizes Customs' implementation, not the constitutionality of obscenity laws. Deficiencies in the system should be corrected: determinations should be made within thirty days, and publications should be released promptly if the government cannot prove its claims within that time. The only concession granted to the appellants was to shift the burden of proof to Customs: "The 'reverse onus' provision under s. 152(3) of the *Customs Act* cannot constitutionally apply to put on the importer the onus of disproving obscenity. An importer has a *Charter* right to receive expressive material unless the state can justify its denial" (4). In other words, the official verdict refuses to countenance the possibility of systemic homophobia in the Customs Act and "conveniently shift[s] the focus away from the possibility that the state is targeting the representations of a marginalized sexual group" (Cossman and Ryman 106).[4] The dissenting judges, however, went further.

The minority opinion held not only that the law had been "administered in an unconstitutional manner" but that "the legislation itself, and not only its application ... is responsible for the constitutional violations" (9–10). They consider that any restriction of such a fundamental right as expressive freedom must be undertaken with care, particularly where this restriction is imposed by prior restraint: "The flaws in the Customs regime are not the product of simple bad faith or maladministration, but rather flow from the very nature of prior restraint itself" (11). Further, they contend that sufficient safeguards should be built into the legislation to ensure rights will not be violated, and that the government has a duty "to justify the actual infringement on rights occasioned by the impugned legislation, not simply that occasioned by some hypothetical ideal of the legislation" (10). Reform at the implementation level would therefore prove inadequate: "The appropriate remedy for this violation of the appellants' constitutional rights is to strike down Code 9956(*a*) of the *Customs Tariff*" (13). Unlike the majority verdict, then, the dissenting opinion goes some way towards acknowledging the lack of accountability in the system and the need for Parliament to redraft the law. But there is no compulsion for the government or the CBSA to attend to the views of the minority.

In the closing argument of the original court case, the Crown's lawyer defends prior restraint as an accepted aspect of Canadian law, going so far as to declare it to be part of what makes us "not Americans" (Fuller and Blackley 178). Prior restraint is applied on the basis of potential risk or harm to "public decency," usually framed in terms of the imagined effect on children or other vulnerable individuals. It requires the exercise of judgment in circumstances where officials are predisposed to target certain materials and groups for surveillance, given that the legal definition of concepts like degrading or demeaning is far from precise and appeals to "community standards." The lingering effects of Canada's Cold War mentality can thus be traced in the succession of judicial decisions in cases like those mounted by Little Sister's that reinforce the status quo. The persistent homophobic link of sexual perversion with political subversion is hard to uncouple. As Elizabeth Grace and Colin Leys argue, the state invokes subversion precisely "to *create* a 'grey area' of activities that *are* lawful, but will be denied protection from state surveillance or harassment by being *declared* illegitimate, on the grounds that they *potentially* have unlawful consequences. In capitalist societies the targets of this delegitimation have been overwhelmingly on the left" (qtd. in Kinsman "Canadian" 114). Once an individual or group has been labelled subversive or a security risk—and by extension excluded from the national collective—it becomes easier to restrict human or citizenship rights (114–15). This appears to be the logic behind the seizure of books like *The Young in One Another's Arms,* where "common sense" might otherwise suggest that material already circulating legally within Canada ought to be exempt from confiscation. As Rule discovered, despite her transference of civic allegiance from the US to Canada, the Canadian state exercises a great deal of control over its citizens through the various laws and institutions at its disposal—including cultural discourses. The example of Jane Rule's lived experience and oeuvre reveals what Reg Whitaker terms the "national *in*security" (35)—most visible when we attempt to cross borders.

Notes

1　"Gross indecency," the offence generally applied to gay anal sex, was not abolished until 1988 (Fuller and Blackley 104).

2　For the full text of the Statement of Claim, see Appendix C in Fuller and Blackley, pp. 197–201.

3　I generally retain the old designation Canada Customs, as the Canada Border Services Agency, merging Customs with other enforcement personnel from Citizenship and Immigration and the Canadian Food Inspection Agency, was not formally created until November 2005.

4　Reporting the final verdict against Little Sister's for *Xtra* in January 2007, Marcus McCann claims that 70% of materials seized by the CSBA are LBGTQ.

Works Cited

Cavell, Richard. "Jane Rule." *Profiles in Canadian Literature* 7. Ed. Jeffrey M. Heath. Toronto: Dundurn, 1991. 159–66.

———. "Introduction: The Cultural Production of Canada's Cold War." Cavell, ed. 3–32.

———, ed. *Love, Hate, and Fear in Canada's Cold War.* Toronto: U of Toronto P, 2004.

Cossman, Brenda, and Bruce Ryder. "Customs Censorship and the *Charter:* the *Little Sisters* Case." *Constitutional Forum* 7.4 (1996): 103–12. *HeinOnline.* 24 July 2010.

"Detained at Customs: Rule Testifies at Little Sister's Trial." Vancouver: Lazara, 1995.

Foucault, Michel. *The History of Sexuality,* vol. 1: *An Introduction.* Trans. Robert Hurley. New York: Vintage, 1980.

Fuller, Janine, and Stuart Blackley. *Restricted Entry: Censorship on Trial.* Ed. Nancy Pollak. Vancouver: Press Gang, 1995.

Goldie, Terry. "Talking Forbidden Love: An Interview with Lynne Fernie." *In a Queer Country: Gay and Lesbian Studies in the Canadian Context.* Ed. Terry Goldie. Vancouver: Arsenal Pulp, 2001. 50–68.

Kinsman, Gary. "The Canadian Cold War on Queers: Sexual Regulation and Resistance." Cavell, ed. 108–32.

———. *The Regulation of Desire: Homo and Hetero Sexualities.* 2nd ed. Montreal: Black Rose, 1996.

"Little Sister's Book and Art Emporium / Censorship / Supreme Court of Canada." http://www.littlesisters.ca/docscc/index_court.html. Accessed 22 July 2010.

Little Sisters Book and Art Emporium v. Canada (Minister of Justice), 2000 SCC 69, [2000] 2 S.C.R. 1120. *Judgements of the Supreme Court of Canada.* http://scc .lexum.org/en/2000/2000scc69/2000scc69.html. Accessed 24 June 2010.

McCann, Marcus. "Little Sister's declares defeat in the wake of 7–2 Supreme Court Ruling." *Xtra!* 19 January 2007. http://www.xtra.ca/public/viewstory.aspx ?SESSIONID=nzvhqtqryza2q145zfb0lbic&STORY_ID=2583&PUB_TEMPLATE_ ID=2. Accessed 21 April 2011.

New, W.H. *Borderlands: How We Talk about Canada.* Vancouver: UBC P, 1998.

Rule, Jane. *Contract with the World.* 1980. Toronto: Insomniac, 2005.

———. *Desert of the Heart.* 1964. Vancouver: Talonbooks, 1987.

———. "The Heterosexual Cage of Coupledom." *BC Bookworld* 16.1 (2001). http:// www.abcbookworld.com/view_essay.php?id=38. Accessed 18 March 2013.

———. *A Hot-Eyed Moderate.* Tallahassee: Naiad, 1985.

———. Interview by Keith Louise Fulton. *Herizons* 6.4 (1993): 28–32.

———. "Labels." *Loving the Difficult.* Sidney: Hedgerow, 2008. 29–36.

———. "My Country Wrong." *Theme for Diverse Instruments.* Vancouver: Talonbooks, 1975. 149–69.

———. *The Young in One Another's Arms.* 1977. Vancouver: Arsenal Pulp, 2005.

Schuster, Marilyn R. *Passionate Communities: Reading Lesbian Resistance in Jane Rule's Fiction.* New York: New York UP, 1999.

Whitaker, Reg. "'We Know They're There': Canada and Its Others, with or without the Cold War." Cavell, ed. 35–56.

sixteen

Strangers in Strange Lands

Cultural Translation in Gaétan Soucy's *Vaudeville!*

Jeffrey Orr

GAÉTAN SOUCY'S POSTMODERN COMEDY of early-twentieth-century New York immigration begins with a beating; or, more precisely, as the opening line puts it, "it all began with a fall" (5). The protagonist, Xavier X. Mortanse, an apprentice demolition man, tumbles 15 metres into a ravine following a brutal kick to the back from his workmates, while he is crouched down, tying his bootlaces. This is perhaps an unusual opening for a comic novel, but well aligned with the book's subtle allegorical undercurrents and intertextual references, a mix of high and low culture that shifts from Milton's *Paradise Lost* to Warner Brothers' children's cartoons, with numerous stops in between.

The book's eclectic intertexuality and shifting cultural awareness attend specifically to the tension between familiarity and strangeness that pervades the Canada–US border, with an exploration of identity and geography that is by turns as frustrating, heartbreaking, and hilarious as the relationship defined by their border. In refiguring both characters and places, *Vaudeville!* invites a reconfiguration and reconsideration of international relationships, personal and collective identities, and cultural familiarities that cross the borders and boundaries of bodies, countries, and communities. Xavier's name suggests the awkward position he occupies at the intersection of the Christian and the Gothic, halfway between Frankenstein's monster and God's son, but in either case, brought back from the dead. The name "Xavier" is Old Spanish for "the new house" (from the ancestral castle of St. Francis Xavier in Navarre), and the name resonates throughout the book as he joins, and is later expelled from, a crew of professional demolition men, only to end his days in physical decay as his internal organs begin to malfunction—a creation that falls to pieces. His middle initial and last name (X. Mortanse) provide the reader with a Latinate hint (confirmed much later in the novel) that he is in fact the creation of a mad scientist, a creature of reanimated body parts, and thus "ex-mortanse," formerly dead.

Early in the hilariously surreal story, Xavier is discovered sitting memoryless on a crate by the harbour warehouses, with a dim conception of himself as a Hungarian immigrant, and taken under the wing of a contemplatively inclined demolition crew boss called "The Philosopher of the Sands of Silence" (11). As a result of the aforementioned fall, Xavier finds a wooden box containing a singing frog, in a plot device that mimics the story of the Warner Brothers animated short film *One Froggy Evening*. After several fruitless weeks on the demolition site, during which his principal occupation is to serve as the whipping boy for those higher up in the Order of Demolishers, he meets a blind beggar who convinces him to take his frog on stage at a vaudeville theatre. Unfortunately, the frog will, as per the Warner Brothers cartoon, only sing when no one is watching, and Xavier is relegated first to busboy in the theatre, and then to punching bag when an aging boxer in the show gets too drunk to enter the ring and is hurriedly replaced by the well-meaning, 45-kilogram protagonist. Predictably, he gets beaten to a pulp in this match, for which the boxing ring has been replaced by a trampoline. After a short period during which it seems he might recover, a visit from the woman he calls his mother reveals him to be a latter-day Frankenstein's monster built by his mother's spurned lover from her recently deceased son's body parts. He is then discovered to have massive internal injuries, misdiagnosed as a lung infection, and eventually dies unnoticed during the triumphal welcome parade in honour of movie starlet Marie Peak-Forde, a reference to Canadian-born Mary Pickford, "America's Sweetheart" of silent movie fame.

This is not an obviously comedic plotline, and strictly speaking it has a rather closer resemblance to Mel Brooks' famous definition of tragedy as "when I cut my finger. Comedy is when you walk into an open sewer and die" (Moncour). The definition may seem reversed in Soucy's work, but in fact it describes the rhetorical relationship very well, particularly the relationship between the reader and the protagonist. Xavier becomes a sort of Everyman; the horrible things that happen to him happen, by an extension of empathy, to us as well.

The immigrant experience of dislocation is also essential to the way in which the book deals with this relationship of empathy between the reader and the main character, and so is the issue of cultural familiarity. Xavier's confusion over, and misconstrual of, the events and attitudes around him, force the reader to rethink and decode the cultural references and landscapes, so that the experience of reading parallels Xavier's immigrant activity of attempting to make meaning of a new and foreign environment. The humour in the novel is often dark, but it springs from a negotiation of empathy rather than *schadenfreude*. We laugh at Xavier's mistaken and off-kilter descriptions of the city because the alienation of the main character within the world of the book is mirrored by the alienation and disorientation of the reader outside the world of the book.

Like the character of Xavier X. Mortanse, the book itself is a reanimated creation built from other parts. The bricolage of cultural referents in the plot, characters, and structure of the story consistently reread and misread other texts; by the same token, Xavier is himself a reconstituted text being constantly translated and misread. His body, itself stitched together from other parts, is, moreover, covered in text carved into his skin. Having read portions of the journal in which his maker recorded the progress of his reanimation, Xavier discovers that "he had to concede that he was well and truly *signed.* On the sole of his foot there appeared, in scarified letters: *Rog. Wond., April 1929*" (414). He later discovers that "[h]is belly and back were covered in graffiti, written on his flesh with quicklime. Including this, under the shoulder-blades: *Christopher Columbus was put in irons for having offered a world!* And on his belly, the most legible, in bigger letters: *I belong to Justine Vilbroquais fore evver*" (427, *sic*). The maker's signature on his foot identifies Xavier as a work of art, something made by and for someone. It transpires that Rogatien Wondell, Xavier's maker, was in love with Justine Vilbroquais, and that when her son Vincent leapt to his death from a window, Wondell attempted to prove his undying love by reanimating the corpse of her son. His body stands as a textual love letter from its maker; Xavier stands in the same relation to the text of the city as we, the readers, stand to the text of the novel. Within the book, Xavier is a cipher, a written figure both empty of meaning and simultaneously full of it, depending on how it is read. Providing a key is an obvious way of alerting the reader to the cipher's plenitude of meaning; not providing the key forces the reader to decipher the figures him or herself by bringing meaning to them from outside the text.

As readers, we share the protagonist's bewilderment with the streets of the city. Xavier watches while the city transforms itself into a madhouse, with people singing and dancing madly, "all with no joy, no good humour, as if a chore had been imposed on them. None except Xavier, who was dumbfounded, feet bolted to the ground" (228). His inactivity gets him beaten by the police with warnings of "Hey nitwit! Move it!" and "It's the National Minute of Being Thrilled to be Alive in the United States of America! Get moving! Do something! Make it snappy or I'll stick you with a fine!" (229).

This use of enigmatic structure, absent a usual one-to-one correspondence with a meaning outside the text, is not what we usually think of with allegory. If, however, allegory is considered more broadly as comprising "the direct address to the reader, shifts between the literal and referential, wordplay, internal commentary making the actions self-reflexive, and the construction of the narrative as an activity parallel to reading" (qtd. in Hunter 167), then it aptly describes Soucy's mode of rhetorical construction. To that list I would perhaps add the act of writing, insofar as both reading and writing are ways of making meaning—a correspondence that will be discussed shortly. Allegory, Quilligan argues, is a particularly self-reflexive and critically self-conscious mode, and "its purpose is always to make its reader correspondingly self-conscious" (qtd. in Hunter 24). Soucy's reader is encouraged to identify with Xavier, not only as a character type of the lovable loser à la Charlie Chaplin's Little Tramp, but also as a kind of proxy for one's experiences of reading the book, and for considering the world outside its narrative structure. This structure not only brings the reader into the empathetic relationship discussed above, but also provides specific contextual interpretive possibilities. In terms of national identities, it also provides a bit of empathetic identification and perhaps self-examination for a slightly smug Canadian audience.

Like Edgar Allan Poe's short stories, which tease the reader with the possibility of an unprovided key to their meaning, the allegorical structure of *Vaudeville!* produces not the overt political comment of, for example, Orwell's *Animal Farm*, but rather a cipher that involves the reader in a process of puzzling out ultimately inconclusive possible meanings. Multiple references from a wide spectrum of high and popular cultural sources create a disorienting blizzard of information, and this places the reader in a situation analogous to that of the new immigrant who must attempt to work out provisional structures of meaning in circumstances of alien information overload, and who will, inevitably, often get it wrong. As the protagonist's friend The Sands (who claims to have spent the past thirty years writing a book despite being completely illiterate) exclaims in a conversation toward the end of the novel, "I've misled people into thinking that I knew when I didn't! and I understood when I didn't! and that I could see when I couldn't see a damn thing!" His interlocutor asks him, "What is it you're talking about?" He replies, "I don't know. About everything, about life. I'm going to die and I won't have understood anything." He is told in reply:

> "[It's] the same for everyone, really. And maybe there's nothing to understand anyway."
> He closed his eyes, put his fist on his forehead as if to drive it in.
> "And yet in there, in *there*, it seemed to me there was something! How many times have I told myself 'that's it, it's going to unblock!' but it was no good, it stayed stuck inside." (404)

For the reader, too, the answer key with which to unblock the meaning of the text is continually elusive.

Xavier's disconcerting encounters with American culture, and our empathetic responses to those encounters, produce the effect that David Leahy describes as "counter-worlding," defined as remaking a dominant imperial centre and simultaneously inviting the reader to "recognize and trouble the ways that the imperial *Other* both interpellates us and is an integral part of our cultures that requires the adoption of paradoxical forms of critique and contestation" (63). *Vaudeville!*, in rendering New York alien and frightening, questions and refigures the hegemonic landmarks and landscape of the city and the country of which it is part. The novel's allegorical narrative structure compels us to look at a culture that seems familiar from the position of strangeness, thereby making non-American readers aware of their difference from that culture in the world outside the book, and making American readers aware of the contingency of cultural comfort, rather than its ideologically naturalized normality. As Leahy notes, "counter-worlding," or alienating the reader from the comfort of feeling *either* the same *or* different, is a means of alerting us to our own "complicity in our own subjugation, to the doubleness of the ways that our desires for progress can make us all 'outsiders' even when we truly believe we are not" (81). Such a reaction to the novel is a prime example of Quilligan's concept of allegory. A situation of estrangement within the novel invites the reader to consider the same kind of estrangement in the world *outside* the novel, so that what remains unsaid becomes a focal point of meaning that the reader brings to the text.

This situation of cultural counter-worlding operates in the context of production in the world outside the text, as well as the world of the narrative. Gaétan Soucy is an award-winning French-language novelist from Quebec who wrote the novel in Japan and Quebec City. Published in French in 2002, it was translated into English by the award-winning anglophone translator Sheila Fischman in 2003. At its inception as a text, then, the book is already involved in multiple layers of cultural difference, translation, and transformation. Paramount among these, perhaps, is the issue of national and linguistic identity. The threat posed by Canada's anglophones to francophone Quebecers is much discussed and well documented, and at the same time, many if not most Canadian and Québécois writers are concerned about American cultural power. By providing an outsider's view of the 1929 economic bubble just before it burst, Soucy not only provides a trenchant cultural critique of the American Dream and American cultural values, but also forces his readers to engage with the ubiquitous American culture as an alien and sometimes hostile force, thereby also asking them to view their own cultural identity with new and alienated eyes, divorced from the context of ideologically normative American cultural production and representation.

The text invites the reader to engage with an unsolvable puzzle by refiguring the shape and history of its pieces to make a new and viable body of meaning. To do so, the reader must bring information from outside the text to bear on the making of meaning inside the text. Such a project can be usefully approached through Walter Benjamin's work. Benjamin draws strong connections among memory, allegory, and translation through the consideration of history and time. For the purposes of a theoretical approach to *Vaudeville!*, three elements of Benjamin's work seem particularly useful. The first is his sense of the use of time in "Theses on the Philosophy of History," in which he asserts that "a historical materialist approaches a historical subject only where he encounters it as a monad ... He takes cognizance of it in order to blast a specific era out of the homogeneous course of history" (254). He takes history to pieces in order to make sense of it through the disorienting encounter with the familiar as something made strange. This sense of violent dislocation from the narrative of progress is, Benjamin says, necessary in order to preserve a piece of the past and to elevate it for (re)consideration. Benjamin applies the same shock of alienation to time that Leahy's discussion of counter-worlding applies to cultural difference. Rather than experiencing a comfortable encounter with the flow of history, the reader of Soucy's novel is constantly reminded of the foreignness of time, place, and culture. Such encounters help us build and rebuild our sense of our own identity, as well as our understandings of others.

This allows us to consider with a critical eye the central place in the novel that the activity of demolition occupies. The monadic cultural setting is literally blasted to pieces as the Order of Demolishers for whom Xavier works blows up the city building by building. Moreover, the society itself becomes fragmented, as the tensions between classes and imposed group identities are exposed in the rubble following each blast.

Soucy's novel seizes on the people and experiences demolished in the race for progress, examining the ruined alternatives to the narrative of capital-"H" history. Xavier's job as a "Demolisher" necessarily brings him into close contact with the people referred to in the book as "The Demolished" and with the detritus of objects rescued and carried by them. In "a vacant lot where a community of demolished had gathered," he encounters "families grouped into clans, and clans into gangs … [H]ad it not been for his work duds, the apprentice would have joined them. Even if it meant lying, even if it meant saying that, like them, he'd been demolished" (77). "The Demolished" here have themselves been blasted out of history, and forced literally to make way for progress. The book picks up the ruined vestiges of their blasted lives to reassess the fairy tale of New York as the immigrant's Promised Land.

The book's sensitivity to such a situation is one of its finest points. "The Demolished" never refer to themselves by this name, and in fact they are only to be seen as such from the perspective of the powers that drive progress and development in the city, and of the people who grow rich from their destruction, such as the shadowy Order of Demolishers. Xavier, although an apprentice of the Order of Demolishers, is also an outcast from them, as his name, Xavier ("new house") suggests. As a poor immigrant himself, he has far more in common with the refugees from progress than with those who tear down their houses, but he is denied acceptance in both groups. Wandering at night through a demolition site, he sees "The Demolished" camped in the ruins of their former tenements, "busy at the tasks of the poor—mending, tightening, joining, stitching; and all around were the sick and the sickly lying on hard luck beds" (33). A persistent theme of the novel is the real lives of those trampled in the rush of progress, and Xavier's condition of being doubly outcast—that is, from both the Demolished and the Demolishers—makes him a scapegoat and thereby endows him with the "weak messianic power" ("Theses" 246) that Benjamin attributes to every generation as a potential to redeem history. Moreover, as the book progresses, Xavier's physical injuries and illness become increasingly pronounced; as we begin to suspect the truth about his parentage, he is himself being physically demolished, until, by the final scene, he is nothing more than an unnoticed piece of detritus in a pit beside the road. Within the world of the book, this end would appear to signal the total failure of Xavier's ability to redeem anything. Within the world of the reader, however, his pointless death produces empathy and identification with the victims of history.

The second Benjamin image I would like to introduce is the well-known description of Klee's *angelus novus* as the angel of history. "Where we perceive a chain of events," Benjamin writes, "he sees one single catastrophe which keeps piling wreckage upon wreckage and hurls it at his feet" ("Theses" 249). Caught in the storm of progress with his face to the past, he is propelled into the future, "while the pile of debris before him grows skyward. This storm is what we call progress" (249). Finally, it is useful to consider Benjamin's assertion in *The Origin of German Tragic Drama* that "in allegory the observer is confronted with the *facies hippocratica* of history as a petrified primordial landscape" (166). Taken together, these passages provide a cluster of images of ruin, from a theorist obsessed with ruins, and Soucy seems to have a similar fascination to that of Benjamin. What binds together these images from Benjamin is the dead, static nature of the past in each of them.

Soucy's book, although it is largely concerned with ruins and fragments of buildings and bodies, is never petrified. Rather, it deals in ruins and fragments that walk and talk—in the case of the main character, created from the ruins and fragments of corpses—and the demolished former tenement. Benjamin's historical materialist blasts the past into fragments to examine it; Soucy blasts it into fragments to reanimate it. The national minute of being happy in America not only alienates the reader, turning him or her into a displaced person within the world of the novel, but also simultaneously fragments and animates the ruins of the shattered narrative of the city. The book translates the experience of one of the most written about locations of the world through the eyes of a stranger. What animates these fragments, then, both in Benjamin's work and in Soucy's, is translation. Lawrence Venuti asserts that "the translator seeks to build a community with foreign cultures, to share an understanding with and of them" (469). As a general statement, this is reasonable; as a description of Soucy's novel, it seems somewhat opposed to the way in which the book actually works. Translation within the book animates the quotidian and overunderstood elements of American cultural production by reminding the reader of his/her foreignness and oddity. In the world outside the text, community is still being built, through the feeling of empathetic alienation that the book produces in the reader. In effect it resists a dominant cultural discourse by estranging it, and, in the process, localizing its pervasive claims to universality. It is, however, important to note the tone of the novel as well. While frequently bleak, it is not simply and unproblematically the United States that operates as an antagonist and destructive force. Rather, it is progress itself, depicted in New York, the twentieth-century capital of progress at the zenith of its power, teetering on the brink of a hubristic fall.

Literally "carrying across", translation is itself a form of migration between languages, places, and cultures. The oldest meaning of the word, "to bear, convey, or remove from one person, place, or condition to another" ("Translate"), refers to the act of moving a saint's bones from one diocese to another for reinternment, and thus bears directly on Xavier's situation as a transplanted and revivified collection of body parts. In this sense, Xavier, as a kind of holy fool, is translated across continents and cultures. As Benjamin argues in "The Task of the Translator," moreover, translation is also the source of an afterlife, providing for literature something similar to what he calls in "Theses on the Philosophy of History" "the weak messianic power of the present to redeem the past" (246). The protagonist, Xavier X. Mortanse, bears the promise of something beyond death in his very name. Rather than an attack on American culture, then, the book provides a reminder of the importance and irreplacability of the past, as well as its ability to shape the present and the future. At the beginning of the book, Xavier, eating lunch with the demolition crew, wonders "if it was indeed his sister—his sister whom he'd left behind, over there in his native land, and missed so much and wrote to every night—if it had been she who had embroidered the pretty pink and yellow sheep that adorned this napkin, or who" (8). As the reader later discovers, there is no sister, and his native land is one he has never seen. The longing that Xavier feels for his imagined homeland of Hungary is in effect the longing for a past that never was. Within the world of the novel, then, Xavier's past existence is not only a fiction, but one that repeatedly determines the course of his major decisions, while the emotions and suffering it causes lead ultimately to an unmarked and accidental grave.

Outside the world of the book, that translational movement of the text gives it a very different value. This is not to say that we as readers are intended to impose an extratextual Québécois identity on Xavier; indeed, the novel seems constantly to be fighting against the imposition of identities. From our position as readers outside the text, however, we *are*, I think, invited to understand that the American identity is not the same as the ideological product that Leahy calls "the USian imperial nexus ... of national, continental, and international policies and values" (63). Rather, the production history of the text, particularly for an anglophone readership, echoes Xavier's translated and endlessly modified biography, in that the cultural contexts of its production make it extremely difficult to assign to it a label of Québécois literature, Canadian literature, or even North American literature. Is a novel written in Japan a Japanese novel? Does an English translation by a well-known Canadian translator turn a Québécois novel into Canadian literature? The point of considering the textual history is, I think, not so much to answer these questions as to raise them, so that "we may better recognize and understand ourselves and what is worth keeping, modifying, and jettisoning of our own *américanité*" (Leahy 68). *Vaudeville!* does not provide suggestions on this front, but the shaking and mixing of cultural background and cultural confusion that it displays and produces within the narrative, like the mixing it suggests through its production history, provide a powerful incentive for us to ask and examine these questions in the context of our lives outside the world of the novel. Xavier's fragmented and ciphered body is a text, tattooed with cryptic statements by his maker. By the same token, Soucy's book is as a face, where men may read strange matters.

The puzzle of allegorical meaning in the book is ultimately unsolvable—that is, there is no final text or ultimate interpretation to which the reader can refer to make sense of the events in the book, nor is there a single historical political event to which it corresponds, in the sense that George Orwell's *Animal Farm* may be said to correspond allegorically to the events of the Russian Revolution. If the translation cannot exist without the original, then neither can the original exist as an "original" without the translation. A translation casts new light on an original work, allowing it to be read in different ways; likewise, the "original" text opens new possibilities for meaning in the translation. As Ian Fairley notes, "Every translated text may be activated as a newly translating text, 'taken across' in order to gloss its original. The original may also gloss the translation" (1040). By the same token, the reader here brings experience of the world outside the text to bear upon it in order to produce meaning within the text, and the text itself casts the reader's own life experience in a different light, allowing those experiences to be reinterpreted in a new way.

In terms of (multi)national identity, then, this reciprocity between the original and the translation opens new possibilities for self-examination, particularly in a readership from the Americas, as a way for "other peoples within the Americas [to] recognize and address our own *américanité* rather than reproducing the role of reactive colonial subjects in a reductive anti-imperial dyad" (Leahy 67). By reading Xavier's story within the novel through a lens of empathetic alienation, we as readers are alerted to the necessity of reconsidering the building blocks of our own identities. Rather than simply opposing USian cultural power, it asks us to consider the ways in which the exchange of ideas has both changed and been changed by geographical and cultural translation across the border; to attend to what is inside the nation *and* inside the self in a manner similar to that with which we attend to the question of what is inside or outside the text, and how that exchange moves back and forth.

Benjamin asserts that translation "serves the purpose of expressing a central reciprocal relationship" ("Task" 73). This is a useful metaphor with which to consider the empathetic act of reading generally, and especially in this sort of disorienting text. "This representation of hidden life," as Benjamin puts it, "in its analogics and symbols, can draw on other ways of suggesting meaning than intensive—that is anticipative, imitating—realization" (73). Hidden lives are the crux of Soucy's work; lives hidden from official histories, but also lives hidden from society, and from oneself. The novel's form, in alienating the reader from the narrative, simultaneously alienates the reader from the narrative of his or her own life, and it does so in a way that provides critical distance, calls for re-examination, and enables a re-consideration of meaning.

Discussing Dionne Brand's *No Language Is Neutral*, Leahy argues that "a narrative of embedded economic and psychic violence ... can also be understood as counter-worlding *Alaméricanité*—after all, America is the birthplace of skyscraper culture—and as perhaps even mocking Canadians' sense of themselves ... as essentially different from USians" (70). The setting of Soucy's novel, at once foreign and familiar to an anglophone North American audience, even if they have never been to New York, creates a tension that requires self-examination in order to understand (though not resolve) it. The translational aspects of *Vaudeville!* thus move back and forth between cultural contexts.

They do so in part by exposing the underpinning of cultural violence that is endemic far beyond the borders of New York, or indeed the New World. The endless of work of destroying and rebuilding is not confined to New York, and the ideological normalization of capitalism often masks the suffering of the people everywhere whose lives are being demolished by the storm of progress. Soucy's novel about the silenced victims of the race for the new is thus an invitation to examine events much closer to home. As Xavier reveals, "Had it not been for his work duds, the apprentice [Xavier] would have joined them. Even if it meant lying, even if it meant saying that, like them, he'd been demolished ... Xavier felt a pang" (77–78).

The representation of the city in the world of this book is clearly not imitative in any realist sense. What it performs, rather, is an extended metaphorical representation of a state of mind. If "the task of the translator consists in finding that intended effect upon the language into which he is translating which produces in it the echo of the original" (77), then in this wider sense of translation as reading, the text produces an effect on the reader that is an echo of the character—"a reverberation of the work in the alien one" (77). That reverberation sets the reader up in an analogous role to that of Xavier, who both translates the culture and the city in which he finds himself, and is himself translated. The reader is thus asked to reverberate in a particular empathetic way, to feel a pang of sympathy as Xavier does, to come to the book as a kind of alien or immigrant without the necessary social and cultural skills and understanding to make sense of it. Specifically, the book robs the reader of the power and comfort of being addressed, instead requiring him or her to reverberate to an alien frequency, and by implication, to consider the processes of transmission and affinity that enable it.

The book's allegorical narrative structure draws the reader into participating in the puzzle of American culture that Xavier attempts unsuccessfully to solve; it also involves the reader in his acts of cultural translation. The frequent references to the Statue of Liberty as "the woman holding aloft her ice cream cone" or "painting her ceiling while clutching a phone book" (72) require the reader to reinterpret his or her own cultural understanding of the context. In this way, the reader is carried across, immigrating to the new and alien world of the text, and metaphorically seeing New York for the first time.

This emigration is, like all emigration, not without discomforts, and it looks back as well as forward. If translation rescues the past by providing it with what Benjamin refers to as an afterlife, it is in the form of conversation between the past and the present. In *Vaudeville!* that conversation is staged geographically through the space of the city and the locations of identity. As old tenements, theatres, and warehouses are demolished to make way for progress, the smooth, linear movement of time is disrupted and torn by intrusions from the past as the demolished protest and excavations for new buildings bring older layers of the city to light. If Xavier's identity is analogous to that of the city in his fragmentary construction, then the city shares his emotional attachment to a dim and misremembered past recovered partially, archeologically, accidentally.

In this alienated translation of the city, even the Statue of Liberty is torn from its cultural pedestal as the quintessential symbol of American freedom and opportunity, and looks back to her home in the Old World, turning her back on the city. As Xavier looks at her "proud and haughty against the horizon" (375) he imagines an alternative world in which "a good life" would bring a sense of compassion and mutual assistance. In a direct reversal of the statue's symbolic meaning, he dreams of "[w]hat the statue would do if she had the slightest bit of justice in her head, instead of painting her ceiling" (374). Rather than standing aloof and isolated, she walks among the poor of the city, panicking the rich and bearing the poor upon her shoulders across the sea to the Old World, where "she would set them down, each and every one, with infinite delicacy in the countries of their birth ... [H]e gazed at the statue of Liberty. She hadn't budged. She still had her indifferent back to the city and its torments" (376).

This longing for an imaginary homeland goes to the heart of issues of identity and understanding in *Vaudeville!* Against the reality of a bewildering exile, the Statue of Liberty becomes an invitation, not to the poor of the Old World, but to the poor of the city on which the statue herself turns her back. It is also an invitation to the reader, and an invitation to liberty in the act of reading. By reversing the signification of the Statue of Liberty, Soucy offers his readers a chance to reverse the normal paths of their own meaning making and to reconstruct the significance of the world outside the book as a new kind of hope, one that is not inscribed with the official discourse of power and history.

In this reimagining of the statue's meaning, her symbolism becomes less a commanding call ("give me your tired, your poor") and more of a dialogue, the subject of which is the forgotten and downtrodden classes of both the Old World and the New, those who, particularly in the historical conception of the Jazz Age, have been written out of history, but whose ranks, in the time of the book, will shortly be swollen by the stock market crash of October 1929. By rewriting the statue's symbolic value, Soucy requires the reader to pay attention to unnoticed and unwritten elements of the historical record and the cold indifference (visually expressed by the Statue of Liberty) with which those realities are ignored and excluded. Cultural translation in this sense casts new light on old narratives and brings to new life the static and settled narrative of the past, while producing a call to change the present. In Soucy's novel, the Statue of Liberty's rewritten relationship to the Old World is a temporal as well as a geographical one; it calls the past to the service of the present and voices a constant desire to revisit the Old World, which the book imbues with the promise of newness. The need to bring the past into the service of the present is a necessary element of self-definition, especially in the disorienting circumstances of the book, for both the protagonist and the reader. Instead of a single trip to the past that settles the matter of identity, however, Soucy acknowledges the impossibility of ever laying meaning to rest.

Forgoing the pleasurable security of a single rewritten history, *Vaudeville!*, like its Frankenstein's monster of a protagonist, produces from its urban surroundings a functional, provisional sense of identity based on eclectic misreadings of multiple places and times. From the vantage point of the present, the city, too, looks back at what Benjamin describes as fragments blasted out of the continuum of history—history brushed against the grain ("Theses" 248). Xavier's immigrant experience, like the experience of the book for the reader, is an attempt to make sense of a present through fragments of a dismembered past in which both time and space are ruptured, in order to reorganize and reassess the smooth flow of historical narrative and the idea of personal identity that is imposed on it and by it.

After another of his numerous beatings, Xavier recalls the first day he became self-aware, in America, sitting on a block near the harbour and gazing at the Statue of Liberty "offering an ice cream cone to someone on the floor above" (72). Xavier's sense of identity is provisional and fluid, produced through his interactions with others and his own sense of strangeness, as he slides into self-awareness "as a body and mind all in one, sitting here, with no memory whatsoever … as if he had been born, conceived, and created all at once, like an angel" (72). As he looks around he sees a confused-looking young man who turns out to be "only his reflection in the big window of a warehouse.

Xavier stood for a long time facing his own image, of which he had no memory either" (72). Likewise, the experience of reading the book, with the reader's connection to Xavier, becomes a kind of confrontation with an unrecognized reflection, forcing him or her to confront an unfamiliar self-image. If Xavier mistakenly thinks himself to be a Hungarian immigrant discovering his own image for the first time and unable to piece together his past, the reader, in his or her empathetic connection with Xavier, is forced to do the same thing. The extratextual element of identity creation, in leaving the reader stranded and alienated through the text, makes him or her re-evaluate from the beginning issues of national identity and ideological development that might otherwise seem natural and unquestioned. The New York City of the book is a foreign city, not just to the protagonist and the other recent immigrants who populate the book, but to the reader as well, and in a way that involves a larger reconsideration of popular cultural values. Many readers will have an image of 1920s New York drawn largely from books such as Fitzgerald's *The Great Gatsby*, in which the rich and elegant float through an idealized world of parties and bootlegged liquor. Such a smooth existence is a far cry from the squalls in which Soucy's characters find themselves adrift. While many of the images of the city have entered North American consciousness, others produce a cultural carnival in which the viewer becomes as disoriented as Soucy's characters.

The identity of both the city and the protagonist are performative acts, improvisations that consistently go off the intended track. Xavier's vaudeville act, in which he displays his singing frog, is a shambles, as the frog refuses to sing when anyone is watching. The city, likewise, is literally a shambles, a tenement labyrinth torn down and remade consistently throughout the book, reinventing itself in relation to other cities and other cultures. This constant remaking of character and setting is likewise carried over to the readers, forcing them to rethink the ways in which they relate to the text, and requiring them to re-evaluate their own expectations and demands. In effect, it produces a continuing responsibility based on various forms of translational dialogue.

If the book opens with a beating and a fall, the story begins an act of retrieval, as Xavier finds the wooden box containing his singing frog. If, as Benjamin suggests, "every image of the past that is not recognised by the present as one of its own concerns threatens to disappear irretrievably" ("Theses" 247), then the book, in a wider sense, is also an act of retrieval, rescuing the past though an act of empathetic translation that works on the basis of a disconcerting dialogue, questioning expectations and constantly remaking its participants in the process. In a similar manner, the textual identity invites a re-evaluation of history and identity across real and imagined borders and communities. In the alienation of the landscape of New York and the misremembering of a fictional past, the book seems inclined to leave us stranded in a new and disconcerting world of identity that, while it may not end well, provides us with a possibility of freedom and exploration in which the symbols of national belonging can be reimagined into new narratives of hope, empathy and self-awareness across and within the space of multiple imagined backgrounds and identities. Rather than considering the book as Québécois literature, or a novel of New York, or an allegory of simple political identity, the book reflects Xavier's ideas when, at the end of the story, he comes to the realization that, "as it happens, I'm a little community all on my own" (428). The vagaries of origin and identity do not stop Xavier from attempting to climb out of the pit in which he both begins and ends the book, and they point the way toward a possibility of self-made identity through which the outsider, the alien, the composite, piecemeal man from nowhere is the most sympathetic possibility for personhood.

Works Cited

Benjamin, Walter. *The Origin of German Tragic Drama.* Trans. John Osborne. London: Verso, 1977.

———. "The Task of the Translator." *Illuminations.* Trans. Harry Zohn. Ed. Hannah Arendt. London: Fontana, 1992. 70–82.

———. "Theses on the Philosophy of History." *Illuminations.* Trans. Harry Zohn. Ed. Hannah Arendt. London: Fontana, 1992. 245–55.

Fairley, Ian. "Parallel Texts." *Encyclopedia of Literary Translation into English.* Vol. 2, M–Z. Ed. Olive Classe. London: Fitzroy Dearborn, 2000. 1040.

Hunter, Lynette. *Modern Allegory and Fantasy: Rhetorical Stances in Contemporary Writing.* London: Macmillan, 1989.

Leahy, David. "Counter-Worlding A/américanité." *Canada and Its Americas.* Ed. Winfried Siemerling and Sarah Phillips Casteel. Montreal and Kingston: McGill–Queens UP, 2010. 62–84.

Moncour, Michael. *Quotationspage.* http://www.quotationspage.com/quote/26965.html. Accessed 2 August 2010.

Soucy, Gaétan. *Vaudeville!* Trans. Sheila Fischman. Toronto: House of Anansi, 2002.

"Translate." *Oxford English Dictionary Online.* 2nd ed. 1989.

Venuti, Lawrence. "Translation, Community, Utopia." *The Translation Studies Reader.* Ed. Lawrence Venuti. London: Routledge, 2000. 468–88.

seventeen

Bodies of Information
Cross-Border Poetics in the Twenty-First Century

Nasser Hussain

IN THE FIRST CHAPTER OF *The Writing of America*, Geoff Ward isolates the term "outwith," as distinct from "outside": for Ward, "outwith" (a Scottish term) avoids the binarism of the English word "outside" and "can point in a more mobile way to a position that can still include *proximity* and *inclusion*" along the English/Scottish borderlands (11, my emphasis). Ward immediately expands his sense of proximity and inclusion to encompass the entire globe (or at least the "our" in "our relationship" with America, writing as he was from the UK in 2002). I do not mean to challenge Ward's position that "we" are "all" to some degree subjects of and to the great shibboleth that is American cultural imperialism, but before we skip too quickly to the global stage, and risk homogenizing reactions to American cultural imperialism (which in itself betrays the degree to which that hegemony has proven successful), I'd like to take this space and time to consider the Canadian example—other than Mexico's, our "outwithness" in relation to America must be paradigmatic.

In terms of cross-border transactions in the context of a book such as this, Canadian "outwithness" (at least in poetic terms) must inevitably invoke the events in Vancouver in 1961 when Robert Duncan's lectures catalyzed a gathering of Canadian poets whose careers would dominate the last half of the century's poetic production in Canada. It would be easy, too easy, to draw national boundaries around the event, and accuse George Bowering, Daphne Marlatt, et al., of "selling out," of adopting a too-American attitude, of being (heaven forfend) un-Canadian. But this does the intelligence of the Tish group a disservice. It is closer to the truth to say that the Canadian poets simply listened, understood, applied, and adapted Projectivist tendencies to their own work. Charles Olson would be the first to applaud a work like *Steveston*, as it links poet to place as fundamentally as *The Maximus Poems* weld Olson to Gloucester, or William Carlos Williams to Paterson.

The Black Mountain/Projectivist/Olsonic emphasis on place and its definition has deeply influenced a number of contemporary practitioners. No less a poet than Ron Silliman has said that at a formative stage in his career, he was "completely under the spell of the Projectivists" (Gregory and McCaffery 255), and out of this clear influence, he has gone on to produce work that Charles Bernstein describes as having "visible borders: a poetry of shape" (39). For a poet so concerned with diminishing referentiality, Silliman's sense of geographic/political borders is clear: he divides his anthology of Langpo into EAST and WEST rather starkly (and there is no question to which nation these orientations apply). But in case we missed the point, Silliman takes great pains to note in the introduction to the anthology that this is an "America-only" volume. While he does not necessarily discount the international writers working in modes sympathetic to or even constitutive of Language poetry (like Steve McCaffery), he does not include them, either (*American Tree* xx). Further boundaries and limits wind their way into Silliman's oeuvre: the Fibonacci-inspired form of poems like "Ketjak"; the geographically bound "BART" (a transcription of all the public language on the SF Bay Area Rapid Transit system); the rule-governed "Skies" (in which he must look up once a day for a month); the simple formal restrictions of "Sunset Debris" (composed only of questions) or "Demo" (in which each line is precisely one sentence long). While these experiments do not belong in quite the same category as Oulipean or Conceptual writing (their formal restrictions are not quite rigid enough; neither do they make a spectacle of the labour expended in producing the work), they certainly do accrete into a "poetry of boundaries." These poems insist on some form of data processing even though a selective principle is always at play, and it is this sense of visible formal boundaries and their violation that drives much of Silliman's work—and we might say the same of Langpo more generally.

Langpo was a photocopied, saddle-stapled affair from 1978, and its attention to the materiality of the word was served by the relative freedom in typesetting available when working with manual technology. Larry Eigner's opening salvo in the first issue, published in February 1978 under the title "Approaching Things," has not lost force in the intervening thirty years, but quite apart from its content, I mean to point to the attention to linearity and its simultaneous subversion in the title to this piece. The title's layout breaks the expected code of rectilinearity and left-to-rightness in a properly Projectivist manner, but the rest of the article hews to the norms of print (Eigner n.p.). Reprinting it in *The L=A=N=G=U=A=G=E Book*, the editors have carefully retained something of Eigner's idiosyncratic typography, and in this moment, we can see the limits that technology imposed on even the most imaginative Language practitioners (Eigner 3). What is important to note here is that even as Langpo announces itself as a radical innovation, it simultaneously inscribes itself into a tradition (that of Zukofsky, Stein, Joyce, and Williams, as opposed to Pound and Eliot) and is bound into the normativity imposed by the materiality of print culture. Such a bifurcated mode of writing as this is not exactly sustainable—at least not until online/new media poetry and poetics emerge.

The Americans-only restriction of *In the American Tree* is relaxed somewhat in *The L=A=N=G=U=A=G=E Book*, and important contributions from Canadian poets Christopher Dewdney and Steve McCaffery are included in this foundational book. McCaffery is an especially prescient example of the restrictions imposed by the technology of writing. Referring to his collaborations with Canadian concrete poet bpNichol under the guise of the Toronto Research Group (TRG), McCaffery writes:

> An obvious side effect of the current regime of personal computers has been a quantum leap in material nostalgia. The handwritten manuscript, the hand-corrected typewritten page, the patchwork paste-up, clipped with scissors and scotch-taped together, are now the valued by-products of an obsolete mode of production, superseded by a method of writing whose new locus is a hyperspace. It is important to remember that TRG was, through its entire history, a non-computer phenomenon whose method of collaboration here outlined would have been radically different with the computer technology available to the individual today. (16)

McCaffery wrote this in 1991, at a time when even the most powerful home computer would have been outperformed by the cheapest PC on the market today. In fact, the very computer he wrote with in 1991 would be subject today to the "material nostalgia" he ascribes to the handwritten manuscript, so quickly and regularly do we make our quantum leaps today.

Darren Wershler-Henry takes McCaffery/Nichol's cutting and pasting to heart: in 1997, in *Nicholodeon: a book of lowerglyphs*, equipped with exactly the kind of personal computer that the TRG lacked, he reconstructed and extended much of the TRG's work.[1] In this book, Wershler-Henry emerges as an inheritor of two traditions: the concrete (via bpNichol), and the theory-driven, non-referential, and oppositional poetics of the Language group (via McCaffery, towing in his wake Stein, Joyce, and Williams along with the freshly translated post-structuralism from late-1970s and early-1980s France). At the same time, Christian Bök was composing his monumental lipogram, *Eunoia*. In "How to Write Eunoia," Bök refers to a moment on his way home from the 1995 "Symphosophia" at Yale (a conference on visual concrete poetry and the contemporary avant-garde) in which he dismissively thinks, "Pfft, I can do this" upon reading Georges Perec's *La Disparition*. The result, *Eunoia*, took up the next seven years of his life. During this time, he also worked toward a doctoral dissertation on Alfred Jarry at York University in Toronto, laboured sixty hours a week at a "retail monopoly disguised as a bookstore" (Bök, *How to* n.p.), and made a name for himself as a sound poet, especially for his compressed, high-speed renditions of Kurt Schwitters's *Ursonate*, entirely from memory. Alongside his first book, *Crystallography* (a book that conflates geological and poetic discourses), Bök clearly represents a tradition of the avant-garde that includes the Oulipo and twentieth-century sound poetry from Schwitters to Canada's own Four Horsemen (which includes McCaffery and bpNichol as core members), with a finger in the Surrealist work that Jarry spawned.

In 1999, Bök and Wershler-Henry travelled to Buffalo to hear Kenneth Goldsmith read his work. A trained sculptor, Goldsmith had turned his attention to language art in the 1990s, and applied the lessons of plastic, sculptural, and visual avant-gardes to language, to the point where he could argue in 2011 that the language arts lag behind other forms of expression. He writes in the introductory essay to his (and Dworkin's) anthology *Against Expression*:

> Nearly a century ago, the art world put to rest conventional notions of originality and replication with the gestures of Marcel Duchamp. Since then, a parade of blue-chip artists from Andy Warhol to Jeff Koons have taken Duchamp's ideas to new levels, which have become part and parcel of the mainstream art world discourse. Similarly, in music, sampling—entire tracks constructed from other tracks—has become commonplace. From Napster to gaming, from karaoke to BitTorrent files, the culture appears to be embracing the digital and all the complexity it entails—with the exception of writing. (*Against* xx)

It might seem strange that Bök, Wershler-Henry, and Goldsmith all found themselves at a dead end in their respective fields—surely, concretism, sound poetry, and extreme formal restriction haven't fallen by the wayside already? In a 2009 interview, Goldsmith refers to the meeting of these three poets:

> It began in 1999 in Buffalo after I gave a reading there and Christian Bök and Darren Wershler drove down from Toronto to see me read. They were Canadian pataphysicists who were involved with concrete and sound poetry, while I was coming out of a text art tradition, but we all saw our respective paths as dead ends. So, we blended these obsessions to come up with a new way of writing just as the Internet was emerging. These strategies as applied to the digital writing environment made sense to us and continue to even more a decade later as the web has evolved. (Sanders Interview n.p.)

At the dead end, wherever the road stops, we find ourselves in a deterritorialized place. Suddenly, the mode of transport that carried us up to this point isn't going to work anymore. At precisely this point, we need to hack a new path through the undergrowth, and like our pioneer ancestors, domesticate the open spaces, transform them into *place*. Whitman may have broken new wood, and Pound may have carved it, but in these days we need to think about clear-cuts, resource management, and planting new forests (see Pound). This is the task of the twenty-first-century poet: to recover the wilderness, to reintroduce some of that Olsonic SPACE back into our overly domesticated places.[2] Buffalo, N.Y.: a short drive across the border from Toronto and the home of the buffalo wing, now has a place in literary history as the birthplace of Conceptual poetry—an exciting forum for writing in new media and formats where formal, bodily, and social boundaries begin to break down and re-form into new practices and identities and a refreshed, global sense of citizenship.

Formal Boundaries

Kenneth Goldsmith is joyfully frustrated by Darren Wershler-Henry's poem *The Tapeworm Foundry*: "Everytime we think we've thought of a new form of writing, Darren's thought of it already" (Perloff interview). *The Tapeworm Foundry* is a single run-on sentence that loops back on itself in an homage to Joyce's *Finnegans Wake*. The text on the last page—

> andor write a book of portmanteaus about an embalmed Irishman in which the last sentence ending in midphrase loops back to link up with the first sentence beginning in midphrase so that the book completes a cycle with itself restarting with the words riverrun past eve and adams but leaving in their wake all the fragments of a language yet to be combined like so much flotsam and (*Tapeworm* 50)

—seamlessly links up with the poem's opening: "or jetsam in the laminar flow" (1). Wershler-Henry's tongue-in-cheek summation of the major features of Joyce's masterpiece obviously leaves out more than it includes, but his sense that *Finnegans Wake* alerts its readers to the recombinant potential implicit in "the fragments of a language" left to us after putting down Joyce's book is crucial to the project of *The Tapeworm Foundry*, and to Conceptual poetics in the main.

Here, I want to draw attention to Craig Dworkin's sense of the *interval* as he applies it in Kenneth Goldsmith's oeuvre, and consider it in relation to Wershler-Henry's work. In "Zero Kerning," Dworkin recalibrates our attitude to Goldsmith's output, which is too often dismissed as unreadable (an implication that Goldsmith has made himself at times), and carefully plots a chart through Goldsmith's work. Dworkin's key is the interval: he writes that "to read Goldsmith's *oeuvre*, at a certain remove, reveals a consistent concern with spacing—with the collapse of distances into equal measures, and the differences and repetitions subsequently legible within regimes of periodic regulation" (10). This concern with spacing, especially the collapse of space (and the attendant collapse of discrete boundaries), is vital to reading *The Tapeworm Foundry*.

The structure of *The Tapeworm Foundry* is, as I've noted, a loop. It leaves little room for rest, constantly streaming from one suggestion to the next and in so doing creating a seamless whole; we could even go so far as to say that it has no formal boundaries. Certainly, its form works against efficient excerpting—any identifiable point in the poem slides into the next without pause. There are no spaces into which we can force a critical wedge, no divisions. And predictably, this radical form extends into the content. While much has been made of Wershler-Henry's out-fluxing Fluxus with his catalogue of activities for the reader (one gathering in the United States took the step of concretizing some of the piece's suggestions), little has been made of the closing of space he makes between the author and the writing prosthesis.

bpNichol's concrete poem "The Complete Works" eloquently summarizes the poetic potential of the most immediate writerly prosthesis. In this concrete poem, Nichol reproduces the layout of a QWERTY keyboard. Interestingly (though perhaps limited by his technology), he does so with a "Courier" type font, instead of reproducing the typically sans-serif lettering on the actual keyboard itself (bpNichol 39). Over and above the "content," the disjunction between the font and the physical keyboard Nichol is typing on represents a subtle indication that the poet is in the moment of typing the poem out—and, if this is the case, then we are witnessing the precise moment at which the border of the body is extended to include the writing prosthesis itself. Here, we can see an execution of Ward's "outwithness" in a concrete form. The object-typewriter isn't "outside" the writer; rather, its "proximity" to the act of composition practically demands "inclusion," this time, as an extension of the writer, co-extensive with him/her. The permutations of the typewriter keyboard are obviously near-infinite, but if possible, the twenty-first-century keyboard, with all of its added functionality (a virtue of being coupled to the computer) might be said to surpass the limits of the manual typewriter, however distant that limit may be. The difference between these interfaces marks out the difference between bpNichol and Darren Wershler-Henry: where Nichol leaves the poetic possibilities of the keyboard latent, Wershler-Henry has it within his grasp, armed with the latest technology, to make a gesture toward manifesting all of them.

The keyboard makes frequent appearances in *The Tapeworm Foundry*. Wershler-Henry suggests that we "litter a keyboard with milletseed so that exotic songbirds might tap out their odes to a nightingale" (*Tapeworm* 1). You could also "remove random keys from your typewriter before you begin to write and then forget which ones have been removed" (5). But the activity of writing is not limited to tapping on a keyboard, or even using a pen. In the world imagined by Wershler-Henry, practically anything imaginable serves as a tool for inscription, by/through which the intentional and egocentric human writer might endlessly and playfully combine and recombine the "fragments of language" for him/herself. For instance, we might carve letters and words "in intaglio onto the surface of a tenpin bowling ball and then throw it down the lane all the while running behind in order to read the text imprinted onto the floor awarding yourself extra points for a strike a spare or coherent sentence" (9). We might also "stuff a copy of the unabridged OED into the hopper of a woodchipper and then read from the resultant spew through a megaphone" (21). We could "hotwire a truck for painting the lines on roads so that you can write in loopy calligraphy on the toll roads of the nation such phrases as god said to abraham kill me a son" (19). Wershler-Henry imagines poetry composed by putting individual words on the bumpers of cars in a parking lot and letting them drive away; "texts resembling the later visual poems of robert grenier" could be accomplished with a pen held not in the hand, but in the anus; or in true Toronto Research Group style, we can "spell it on the floor in alphabits and then pour milk on it and then read it by rolling your body across the text" (30–31).

The volatility of these hypothetical modes of composition lies less in the text that might be produced than in the activity itself: a radical renunciation of the traditional writing process that imagines a seamless transition of an internal and subjective "experience" from mind to hand and from there to paper. Wershler-Henry's prosthesis of choice is the personal computer. The drastic interventions he proposes for writing all share, to some degree, the imposition of a machine between the writer and the writing: bowling balls, washing machines, wood chippers, and those trucks that clog the Ambassador Bridge that connects Windsor, Ontario, to Detroit, Michigan, all stand as replacements for the Underwood, or the pen. Early in *The Tapeworm Foundry*, we are given a hint of what is to come:

> andor use a dotmatrix printer to sound out a poem in which each line is a series of pauses whose length is determined by formatting codes and then record the squeal and lurch of the printhead moving across the paper and then replay the noise and then have it transcribed as chamber music for cello or voice (1)

Along a similar line, Janet Murray recalls a similar experience as a software designer for IBM in the 1980s, when the engineers put the giant, cumbersome, and primitive machine to a more "inspired" use:

> One day the icy, clamorous cardprinter room was turned into a whimsical cabaret: a clever young hacker had created a set of punch cards that worked like a player piano roll and caused the card reader to chug out a recognizable version of the Marine Corps Hymn: bam-bam THUMP bam-THUMP bam-THUMP THUMP-THUMP. All day long programmers sneaked away from their work to hear this thunderously awful but mesmerizing concert. The data it was processing was of course meaningless, but the song was a work of true virtuosity. (3)

Twenty years separate Murray's encounter with the singing machine at IBM and Wershler-Henry's experiment, but they share important points. Again, the "value" of the song is not precisely in the tonal quality of the performance, but rather in the possibility for the machine to do it *at all*. In Language poetry, the same applies—we are meant to focus as much (if not more) on the *operation* of the poem, bearing witness to its constructedness in language, as we are on its semantic content. The pragmatic, data-processing function of the machine is subordinated: the machine is now an instrument in a much larger orchestra.

The Tapeworm Foundry behaves in a similar manner, but with a more intimate and collaborative edge. When the poet stops composing and silences himself, the music of the machine—that white noise and hum of the personal computer running parallel to the act of composing poetry in the twentieth century—comes to the forefront. As the poem progresses, we encounter an extended passage that is announced by the possibility that Wershler-Henry might "have [had his] computer make it recombinant for a while" (*Tapeworm* 28). The lines immediately following this announcement bear consideration:

> andor have your computer make it recombinant for a while andor drop a
> player instead of running around a bus depot and then touch a detailed
> concordance of the dictionary in the same way you get gertrude stein
> to declare it good andor write a series of theories about their legs rather
> than the tarot at the beginning of long sheets in alexandria and then
> build a statement about a book of lines for a victim in a long run of the
> dead andor use the letter tiles from the house of keats in every copy of
> the accidents that you make famous andor construct real poems in silky
> pants and then stuff a statement about the streets into a book that really
> knows what people want to say about two trains and or replace them
> photographically and then rewrite don quixote with any three initials
> for apollinaire andor (28)

This highly disorienting word salad continues until page 31, when the poem suddenly announces that it will "stop being recombinant for a while." We immediately move *back* into the pun-laden and recognizably human mode of composition that marked the first twenty-seven pages, when the poem declares,

> andor stop being recombinant for a while andor drive over the pages of
> it in your parking lot before you bind them andor record a drum n bass
> version of an opera by Emmett Williams andor make it nude (31)

These three pages (between 27 and 31) are precisely the moment at which the human author hands his/her compositional duties over to the machine, and the results are astonishing. Christian Bök describes these lines as the kind of "falderal written by the mechanism," which "invariably outclasses dog-gerel written by the rhymster" ("Piecemeal" n.p.). Wershler-Henry's computer demonstrates perfect spelling and is composing grammatically and poetically perfect "sentences" (given the conjunctive structure of the *Tapeworm*). Or again as Bök writes, the computer is "syntactically loyal but semantically opaque" (Piecemeal n.p.).

That we can distinguish between the human and the inhuman portions of the poem is not a failure (even though Turing might say otherwise); rather, the success of *The Tapeworm Foundry* lies in the collaboration and coupling of man and machine in the production of a poem. Perhaps the distinguishing characteristic of the poem is the curious conjunction "andor," a melding of the paratactic and the binary, which, in its simultaneity presents neither option as preferential. The reader can always choose between considering a gestalt reading of the work, skimming along its surface, *and/or* descending into any single scenario between the copulas, "eloping along" any one of the "bottomless discourses" that the poem suggests (1). By eliminating the slash mark between the two conjunctions—that last vestige of the space "between," or Dworkin's "interval"—the "andor," meaningless in itself, metamorphoses into an interstitial sub-machine, the coupling agent without which the poem cannot operate, andor signals the same necessity for the reader in the world. Without the interval, space, or slash, borders are bypassed rather than crossed.

Bodily Boundaries

If *The Tapeworm Foundry* signals a closing of spaces between discrete objects in the phenomenological field (especially if an inanimate computer can lend a "hand," so to speak, in composing a poem), then we may be coming to a point at which the term "prosthetic" is insufficient, especially if it is taken to imply that the machine is in the *service* of the human poet. Conceiving our relationship with our prosthetics as a collaboration (in which our extensions and our selves work in a looping, "feedback" relationship) allows us to embrace and enfold one another, giving equal credit to the meat and the machine as it appears in both sides of the partnership. Where Bök differs from Wershler-Henry is in his attempt to mimic the sonic value of the "white noise" of technology with his all-too-human laryngeal and labial apparatus, rather than enlisting the machine itself to write (or perform) the poem. In this sense, Bök enfolds the machine, and tries to speak to it in a language it might understand rather than programming the machine to try and communicate to a human audience.

Of course, there is no available method that would determine whether these imagined androids will find "meaning" in Bök's poem, but *The Cyborg Opera* is a noteworthy gesture in their direction. As of this writing, only snatches of the overall work have surfaced in performance—generally as a kind of encore after a reading from *Eunoia*. The "rough takes" that have been recorded are "Motorized Razors," "Mushroom Clouds," and "Synth Loops." Conceived of as a kind of exercise in "one-upmanship" with regard to the *Ursonate*, *The Cyborg Opera* refines and focuses Dadaist sound poetry techniques into a more rigorous and semantically relevant/comprehensible form, although they are no less playful. Where Schwitters offers a score for a human voice unfettered by the constraints of referentiality (a document that only holds force for the performer), Bök's sound poems torque referential language and seek out the sonic play that can be accessed in "normal discourse."

Work like Kurt Schwitters' *Ursonate* and Hugo Ball's *Karawane* are precisely the models that inspired the Toronto Research Group and the Four Horsemen in Canada, and that have been passed down, transmitted, and reconstructed by other artists in a relatively undiluted fashion from Dada into the late twentieth century. This is the art that allowed Bök's predecessors in sound poetry to conceive of their work "within a primitive, if not infantile, humanism, one which supposedly returns the performer to a much more 'integrated' experience of the self" (Betts interview 60). What I notice in Bök's reduction of the formulaic sound poetry experience is a simple truth: while sound poetry enacts what may well be an integrated experience for the performer, the audience is always at a remove from that experience. There is no common ground, no medium between the work and the spectator. We are enlisted merely to watch the sound poet undergo his/her "integration," not to participate in it or make our own connections with the work as it unfolds. Sound poetry of this utterly non-referential type might be understood as a self-involved excuse for exhibitionism (as the performer serves up his/her "libidinal outbursts") coupled with a sanctioned voyeurism on our part.

However, Bök's sound poems treat the matter more democratically. Rather than reaching out for some unimaginable and unrecoverable primitive experience, he looks to his immediate context for his source material. "Mushroom Clouds," for instance, is a sound poem "inspired by the acoustic ambience of Super Mario Bros. by Nintendo," and in this piece, Bök chooses "silly words from the popular culture of globalized capitalism, doing so in order to suggest that … life itself has taken on the cartoonish atmosphere of our pinball arcades" (Betts interview 59). To Bök, the arcade we live in sounds something like the following excerpt from "Mushroom Clouds":[3]

```
yo-yo Tokyo peyote

okay
opium Pinocchio

go-go dance akimbo

baby
bebop obliggato
```

pop a pill to play
Day-Glo pinball

   pogo-jump
a ping-pong
   ball

   judo-kick
a ding-dong
   bell

lob a bomb to bomb
Pop-Art gewgaws

Ubu buys Enola Gay

pygmy lollapalooza

zoo
kazoo bazooka

big
igloo palooka

kooky gobbledygook

eureka kabuki

yucky
blue buckaroo

kinky
pink pachinko

cuckoo kaboom

```
bikini kahuna

burka
play peekaboo

karma
boom babushka

voodoo vavoom
```

In his performance (captured at the "Segue Reading at Double Happiness," 19 May 2001), when Bök swings into the "eureka kabuki" lines of the poem, there is an audible twitter of laughter from the audience—they are clearly tickled by the piece. This laughter is apparently not an uncommon occurrence at a Bök performance: Betts noticed the same thing happening at a performance of the poem at a café in Toronto, and asked the poet to speak to the source of the humour in the poem. On this point, Bök speculates that the laughter is primarily a response to the onomatopoeic "goofiness" of the work, copying the "bloops and bleeps" of the arcade game, but also that the audience may "be responding in some way to an experience of the 'uncanny' while watching a comical human behave like an artsy robot; moreover, the silliness of the poem does contrast with its overtones of atomic horror, and the audience may be laughing at the 'mordant' ironies of an artist shouting 'aw-shucks!' at the shock-and-awe campaign of nuclear détente" (Betts interview 60). What is important to note in this case is the manner in which Bök strips words of their referentiality without damaging the words themselves: works like "Mushroom Clouds" and "Motorized Razors" (which features lines like "berserkers curse each law which causes rust on scissors") are no less "senseless" than Schwitters's work. However, by arranging his lexicon sonically, all the while tuned to the concept that informs the entire work (whether he is reproducing the sound of an electronic game, or the grind of a robotic razor), Bök presents the raw material of the work to his audience such that they can joyfully participate in and react to it; thus, the voyeuristic constraints can be loosed, so to speak, and the passive spectatorial economy of peering at the poet in the throes of his own onanistic performance can be redefined or even transcended. Ultimately, we see Bök moving the project of sound poetry away from a quasi-mystical, Dadaist form of gnosis and toward a more concrete linguistic praxis, one based in a transnational frame of cultural reference.

Bök's latest proposal is for a project he calls *The Xenotext Experiment*. With it, he intends to exploit new breakthroughs in the field of biochemistry in order to implant a bacterium with an original poem that will be translated into genetic code. Bök and his collaborators have pitched the idea along some decidedly unartistic parameters. The aesthetics of the project are downplayed in favour of the *Xenotext Experiment*'s potential to work out new directions in data storage for a variety of corporate and technological applications. On one occasion, they presented their work in these terms:

> The researchers hope that their unorthodox experiment might serve to integrate science and poetics—two domains that might not have otherwise had any reason to interact, except under the innovative conditions of this artistic exercise. Not only do the two thinkers hope to explore the aesthetic potential of a "literary genetics," but they also hope to refine methods for the biological encryption of data—methods that might be applied to domains as varied as cryptography, epidemiology, and agrobusiness. The researchers hope to demonstrate that, if scientists can perfect the process for implanting lengthy, textual information into an organism, we might not only provide a secure method for delivering secretive documents, but we might also "watermark" cells in order to track the movement of microbial diseases or botanical products. (Bök, "Xenotext" 228)

Bök hopes not only to store his poem as a genetic code, but also to implant it in the bacteria in such a way as to stimulate it to create a new protein, one that could be extracted and deciphered, making the organism "a machine for writing a poem" (Voyce interview 65). Interdisciplinary at every level, Bök envisions the *Xenotext* manifesting itself in a number of different guises and genres:

> I foresee producing a poetic manual that showcases the text of the poem, followed by an artfully designed monograph about the experiment, including, for example, the chemical alphabet for the cipher, the genetic sequence for the poetry, the schematics for the protein, and even a photograph of the microbe, complete with other apparati, such as charts, graphs, images, and essays, all outlining our results. I want to include (at the end the book) a slide with a sample of the germ for scientific inspection by the public. (64)

Into the framing device of the "artfully designed monograph," Bök is inserting a variety of discourses that might otherwise be outside the boundaries of the poetic. Charts, ciphers, and schematics: *The Xenotext Experiment* might ultimately appear more like a biology textbook than a work of poetry. But, as is the case with the poets considered here, blurring the boundary between the poetic and the non-poetic is precisely the point. While Bök has clearly made strides in this direction with, the advance that I see as most significant in the case of *The Xenotext Experiment* is his wish to bind the composing germ into the book. The missing presence of the poet, or the chirographic "trace," or the stark presence of the machine in *The Tapeworm Foundry*: all these gestures in *language* are superseded by the real physical presence of the "writer," however microscopic.[4]

More than a decade after claiming that contemporary poets might need to begin mastering "machinic dialects," Bök has successfully transformed himself into a molecular biologist and is using scientific discourse to intervene at the most basic scriptural level of all—genetic code (*After* n.p.). If he manages to complete this project, becoming "a poet in the medium of life" (Bök, Voyce interview 62), then we will have a new model with which to examine the interplay and boundary between surfaces and depths. Where Wershler-Henry offers an escape from the "surface" of a paragraph by proposing that we "elope" along bottomless discourses (as I've noted earlier), Bök implies that a similar dynamic can be located in the body itself. In biological terms, the most internalized part of our anatomy is surely the genetic code, but its messages are both "written" and "read" at the level of the body-as-a-whole. The information making my eyes brown is recorded in the innermost recesses of my body, and it is these interior surfaces that Bök proposes as a possible new expanse for inscription. Poetry is no longer a matter of mimesis, or the imposition of arbitrary rules in order to refocus attention on the cognitive processes embedded in the reader: *The Xenotext Experiment* enlists the biochemical processes of life itself, the mechanics of cellular division, in the production of art. Regardless of its successes and failures, *The Xenotext Experiment* points toward a future in which literature is, at its deepest conceivable level, an embodied process.

Social Boundaries

Kenneth Goldsmith is, alongside Wershler-Henry and Bök, the foremost spokesperson for Conceptual practice. Coming out of a text-art and sculptural tradition, his radically "uncreative" practice has produced some of the most challenging writing of our time, up to and including pushing the boundaries of what constitutes "writing" in the first place. His "American Trilogy" (*The Weather*, *Traffic*, and *Sports*) is built from transcriptions of a year of weather reports from station WINS 1010 and a year of traffic reports that Darren Wershler-Henry rightly identifies as a "key aspect of New York"; *Sports* was "transcribed from digital audio, more precisely from the WFAN broadcast of the game on the YES (Yankees radio) Network," ("American Trilogy" n.p.). Alongside the monumental *Day* and the upcoming *The Day* (both transcriptions of the *New York Times*), this "American Trilogy" seems remarkably localized; in many ways, we could refer to these books as the "New York" trilogy. Yet how is it possible to think of these pieces as somehow representative of a nation, especially given their extreme geographical constraints? We might read "American" as a metonym for "culture," but this seems insufficient at best, and reductive at worst; obviously, there is more to America than what happens in New York.

Rather than arguing about the problematics of representation or reference, it is the point of Conceptual poetics to free language from its original contexts. For Conceptual writing, the act of pouring this linguistic material from one container into another effectively liquefies the localized and instrumental use of language, injecting it into the larger national, transnational, and global flow of depersonalized information—all in the service of highlighting its intrinsic formal and aesthetic properties *as information*. In this final section, I'd like to consider Robert Fitterman's 2010 book *now we are friends* as an example of how the local and personal boundary is actually part of a relatively border-free concept of a "culture."

Goldsmith's oeuvre and, more importantly, the processes that have determined these works have allowed a new generation of Conceptual writers to emerge and have also enabled older works like Benjamin's *Arcades Project* to be recontextualized into a new canon of uncreativity.[5] The process of copying extant language, especially with the computerized tools at our disposal, is as much about preservation as it is a method of reframing for a deliberate defamiliarizing effect. The epigraph to *now we are friends* is a short excerpt from Vito Acconci's text of the performance titled "Following Piece" from 1969, in which he chose random passersby and followed them until they entered a private space into which he could not legally follow. If Acconci's performance is the piece that turns stalking into an art form, then Fitterman's book is a "Following Piece" for the twenty-first century—and the boundary between the public and private isn't nearly as unambiguous as a closed door anymore.

The paperback 2010 edition of *now we are friends* makes explicit reference to Facebook on its cover, and the editor's note also discusses the notion of privacy in the age of the social network. (That note was written, apparently, at 11:31 p.m. on Monday, 11 October 2010, again highlighting the local and singular presence of the writer in time, but in the now so-familiar-as-to-be-invisible format of an email, detailing date, subject, and delivery system.) What Fitterman embarks on in the book is a gargantuan project of online stalking, and his chosen subject is the average cyber-Joe, Ben Kesseler:

Who is Ben Kesseler?

I have been an entrepreneur and interested in the web and technology since an early age. Currently, I am studying Business Administration with a concentration in Marketing at the Lebow College of Business at Drexel University.

I have proven experience in many fields of marketing including branding, advertising and public relations. Currently, I am very interested in social media marketing and blogging. I strongly believe that a brand must have complete transparency, an authentic and friendly personality and image to compete in the current marketplace.

> I am the co-founder and editor of Unbreaded, an online publication that explores the craft of fine sandwiches.
>
> …
>
> To find out more about me and interact with me, why not say hi? You can find me on Facebook, Twitter, FriendFeed and LinkedIn. (11–12)

The first chapter continues for the next thirty pages, documenting with "flat lined obsessiveness" the detritus of language that Ben Kesseler has left behind in his online wake. Out of these shards we can quite easily reconstruct a portrait of the sandwich blogger as a young man, but, of course, this is merely a performance of the self, a "cubist collage" of selves, each angle appropriate to a given hyperspatial "community" as shifts in linguistic registers are rendered obvious between each facet of the contemporary online subject (Fitterman 9).

The second chapter considers "other ben kesselers" and opens with the very real condition (in our Google age) of being "confused with that other Ben Kesseler" (41).[6] Chapter 3 deals with Ben's friends, and we are presented with michelle deforest's paratactical list of interests, including "Neon signs that say WIGS (or INTERNET)" (53), and Rich Sedmak's thoughts on "What's strategic for Facebook?" (55), and Tina Dividock's stats as she plays for the "Drunken Whores" house cricketing team (76). As we scan these pages of bare statistics and names, documenting a given player's "MPR" and "improvement," we must sooner or later ask: How is any of this relevant to *me*? Perhaps it is in the final chapter that we find an answer, as the network extends to Ben's friends' friends, including the minor movie star Rae Dawn Chong—and it is in this moment we can see how borders melt in hyperspace: Chong is *connected*, and her cyber-profile (copied from her IMDB page) takes its place alongside (although we must be careful when we use such orienting language in this case) Ben Kesseler's autobiography on the Web. From Rae Dawn Chong, outward—or, "outwith," even into our inboxes.

In a manner properly Joycean, or tapeworm-esque, I return to my opening comments and propose that we now have a way of thinking though Ward's "outwithness." What is more proximate than our prosthetics? What is more "included," enfolded into ourselves, than the code with which we are expressed on a genetic level? The borderlines that define the subject relative to the object, and the signs that constitute the subject itself, appear now to have practically negligible "intervals" separating them from one another. In this interpenetrated field, it comes as no surprise to find writing like Fitterman's emerging. *now we are friends*, in its clinical reframing of extant online fragments, makes it clear that far from peering at one another across a border, we are *connected*, and that in those connections, there is a poetry of sorts. Preserved in print, what emerges is a radical reformulation of the expressive human subject. We are released from the limitations of Projectivist spatiality and its attendant concerns with borders, and find ourselves instead networked and stored in servers and books without boundaries, be they geograpic, bodily, "andor" social. Now, we are to be read as the result of a conglomeration of the poetic, the prosaic, the inane, and the instrumental. We can begin to conceive of ourselves anew: as bodies of information, to be moved—and in that movement, we simultaneously redraw our borders.

Notes

1 For instance, see "R.I.P T.R.G." (a reconstruction of the TRG's satirical photo-essay "Nary-A-Tiff," reproduced in *Rational Geomancy*).
2 See Franklin and Steiner's introductory essay "Taking Place: Toward the Regrounding of American Studies" from *Mapping American Culture* for a trenchant discussion about the distinction between "space" and "place."
3 My thanks to Christian Bök for supplying me with this poem and his permission to reproduce it in this chapter.
4 On page 85 of *Rational Geomancy*, McCaffery (or possibly his assistant/s) handwrites the phrase "this phrase" into each copy.
5 See the list of contributors to "Against Expression" or the online archive at Ubu.com for a sense of this body of work.
6 Certainly, with a name like "Nasser Hussain," I find myself practically invisible online, considering the dominant cyber-presence of the English cricketer of the same name. After the England team won the Ashes in 2010, my Twitter account was inundated by cricket fans wishing me well on this happy occasion.

Works Cited

Bök, Christian. "How to Write Eunoia." *Broken Pencil.* http://www.brokenpencil.com/view.php?id=4732. Accessed 19 April 2002.

———. Interview with Stephen Voyce. *Postmodern Culture* 17.2 (2007). http://www3.iath.virginia.edu/pmc/current.issue/17.2voyce.html. Accessed 19 April 2002.

———. Interview with Gregory Betts. "Welcome, Human, 'The Cyborg Opera': An Interview with Christian Bök." *Open Letter* 12.9 (2006): 55–61.

———. "After Language Poetry." *UbuWeb Papers.* http://www.ubu.com/papers/oei/bok.html. Accessed 2 July 2013.

———. "Mushroom Clouds." *Segue Reading at Double Happiness, NY.* PennSound, 2001. MP3 file. http://writing.upenn.edu/pennsound/x/Bok.php. Accessed 19 April 2002.

———. "Nickel Linoleum." *Open Letter* 10.4 (1998): 62–74.

———. "The Piecemeal Bard Is Deconstructed: Notes Toward a Potential Robopoetics." *Object 10: Cyberpoetics, UbuWeb Papers*, 2002. http://www.ubu.com/papers/object.html. Accessed 19 April 2002.

———. "The Xenotext Experiment." *SCRIPTed: a Journal of Law, Technology and Society* 5.2 (2008): 227–31.

bpNichol. "The Complete Works." *As Elected: Selected Writing 1962–1979.* Ed. Jack David. Vancouver: Talonbooks, 1980. 39.

Dworkin, Craig. "Zero Kerning." *Open Letter* 12.7 (2005): 10–20.

Eigner, Larry. "Approaching Things." *L=A=N=G=U=A=G=E* February 1978. http://www.eclipsearchive.org/projects/LANGUAGEn1/pictures/001.html. Accessed 19 March 2013

———. "Approaching Things." *The L=A=N=G=U=A=G=E Book*. Ed. Charles Bernstein and Bruce Andrews. Carbondale: Southern Illinois UP, 1984. 3–4.

Fitterman, Robert. *now we are friends*. http://www.truckbooks.org/pdfs/Fitterman_NWAF.pdf.

Franklin, Wayne, and Michael Steiner, eds. *Mapping American Culture*. Iowa City: U of Iowa P, 1992.

Goldsmith, Kenneth. Interview with Katherine Elaine Sanders. "So What Exactly Is Contemporary Writing: An Interview with Kenneth Goldsmith." *Bomblog* 2 October 2009. http://bombsite.com/issues/1000/articles/4534. Accessed 19 April 2002.

———. Interview with Marjorie Perloff. "A Conversation with Kenneth Goldsmith." *Jacket 21* February 2003. http://jacketmagazine.com/21/perl-gold-iv.html. Accessed 19 April 2002.

———, and Craig Dworkin, eds. and intro. *Against Expression*. Evanston: Northwestern UP, 2011.

Gregory, Sinda, and Larry McCaffery, eds. *Alive and Writing: Interviews with American Authors of the 1980s*. Urbana: U of Illinois P, 1987.

McCaffery, Steve, and bpNichol. *Rational Geomancy: The Kids of the Book Machine*. Vancouver: Talonbooks, 1992.

Murray, Janet H. *Hamlet on the Holodeck: The Future of Narrative in Cyberspace*. Cambridge, MA: MIT P, 1997.

Pound, Ezra. "A Pact." *Lustra of Ezra Pound*. London: E. Mathews, 1916.

Silliman, Ron. *In the American Tree*. Orono, Maine: National Poetry Foundation, 1986.

Ward, Geoff. *The Writing of America: Literature and Cultural Identity from the Puritans to the Present*. Malden: Polity, 2002.

Wershler-Henry, Darren. *The Tapeworm Foundry, and/or the Dangerous Prevalence of Imagination*. Toronto: Anansi, 2000.

———. *Nicholodeon: A Book of Lowerglyphs*. Toronto: Coach House, 1997.

———. "Kenneth Goldsmith's American Trilogy." *Postmodern Culture* 19.1 (2008). http://muse.jhu.edu/journals/postmodern_culture/v019/19.1.wershler.html. Accessed 19 April 2002.

eighteen

Bordering on Borders
Dream, Memory, and Allegories of Writing

Lynette Hunter

THIS CHAPTER EXPLORES WHY sentient beings make borders, what kinds of borders they make, and the implications of those distinct kinds of borders for ways of being and thinking about our selves. It explores dream as a place that embodies difference, memory as a process of situating that embodiment, and allegories of writing as a way of building a situated textuality that enables allegories of reading. It will first consider significations of "border" and "bordering," or the performativity of the border, and will turn to commentary on memory and story and to discussion of storylines from traditional knowledge practices to think further about the embodied social knowledge that is wrapped up in the process of bordering and its articulation in the work of dream, memory, and allegory. The chapter then turns to the poetry of Judy Halebsky to study her poetics of dreaming, and to recent work by Daphne Marlatt to study the poetics of memory. Each writer thinks textually about the ways words become allegories of somatic experience and performances of bordering.

Borders are sometimes rigid, sometimes flexible, at times inclusive, at others exclusive—often all at the same time. Some borders close me down, require me to behave in certain ways, yet what I am interested in here is the process of bordering and the work of dream, memory and the process of mapping that is allegory: storylines that orient the self with respect to the ecology of life, become an embodied set toward the people, things, and landscapes around us, and prompt us to engagement.

Consider the border that skin makes: we are covered by it, and it is both a delineation of who we are and what we are not, as well as a place where "we" intermingle with the rest of the world outwith the body, the skin being the second largest breathing organ of the body. The skin marks a cut between self and not-self, the Buddhist Phat, or the way we exist as different entities at the point we also realize we are one. If skin is a border, it is not the border as liminality where the fixed is deferred, but the border where we make difference, create identity through embodiment of our recognition that we are not something other/else. I call this engaged border: bordering.

A border, as Etienne Balibar, who also writes on "transindividuality,"[1] said in 1991, just after the Wall came down, is not there until we make it: "The theorist who attempts to define what a border is is in danger of going round in circles, as the very representation of the border is the precondition for any definition" (76). Neither is difference there until we make it. The making of engaged difference (a process embedded in Derrida's *différance*) leads to value because as we recognize that we make the difference, we have to take responsibility for it, which is an indication of, as Peggy Kamuf writes, "the impossibility of a *position* which is *not already a relation*" (qtd. in Gatens and Lloyd 188). Responsibility leads to valuing, and values give us agency, provide the moral energy to act or speak, and the energy of words and action carries affect and knowledge. The process defines our self as collaborative.

A border is also a performance of different kinds of identity and self that realize different kinds of rhetoric. Whether national, regional, or personal, borders are made up through rhetorics of representation as well as through rhetorics of presence and performativity. Doreen Massey's *For Space* is one of the more extensive studies of the rhetorics of situated knowledge and their relation to borders. It explores the material relations of space that can dislocate the representations that assume that locales, cultures, and nations have "an integral relation to bounded spaces, internally coherent and differentiated from each other by separation" (64). Massey argues that new ways of thinking about space can disrupt the totalizing claims of liberal humanism and neoliberal globalization, which base themselves on that notion of bounded space. Central to this new materiality is a multiplicitous awareness of "stories-so-far" that prompts us into "the continuous production and reconfiguration of heterogeneity in all its forms" (61). These stories require a redefinition of time/space elements[2] that posit a non-verbal rhetoric of presence and performativity.

Borders are to do not only with the geography of rhetoric, but also with affect. One of the enduring moments of my life was reading David McFadden's *A Trip around Lake Erie*. I had immigrated to Canada, aged ten, to live in Hamilton, where I spent my teenage years. McFadden's book described the south shore of Lake Erie allegorically, as a marsh draining down in a pale wash of light, as if into a different dimension (20). This was, and to some extent still is, exactly how I *felt* about the "other side of the border," and I experienced a shock of recognition in this mutually felt body memory for the United States. I *feel* differently about the US–Mexico border, to which I'm now quite close, than the US–Canada border, which is different again from the Canada–Alaska border in Yukon. I *feel* differently about the Canada–China sea border than the Canada–Europe border, which is mediated by the Grand Banks and hundreds of years of fishing traffic with which I'm familiar. And what about ice? All that increasingly coming and going of just about solid territory at the border between Canada–Greenland or Canada–Russia, borders that are sometimes there and sometimes not.

These actual borders are not necessarily the ones about which I feel most strongly. I tend to recognize, realize, make real those I'm personally involved in making, for example, during my travel down Highway 41 between Pembroke and Kingston. As I drive down the highway on my way home to a small village called Denbigh, I go over the top of a hill and—I'm *there/here*. It's a visceral feeling affirmed by a sign that announces Addington Highlands Township and the start of a potholed road, but many people will travel the same road and not experience that feeling. I've made a border, and engaged in a process of that making, the way it makes me feel; I've made a difference, crossed a border, come home. Just so, in teaching Canadian literature in Britain or the United States, I'll be reading along with a group of students, and because they usually recognize the language, English, and think of it as their own, and are imbricated into the heteronormative nation-state that determines so many countries around the world, they feel familiar with the text. Suddenly they miss a feeling, a possibility for difference. "Aesthetics" means "feeling," that embedded somatic response to things in the world. And at times, the students find a difference collectively, where I do not. Not making that difference is problematic, on their part or on mine, and I see my work as an educator as largely being to alert myself and my co-workers to ways that encourage that making, generate those feelings.

"Home" is just as open to representative or performative rhetorics as "border." Massey would argue that nostalgia for "home" insists on the past in a way that can rob others of their stories. If we have a fixed idea of "home" in mind, we deny the possibility of change, of the way others' stories may well have made a difference to the space and time we remember. Yet many people feel an affective need for "home," and Massey suggests that it is only when nostalgia denies other stories that "it is indeed 'nasty'" (124). The ways these performative and affective feelings happen is the process I'm here calling "bordering," and dream is a central part of its making.

Dream, and its connection with storyline, orients the self with respect to the ecology of life. Together, dream and storyline become part of our physiology, part of our social constitution, part of the way we negotiate a situated positionality in our daily lives, and part of the way we make situated textualities to articulate that positionality. But prior to negotiation, a privileged activity, is otiation: generally understood as "lazy" or "leisured" depending on class position, but curiously also signifying "something that is not contributing to the state of things." Dream, as we retain it in "daydream," is otiose and therefore a tool for those not included in the state. In turn, memory makes the embodiments of dream into textual mappings of many kinds. In the situated textuality of allegory in particular media, memory works through a rhetoric of forgetting. What is remembered with certainty overwrites the stories of others, yet forgetting is a process of remembering in the present that makes stories in collaboration. I am here exploring writing, telling, listening, and reading. The process is spiral, for dream is an embodiment with which the memory needs to interact, and the situated process of that interaction is the bordering of story, the allegory of dream, that in turn becomes embodied in the reader.

Peter Kulchyski uses the phrase "storyline" to describe an Aboriginal word-craft that speaks both back to and alongside the "certain kind of writing that is the state" (37). Storyline is generated, he suggests, by dream—not the dream of the "unconscious," not part of the repressed, but in the present. This kind of dream is not a set of images discarded by mass culture,[3] but a living memory of the collective. In my own words, it is involved not in rhetorics of representation but in rhetorics of presence/presents/gifts. It generates "a story that is a way of seeing, a story that reveals, makes visible, the limits of a way of seeing" (32–33). Working from Michael Taussig's concept of "implicit social knowledge," Kulchyski notes that the form—what I would call "textuality"—in which the images make that knowledge is a critical feature of the value it generates and the knowledge that results.[4]

Turning to implicit social knowledge and traditional knowledge in Indigen-ous communities enables thinking about borders/bordering as the direct link made by people commenting on the connection of these knowledges with particular rhetorics of story. Situated knowledge theory, which has much in common with these epistemologies, tends to neglect the need for a textuality to convey the knowledge, yet without a textuality there can be no communi-cated knowledge. Massey, for example, speaks of the need for texts to be "a place within continuous and multiple processes of emergence" (54), as if this were an odd challenge to a status quo of the text, whereas it is the basis on which "literature" rests, and in which many critical readers engage. Whereas disciplinarity has kept situated knowledge theorists from benefiting from cen-turies of work on poetics, in Aboriginal studies, social effectiveness is often closely aligned with engaged texuality.

Louise Profeit-Leblanc calls the "first face" of story "ancestral memory," knowledge of the myths needed for survival that establishes "strength," gives young people "the continuous training and education about how not to be afraid of what lies before you, what lies around you, what's in your environ-ment" (49). This kind of story is "true," but as Jim Cheney points out, quoting from other comments made by Profeit-Leblanc, truth is here "'responsibly true' (a 'responsible truth'), 'true to what you believe in,' 'what is good for you and the community'" (92). In the West, this is historically the definition given to the truth of rhetoric rather than the truth of rational logic, often delineated as the "good,"[5] "probably the best for the moment" (see Hunter, *Rhetorical* ch. 2), a sense of truth as a negotiated feeling in communities of difference.[6] Cheney suggests that this kind of world outlook creates a "ceremonial world" in which there is an "agnostic" relationship between map and territory, so that map is not fixed. A ceremonial map provides an "ethical-epistemological orientation of attentiveness (*respect*) rather than an epistemology of control" (94): a bordering rather than a border.

Another central element of the commentary on implicit social knowledge, or traditional knowledge, that is missing from accounts of situated knowledge is the importance of listening (see Nunavut Arctic College). The elders I have worked with briefly always talk about the first skill in storytelling being the ability to listen (Hunter, "Equality" 57); as Kulchyski also notes, most elders are concerned that people do not listen as much as they used to (35). I would extend this concern to reading—not the functional ability to read, but the skill of reading with an engaged, feeling body. Both listening and reading have etymological roots in being attentive, or attending to, the material at hand, having an attitude of care, respect, and interaction with the material.[7] While to "listen" is to keep silence and to "read" is to advise or suggest, reading *as* listening is the work I'd call attention to here.

Situated knowledge theorists articulate careful theories about borders and bordering, calling on story to support the latter. Yet stories can be fixed and unfixed and in the process of making. They are not necessarily in one rhetoric or another, but are historically contextualized so that some strategies and devices become more or less appropriate to static, relational, and processual events. The rhetoric of traditional knowledge, which understands this, involves how the story is told socially and contextually as well as orally or verbally. In this chapter, I would like to bridge from the insights of traditional knowledge as a process of bordering, through Kulchyski's insights into state stories and dream stories, to respond to Massey's call for a text that responds to process, what I call a textuality. I want to delineate bordering from border not only as a desirable process but also through particular textualities with particular rhetorics. Poetics is the field in which language is in process, but this textuality does not underwrite its ability to enable bordering in all socio-cultural situations. Poetics needs a rhetorical stance that sets it toward that bordering, a stance generically named allegory.

The chapter works through two particular engagements of textuality, my reading of two writings, in which I attempt to explore the rhetorical strategies used by each writer to enable a process of reading/listening, and my own strategies for enabling the materiality of embodied affect in the writing of this reading. The writer writes, bodily engaging the world with dream through memory into the word. The reader reads, bodily engaging the word through similar strategies into the world. The reader only engages the body when they retell the words, just as traditional knowledge imparts that the listener only engages the body when they retell the words. A text can sit in the body for years before it somatizes into dream, impelling memory to materialize it into retelling, into making it present, into mimesis. And if you work on that reading as allegory then you make just one particular reading, a reading in process so that as the particulars change, as they must with the movement of the earth, so the reading changes.

Dream and a Textuality of Embodiment

Judy Halebsky, in *Japanese for Daydreamers*, and Daphne Marlatt, in *The Given*, focus on the borders between humans, between humans and the natural world, between humans and the man-made world, and on the different ways we textualize these borders: the moment's version of poetics. In these texts, the borders between humans and non-humans have many more apparent resistances than do humans or man-made objects. They offer an elusiveness and enigma from which we can learn about making differences that we can apply to other interactions. Articulating those differences within a situated textuality draws on and develops rhetorics of allegory.

These writers make us go back to dream to grapple with the embodied knowledge of other people and the world—dream as a felt experience that provides an analogy to a somatic bordering that both limits and dissolves any autonomous sense of self. The interaction with the natural world is perceived as immediate, somatic, and in the moment. The interaction of human with the natural world is one of hoping for a similar bordering, holding not only the promise of making difference, creating value, finding responsibility, but also the hope that the process engages us, makes us immanent in each other. Dream holds vestiges of this experience that are rehearsed in ritual. Marlatt and Halebsky not only hope but also enact/perform bordering in their writing. Halebsky meditates on translation, on the way bodies engage with what has happened in dream so that translation becomes a form of re-membering in the present; Marlatt meditates on memory and forgetting, re-membering as an active connection between what has happened and words. They elaborate rhetorics of allegory in translation and forgetting.

Judy Halebsky's *Japanese for Daydreamers* works on the process of translation to explore the poetics of dream and embodiment in a series of poems that engage with haiku by the Japanese poet Basho. Translation could be considered a fundamental recognition of difference, given that no translation can ever be exact. Halebsky's writing suggests that translation is a process of dreaming the world-to-be-translated into embodiment that yields an engaged textuality. The poems in this collection move between English and Japanese, making a space for dream, for a rehearsal of the unknown in the body that makes difference. The process is continually bordering on what-is-said and what-cannot-be-said, engaging the reader, who may read silently or aloud, in valuing the feeling prompted by the textuality.

The first poem presents the Japanese characters followed by a translation: "Oh sky, a little bit even, fly not" (3). The poem's movement generates another translation that has passed through the body of this poet, and through the reading of the reader, into the final line: "I cannot fly in the sky at all" (3). Reading through the poem, a reader feels the embodiment when responding interactively to the textuality. The first stanza:

> You can move between French and English
> put the table in the kitchen
> and the soft red chair by the window (3)

opens with regularity and balance, wisps of childhood French lessons, simple sentences that speak to me now of the cultural translations I make whenever I go to France or to England. It shifts from the basic "put the table in the kitchen" to the more complex third line, which may have an understood verb "and *put* the soft" or may just be a observation, and which has ambiguous qualifiers: Is the red chair "soft" or is the chair coloured in "soft red"?

The second stanza:

> but with Japanese you can't bring what you already have
> like the words: me, you
> or how to count: 1 bed, 2 chairs, 3 days (3)

The length of the first line strung right out across the page dissolving the line-end effect with a physical enjambement. If I engage the textuality and break the jam, bend the arm at the elbow, I realize the first line is a definition, that there is no Japanese word for "to bring what you already have." But also, "what you already have" are words like "me, you" and numbers with nouns. Implicitly, they too elude translation, do not exist in the other language and culture. In their place things exist differently. What this difference is we do not know, but we have made a border between us and it by understanding that we cannot translate.

The third stanza:

> an airplane takes off from Sacramento
> I lie at an angle so I can see the fig tree out the window (3)

The translating body is situated, in Sacramento, watching airplanes, changing the angle of vision "to see the fig tree out the window." Or is this the physical movement the translator engages in to think through the way to speak of "sky" in Japanese, to translate Basho? Either way, the words impel me to bend into the movement, to rehearse it through my own body to grasp a possibility as I translate from the poem to me. I almost want physically to cock my head, strain my neck to see just a "little bit of sky."

The fourth stanza:

> arms for wings
> ears for songs
> 3 days for water
> sleep for sleep
> chocolate for chocolate
> vodka for vodka
> kanji for death
> death for surrender
> surrender for sleep and 10,000 years (3)

runs through a list—are these passing thoughts as the eyes stare into the sky? are they translations from English to Japanese, Japanese to English? are they literalizations of syllabic characters? meditations or memories on words and different languages? They begin with a possible translation for "fly"—"arms for wings"—and then slip into a series of associations that eddy daydream-like from one to the next, morphing from an inserted Japanese word "kanji" to death/surrender/sleep and 10,000 years, as if leading into unknown territory.

The fifth stanza:

> the sky is (o for honorific)
> a little bit (silent syllable) even
>   (I (implied) cannot fly (3)

returns to the literal text and formally addresses its physicality. The ellipses cordoning off an analysis of certain elements, which we know from the ambiguity of the first stanza, are uncertain when out of context, and what is the context here? The eddying list in stanza four seeps through the tension of this grammatical/syntactical structure to release the final line, the sixth stanza, "I cannot fly in the sky at all," which leaves the haiku behind and floats on the page with the curious sense that even if you only had a bit of sky—rather than the whole thing—you still couldn't fly in it. There is no significance to a depth and breadth of the sky, only the human limitation in face of it.

The process of translation passes through the particular body of the translator, eddying through daydream into words as it passes from narration to association to analysis that breaks apart into new words. The eighth poem, "Zen Monks Talking Big," has a structure similar to the first, but adds the roman characters for the Japanese syllabics, partly to foreground the last word "yo." "Yo," which means "yup, that's what it's like" or "as I said" or "hi there" in North America, turns a literal, formal translation of

> watching the lightening
> those who share simply
> are noble

into a different, deadpan translation:

> high brow talk
> over the lightning
> such a pity (11)

Each of the poems in this collection presents other processes of embodiment for translation. For example, the second poem "W [this is a broken letter preceded by the Japanese character for "woman under trees"] oman Under Trees" takes us through a fugue study on the Japanese character for "woman" as the writer assesses the impact of translation on her maturing person:

> you might not think these aren't my words
> not my body, not sounds that shaped me
> when I was growing through shadows on the wall (4)

We learn from the following poem "Folksong (translation)" that "shadows" are the words the translator finds for the reality of existence in the first language.

"Woman Under Trees" takes us physically through the Japanese characters for different kinds of woman, their transliteration, and a possible translation, in a layout recalling concrete poetics that releases the final stanza:

> these words flood into the river
> they are trees that rise uprooted
> they are butterflies in the trees (4)

The epigraph to the collection is a translation of a Basho haiku by Robert Hass: "A caterpillar, / this deep in fall – / still not a butterfly" (1). It reminds us that a butterfly is a realized potential. Still later, the poem "Water Voices" quotes from poet Claude Roy, "I will only say that poets are like trees: / they are all united by their roots in the earth / and their branches in the sky" (9). Bringing these to the final stanza of the second poem affirms its sense of generative flooding, of words maturing through the body of the poet into poems, and of the woman's body realizing its potential.

"Water Voices," dedicated to "Anatole Lubovich, poet and translator," insists not on the tree that is the poet but on water, saying, "a water heart / means how to swim" (9): "water heart" is the transliteration from the Japanese characters; "how to swim" is the translation. The physical image of the character, its transliteration, its translation, can be read as a single "character" in itself, that generates a list of other possible translations and a series of haiku:

> how to float with no mooring
> the jasmine in Berkeley in December
> the gingko leaves yellow in all corners of the street
> the way we prop ourselves up to dawn (9)

before returning to three more "characters" in which "water people" = "what you tried to carry," "water voices" = "the sound of water," "water people talking" = "a love song." Water is the first element, the energy for action, the sense of floating anticipation, the lightness of laughter, the reason we bother to wake up.

Other poetic strategies work from the sound or shape of the words, at times importing mathematical symbols that change the shape of the meaning, at other times offering multiple translations of the same Japanese syllabics. "Read Me Where I Lie" plays even in the title with the ambiguity of the body and the word, for "lie" is to lay down the body as well as to deceive. This poem and the next, "Landscape," underline the embodied process of translation. "Landscape" laments that "the dictionary is out of words, out of pages," and continues, "let me dream the blank pages that were once a dictionary" as the poet searches for the words in the body (23). The search is "desperate," yet in comparison with "Oakland / where no one has what they need," perhaps gains a context that yields:

> in Japanese there's a character that means searching for
>   something
> and a different character
> that means searching for something you've lost (23)

Oakland, with its substantial African American population living the crises of black American life, keeps what people "need" in perspective. Not only do these crises, which negate Afro-American access to the world of efficacious words, make possible any kind of modern civic life, but the crises also remind more privileged others of their capacity for translation. Dream becomes a place where, for this relatively privileged writer, both those characters—for "something" and for "something you have lost"—can be embodied, even as the dictionary remains "still blank." If the dictionary is the repository of "already said" words, the poetics of translation materialize the embodiments of dream in words. Translation becomes a kind of remembering.

"Read Me Where I Lie" notes:

> Sensei doesn't like me changing the words
> breathing my angle into them
> bracing them into my shape (22)

Sensei wants the poet to say what love song "actually" means, that translation is a series of grade points, "he wants me to tell you / a different kind of love song" to the translation that lets:

> the words come underwater
> breathed in like air
> seeded to spruce, to elm, to fir (22)

Outwith the words, or the translating process, there is a natural world that simply "is" in a way that the daydreaming body nearly, simply "is." But the world of nature is also a place with more evident resistance to human beings than other humans, or even other man-made objects. We can learn more acutely about the way we make difference from the way the physical elements around us insist on their elusiveness. That natural world begins in water, in the "water lung" of birth that speaks in the final poem "Down the Mountain" before it becomes the "paper lung" of poetry. It provides the writer with a world in which translations are made in the moment, where she can see the trees ripped from Stanley Park in "Stanley Park with my Father, 2006," and read their translation of her relationship, through the time and space that they encapsulate, into a way of making that relationship for herself. Or the immediacy of

> birds in flocks on the trees
> each one urgent and shouting
> if not here, then here (19)

a cacophony of noise that goes nowhere, but is everywhere, arresting time in the sound and space of "here"—or the cicada's call that "pierces the stones" at the same time as "the rocks hear/ the sound of the cicadas" (18).

This world runs alongside the familial and the civic, just as the world of her body, becoming a "home for worms / a nest for moths" (21), lives at the same time as she is remade by her family into "queen of cakes," "queen of waking dreams, the queen of lost mittens." There is an insistent parallel between the natural and civic worlds, with the natural providing a "limit case" of what cannot be known.[8] Even as human beings change the natural world they do so with complete lack of interaction; nature doesn't "speak back" in its terms, but in terms that we attribute to it. The city, as Massey notes, is a "human–nonhuman negotiation of place conducted, on the human side, within an overweening presumption of the ability to conquer" (161) the natural. Hence the ongoing fascination of what it might be saying, and that concept, too, is anthropomorphic. The natural is also at the same time a reminder that human beings are part of an ecological system, a "oneness," that just because we can never comprehend it, is never complete.[9]

The collection ends with "Down the Mountain," where the ghost of trees makes possible the words of her "paper lung" (24):

> whatever I came with exhausted
> I pass through these pages like a ghost
> whatever I came with I spent

"exhausted" being emptied as well as tired, "spent" being tired as well as emptied. The lines recall the first poem's statement "with Japanese you can't bring what you already have," or that poets can "carry" feeling even though they cannot bring it. "To bring" implies that we bring an object or a person or a memory of a finitely locatable thing with us, "to carry" implies a process. This poet has carried the process of translation in her body, formed from the somatic responses of dream and daydream into the words that are embodiments of her voice. The poetry cannot bring with it another reality, but it can invite us into the reality of the writing body, a textuality with which we need to interact in a present-time allegorical reading that attends with care, that listens and rehearses those words in our own body.

Memory and a Rhetoric of Forgetting

Daphne Marlatt's The Given is an elegy, or a ritual of remembrance, for her mother, the city through which she knows her, and the wider environment. A fugue meditation on home, the homeless, ideological pressures, and war, it's an exploration of memory and forgetting, and a glancing interaction with an alongside world of natural and spiritual significance. The text also becomes an exploration of the way a modern city insists on borders, borders that include and exclude, but also on the material reality of borders that make some people inhuman (here, women and the destitute) and that could not exist at all without the defined-as-non-human body of the slave. As the "home" is the unacknowledged shadow of the civic state, the wife an unseen and unnamed labourer who enables capitalist profit, the text offers exploration of the way home is a certain kind of territory from which one could become homeless, but it also offers home and homelessness as a process of openness to change, a challenge to the definitions of the city.

The writing explores the way memory, like the "certain writing that is the state," insists on certain interpretations and is dislocated when these are disallowed. It asks, what do memories overwrite if they persist? It's not a matter of denying the past, but of engaging with it, knowing that we understand it from the needs of the present, and keeping this knowingness present and part of the process. The textuality follows the way happenstance happens, the way chance keeps us in the moment, the way the indecipherability of the natural world and its radical difference keep us honest about our systems of man-made privilege, the way a good memory becomes a forgetting, so that the present can be present, that knowing the making of memory in the present prevents the rush of certainty. And it is also about the somatic experience generating memory and forgetting and the glimpses of that feeling afforded by the indecipherability of ritual.

The book has five parts: in part one, or "Seven Glass Bowls / [*overture*]," the writer begins to delineate the different points in time that will layer this story, maps the feeling into words through strategies of somatic memory—the central point being the day her mother is found dead at home, which is in the relatively distant past to her act of writing. In the second section, "1953 / [*act one*]," a childlike narrative voice surfaces as the main point of reference, in the year of 1953 when the second Narrows Bridge was begun between the North Shore and Vancouver. The third section, "Out Of The Blue / [*intermezzo*]," takes us back to the moment of the mother's death, opening out the connections between the mother's body and the city. The fourth section, "1958 / [*act two*]," combines the fall of the bridge with the narrative voice of a young teenaged girl coming to terms with sexuality and with an increasing sense that something is wrong with her mother. The final section, "Late In The Day / [*finale*]," explores the process of forgetting as time collapses into the present space of her relationships with other people, the city, the natural world.

"Seven Glass Bowls / [overture]"

The section begins with "you remember—what is it you remember?", and continues, "the feel of home, that moment of coming into your body, its familiar ache and shift" (1). The prosody is broken into cohesive "paragraphs," or perhaps somagraphs, since they carry the embodied moment. Later in this first somagraph, the speaker says, "in the still of the day" "we," possibly the writer and her partner, "bring something to burn" to create a ceremony that "ribbon[s] through the days we share. and share, continuous, with what is gone" (2). Later in overture the reader returns to "in the stillness of morning. we set out seven glass bowls with a tea-light in the middle—two waters, a flower, incense, flame, perfume, food, music. pour water through inner turbulence. watch it brim luminous in each transparent dish. watch it through our muddied implicatedness" (12–13). This ritual draws the "we" together, offering an alongside world that brings luminescence to the turbulence of the way we are implicated in the net of the world, the mess of our situatedness present with the energy that generates it. Later, in the finale, we return to the image "in the still of almost evening, something to burn for those who have left, who go on burning in us. tsa sur. brimming bowls and incense. water and light" (98), suggesting that the ceremony is one that commemorates, remembers, and—as we shall discover—also forgets, the dead.

The opening *overture* then takes us immediately back with "it was July ...," the kind of day that calls "the body out to play ... re-arisen, chickadee's two-note shrill euphoric, *here* / *i'm here*" (2), "this *joyant* pouring in with sun across a kitchen nook amist with memory smoke" (2). In the midst of "that morning of liquid flight" her father calls and says "i can't wake her up" (2). At this point the poetics move on to a two-line arrest of attention, possibly in the now, possibly in the past:

> and birds, in the corner of an eye as i stared unfocused at their
> skywriting: flap flap, soar. their Sanskrit.

On first reading it is difficult to tell how to read these lines, but already we follow this writer's turn to the natural world when she looks for images to carry feeling, whether it is the chickadee in the centre of her focus of the joyant day, or the unfocused flapping of bird wing that speaks possibly of shock, possibly of a memory-state, possibly of the shift in set toward[10] the world with which death leaves us.

The arrest spins out rapidly into a series of moments of recall and feeling for several somagraphs, spilling into the writer's comment that this is

> rapid overlay, one place-time on another, as if we're actually in the
> movement between, memory cascading its light-drenched moments and
> then suddenly that single jet of recognition, parallel perhaps, that allows
> us to see, paradoxically, this place we're in the midst of ...
> *incredible, conflicting with explanation.* (4)

Memory layers feeling on feeling, present sense of past experience on past experience, and throughout *overture*, voice, quotation, letters, directly reported speech, indirect description, remembered observation, song, commonplace, formal speech, gendered speech, visual image, and most vibrant the staccato conversations and poetic interventions, build that insistent Marlattian prosody that turns prose into a river. The layers are strung on a fugue-like repetition of "home." From "the feel of home," to "to feel at home," "coming home," "going home," "homing in," "home and the closeness of the beloved," "so where is home for you?", the prosody is interrupted, sometimes at moments of intense feeling (where words fail?) with that alongside world. For example, remembering coming into the room and seeing her mother's body "like a child's" gives way to

birch-waver, pine-sway. Animated talk of struck glass. Rhythmic gusts
bending the length of trunks away from our neighbour's porch. (13)

This shift turns into "*furor scribendi.* rapid, with frantic signage, pine jostle
green behind." It is as if there are two different kinds of writing going on: the
"waver, tremble" of the "restless filigree of leafless birch," and the writer "still
getting used to this particular sense of history as missed story, shadowing
place" (5).

Not all shadows—here the remnants of the actual body, analogous to the
actual reality of Halebsky's Japanese that is shadowed by her English—are
beneficent. Marlatt's writer tries self-consciously not to pass on the "shadowy
figures" of confining, gender-specific maxims with which she grew up. But the
presence of the body in her memory becomes increasingly more problematic.
Set against an intimacy recalling "a splotch of robin's egg blue on the soft sag
of her cheeks" (3), is the "underlay, as if / her body under the / lay of the city
under / lies it" (4). Set suddenly in contrast with the "love" for her mother is
the awareness of the dead body, and "what to do with the body?" (7), and later
"what to do with the body? // (we didn't know)" (14). Set alongside the present,
with its "outrageous birdjoy all around" (20), the cats, dogs, and sunshine, is
the question of what to do with the words: "if all this is a sign, what does it say?
one seme, one phoneme even?"; "*description.* this writing around" (19). The
writer, aware that as she remembers her mother, she is mapping her present
geography and relationships, is "bordering" in particular with the person with
whom she makes her home in the present.

By the close of *overture* the mother's body is "impossibly there and not
there" (20), and "dumb," without words, and "released from her story." The
writer's final line, "now I remember mum's the word" (21) folding "mum" into
"mother," with mum / = mom (according to mother), as the sign of the journey through memory to "mum's the word," the silence, but also the "word":
what's the right word? The word is central to memory, the word is what you
remember in making present. *The Given* is of course the writer's story, and no
one else's—until the reading.

1953 / [*act one*] – Out Of the Blue / [*intermezzo*] – 1958 / [*act two*]

The second part, 1953 / [*act one*], opens with the words:

only she, to begin with, she which means about – and so begins the long
pulling of a thread from the trammel that underlies all this, the way any of
us are tangled in the past. (23)

A trammel is a fishing net, a strategy to catch some things but not others, a net
offering a kind of loose map of an area, and a net disintegrating as a thread is

pulled out, becoming a tangle, a messy mapping. But trammel is also to bind up a corpse, and the line recalls the comment that her mother's body underlies the city, so thinking about the city will help her think about her mother, as well as suggesting that the city is built on the broken body of her mother.

The mother's "letters home" are intercut with the young girl's diary extracts, and the layers of memory writing to which we were introduced in part one—with the difference that there is little present-day commentary. Throughout this initial memory-mapping of her childhood pathways and geography, the writer is concerned more and more with words. Advertisements advising "*KEEP YOUR HUBBY HAPPY*" (24), and headlines about "happy, comfortable homes and well-ordered families" (34), "The Little Woman" (37), the bridge that is to be built from the North Shore, and the social mores of god and society, pepper the pages with solid black type and alarming fonts.

Yet the girl-voice is concerned not with the certainties of headlines but with the secrets of words. She knows even at this stage that words are potential rituals, writing and unwriting at the same time. One of her first direct considerations is a quotation from Pauline Johnson's story of "The Two Sisters." The young girl is already familiar with this "Pauline" and enchanted that she now knows the "secret name" for the mountains that everyone else in her world calls "The Lions" (31). There are accounts of the writing she undertakes in her "*School Girl's Diary*" (32), of the quite different angular font found in her "red scribbler hidden on the bookshelf inside a copy of the *Girl's Own Annual*" (33), and of the training of her writing through "MacLean's Method of Writing," which ensures she gets the "right, the Canadian, slant on it all. getting it right" (34). Her book by Pauline Johnson has the author's name "hand-burnt" on the cover "as if skin might absorb the words inside"—"new words, and old words she thought she knew, put together strangely" (35).

The girl-voice continually tries to find out "which words count" (36), knowing already that there are "(no words)" for feeling, "no accounting for—" (30). She asks insistently, "but what does it mean?" (37), picking up on her mother's ambivalent explanations: "that's what she's saying. but of course that isn't what she really means" (38). She asks her mother about interpretations of foreign words, or nonsense words such as "Marezy doats and dozy doats / and liddul lamzy tivy," to which her mother responds "well listen to the words" (42). The secret power of words pops up in unexpected places, such as the messages on "heart-shaped candies" (42) written on with that hidden font from her scribbler as if it conveys special significance.

All of this enriched, powerful, and exciting writing goes on at the same time as the alarming headlines. The girls are trained to be decorous readers: they carefully cover their books with paper, print their names on the front, and contain the contents within a "subject" (46), but as the year progresses these covers become filled with squiggles and doodles, scribbles and erasures, as they make them their own by transgressing their borders. At the end of the year they tear off the covers, "surprised at how anonymous and new they looked. how suddenly not ours" (46). Our words make the page our own, not only as we write but also as we read. Reading becomes a curiously ephemeral analogy for writing, underlining their codependence.

The *intermezzo* "Out of the Blue" returns us to the question of "what to do about the body?", extending it out to the body of the city, the body of a mother, the body of a lover, one's own body, asking, "where does the perceiving body begin and end?" (52). Like skin, the body's perceptions are processes of melding, bordering. In "*act one*" the voice speaks of the smells around her as "traces body-memory will rise to greet" (25), smell being a perception that enters the body in a quite particular and material sense. Here the dead body of the mother releases many other bodies—the mother's own, increasingly depressed, the "blue lady"—those of people in the street, people on the street, and people remembered from the street.

There's a way that this layering, this "palimpsest of removals" (49), what the writer calls at one point "streets of layered lives, lapidary, set in cement. the remains of stories" (55), becomes a meditation on how human beings build their worlds. Palimpsests are paradoxes, both overwriting past writings and harbouring their utterances. Her mother may have made a home for her and her sisters, but it is only sometimes a home for herself. She is curiously homeless at home, almost made homeless by the home, just as the bodies

> asleep on church steps, in doorways, under overpasses. bodies
> at sea in the streets
> of this city of reconstruction. unhoused: unnamed. collapse
> of social bedrock
> underneath. (57)

Yet the detritus of human lives, from a burned futon to an old boot, is set against this "*world-class city*" (56), just as the depressed body of her mother, the dead body of her mother, is set against the orderliness of her "mushroom"-coloured satin brocade cushions. Somewhere the human attempt to build a home has gone awry, has not listened to the body and its necessary ecology. The modern city, and its need to capitalize, defines certain people as privileged and others as inhuman. Those not participating in the economy of the modern home are rendered homeless.

Marlatt, like Halebsky, grasps at the inability of human beings to translate from the natural world. When "bird books" try to do so or others try in other forms, "the vowels are all wrong"; they cannot yield "spring's piercing call to bliss" (40). Yet it is the gulls' "wheel and cry above the dumpsters," their "lunge of desire" (52) with its fabulous quality of rebus and homophone that correlates lung and lunge, that leads the writer to the perceiving body. The bodies in this part of the written text are "incontrovertible" links to the natural world; the body "does not lie" (50). Especially, it seems, the interaction between the mother-daughter body, "the maternal body the first one home re-enters. walks in through the door to its embrace. familiar palimpsest of smells" (62), which, like a bird call suddenly heard in the heart, is "there, out of the blue" (49). Those memory flashes that carry intense embodiments into the present, embodiments of her mother not as the blue lady but as someone present and vital, leave the writer not in "the blues. the dumps, the mopes, the megrims" (59), but alive with that presence.

In "1958 / [*act two*]" the bridge that was called for and described in "1953" collapses, taking with it the lives of many people, including the father of the young girl's best friend. This part, from a more observational perspective of a teenager, is thoroughly taken over by the headlines, advertisements, and billboards that tell people how to live, that still focus on the nuclear bomb, the city, the destitute, and the perfect urban wives. *act two* acquires more of a narrative drive than the previous sections as the reader engages with the emerging sexuality of the young girl, the tragedy of the bridge collapse, and the off-hand response of the mother that finally gets the girl asking, "what's wrong with Mom?" (93). Even "Dad's red roses don't seem to help a Blue Lady" (89). The densening personal narrative with its diary entries in a "new Hilroy scribbler" (67) jostles with the signs and statements of a civic state that is trying to shape individuals into easy moulds.

There is far less explicit commentary about writing, words, or the natural world; Pauline Johnson surfaces just the once when the young girl wonders whether Johnson's story had been "fudged" (92), whether there was still a curse on the waters and the bridges over it. The mother thinks so, saying, "Fate had a hand in this, you mark my words" (91). Later a voice says, "*if only I could sleep. just a few hours. The Moving Finger writes—so many words, so many words all night. The Moving Finger writes—and it's indelible. who next?*" (92). Omar Khayyam's, or rather Edward Fitzgerald's, translation of "The Rubaiyat" is often read as a statement that we are responsible for our own futures, but here that interpretation is a reader's memory coming second to an indication of a vengeful Fate hungry for disaster. As the writer tells the reader in the following part, "disaster fear. dis-astre. / up against the stars and their foregone orbits. conclusive" (99). This kind of disaster is written, the words realizing the actuality indelibly. Words determine our lives, write our path to death. This perspective seems not only to be that of the mother, but of a shadow lingering over the teenager as she begins to realize the implications of the power of words, that their certainties not only empower her but also control her, either way they subject her to the society around her. A reader in the moment of reading the book has subtle access to the way memory works as a process in the present.

A reader is the present of the text. Here, this reader experiences not only the double bind of the certain borders of the state but also the way the writing of this text attempts to make uncertain possibilities, borderings, out of this knowledge.

Late in the Day / [*finale*]

The final part of the book opens with:

> you forget—what is it you forget?
> not deliberately. contours of memory-landscape, significant features of its
> stories shift with the years, eroded by changing weather systems. so
> home, so the more and more homeless, now that it's late in the day. (97)

Memory finds an event as "past," but as it becomes aware of others' memories it experiences that event as a process of interaction, so that it becomes a happening in the present moment. Becoming aware is dependent on how well trained we are in recognizing that we make difference, can then value it and be responsible for it. A curious thing about memory is that often the more you remember the more you forget: to re-member is to change the body—put it in the present, in the moment—and to leave the body that was, behind, to forgo the getting together of that body. Halebsky translates "to remember," noting it "also means to learn" (10), and tells us that "to forget" in Japanese is made of the characters signifying "rush + heart" (8). In this reading, to forget is to rush the heart forward into the present. Much of Marlatt's *finale* opens out the process of forgetting as living in the present, using words to explore where the body is situated alongside social pressure, to understand its energy and its emptiness. This is to be well trained in practising the good rather than seeking the true.

Both the spoken and unspoken words of the book are about the mother's death, but the reader finds here why this is so problematic for the writer. All living creatures die, yet in the writer's mother's death was a life that may have been ended on purpose. But is this a fatalistic result, "pre-ordained, fatal attraction?" (105), as the doctor says, "quite common in women" (104)? Or is it specific to her mother? Suicide can leave the left-living with a rejection, or as the writer says about her father, with guilt. Yet the writer clearly has memories that lead her to believe that the death could have been suicide. The writer-daughter takes us back to a moment when the mother says with an "embarrassed edge" that "they" "were out to get her" (101). The narrative has already looped back to the time she and her mother are painting the nursery blue, when she asks the mother what she means, and the mother says, "because I'm still here," leaving the daughter to wonder, "what does *mean* mean?" (99). And when the writer and her sister hunt at the deathbed "for a note, a letter, a string of words to explain her body," all they find is: "*they are too strong for me* it said.

that's all it said. a private scrap of paper" (112). Suicide? perhaps and perhaps not. The mother certainly feels abandoned, as she says, "who am I supposed to keep the homes fires burning for?" (106). She "didn't marry a *house*" (105), she's not "just a housewife. *not a parasite ... a bum*," but she became "a stifled bomb. deactivated" (108).

Marlatt's *Given* explores remembering as a kind of coming home, only to open out the rhetorics of repression, of nostalgia, and of self-identity that it can yield. Forgetting becomes a way of coming home that does not rob others of their stories. Massey's analysis of the City of London can be read through Marlatt's metaphor of the body of her mother underlying the city of Vancouver. Her mother is made homeless by the city's trajectory of finance and global power, just as the homeless on the streets are necessary to the success of that city, and just as London's success is a massive collision of trajectories, which depends on a "dynamics producing poverty and exclusion" (Massey 157). These people are made homeless because their stories are stolen. The homeless are without a home because they do not have the power to negotiate their own stories and, as Massey notes, this "antagonism" is denied (157). However, to have a home can become a privileged yearning for a version of the world where we do not have to engage, what Massey, citing Chantal Mouffe, calls "politics without adversaries" (86).

This paradox is the paradox of recognizing the appalling structure of the civic state; at least, for a middle-class white person in North America it's a paradox: the standard of living, cleanliness, access to foods, concepts of aesthetics, cultural and social pathways, being built on the necessity for poverty. For a black person on this continent it is the condition of fungibility, of the impossibility of humanity for black people if the civic state is to exist in the first place. For the "homeless" of any kind, the paradox is the condition of exclusion. For the mentally ill woman whose death is being re-membered, it is the loss of the "home," the story for which she thought she was made, and which she thought she had to perpetuate. But the writing pursues another way of making home. It points to another paradox. Homelessness could also be a process of consistently trying to ensure that the home is open, not fixed. We have no "rights" to home, we can only continue to make the present. In a sense the process of making the present is a kind of home.

Homelessness is the paradox of both not listening to the body's story, and listening to it too intently as defined by the civic state. To be homeless is both to have been ignored, not listened to, made abject, living on the other side of the border, and to be in an ecological relation, an ongoing process of situatedness. Yes, in the short term it is important to recognize the structural conditions that make abjection, because these could be ameliorated or changed. Without that recognition the idea of ecological relation may become a way to justify the inequities of structure: that a person is homeless "simply" because they have chosen to be so. But in the long term the person who "recognizes" abjection is also complicit in creating it, a person can only "choose" homelessness if the condition has already been made possible by their exclusion. The long term displays the interconnectedness of all things, and the other sense of homelessness as the recognition of the territorialization of home, the need for continual process, bordering on borders.

Making a home by bordering is also a task the writer is undertaking for herself as she re-members and forgets. She walks the streets mapping both the personal history and the city itself where so much building is going on over the past, leaving "memory deconstructed" by "crane erections towering" (101), as the city maps over other stories. As she walks she sees the "unhoused people" (106), oddly also "people encased," the excluded homeless making borders around themselves, "trying to make some semblance of home on the street" (107). Juxtaposed with this errant walking is more and more of the way in which she is making a home for herself with her partner, turning an empty house into a home. Memory glances off the body to make words that recognize the differences. About halfway through *finale* the writer says, "you are gradually speaking less and less of elsewhere. that sharp pang of the place you didn't want to leave is fading. the you i know stretches its recognition network into these streets" (102), as if she recognizes that her past self is now so different that it is a "you" not an "I." This is no certain new "I" but one in a bordering process, as "connections splay out between images, cross thought traffic, don't form throughways or one-way sense" (107). She has the privilege to not-border, to make, to write, just as I have the privilege to make while reading.

It's late in the day to be re-membering her mother who died many years ago, and the writer at one point asks "why now?" (106). Yet the process of re-membering, orienting herself to her mother by way of her sense of "home" or of the city, opens the door to the paradox of home and homeless and how the city creates it. Re-membering means memories not only of a personal past but also the body memory of many pasts, in their contexts of social and political landscape. When she tries to map her mother, she maps those landscapes, releasing in her mind those who do not fit the city, the mapped over, such as her mother and social others, whose covering up both critiques the modern city and recognizes it as a site for change. And it's late in the day to remember that when you change a city you change its people. It's late in the day to remember that when you change an environment you change the whole earth. Yet it's right now that she does this for: writing, bordering, making the present day, today, here.

The present leaves her "not home. never at home in what remains. yet caught in the here of it" (115), that word "here" recalling the alongside world of birds, trees, nature. *finale* is frequently arrested by the writer's attention to

> the body of this earth. tufted pine branch swirl multidirectional. crossed
> by the shadow of a wind-tossed crow. (107)

or, recalling *overture*, the connection of that world with writing:

> so what were they writing, those birds, with their flourishes hieroglyphic?
> their feathered liftoff into the eye's vanishing point? (109)

It's as if for this writer's body the indecipherability of the natural world generates a landscape for the present: "here, i said. i was always saying here" (115).
Like words, which human beings make both fateful and strange like that other
map, the cartograph, which emerges from *chartus*: both the piece of paper on
which the map is drawn and potentially fixed, and the cards in a deck of cards,
full of chance and fate. It's the chance words, words in the present, that turn
memory material into the writing by forgetting the words of the past. This is
writing that takes time, enacts or embodies the enigmatic movement of people
from body to memory to word that allows us also to rehearse the text in our
readings. Birds, in contrast, are simultaneous with their being. Like Halebsky's
birds that are "here and here," Marlatt's sing and are here. The last memory the
writing gives us is of the writer escaping from the house of her mother's death
and suddenly:

> small tree—i recognized its shimmering. in it a single sparrow, head
> cocked eyeing me. i stop headlong as it opens its beak to pour out all that
> the room, her body, her house, could not. home free. (115)

The bird and its song are all that her mother could not say, all that this book
has moved into saying, toward understanding the complex paradoxes of "home
free." The birds have no memory; they need no translation.

Both Halebsky and Marlatt work with an alongside world of earth, birds, and
trees, that attains a presence, a coalescence of time/space that usually eludes
sentient beings but reminds them not to settle for less than intense presence.
For Marlatt, walking the city becomes a meditative exercise to re-member the
body in the present through memory of her mother, a meditation that encap-
sulates the writing in the ceremony of the glass bowls, with their water and
light taking on a more particular difference in daily life than even the natural
world. For Halebsky, the impossibility of translating from the natural world
offers a reminder that the body is always in the present, coming from water
and, possibly, going to sky.

These writers tell a story about the way the body is present moment to
moment. They tell a story about presence as engagement with the material
world. They tell a story about writing as an ongoing process in a human world

that halts that engagement in multitudes of different places, creating borders that are supposed to support specific identities rather than making borderings of collaborative identities. The writing tells us not only about the attempt to keep the writing in process, but also about the ways in which the human world halts that process into stasis, tries to make it a space without time. It also tells us about the ways in which that writing can release the stasis into other processes. The writing is, in other words, laying out the different rhetorics of borders and bordering, and exploring the connection of the latter with dream and memory, the embodied affect and image of the material world.

The reading is trying to listen to what the writing is saying, trying to engage affectively, somatically, so that the words are treated as material, as resiliently other. In an allegorical stance, we make them different and in doing so define our self. Affect here is not human sympathy but a recognition of the differences we make between our self and other people and materials, differences that change us and for which, once recognized, we need to take responsibility. Both the writing and the reading explore the way engaging with the natural world reminds us of the possibilities in engaging with the material artifact. Engagements with the natural world remind us of the limitations of our ways of knowing, and the importance of keeping the process of knowing going. Maps can halt, and maps can open the door. The word can be certain or ceremonial in an early modern sense of the word that echoes its use in traditional knowledge. Borders can chart territory or trigger ritual, make a border or engage in bordering.

Somewhere among the body, the memory, the act of writing and the story is the palimpsest of life, the layered time/place of here that becomes the embodiment in which the reader encounters the dream and makes allegory. The process is one of bordering on saying something, a process that has no mark, limit, or end, except another reading in the present, another embodiment. Writing as a process borders on reading, a process in which we feel our skin, feel where we make our differences. We engage in performativity, are affected, where we make that cut between self and not-self that is always permeable, always simultaneously one, always bordering on borders.

Notes

1 "Transindividuality" underlines a concept of self that does not stop with the skin (see Balibar qtd. in Massey 188).

2 See Massey on contemporaneity and coevalness (10), and constitutive complexity (125).

3 Kulchyski cites Walter Benjamin on dream not being unconscious but conscious and part of the present (32).

4 Kulchyski stops short of looking at the poetics of the word, the actual process of verbal, especially graphic, articulation.

5 See, for example, both Levinas and Murdoch.

6 See Nancy for an analysis of the way communities need to base themselves around disagreement rather than unity to continue to develop; see also Cockburn.

7 *The Oxford English Dictionary* defines "attentiveness" as a key element in both listening and reading (listen v., read v.).

8 Wittgenstein's joke on "what is the case" throughout, when we can never know what is the case, in *Tractatus Logico-Philosophicus* (1921).

9 See Morton on object-oriented ontology and the concept of the "withdrawn."

10 A "set toward" hegemonic structures is a positionality that is not generated in response or relation to those structures but nevertheless builds a fictional stance toward them.

Works Cited

Balibar, Etienne. "What Is a Border?" *Politics and the Other Scene*. Trans. Chris Turner. 1993. London: Verso, 2002. 75–86.

Cheney, Jim. "The Moral Epistemology of First Nations Stories." Jickling 88–100.

Cockburn, Cynthia. *The Space Between Us*. London: Zed, 1999.

Gatens, Moira, and Geraldine Lloyd. *Collective Imaginings: Spinoza, Past and Present*. London: Routledge, 1999.

Halebsky, Judy. *Japanese for Daydreamers*. Georgetown: Finishing Line, 2008.

Hunter, Lynette. "Equality as Difference: Storytelling in/of Nunavut." *International Journal of Canadian Studies* 30 (2004): 51–81.

———. *Rhetorical Stance in Modern Literature*. London: Macmillan, 1984.

Jickling, Bob, ed. "Telling Our Stories." *Canadian Journal of Environmental Education* 7.2 (Spring 2002).

Kulchyski, Peter. *Like the Sound of a Drum: Aboriginal Cultural Politics in Denendeh and Nunavut*. Winnipeg: U of Manitoba P, 2005.

Levinas, Emmanuel. *Otherwise Than Being: Or Beyond Essence*. Trans. Alphonso Lingis. Pittsburgh: Duquesne UP, 1998.

Marlatt, Daphne. *The Given*. Toronto: McClelland & Stewart, 2008.

Massey, Doreen. *For Space*. London: Sage, 2006.

Morton, Timothy. "An Object-Oriented Defense of Poetry." *New Literary History* 43 (2012): 205–24.

Murdoch, Iris. *The Sovereignty of Good*. Cambridge: Cambridge UP, 1967.

Nancy, Jean-Luc. *The Inoperative Community*. Minneapolis: U Minnesota P, 1991.

Nunavut Arctic College et al., eds. *Interviewing Inuit Elders*, vol. 1: *Introduction*. Iqaluit: Nortext, 1999.

Profeit-Leblanc, Louise. "Four Faces of Story." Jickling 47–53.

Notes on Contributors

JENNIFER ANDREWS is Professor of English at the University of New Brunswick. She is the author of *In the Belly of a Laughing God* (U of Toronto P, 2011) and co-author of *Border Crossings: Thomas King's Cultural Inversions* (U of Toronto P, 2003) and has published numerous articles on English-Canadian and American literature. She is working on a new monograph titled *Americans Write Canada*.

CATHERINE BATES is a Research Fellow at the University of Huddersfield. She has particular research interests in Canadian literature, autobiography, and figurations of the urban and waste. She has published articles on the work of bpNichol, Robert Kroetsch, Marian Engel, Alice Munro, and Michael Ondaatje and is working on two monographs, provisionally titled *Alibis, Decoys and Back Doors: Robert Kroetsch's Subversive Life-Writings* and *Regarding Discard: Representing Waste in Contemporary Canadian and US Literature*. She is the founder of the Yorkshire Network for Canadian Studies and the Deputy Director of the Leeds Centre for Canadian Studies. She also runs an environmentalist reading group in Yorkshire called Green Reads Leeds.

SUSAN BILLINGHAM is Associate Professor in Canadian Studies at the University of Nottingham. Recent and forthcoming publications include essays on Trish Salah's *Wanting in Arabic*, Elizabeth Ruth's *Smoke*, and Daniel David Moses's *Indian Medicine Shows*. She is currently developing a new project on queer pedagogies and young adult literature.

MAGGIE ANN BOWERS is a Senior Lecturer in English at the University of Portsmouth specializing in the fields of comparative multiethnic, postcolonial, and cross-cultural writing of North America and Britain. She has published articles on African American writing and Native American writing as well as comparative studies of Asian diasporic writing of America, Canada, and Britain. She is the author of Routledge's New Critical Idiom volume *Magic(al) Realism* and is a co-editor of the multilingual postcolonial volume *Convergences and Interferences*. She belongs to the Centre for the Study of Literature at the University of Portsmouth, the UK Native Studies Network, the Network for the Studies of Culture across the US/Canada Border, and the Postcolonial Studies Association. She is currently involved in the European-wide project "Imaginary Europes."

JAN CLARKE is an Associate Professor of Sociology at Algoma University in Ontario. Her research and teaching interests include critical analysis of health care systems; feminist science and technology studies; critical pedagogy; and women and work. Jan is a member of the Culture and the Canada–US Border Network and co-organizer of the 2013 CCUSB Straddling Boundaries conference at Algoma University.

LEE EASTON has been working collaboratively with Kelly Hewson for over a decade pursuing their common interests in film studies, pedagogy, and reception theory. They have published in journals such as *Ariel* and *Reception*. In addition, he has published articles and essays related to science fiction and comic books. He is Associate Dean in the Faculty of Humanities and Social Sciences at Sheridan College Institute of Technology and Advanced Learning. He leads the School of Communication and Literary Studies.

JOANNE C. ELVY has taught survey courses in the Humanities Division at Algoma University (Sault Ste. Marie, Canada), including photographic arts, world cinema, and Latin American history. She holds a B.A.A. in Photographic Arts (Ryerson, 1985), an M.Ed. (Queen's, 2000, Cultural Studies), and is currently writing her Ph.D. on the role of women in the 1961 Cuban Literacy Campaign (University of Toronto). Published work ranges from the role of arts-informed research in the academy (*Journal of Teaching and Learning*, 2011) to a survey of Cuban national identity post-1959 (La Revista Latinoamericana de Estudios sobre la Historieta, 2008).

ZALFA FEGHALI recently completed her Ph.D. in American Studies at the University of Nottingham and is now Lecturer in Modern American Literature at Canterbury Christ Church University. Her research has focused on reading as a civic act and on the articulation of alternative, queer models for citizenship, as well as comparative approaches to border studies. She has broad research interests in contemporary American, Canadian, British, and Irish fiction and poetry.

JADE FERGUSON is Assistant Professor of English at the University of Guelph. Her teaching and research focus on nineteenth- and early-twentieth-century North American literature, critical race theory, and new southern studies. She is currently working on a book-length project on cultural representations of lynching in Canada titled *Lynching in Canaan: Race, Property, and Violence in Canadian Literature and Culture.*

LUIS RENÉ FERNÁNDEZ TABÍO is a Senior Professor and Researcher at the University of Havana. He is leading a project on Canadian Studies at CEHSEU. His primary areas of research are the US and Canadian economies; Inter-American relations and integration; US–Cuba and Canada–Cuba relations and economic relations; Latin American migration to the US; and Canadian border-security problems and their consequences for international relations. He is collaborating with Canadian scholars on a book about Cuban–Canadian relations.

KELLY HEWSON joined Mount Royal University in 1993. Since then, she has taught a range of the English Department's offerings, her particular areas of interest being postcolonial literatures and film studies. Her recent scholarly work, some produced in collaboration with her colleague, Lee Easton, has focused on the affective turn in pedagogy; student spectators and American film products; ice hockey and the imagined Canadian nation; reparative reading practices; and resiliency thinking.

LYNETTE HUNTER has worked for many years on Canadian Studies, particularly Canadian literature. Her books on this topic include *Outsider Notes* (Talonbooks, 1996) and *Disunified Aesthetics* (McGill–Queen's UP, 2014). She currently works at the University of California–Davis, where she is Director of the Graduate Group in Performance Studies. Her recent research combines an exploration of the political rhetorics developed by communities new to Western liberal state structures, with the textuality of traditional, tacit, embodied, and situated knowledges.

NASSER HUSSAIN teaches literature and creative writing at Leeds Metropolitan University and York St. John University in the UK. His research interests include performance poetry, conceptual writing, and narratives of "crossing" America.

SARAH A. MATHESON is Associate Professor in the Department of Communication, Popular Culture, and Film at Brock University. She is co-editor of *Canadian Television: Text and Context* (Wilfrid Laurier UP, 2011). Her work has appeared in *Canadian Journal of Film Studies* and *Film and History* and in anthologies such as *Programming Reality: Perspectives on English-Canadian Television* and *The Tube Has Spoken: Reality TV and History*.

JEFFREY ORR is an associate faculty member of the Communications Department at Royal Roads University, Victoria, BC. He works on communications and relationships between visual and narrative media.

GILLIAN ROBERTS is Associate Professor of North American Cultural Studies at the University of Nottingham in the UK. She is the author of *Prizing Literature: The Celebration and Circulation of National Culture* (U of Toronto P, 2011) and has recently completed a monograph on cultural representations of the Canada–US border. She is Co-Investigator of the Leverhulme Trust–funded Culture and the Canada–US Border international research network.

SARAH E.K. SMITH is a Ph.D. Candidate (ABD) in the Department of Art at Queen's University. Her research scope is modern and contemporary visual and material culture, with specific interest in the relationships among culture, economics, and globalization. Her dissertation, *Art and the Invention of North America, 1985–2012*, examines the responses of Canadian artists, curators, and museums to the 1994 implementation of the North American Free Trade Agreement. Her writings have been published in *Public, Canadian Review of American Studies,* and *Inuit Art Quarterly.*

MAUREEN KINCAID SPELLER is a Ph.D. Candidate in the School of English at the University of Kent. Her research focuses on "ethical Native criticism," taking account of the intellectual traditions and experiences of Indigenous peoples in considering the work of Native authors based in North America. Her broader research interests include the representation of Indigenous peoples in the Euro-American media and the history of early encounters between European explorers and Indigenous peoples in the Americas.

DAVID STIRRUP is Senior Lecturer in American Literature at the University of Kent. He is the author of *Louise Erdrich* (Manchester UP, 2010) and co-editor of *Tribal Fantasies: Native Americans in the European Imaginary, 1900–2010* (with James Mackay, Palgrave, 2013) and *Enduring Critical Poses: Beyond Nation and History* (with Gordon Henry, Jr., SUNY P, forthcoming). His publications also include essays and book chapters on a range of contemporary Native American and First Nations writers and artists. He is Principal Investigator of the Leverhulme Trust-funded Culture and the Canada–US Border international research network.

Index

Books in the Cultural Studies Series
Published by Wilfrid Laurier University Press

Slippery Pastimes: Reading the Popular in Canadian Culture edited by Joan Nicks and Jeannette Sloniowski 2002 / viii + 347 pp. / ISBN 0-88920-388-1

The Politics of Enchantment: Romanticism, Media and Cultural Studies by J. David Black 2002 / x + 200 pp. / ISBN 0-88920-400-4

Dancing Fear and Desire: Race, Sexuality, and Imperial Politics in Middle Eastern Dance by Stavros Stavrou Karayanni 2004 / xv + 244 pp. / ISBN 0-88920-454-3

Auto/Biography in Canada: Critical Directions edited by Julie Rak 2005 / viii + 280 pp. / ISBN 0-88920-478-0

Canadian Cultural Poesis: Essays on Canadian Culture edited by Garry Sherbert, Annie Gérin, and Sheila Petty 2006 / xvi + 530 pp. / ISBN 0-88920-486-1

Killing Women: The Visual Culture of Gender and Violence edited by Annette Burfoot and Susan Lord 2006 / xxii + 332 pp. / ISBN-13: 978-0-88920-497-3 / ISBN-10: 0-88920-497-7

Animal Subjects: An Ethical Reader in a Posthuman World edited by Jodey Castricano 2008 / x + 314 pp. / ISBN 978-0-88920-512-3

Covering Niagara: Studies in Local Popular Culture edited by Joan Nicks and Barry Keith Grant 2010 / xxx + 378 pp. / ISBN 978-1-55458-221-1

Imagining Resistance: Visual Culture and Activism in Canada edited by J. Keri Cronin and Kirsty Robertson 2011 / x + 282 pp. / ISBN 978-1-55458-257-0

Making It Like a Man: Canadian Masculinities in Practice edited by Christine Ramsay 2011 / xxx + 342 pp. / ISBN 978-1-55458-327-0

When Technocultures Collide: Innovation from Below and the Struggle for Autonomy by Gary Genosko / Forthcoming 2013 / x + 212 pp. / ISBN 978-1-55458-897-8

Parallel Encounters: Cultural at the Canada–US Border edited by Gillian Roberts and David Stirrup 2013 / viii + 346 pp. / ISBN 978-1-55458-984-5